M000072751

Over-The-Counter Drugs

and Pharmacy Products

Max R. Leber R.Ph.

Robert W. Jaeger, B.S. Pharm.

Anthony J. Scalzo, M.D.

Celestial Arts
BERKELEY, CALIFORNIA

A number of products are listed in this book as banned by the U.S. Food and Drug Administration for use in a particular over-the-counter (OTC) product category. Specifically, the use of a "banned" ingredient means that the "FDA has determined that the presence of these ingredients in an OTC drug product would result in that drug products not being generally recognized as safe and effective or would result in misbranding" (55 FR 20434). This affects only the use of the listed ingredients as active ingredients for the specific indications listed and does not mean that an ingredient cannot be used in another product for a different indication. Also the FDA recognizes that some ingredients have valid uses as inactive ingredients. Some ingredients listed as "banned" may also have valid uses as pharmaceutical necessities in over-the-counter products.

This final ruling on certain ingredients is a result of the FDA's published rulemaking in the Federal Register of May 16, 1990 (55 FR 20434) which encompassed all Category II and Category III active ingredients for which the periods for submission of comments and new data following the publication of a notice of proposed rulemaking had closed and for which no significant comments or new data to upgrade the status of these ingredients had been submitted by manufacturers. For more information on these rulemakings consult the Federal Register of November 7, 1991 (55 FR 46914).

Copyright © 1994 by Max R. Leber R.Ph., Robert W. Jaeger, B.S. Pharm., and Anthony J. Scalzo, M.D. All rights reserved. No part of this book may be reproduced in any form, except for brief review, without permission of the publisher. For further information, you may write to:

Celestial Arts Publishing
P.O. Box 7123
Berkeley, California 94707

Cover by Fifth Street Design
Text design & production by Star Type

Library of Congress Cataloging-in-Publication Data

Leber, Max.
Handbook of over-the-counter drugs and pharmacy products / Max R. Leber, Robert W. Jaeger, Anthony J. Scalzo.
p. cm.
Includes index.
ISBN 0-89087-734-3
1. Drugs, Nonprescription—Popular works. 2. Health products. 3. Consumer education. I. Jaeger, Robert W. II. Scalzo, Anthony J. III. Title. IV. Title: Over-the-counter drugs and pharmacy products.
RM671.A1L43 1994
615'.1—dc20 94-23405
CIP

Printed in the United States

First Printing, 1994

1 2 3 4 5 6 / 99 98 97 96 95 94

Introduction

People want to provide their own health care to the extent that it is possible. This fact makes over-the-counter (OTC) drugs and pharmacy products a very important part of our health care system. Another factor that makes OTC drugs a dynamic part of modern medicine therapy is the "switch" phenomenon. This refers to the legal reclassification of a drug from prescription-only to nonprescription status, bringing it into the OTC category. Considering both OTC drug product ingredients and dosage strengths, more than 400 OTC products that were prescription-only status in 1978 are available as OTC today. The national trend toward increased self care will fuel more prescription-to-OTC switches in the near future. Self care, often with OTC products, is the largest and least costly component of any health care system.

In addition to prescription-to-OTC switches, each year "new" products, with unique brand names, enter the over-the-counter market and many contain the same ingredients that have been used over the years in other products. In fact, while there are hundreds of thousands of brand names on the market, there are only about 700 ingredients used in these products. But since manufacturers can mix and match ingredients and amounts within reason (and under the scrutiny of the U.S. Food and Drug Administration), the number of combinations seems endless. Cosmetic products are even more varied since the industry selects from more than 5,000 different ingredients. Some of the most commonly encountered ones are explained in this book.

To help make sense of all this, each chapter of *The Handbook of Over-The-Counter Drugs and Pharmacy Products* groups items together similar to the way they are found on pharmacy, drug store or supermarket shelves (60 percent of sales are at non-pharmacy outlets), such as cough and cold medicines, dental and mouth care, shampoos and hair products, stomach medicines, first aid and infection care, and so on.

This handbook was written to encourage people to read the label on drug and sundry products. Simply note an ingredient from the label and find it in the index of the book. This will help one derive the most benefit from any over-the-counter product.

The book focuses on ingredients so that brand names and generics can be compared on an equal basis. In this way a choice for the least expensive, but comparable quality product can be made.

Over-The-Counter Drugs

There will always be limits with the use of over-the-counter drugs. These limitations are spelled out in this handbook as clearly as possible. The book is not a substitute for consultation with a physician or other health professional, particularly when a health problem persists over a period of time or where children are involved.

Table of Contents

1

Alcohol

Many of the larger drugstores have a liquor section, and they do a substantial amount of business. **ALCOHOL** is a drug, and an extremely active one. It is a central nervous system depressant and when combined with certain chemicals can cause undesirable problems. In the United States in the 1990s there is a trend toward wine and low alcohol products, like wine coolers. Keep in mind these are still alcoholic beverages, even though they are sometimes offered like soft drinks.

Alcohol and Drug Reactions

Although consumers may be wary of drinking alcohol when taking a prescription drug, they may not be so cautious when it comes to taking what they believe to be "milder" nonprescription products. Many popular cough and cold remedies contain **ANTIHISTAMINES**; some also contain alcohol. Antihistamines, which are used to treat allergies and prevent motion sickness, have a tendency to cause drowsiness and lessen coordination. Anyone who plans to treat a cold with a "hot toddy" and an over-the-counter antihistamine product will increase their drowsiness and make driving or operating machinery very hazardous. Drug-alcohol reactions can range from minor drowsiness all the way to loss of consciousness and death. Just how much a person is really affected by a mixture of alcohol and drugs depends on their ability to metabolize alcohol and drugs. Size, body weight, age, sex, and state of health all make a difference. For example, recent evidence indicates that even small amounts of alcohol (just three beers over two days) can cause a tenfold increase in the rate of human immunodeficiency virus (HIV) multiplication. These relatively small amounts of alcohol also impair the body's resistance to HIV, thus rendering HIV-infected persons more likely to develop AIDS in a short, rather than a long time. HIV-infected persons should avoid alcohol completely to improve their chances of survival.

Another thing to remember is that alcohol is not the only ingredient in an alcoholic beverage. All alcoholic beverages contain other ingredients that provide the characteristic color, odor, and taste of individual beverages. More than 400 chemical compounds have been identified in various alcoholic products. In fact, it has even been suggested that these other chemicals, known as "congeners," may be the cause of symptoms of hangover. These chemicals also share the possibility of interacting with any medicines that are being taken. Nobody really knows anything about these kinds of interactions, so it's really a sensible idea to avoid alcohol when taking medications to treat an illness or symptom. Additionally, many wines contain sulfites which may cause allergic symptoms in some individuals.

Alcohol-Containing Products

Many people are in alcohol treatment programs and may take medicine to lessen their craving for alcohol. If alcohol does come into contact with this medicine, it causes a reaction that ranges from nausea and vomiting to shortness of breath. While people who are intent on breaking their alcohol habit will avoid drinking, they may not realize that many products, especially cough syrups, contain an alcohol base. For example, these popular cough/cold remedies contain the following amounts of alcohol:

- *DIMETAPP ELIXIR* 2.3%
- *DIMETAPP DM COLD & COUGH ELIXIR* 2.3%
- *BENYLIN COUGH SYRUP* 5%
- *BENADRYL ELIXIR* 5.6%
- *TYLENOL EXTRA STRENGTH LIQUID* 7%
- *COMTREX LIQUID* 20% (40 proof)
- *NYQUIL* 25% (50 proof)

Most drug makers have reduced the alcoholic content of over-the-counter products to the absolute minimum necessary to get medicines used in the product to dissolve. If the alcohol isn't necessary for this purpose, they have taken it out. Only a couple of products, like *NYQUIL*, use alcohol as an "active" ingredient, that is, the sedative effect of alcohol may be part of the way the product does its job. It's easy, however, to find a nonalcoholic formulation in just about any over-the-counter category. Most children's products now are also alcohol-free. Many pharmaceutical manufacturers are now listing "inactive ingredients" on the label, and this will tell everything that is in the final formulation, including alcohol.

Alcohol and Blood Alcohol Concentration

One question people ask pharmacists is: What is a safe amount of alcohol to drink, provided no medication is being taken? In order to measure the amount of alcohol in the blood, a blood test can be taken called a **BAC** (blood alcohol concentration). But how do we know, when we are having a few drinks, how much alcohol is actually in the bloodstream? There is a rule of thumb that most people can go by, based on how many drinks are consumed in a given amount of time and how much an individual weighs. The following chart shows how many drinks are required for persons of various weights to become intoxicated.

AREA 1—Blood Alcohol Content up to 0.05%
(Caution Required)
AREA 2—Blood Alcohol Content above 0.05%
(Driving Impaired)
AREA 3—Blood Alcohol Content 0.10% or more
(Driver Intoxicated)

Body Weight (In Pounds)	Number of Drinks (1½ ounces whiskey or 12 ounces beer) in a Two-Hour Period		
	AREA 1•	AREA 2•	AREA 3•
100	1-2	3-4	5-12
120	1-2	3-4	5-12
140	1-2	3-4	5-12
160	1-2	3-5	6-12
180	1-2	3-5	6-12
200	1-3	4-5	6-12
220	1-3	4-6	7-12
240	1-3	4-6	7-12

However, the risk of intoxication increases when taking certain kinds of medication whether over-the-counter products that contain antihistamines, such as cold remedies and sleeping aids, or prescription tranquilizers and sleeping pills.

Hangover

Through all of recorded history man has been plagued by the medical aftereffects of overindulgence in alcoholic beverages. People have swallowed owl's eyes, raw eggs, fish, ashes from various woods; worn garlands of celery or parsley around the neck; rolled naked in the snow, roasted in saunas, inhaled oxygen, and tried almost anything if there were even the most remote possibility that it would relieve the suffering of hangover. Even alcohol has been recommended ("a little hair from the dog that bit you") since one theory is that the symptoms of overindulgence start when blood levels of alcohol begin to recede. However, it is currently believed that one of the breakdown products of alcohol, acetaldehyde, is responsible for the hangover syndrome. Symptoms of hangover usually do not appear for several hours to a day later. Drugs that have been used over the years to treat hangover are pain relievers for headache, antacids for stomach distress, and caffeine for fatigue or dullness. Plain **ASPIRIN**, which has been a stand-by for treating hangover can be irritating to the stomach. Alcohol can wash away the stomach's protective coating, making it more susceptible to the irritating effects of aspirin. Over-the-counter preparations for the relief of hangover contain two or more ingredients, since no single ingredient will relieve all of the major symptoms of this malady. The Food and Drug Administration's OTC Miscellaneous Drug Products Panel concluded that the use of certain combination products are effective and safe in treating hangover. These products include combinations of **ASPIRIN, CITRIC ACID** and **SODIUM BICARBONATE**, such as found in *ALKA SELTZER* (in this combination the active pain reliever becomes **SODIUM ACETYLSALICYLATE**, which does not cause the same gastric erosion or stomach bleeding that plain aspirin does); and **ACETAMINOPHEN, CITRIC ACID** and **SODIUM BICARBONATE**, the ingredients in *BROMO SELTZER*. The use of **ACETAMINOPHEN** combinations offers an alternative, since it is less likely to affect the lining of the stomach.

Even though hangover can occur in some people with low uses of alcohol it is something to be avoided. It can be prevented by consuming less or no alcohol, drinking alcoholic beverages only when food is present, pacing oneself at not more than a drink per hour and alternating with nonalcoholic or low alcohol beverages which are now commonplace in drinking establishments and restaurants.

2

Bottled Water

Bottled water has had its share of problems in recent years. In February of 1990, the well-known *PERRIER BOTTLED WATER* was found to contain excessive amounts of **BENZENE**, a known cancer-causing chemical. This problem was caused by faulty filtration and the manufacturer of the water recalled its entire worldwide stock after the chemical was detected. Benzene in levels of 12.3 to 19.9 parts per billion were first detected by the North Carolina Department of Agriculture during routine testing. EPA standards require that levels of the chemical in drinking water not exceed 5 parts per billion.

According to the FDA's health evaluation board, the excessive levels found in the Perrier did not pose an immediate health hazard. The board said that consumption of 500 milliliters (about 16 fluid ounces) of the water each day over many years could pose a lifetime cancer risk of one in a million.

Benzene and other chemicals are naturally present in small amounts in the source of the water, a natural underground mineral spring in Vergeze, France. The company separates natural gas from the water, then filters out impurities such as benzene, and remixes the water with the purified gas to give Perrier its fizz. The filters, however, had not been changed regularly, and benzene eventually seeped through with the gas into the water. The manufacturer said that filters where the gaseous water first hits Perrier's processing system were changed, and a stringent schedule for replacing filters was maintained. Monitoring has turned up no more traces of benzene, and production has resumed.

Other manufacturers have gotten some unfavorable publicity regarding charges that their so-called "spring water" is nothing more than water right out of the tap. It is the Food and Drug Administration's responsibility to regulate the manufacture, sale and safety of bottled waters.

In spite of all this, more and more drugstores are carrying bottled waters, but all bottled waters are not equal. More than 700 different brands of bottled water are available in the United States. Some are carbonated and some are not, some are natural and others processed. Some taste refreshing and pure, other taste like medicine. One thing is sure: they are not inexpensive. As a rule, imported waters cost more than domestic brands. In either case, it is important to know what the bottled water is supposed to do and then to read the label carefully to make sure that it does it.

Many people prefer bottled waters to tap water because of the taste. Others are concerned about the chemicals put into our drinking water to purify it. Some people drink bottled waters for health reasons, because some brands are high in mineral content. And some people simply buy bottled water to have in case of an emergency or catastrophe in case tap water is shut off or contaminated. Finally, some people just like to use bottled distilled water in their home appliances, such as irons and coffee makers, to avoid the buildup of minerals.

Below are the types of water that are bottled. All are pure, but not all come from natural springs. Many American brands are simply bottled tap or well water that has been chemically treated or purified. They use terms on their labels like "spring fresh," "spring-pure," or "formulated"; these words mean that the water is not from a natural spring. Another description that appears on the label of bottled waters is "natural spring water," which means that it comes to the earth's surface by its own force without being pumped out. Such water is naturally rich in small amounts of vitamins and minerals. There are two types of natural spring water, still, or noncarbonated and carbonated with natural gases from the ground. The advantage of natural carbonation is that it stays in the liquid for a longer period of time than does added carbonation.

The International Bottled Water Association (IBWA) has petitioned the Food and Drug Administration to establish stricter guidelines for bottled water because of the confusing and misleading terms companies use to describe their products. After studying the situation, the FDA proposed standard definitions which are listed here.

Under proposed regulations, **ARTESIAN WATER** would be considered water that is drawn from a well that taps a confined aquifer (a water-bearing rock, rock formation, or group of rocks) in which the water level stands above the natural water table.

DISTILLED WATER would be bottled water that has no minerals because it has gone through a process in which the water is changed to a vapor and then converted back to a liquid, it has no flavor. It is the type of water used in irons, humidifiers and other home appliances because it does not create a build-up of mineral deposits that may clog the appliance.

PURIFIED WATER would be water that is produced by distillation, deionization (passing water through resins that remove most of the dissolved minerals), reverse osmosis (the use of membrane filters to remove dissolved solids), or other suitable methods, and that meets the most current pharmaceutical standards for "purified" water.

SPRING WATER would be bottled water obtained from an underground formation from which water flows naturally to the surface, or would if it were not collected underground through a bore hole where a spring emerges.

WELL WATER would be defined as water that comes from a hole bored, drilled, or otherwise constructed in the ground to tap an aquifer.

MINERAL WATER, which was previously exempt from bottled water quality standards, would be water that comes from a source tapped at one or more bore holes or springs originating from a geologically and physically protected underground water source.

The proposed regulations would continue to exclude products labeled as **CLUB SODA** or **SODA WATER** (filtered, carbonated tap water with mineral salts added to provide taste which is high in sodium, 30 to 65 milligrams per 8 ounces), **CARBONATED WATER** (same as "sparkling" water and usually high in sodium), **SELTZER WATER** (same as "club" soda without the added salts) and **TONIC WATER** because they are considered soft drinks.

An important fact to remember is that, in general, bottled waters will not have the benefits of the fluoridation process of municipal water. If bottled water is used exclusively as the source of all drinking water, fluoride deficiency and dental caries may occur, especially in children.

3

Contraceptive Products

Half of all pregnancies are unplanned. Even so, recent trends toward smaller families in the United States suggest that more and more people are using some sort of birth control method. Of course "the pill" is the most significant means of contraception and, since its development by Gregory Pincus and introduction in 1960 by G.D. Searle and Company, it has been used by over 60 million women worldwide. But as safe as the pill is for most healthy, non-smoking women, it is still not safe for all women. The risk of serious illness and death increases significantly for certain groups:

- Women who smoke—particularly those over 35 who are heavy smokers (more than 14 cigarettes a day)—have a significant risk of heart attack and stroke. This risk increases with age. Women who use oral contraceptives should not smoke.
- Women who are obese or have underlying health problems, such as diabetes, high blood pressure, or high cholesterol, also have a significantly increased risk of serious side effects from using the pill.
- Women who have a history of blood clots, heart attack, stroke, liver disease, or cancer of the breast or sex organs should not use oral contraceptives.

Fortunately, alternatives to the pill are available. True, they are not as convenient as the pill, but they work. As a matter of fact, many pharmacies are developing family planning centers in which personnel are available to answer questions and to show the different types of products that are on the market. While the pill is available on prescription only, most other contraceptive products are available without prescription for both men and women.

Condoms

A condom is a contraceptive device now used by either sex and is a very popular method of birth control. The *REALITY* Female Condom was approved by the FDA in April 1993. Condoms used to be kept behind the prescription counter. Men and women asked for them by a variety of names, such as bags, balloons, rubbers, safes, skins, and prophylactics.

Nowadays, most drugstores have a display right out in the open. This raised eyebrows among some people right up until the time that concern over **AIDS** (autoimmune deficiency syndrome) became widespread, about 1981. Keep in mind that it may still be embarrassing for some people to ask for condoms. Now they can be purchased without the anxiety of having to ask someone. Interestingly, women buy them more often than men. And many people feel they are a very necessary routine protection, particularly with the very real danger of **AIDS**. Condoms are simple to use, harmless, inexpensive, and very effective. They offer two kinds of protection: against pregnancy and against sexually transmitted diseases (**STD**s). As a matter of fact, they are the only contraceptive method that effectively prevents sexually transmitted disease.

Male condoms are usually made of rubber (latex), but some are made from animal intestine and are called "skins." Products made from animal intestine, such as *FOUREX* and *TROJAN NATURALAMB* condoms are not recommended if the concern for protection is against **AIDS**. Only the latex condoms give positive protection against penetration by the **AIDS** virus. Natural skin condoms are about four times as expensive as latex condoms. Although all condoms provide a high degree of protection against conception, accidents such as tearing or rupture of the condom do happen. Two techniques help prevent the condom from bursting: Let it extend about an inch beyond the end of the erect penis to hold the semen. If lubrication is necessary, use one of the water soluble lubricants, such as *K-Y JELLY*. Never use Vaseline or any other petroleum product; they may react with the rubber and deteriorate it. Even though condoms are very effective, there are a number of pregnancies reported each year due to misuse of these products (see table page 19).

The *REALITY* Female Condom consists of a lubricated polyurethane sheath with a flexible polyurethane ring on each end. One ring is inserted into the vagina much like a diaphragm, while the other remains outside. The female condom may offer some protection against sexually transmitted diseases, but for highly effective protection, male latex condoms must be used. In a six month trial, the pregnancy rate for the Reality Female Condom was about 13 percent. The estimated yearly failure rate ranges from 21 to 26 percent. This means that about one in four women who use *REALITY* may become pregnant during a year.

Vaginal Spermicides

Chemicals used as contraceptive agents or spermicides (sperm-destroying chemicals) have been used for thousands of years. Even the Egyptians used different substances as pastes and creams to be placed in the vagina such as honey, olive oil, animal dung and the oils from plants. Modern spermicides are very effective, and are generally reliable when properly used. They may be used alone as the sole method of contraception or in conjunction with a vaginal diaphragm or even a condom. Contraceptive chemicals are designed for use by the woman and are inserted into the vagina by various means prior to sexual intercourse .

Since an English pharmacist formulated the first commercial vaginal contraceptive suppository in the 1880s of cocoa butter and quinine, no less than 35 different chemical substances have been used commercially as vaginal contraceptives in this century. All but a few have been abandoned in the United States due to poor effectiveness or risk of poisoning. After reviewing the available spermicides on the market the FDA panel on nonprescription contraceptives and other vaginal drug products published its recommendations and found only three chemicals safe and effective for OTC use. Detergents (or surfactants) are the most effective spermicides. Detergents have the ability to destroy cell membranes and other internal cell parts of the sperm. But why the damaging effect of the detergent is only limited to the sperm and avoids other cells, such as the cells which line the innermost part of the vagina or cells of other tissues, is not known. The protective effect of vaginal mucous probably plays a role. The most popular detergent used, **NONOXYNOL-9**, is well absorbed from the mucous membranes of the vagina into the blood stream. It is presently believed that this chemical is not harmful to a developing fetus in the event that pregnancy should occur during use. A panel of scientists at the United States Centers for Disease Control has concluded that available studies do not support a link between vaginal spermicide exposure and an increased risk of birth defects. An FDA panel has also found no association between spermicides and birth defects of any kind. Since studies do not point to an increased risk of birth defects from use of spermicides in vaginal contraceptives warning labels (which some groups had proposed) on such products are not warranted, according to FDA's Fertility and Maternal Health Drugs Advisory Committee.

Spermicides are applied or inserted vaginally. They are available in creams and gels, along with an applicator. The applicator is filled and inserted into the vagina. Also available are foams that are in aerosol containers and are accompanied by an applicator. Suppositories have been available for some time now. Another form of vaginal contraception is a product called *TODAY.* Made of white polyurethane foam, it was approved by the FDA in 1983. It is a disposable vaginal contraceptive sponge permeated with the spermicide nonoxynol-9. The sponge provides a barrier to the cervix, the necklike opening to the uterus. Semen is absorbed by the sponge and spermicide is released even during multiple acts of intercourse. The sponge is effective for up to 24 hours and it must remain in place for at least 6 hours after intercourse.

The choice depends on personal preference. The creams provide greater lubrication during intercourse. The jelly is easier to remove because it is completely water soluble and dissolves. Foams do not help lubricate but are undetectable during use. The sponge is convenient because it can be inserted hours before and in anticipation of intercourse, allowing for more spontaneity between partners. All of these products contain a spermicide to kill sperm. Also, a little known fact is that all the vaginal spermicides kill the **AIDS** virus.

Products designed to be used without a **DIAPHRAGM** are *CONCEPTROL GEL*, *DELFEN*, and *EMKO*. Vaginal contraceptives that are used with a diaphragm are *ORTHO GYNOL* and *GYNOL II*. *ENCARE* and *SEMICID* are suppositories and, like the foams and jellies, contain a spermicide, **NONOXYNOL-9.**

ENCARE VAGINAL CONTRACEPTIVE SUPPOSITORIES effervesce when inserted. This is claimed to better cover the area to be protected. To determine a tablet's freshness moisten it with a drop of water. If the tablet begins to bubble, insert it immediately. The main advantage of suppositories is that they are easier to use. With most of the other vaginal contraceptives, you must deal with a tube and applicator, and sometimes a diaphragm; with the suppository, that's all there is. But be careful! These suppositories have accidentally been inserted into the urethra, the urinary tract from the bladder. This is a very dangerous mishap and requires immediate medical attention. Follow product directions carefully and pay attention to the manufacturer's precautions.

Store all of these products in a cool, dry place; they should be used within a six-month period.

About ten to twenty pregnancies are reported for every 100

women using these products. This is simply because of misuse of these products. When using cream, foam, jelly, or suppository, it must be applied less than one hour before sexual intercourse and should remain in the vaginal tract for eight hours afterwards. Before each subsequent intercourse, an additional application or suppository should be inserted.

As with any applied chemical, irritation of the vagina and penis may occur. In that case, discontinue using the product.

Spermicide Ingredients

MENFEGOL is a synthetic detergent made from petroleum starting chemicals also known as **p-METHYLPHENYL POLYOXYETHYLENE ETHER**. It is usually found in products where the chemical is applied as effervescent vaginal suppositories. It is strongly spermicidal and animal studies indicate it to be nontoxic and nonirritating. Developed in Japan and produced at Eisai Laboratories, it is a liquid at room temperature and is technically referred to as a nonionic surfactant (a type of detergent).

NONOXYNOL-9 or NONYLPHENOXYPOLYETHOXYETHANOL is a nonionic surfactant, or a detergent, and a liquid at room temperature. Made synthetically from petroleum chemicals, it is unquestionably the most frequently employed spermicidal chemical in vaginal contraceptives.

OCTOXYNOL is a synthetic detergent which is manufactured from petroleum chemicals and belongs to the nonionic surfactant class of detergents. Normally a liquid, it is incorporated in jellies and creams for use as spermicide. Some douches also contain this ingredient, but not for use as a vaginal contraceptive. Since this is a detergent, it is used in douches for its spreading, not spermicidal, properties. This makes it easier for the product to spread over the vaginal mucous membrane and penetrate the folds of the vagina. It is a spermicide more often used in combination with a vaginal diaphragm since its physical characteristics make it more suitable for dispersion in conjunction with a sperm blocking device (see Chapter 11, Femine Hygiene).

Douching

Flushing out the vagina immediately after intercourse to remove semen is an age-old method of attempting to avoid pregnancy. Unfortunately, this after-the-fact method is totally unreliable. The idea behind the practice is to remove the semen before it enters the uterus. However, sperm can reach the mouth of the uterus within 90 seconds after ejaculation. There are a number of douche products available: *MASSENGILL DISPOSABLE DOUCHE*, *MASSENGILL DOUCHE POWDER*, *SUMMER'S EVE VINEGAR AND WATER*, *MASSENGILL VINEGAR AND WATER DISPOSABLE DOUCHE*, and *TRICHOTINE* liquid and powder. They should be used for hygienic purposes, not for contraception (see Chapter 11, Feminine Hygiene).

Natural Family Planning (NFP)

Natural family planning includes the rhythm method, or periodic abstinence from sexual relations during the ovulation period of the female cycle. It is one of the least effective methods of contraception.

However, if a woman has a regular menstrual cycle, there are benefits to this method. The time of ovulation is established by charting changes in the basal body temperature. Take an oral temperature at the same time each morning, just before rising (the basal body temperature). Record the temperature each day during the entire cycle. When ovulation begins, a woman's basal body temperature drops slightly, followed by a rise of about 0.5°F over 24 to 72 hours. Theoretically intercourse should be avoided for two days prior to ovulation, the day of ovulation, and one day after ovulation. However there are many variables affecting body temperature. For instance, the temperature normally varies throughout the day. On the other hand, if there is a cold or flu, there may be a change of temperature having nothing to do with ovulation.

The cervical mucous method, also called the Billings method, is another means of natural family planning that enables a woman to determine the fertile and infertile times of her menstrual cycle. A woman or couple is then able to make decisions to avoid or achieve pregnancy based on the presence of mucus or dryness at the opening of the vagina. This method also gives the woman invaluable insights into the events which occur during her menstrual cycle. It is important to recognize the fact that fertility is dependent on both the male and female. However, in this book only the woman's fertility is discussed.

The cervical mucous method consists of checking for discharge at the opening of the vagina. If a discharge is present, she needs to record its consistency, color, and sensation and to note any changes which may occur in the discharge from one day to the next.

The menstrual cycle begins with the menstrual flow. Following the flow is usually a period of days that are free of vaginal discharge. Then begins a discharge of thick, sticky or tacky, and cloudy mucus. This discharge changes over a period of days to become clear, stretchy, and/or lubricative. This clear mucus is known as "peak-like" mucus. The last day of clear mucous discharge is called the "peak." This is the most fertile time. Following the peak there is a dramatic change in the mucus, due to the drop in estrogen levels and the increase of progesterone which occurs after ovulation. The remaining days of the menstrual cycle are usually days in which no vaginal discharge appears.

There are many health benefits to women using the cervical mucous method. Some women have been able to determine, and therefore secure treatment for, vaginal infections and cervicitis, by learning to distinguish whether their observations of the vagina reveal a normal sequence of events or a possible disease process. Therefore, a woman using this method provides herself with a useful reproductive-health screening tool. Also, she can become familiar with the length of her menstrual cycle and the duration and amount of menstrual flow, recognizing the effects of illness and stress on the process. Since the occurrence of menstrual periods follows ovulation by an average of fourteen days, a woman using this method learns to expect her period in twelve to sixteen days after her peak.

Ovulation predictor kits are now available over-the-counter in drug stores. Kits like the *Q-TEST OVULATION TEST* and *ANSWER OVULATION TEST KIT* can accurately "predict the day a woman is most able to become pregnant." Therefore, a couple can use NFP to achieve or avoid pregnancy. If they wish to avoid pregnancy they should not have genital contact on fertile days. If they wish to achieve pregnancy they will have intercourse on fertile days. The effects of drugs, nutrition, stress, and light on the menstrual cycle are areas of research to which NFP lends itself and which are currently being investigated.

In conclusion, NFP is not a very effective means of birth control, but it can be an invaluable health tool. It is useful during a woman's entire fertile years and through menopause. Learning NFP requires frequent follow-up visits with a trained instructor during the early stages or using one of the kits available in drug stores. Regularly scheduled follow-up visits with a physician are recommended to reinforce and re-evaluate the woman's or the couple's understanding of the technique.

The following table gives the effectiveness rates of the various forms of contraception (based on the number of pregnancies per 100 women per year of use).

Method	Estimated Effectiveness
Sterilization	99+%
Implant (Norplant)[1]	99%
Injection (Depo-Provera)[1]	99%
The pill (estrogen, progestin)[1]	98%
"Mini-pill" (progestin alone)[1]	97%
Male condom with vaginal spermicide	97%
IUD[1] (intrauterine device)	94-97%
Male condom alone	85-88%
Diaphragm with spermicides[1]	82-94%
Cervical cap with spermicide[1]	82%
Female condom alone	74-79%
Vaginal sponge	72-82%
Vaginal spermicides alone	70-80%
Periodic abstinence (rhythm)	53-86%
No contraception	20-40%

[1] While these prescription items are not discussed in this book, they are listed here for comparative purposes.

4

Cosmetics

It is really not so strange to find a section on cosmetics in a book about drugs. For centuries cosmetics were basically meant to be products that helped people look good. In fact the word "cosmetic" from the Greek "cosmos," meaning "order," eventually was applied to cosmetics used to "order" or "adorn" a person. But modern cosmetics have evolved into products of health and hygiene and some have even been reclassified by the Food and Drug Administration from cosmetics to drugs. Sometimes it is difficult to distinguish between the two. Depending on how a manufacturer intends for a product to be used, the kinds of ingredients used, or both, will determine whether the FDA will consider it a drug or a cosmetic (or both).

Although most cosmetics on the market today are hypoallergenic (which means they are low in allergens), **ALLERGIC REACTIONS** and **IRRITANT REACTIONS** still do occur. But, considering the number of cosmetic applications made daily, cases of serious allergic or toxic reactions to cosmetics are rare. The frequency of adverse reactions to cosmetics that require a physician's care is approximately 210 per one million cosmetic products purchased, according to information from a Food and Drug Administration survey. Skin care products, such as facial cleansers and moisturizers, are associated with the largest number of cosmetic allergic reactions. Hair preparations in general, including hair dyes, form the second largest group, and facial makeup, such as foundation and blush, is third. As for the types of ingredients that cause the allergic reactions, fragrances and fragrance ingredients are responsible for the greatest number. Preservatives are next, followed by **PHENYLENEDIAMINE** (found in hair dyes), **LANOLIN**, the hair-waving ingredient **GLYCERYL MONOTHIOGLYCOLATE**, and **PROPYLENE GLYCOL** (a skin softener).

IRRITANT REACTIONS commonly occur the first time a person comes in contact with a particular cosmetic, while **ALLERGIC REACTIONS** generally develop after continued use. Whether liquid, pressed powder, or solid cake cosmetic is used, you may develop a reaction if used too often or too heavily. Most cosmetics counters have a sales clerk who knows even more about these products than the pharmacist.

Some perfumes may react with the skin to form a new chemical that causes irritation, such as **FORMALDEHYDE**. Although one does not associate perfume with formaldehyde, the reaction sometimes occurs.

Reactions to soap, cosmetics, and other beauty aids can be a problem for anybody. The first and most obvious step is avoidance of irritating or allergenic products. Second, do not do anything to further irritate an area that is already affected. And third, use cool water compresses on the affected area for five to ten minutes several times a day. Over-the-counter hydrocortisone creams or ointments, such as *CORTAID*, can be used for relief of irritation.

Cosmetics are formulated from very sophisticated chemicals and methods. They are sensitive to light and heat just like food products, and in some cases will become rancid, just as food will. Cosmetics other than perfumes, toilet waters, and the like deteriorate with age. The older the cosmetic, the more susceptible it is to bacteria and the more likely you are to get a bacteria-caused reaction. Don't buy more than you can use in six months. Keeping makeup in the refrigerator will slow its deterioration.

Also remember that, no matter what cosmetic, it is designed for use on healthy skin. Applying any cosmetic to an area that is already irritated may cause further problems. As always, if the problem persists for an abnormal length of time, see a doctor.

Women are finding more and newer products at the cosmetic counter. Traditional fingernail polish removers are side-by-side with newer polish-removing gels.

There are also a variety of ways for removing makeup, with soap and water treatment being the most common. But as that sometimes leaves the skin dried out, it often can be an advantage to apply a cream moisturizer to the face after washing it. And of course there is the old stand-by, cold cream. After applying it to the face it should be wiped away with a tissue. This method of removing makeup does have the advantage of keeping the skin moist. Another way is to use the newer cream cleansers that rinse off with water, such as *REVLON CLEAN & CLEAR CLEANSING GEL* or *AVON DAILY REVIVAL CREAM CLEANSER.* These products keep the skin soft and lubricated.

Colorants Used in Eye, Lip and Other Makeup

The eyes and the mouth, both leading features of the face, have been painted and adorned with pigments since the dawn of recorded history.

Today colorants find most of their application in eye and lip makeup. In fact, eye makeup may involve formulas that use concentrations of pigment upwards of 80 percent, the remainder being binder. This is in contrast to colors used in food and drugs where seldom more than a few to several hundred parts per million of color is used to achieve the desired result.

It is this use, more prominent today than ever before, that makes it particularly important that coloring agents are safe and non-toxic since absorption into the bloodstream might occur through the mouth and mucous membranes of the eyes. Historically, coloring agents were used indiscriminately for facial and body adornment with little or no attention being paid to the harmful physical effects, either internal or external. For this reason the use of colors in personal products is increasingly affected by legislation, particularly in the United States. Manufacturers have the burden to provide data to support their claim that the colors are safe. If the data is not forthcoming, colors may be banned. Ideally the cosmetic and toiletry industry wants to establish positive lists of substances which can be used, but the industry claims that this is sometimes impossible due to inconsistencies in the actions of government agencies and by misunderstandings of what science is capable of. The use of color in cosmetics is chemically and technologically complex. Imagine how difficult it is to get a certain color to work when it depends on so many things, like: will it dissolve in the vehicle used to apply it, the presence or absence of moisture (perspiration), temperature of the skin, temperature of the environment, friction and so on. All of these factors, and more, are taken into consideration after the colorant has been shown to be safe and nontoxic.

Colorants are usually divided into various types. 1) natural (animal, vegetable or mineral) soluble dyes, 2) synthetic (man-made) soluble dyes, 3) natural (animal, vegetable or mineral pigments, 4) synthetic (man-made) pigments, and 5) natural and synthetic "lakes." The use of the term "dye" means it is soluble in either water or chemical solvents that are used to apply the cosmetic. In contrast, pigments are color additives with little or no solubility in water or chemical solvents. "Lakes" are water-soluble dyes absorbed on a suitable substance, like **ALUMINA HYDRATE** (see below), in the presence of a suitable metal salt, such as **ALUMINUM CHLORIDE** (also see below). This interaction may involve the precipitation of a final color. In any case the resultant color is not dissolved in water or chemical solvents. The development of lakes has considerably extended the range of colors available in the production of cosmetics.

There are other distinctions between color additives. From a legal standpoint they can be divided into two groups. Those "listed" for use and those "provisionally listed." "Listed" additives are those that have been sufficiently evaluated to convince the FDA of their safety in the intended application. "Provisionally listed" colorants are dyes and pigments that, while not considered unsafe, have not undergone all the tests required by the Color Additives Amendment of 1960 to establish their eligibility for 'permanent' listing. This 1960 law set up a pre-market approval system for new color additives and required determination of safety of all color additives already in use. A previous law, the Federal Food, Drug and Cosmetic Act of 1938, instituted some of the more important practices observed by the color manufacturers and users. For example, it provided that synthetic (man-made) color additives be listed and certified for purity and safety before being used in food, drugs, or cosmetics. Among other things, this law created three categories of what were called at the time "coal tar" colors because of their synthesis from the chemicals found in coal tar (now prepared from petroleum chemicals): **FD&C** colors—those certifiable for use in coloring foods, drugs, and cosmetics; **D&C** colors—dyes and pigments considered safe in drugs and cosmetics when in contact with mucous membranes or when ingested; and **Ext. D&C** colors—those colorants that, because of their oral toxicity, were not certifiable for use in products intended for ingestion, but were considered safe for use in products externally applied. These abbreviations are used in the colors described below.

Colorants and Cancer— The Delaney Dilemma

Under the Delaney Clause of the 1960 Color Additive Amendments, the FDA cannot approve color additives shown to induce cancer in humans or animals in any amount. Many government officials, however, believe that the inflexibility of the Delaney Clause should be replaced by a standard that allows for what may be an insignificant cancer risk. Advances in technology and the ability to detect minute quantities of cancer-causing chemicals in foods and cosmetics may make the risk standard of the Delaney Clause unnecessarily stringent in some cases. In some cases, banning chemicals, such as dyes, has been based on the legal requirement and not on the basis of risk to the public. In some cases the cancer risk posed is so low that it is hard to calculate. For example, a government review panel had assessed the worst-case risks for externally applied drug and cosmetic used for **D&C ORANGE No. 17** as one in 19 billion (that is, exposure to external cosmetics containing **D&C ORANGE No. 17** may cause at most one additional case of cancer in 19 billion people over a 70 year lifetime of exposure). Under the Delaney Clause the courts have ruled that even these dyes must be banned, because the Delaney Clause does not contain an exemption for cancer-causing color additives with only trivial risks. Because of this, new legislation has been proposed that would substitute a "negligible risk" standard for the "zero-risk" standard, such as that described in the Delaney Clause.

The colorants listed below will give some idea of what you are getting when you see it on the label of your cosmetic:

Colorant Ingredients

ALKANNIN, also called **ANCHUSIN, ANCHUSIC ACID** or **ALKANNA RED** is a naturally occurring coloring principle found in the plant *Alkanna tinctoria*, an herb with hairy leaves and blue or purple trumpet-shaped-flowers. It is native to Hungary, Greece and the Mediterranean region. Alkannin has been shown to be nontoxic when fed to animals. It is approved for use as a food and cosmetic dye by the FDA.

ALUMINA HYDRATE or **HYDRATED ALUMINA, HYDRATED ALUMINUM OXIDE** or **ALUMINUM HYDROXIDE** is a white, odorless, tasteless, powder which is found in nature in the mineral bauxite. Used as a white colorant in eye makeup, it is commercially produced from the mineral. It is not absorbed from the skin and is considered nontoxic. It is approved for use in cosmetics by the FDA.

ANNATTO or **ANNATTO EXTRACT** is a naturally occurring material from the annatto tree (*Bixa orellana*), a large, fast growing shrub cultivated in tropical climates, including parts of South America, India, East Africa, and the Caribbean. The tree produces large clusters of brown or crimson capsular fruit containing seeds which are coated with a highly colored resinous substance that is the raw material for this colorant.

AMARANTH is a synthetic dark red-to-purple powder soluble in water and most organic solvents. It is a suspected cancer-causing chemical and use has been discontinued in foods, drugs and cosmetics. Formerly called **FD&C RED No. 2** or **RED DYE No. 2**.

BETA CAROTENE is a relative of the naturally occurring carotenoid (a class of pigments found in higher plants, e.g. carrots), **CAROTENE**. It is the pigment responsible for the color of many products obtained from nature, such as butter, cheese, carrots, and certain cereal grains. For commercial use it is synthetically made from acetone. It is one of the first natural colorants that was prepared synthetically. Beta carotene is available in pure form as dry, reddish-violet crystals.

BISMUTH CARBONATE or **BISMUTH SUBCARBONATE** is a white, tasteless, odorless powder that was made at one time for use as a pigment synthetically by adding ammonium carbonate to a solution of a bismuth salt. Bismuth is a metallic element. It is no longer listed as approved for use by the FDA.

BISMUTH OXYCHLORIDE is a pigment commonly found in eye makeup formulations. It is a white, lustrous, crystalline powder which is insoluble in water. It can be made synthetically from simple salts of the metallic element, bismuth. It is used to coat mica in eye makeup to achieve pearlescent effects. Used in lipstick, nail polish, eye makeup and numerous other cosmetics.

BIXIN is the chief coloring principle found in the oil or fat extracts of annatto seeds (see above). It is a naturally occurring brownish-red crystalline material.

CANTHAXANTHIN is a synthetically made carotenoid (a class of pigments in higher plants, like carrots) color additive. It occurs in nature and was first isolated from an edible mushroom (*Cantharellus cinnabarinus*). In its pure form it crystallizes as brownish-violet shiny "leaves." Canthaxanthin is only approved for use in cosmetics applied to the skin. It was recently sold in health food stores as a chemical means of obtaining a suntan until banned because of suspected toxic effects in humans. Canthaxanthin has been reported to cause damage to the liver and the eyes. The skin coloration is not quite the golden brown tan one would expect from basking in the sun anyway. It is a dingy yellowish hue which most people do not find attractive.

CARAMEL also called **NATURAL BROWN 10** is burned sugar. It is prepared from a controlled heat treatment of dextrose, and other approved sugars, including sucrose (table sugar). While it is approved for use in cosmetics, its main use is in food and drugs.

CARMINE is a red "lake" (see introduction) extracted from cochineal (dried insects of the species *Coccus cacti*, a variety of shield louse). This is an insoluble material and was used in early lipsticks. It produces a much less intense coloring than the synthetic red pigments now used more often. Carmine is useful for producing pink shades in rouge and eye shadow. It is considered safe for use around the eyes by the FDA.

CAROTENE occurs naturally in plants, such as algae and carrots, as an orange-yellow pigment and can be isolated as dark red crystals that are insoluble in water. Actually carotene is a member of a large class of pigments called carotenoids. It has the same basic molecular structure as vitamin A and is transformed to the vitamin in the liver of animals.

CHLOROPHYLL is a naturally occurring pigment commercially obtained from alfalfa (*Medicago sativa*), a clover-like plant of the pea family. However, it is found in the chloroplasts of all green plants, in certain bacteria, and in other organisms capable of photosynthesis.

CHROMIUM HYDROXIDE GREEN or **PIGMENT GREEN 18** is chemically hydrated **CHROMIC SESQUIOXIDE**, a powdered, bluish and brilliant green pigment prepared synthetically by the roasting of potassium or sodium dichromate (a salt of the metallic element chromium) and boric acid. It is approved for external use only but may be employed in makeup intended for use around the eyes.

CHROMIUM OXIDE GREENS or **PIGMENT GREEN 17** is chemically chromic sesquioxide, prepared synthetically from boric acid and a salt of the metallic element chromium, potassium dichromate. It is a yellowish-green pigment approved for use in eye makeup.

COCHINEAL EXTRACT or **NATURAL RED 4** is the concentrated solution obtained after removing the alcohol from a water-alcohol extract of cochineal, which is the dried bodies of the female insect *Coccus cacti*, a variety of shield louse. The cochineal insect lives on a species of cactus, *Nopalea coccinelliferna*, native to Mexico.

COPPER POWDER is a very fine, free flowing metallic powder made from virgin electrolytic copper. Small amounts of these "lubricants" are used for employment in cosmetics applied around the eyes.

D&C BLUE No. 4 is also called **ALPHAZURINE FG** and is a dye synthetically prepared from petroleum chemicals. It is listed as safe by the FDA for externally applied cosmetics only.

D&C BROWN No. 1 or **RESORCIN BROWN** is prepared synthetically from petroleum chemicals and listed as safe for externally applied cosmetics only.

D&C GREEN No. 5 or **ALIZARINE CYANINE GREEN F** is listed by the FDA as safe for use in all cosmetics. It is made synthetically from petroleum chemicals.

D&C GREEN No. 8 is also known as **PYRANINE CONCENTRATE** and is approved for externally applied cosmetics only in limited concentrations.

D &C ORANGE No. 4 or **ORANGE II** is listed as safe by the FDA for use in externally applied cosmetics and is made from petroleum chemicals.

D&C ORANGE No. 5 or **DIBROMOFLUORESCEIN** is listed as safe when allowed up to 5 percent concentration in lipstick and other lip cosmetics. It may also be used in ingested mouthwashes and dentifrices. It is an artificial dye made from fluorescein (a chemical made from petroleum) and bromine, the element.

D&C ORANGE No. 10 or **DIIDOFLUORESCEIN** is listed by the FDA as safe for use in external cosmetics. It is synthetic and made from fluorescein and iodine, the element.

D&C ORANGE No. 11, also known as **ERYTHROSINE YELLOWISH SODIUM** is a synthetically made dye and is listed by the FDA as safe for use in externally applied cosmetics.

D&C ORANGE No. 17 or **PERMATONE ORANGE** has been banned by the FDA even though its cancer-causing risk is trivial. While there is no risk to humans, the Delaney Clause has forced FDA to abandon it as "safe." It was allowed only in externally applied cosmetics, and it is made synthetically from petroleum chemicals.

RUBIN B is a synthetic dye from petroleum chemicals listed as safe for use in all cosmetics except those intended for use around the eye.

D&C RED No. 7 or **LITHOL RUBIN B CALCIUM** is a synthetically made dye from petroleum chemicals and is listed by the FDA as safe for use in all cosmetics except those intended for use around the eye.

D&C RED No. 8 or **LAKE RED C** has recently been banned. While it only poses a cancer risk of 1 in 60 million, the Delaney Clause is not flexible enough to permit its continued use. It was used in all cosmetics except those intended for use around the eye. It is made from petroleum chemicals.

D&C RED No. 9 or **LAKE RED C BARIUM** is a synthetically prepared dye from petroleum chemicals. It is no longer listed as safe even though it poses a negligible cancer risk in humans. It was used in all cosmetics except those for use around the eye.

D&C RED No. 17, TONEY RED or **SUDAN III** is listed as safe for use in all externally applied cosmetics except those intended for use around the eye by the FDA. It is synthetically made from petroleum chemicals.

D&C RED No. 19 or **RHODAMINE B** is synthetically prepared from petroleum chemicals and has been banned by the FDA for use in externally applied cosmetics. The Delaney Clause required the ban, even though this chemical was supposed to cause at most only one new cancer in 9 million people over a 70 year lifetime of exposure.

D&C RED No. 21 or **TETRABROMOFLUORESCEIN** is a synthetic dye made from petroleum chemicals and is listed as safe by the FDA for use in all cosmetics except for those cosmetics intended for use around the eye.

D&C RED No. 22 is also known as **EOSIN Y**. It is a synthetic chemical from petroleum chemicals and is approved for use by the FDA in all cosmetics except for those cosmetics intended for use around the eye.

D&C RED No. 27, TETRABROMOTETRACHLOROFLUORESCEIN is a synthetic dye manufactured from fluorescein and a combination with the element halogen gases bromine and chlorine. It is listed by the FDA as approved for all cosmetic uses except for those products intended for use around the eye.

D&C RED No. 28 is also called **PHLOXINE B** or **CI ACID RED 92.** It is a synthetic dye from petroleum chemicals approved for all cosmetic uses except for those products intended for use around the eye.

D&C RED No. 30 or **HELINDONE PINK CN**. This dye is approved for all cosmetic uses except for those products intended for use around the eye. It is listed as safe by the FDA and is made synthetically from petroleum chemicals.

D&C RED No. 31 or **BRILLIANT LAKE RED R** is a synthetically made dye. It is the calcium salt of a petroleum-based starting chemical. The FDA lists it as approved for all externally applied cosmetics except for those products intended for use around the eye.

D&C RED No. 33 or **ACID FUCHSINE** is allowed in cosmetics in limited quantities and is provisionally listed as safe by the FDA. It may be used in all but eye cosmetics. It is made from petroleum chemicals.

D&C RED No. 34 or **DEEP MAROON** is listed as safe in externally applied cosmetics, except those applied to the eye. It is an artificial dye made from petroleum chemicals.

D&C RED No. 36 or **FLAMING RED** is a chemical dye made from petroleum starting chemicals and it is only provisionally listed as safe by the FDA pending further studies on safety. It may only be used in limited quantities in all but eye cosmetics.

D&C RED No. 37 is also called **RHODAMINE B-STEARATE** is a derivative of **D&C Red No. 19**, discussed earlier. Both are made from petroleum starting chemicals. It is listed as safe by the FDA pending further studies. It may only be used externally in all but eye cosmetics.

D&C VIOLET No. 2 or **ALIZUROL PURPLE SS** is a synthetic dye listed as safe by the FDA for externally applied cosmetics. This does not include products intended for use around the eye.

D&C YELLOW No. 7 is **FLUORESCEIN**, a dye made from resorcinol and phthalic anhydride, another petroleum chemical. It is an orange-red crystalline powder which in solution will exhibit an intense, greenish-yellow color by reflected light and an orangish-red color by transmitted light. It is of low toxicity and is listed as safe by the FDA for use in externally applied cosmetics, except for those products intended for use around the eye.

D&C YELLOW NO. 8 is also known as **URANINE** or **ACID YELLOW 73**. It is the sodium salt of fluorescein. It also is listed as safe for externally applied cosmetics, except eye make-up.

D&C YELLOW No. 10 is **QUINOLINE YELLOW** or **ACID YELLOW 3** and may be used in all except eye cosmetics in limited quantities. It is made synthetically from petroleum chemicals. The FDA has listed it provisionally until further studies confirm its safety.

D&C YELLOW No. 11 or **QUINOLINE YELLOW SS** is a synthetically made dye. It is derived from petroleum starting chemicals. It is listed as safe by the FDA for external cosmetics only except for those products intended for use around the eye.

DIHYDROXYACETONE, found in products like *BAIN de SOLEIL* is a synthetic chemical employed as a colorant in the sense that it is used for "synthetic" suntans. It is approved for external use only. Dihydroxyacetone or **DHA** does indeed form brownish-yellow pigments in contact with amino acids (building blocks of protein) and other chemicals in the skin, however most of these color bodies are yellowish and not particularly attractive on the skin. The coloration formed does not require light or oxygen and it is not easily extracted from the skin, suggesting that it is not a simple physical adhesion of a pigment to the skin surface. It is, as far as is known, a safe, nontoxic practice.

EXT. D&C VIOLET No. 2 is also known as **ALIZARINE VIOLET** and is synthetically made from petroleum chemicals. The FDA lists it as safe for external use only except for those products intended for use around the eye.

EXT. D&C YELLOW No. 7 or **NAPHTHOL YELLOW S** is listed as safe for all externally applied cosmetics except eye makeup. It is made synthetically from petroleum chemicals.

FD&C BLUE No. 1 is also known as **BRILLIANT BLUE.** It is approved for all cosmetic uses except eye makeup. The dye is made synthetically from petroleum chemicals. It is also permanently listed as safe for use in food and ingested drugs and has not been found to cause cancer in animal studies.

FD&C GREEN No. 3 or **FAST GREEN FCF** is a synthetic dye made from petroleum chemicals and listed as approved for all cosmetic uses except in products intended for use around the eye.

FD&C RED No. 3 or **ERYTHROSINE** is a brown powder in appearance that makes a cherry red solution in water. The FDA no longer permits it as a straight color in cosmetics or externally applied drugs, or in any "lakes" of **FD&C Red No. 3.** It is still listed for use in ingested drugs, such as *PEPTO-BISMOL* and some foods. The dye is manmade.

FD&C RED No. 4 is made from petroleum chemicals and is only listed as safe for externally applied cosmetics, except those for use around the eye.

FD&C RED No. 40, ALLURA RED AC or **CI FOOD RED 17** is made synthetically from petroleum starting chemicals and is listed as safe for all cosmetics, except eye makeup.

FD&C YELLOW No. 5 or **TARTRAZINE** is a synthetic dye that has received a great deal of publicity with regard to its use in drugs intended for oral use. It was used extensively in the past but much less at present. It is approved for use in all cosmetics by the FDA. Studies have shown that it does not cause cancer in animals, but since it causes allergic reactions in some people, the FDA requires its listing on food and drug labels.

FD&C YELLOW No. 6, SUNSET YELLOW or **CI FOOD YELLOW 3** is made from petroleum chemicals and is provisionally approved for safe use in all except eye cosmetics.

FERRIC OXIDE, IRON OXIDE, SYNTHETIC IRON OXIDE, PIGMENT BLACK 11, PIGMENT BROWNS 6 and **7, PIGMENT YELLOWS 42** and **43** and **PIGMENT REDS 101** and **102** are all as one of the names implies, made synthetically. The naturally occurring oxides are unacceptable as a color additive because of the difficulties frequently encountered in purifying them. The major use of iron oxide as a colorant is in eye makeup and face powders. The various colors are prepared by chemical treatment and mixing the different types. It is currently approved as safe and nontoxic by the FDA.

FERRIC AMMONIUM FERROCYANIDE is a blue pigment obtained synthetically from inorganic chemicals, iron, ammonia and cyanide. It is approved for use around the eyes and is listed as safe and nontoxic by the FDA. The cyanide portion of the molecule is bound to the rest of the chemical in such a way that it does not pose any risk of cyanide poisoning under any circumstances.

FERRIC FERROCYANIDE or **IRON BLUE** is a blue pigment made synthetically and approved for use in eye makeup for external use only. The cyanide part of this chemical is bound in such a way that there is no risk of cyanide poisoning from use in any way.

GUANINE is a crystalline substance from the scales and body of various fish, including herring. Technically, guanine is not a colorant but instead is used to produce iridescence in the final product. The hue of the colorant varies greatly with the amount and type of pigment found in the fish scales. In nature, fish scales produce pearlescent effects due to the platey crystals of guanine producing an optical effect. The critical spacings between parallel layers of guanine platelets will interfere with visible light. This gives rise to a color phenomenon known as "interference reflection." This same effect can be seen quite clearly in a soap bubble. In its pure form, guanine is nontoxic, but there are reports of it causing skin irritation. This natural source of pearlescence has been used in nail lacquers in the form of a suspension of nitrocellulose (see page 42) and butyl acetate (see page 39). It is approved for use in make-up around the eyes.

HENNA is a shrub (*Lawsonia inermis*) native to Africa and Asia and widely cultivated in other parts of the world. The dried leaf is used in numerous hair care products but is no longer added to lip and eye colorants. Prolonged use of henna on the hair would turn the hair orange-red unless henna is mixed with other dyes to obtain different shades. To obtain a long lasting color the henna preparation must be rendered slightly acid. It is "permanently listed" by the FDA as an approved colorant for use in hair products only.

INDIGO or **SYNTHETIC INDIGO BLUE** is a dark blue, crystalline powder with a bronze luster that is now made synthetically. It was prepared at one time from plants of the genus *Indigofera.*

MICA is a white powder obtained from the naturally occurring mineral muscovite mica, consisting predominantly of a potassium aluminum silicate. It is used with other pigments to obtain a pearlescent effect in cosmetics.

TITANIUM DIOXIDE, TITANIC EARTH or **PIGMENT WHITE 6** is the whitest, brightest pigment presently known. As the oxide of titanium, a metallic element, it exists in nature in three crystalline forms anatase, brookite, and rutile. Anatase is the commonly available form. However, only synthetically prepared titanium dioxide can be used as a color additive. It is widely used in lipsticks, nail enamels, face powders, eye make-up and rouges in various amounts. It is safe and nontoxic.

ULTRAMARINE BLUE or **PIGMENT BLUE 29** is prepared synthetically from ultramarine green by further heat treatment in the presence of sulfur. It is approved for use around the eyes and is safe and nontoxic.

ULTRAMARINE GREEN or **PIGMENT GREEN 24** is synthetically prepared by heat treating and very slow cooling of various combinations of the naturally occurring minerals kaolin (aluminum silicate clay), silica, sulfur, soda ash, and sodium sulfate plus a carbon-based reducing agent such as charcoal pitch. It is approved for safe and nontoxic use around the eye in makeup.

ULTRAMARINE PINK is prepared synthetically from ultramarine violet (see below) by treatment of the latter with a mineral acid, such as hydrochloric acid. It is safe and nontoxic for use around the eyes.

ULTRAMARINE RED is made synthetically from ultramarine violet (see below) by treatment of the latter with a mineral acid, such as hydrochloric acid. It is safe and nontoxic for use around the eyes.

ULTRAMARINES are synthetic, inorganic pigments that are basically composed of sodium alumino-sulfosilicates. They have been developed by the cosmetic industry to duplicate the colors found in the naturally occurring semiprecious gem, Lapis lazuli, or lazurite, which has been used in personal adornment since ancient times. The ultramarines are manufactured from naturally occurring minerals and clays by heat and chemical processes. For their intended uses they are considered safe and nontoxic.

ULTRAMARINE VIOLET is developed synthetically from ultramarine green (see above) by chemically treating with ammonium chloride for several days at elevated temperatures. Like other ultramarines listed above it is approved for use in cosmetics around the eyes.

UMBER is a naturally occurring dark brown earth composed of ferric oxide, silica, alumina, manganese oxides and lime. Different shades of brown can be produced by burning umber (burnt umber).

ZINC OXIDE or **PIGMENT WHITE 4** is a white or yellowish-white odorless powder that is nontoxic. Of all the white pigments used in the cosmetic field, zinc oxide is considered one of the most important. Zinc oxide has many advantages such as brightness, adhesiveness, and even therapeutic properties of being antiseptic and astringent. It is used in face powders, rouges and eye makeup extensively.

Nail Products

Nail products include lacquers, lacquer removers, hardeners, nail elongators, cuticle softeners and creams. All of these are concerned with the cleansing and preparation of the nail and its decoration. The health risk from nail products is considered low to moderate, based on FDA reports concerning adverse reactions. Dermatitis from nail products, the most common reaction, may appear on the eyelids, lower part of the face and the neck, and upper chest most frequently, although, other parts of the body may be involved, but more rarely. More than half of the reports of adverse effects from nail cosmetics are due to nail polishes. The functions of chemicals most popularly formulated in nail cosmetics and their tendency to produce adverse effects are described below. Some of the individual ingredients offer no striking cosmetic advantage to the consumer, in fact, some are used for lack of a safer, equally effective alternative. But they continue to enjoy wide application in the cosmetic industry because of their important chemical properties, that is, the ingredient is a good solvent for other chemicals in the formulation, increases durability, etc. In these cases, a minimum risk is accepted by the Food and Drug Administration, and the public, for the purpose of obtaining the overall cosmetic benefits offered by a particular product.

Nail Product Ingredients

ACETONE is a chemical that is obtained by fermentation or by chemical synthesis from isopropanol (rubbing alcohol). It has a very characteristic odor. Acetone is used in both nail polishes (as part of the solvent system) and in nail polish removers since it is quick acting, fast removing and fast drying. A couple of examples are *REVLON EXTRA FAST NAIL ENAMEL REMOVER* and *SALLY HANSEN KWIK OFF NAIL COLOR REMOVER.* Acetone is the best solvent to dissolve the lacquers used in nail polishes after they have hardened on the nail. Cosmetically, however, it is undesirable since it is a very harsh solvent, removing natural oils, turning the skin white and leaving the nail brittle. In some "non whitening" formulations water is added to moisturize the nail and to slow the drying action by acetone so as not to leave the nail white. Acetone can be absorbed into the body following ingestion, absorption through the skin or inhalation. In overdose, it causes central nervous system depression (drowsiness, confusion, and coma). However, there is little or no risk of substantial absorption during the routine use and application of nail polish and polish removers. Local effects are more likely following frequent use, such as drying and cracking of skin leading to irritation and possibly infection. Long term harmful effects, other than those just discussed are not known to occur even from repeated use.

BEESWAX is a natural wax from the honeycomb of the bee. It is added to polishes to provide body and richer texture to the finished product, but adds little, if any, cosmetic value for the user, other than making the formulation easier to apply. A typical product employing beeswax for this purpose is *PROFESSIONAL CUTICLE MASSAGE NIGHT CREAM BY REVLON*. Beeswax is completely non-poisonous, but because it is a naturally occurring and complex substance, it has been reported to cause a few adverse skin reactions when applied in facial cosmetics. It has not been known to cause any adverse reactions when applied in nail products.

BUTYL ACETATE is a colorless, flammable liquid with a fruity odor. It is made synthetically from alcohols and acetic acid (the primary component of household vinegar). Used in nail polishes *(REVLON'S LIQUID NAIL WRAP)* and removers *(REVLON'S 'WONDER WEAR', ADHESIVE BASE COAT)* it is a slower solvent for nitrocellulose, a lacquer used in many nail polishes, but it is not as irritating to the skin as acetone. It is moderately toxic by ingestion, causing drowsiness if accidentally swallowed in overdose. It has been reported to cause only minor skin irritation in some individuals, and this is due to the inherent, irritant properties of the chemical.

CAMPHOR is obtained naturally by steam distillation of parts of the camphor tree, *Cinnamomum camphora*, native to Taiwan and other parts of eastern Asia and naturalized in other parts of the world. It can also be made synthetically from a hydrocarbon obtained from oil of turpentine. Camphor is used in nail polishes as a plasticizer of certain resins, such as nitrocellulose (see below). Plasticizers provide a functional rather than a cosmetic value for the consumer by increasing the flexibility and toughness of the resin, thus improving the end product in the way that it wears on the fingernail. Thus, a product like *SALLY HANSEN'S SUPER SHINE SHINY TOP COAT*, which claims to add shine to nail enamel, uses camphor for this purpose. Camphor can be extremely poisonous when taken internally, however, it presents no health hazard in the small percentages used in nail polishes when applied topically. A naturally occurring plant substance, camphor has been reported (rarely) to produce a rash in sensitive people.

CETYL ALCOHOL is a white, waxy solid at room temperature. It is made synthetically from naturally occurring fatty acids and referred to as a fatty alcohol. Widely used in face creams, lotions, lipsticks, and nail polishes, it is an emollient (skin softener) and product thickener. *REVLON'S PROFESSIONAL CUTICLE REMOVER* uses cetyl alcohol to soften the cuticle that it comes in contact with, reducing irritation from other, harsher chemicals in the formulation. Cetyl alcohol is nontoxic and has not been reported to contribute to any adverse effects in nail cosmetics.

DIMETHICONE COPOLYOL is a synthetic polymer and a water-white, viscous, oil-like liquid. It is an emollient which lubricates cuticle and surrounding skin tissues. This is particularly important in polish removers, like *L'OREAL'S 'NAIL METHODE' GENTLE NAIL ENAMEL REMOVER*, where it is used as a skin protectant and a vehicle for other ingredients. It is nontoxic and has not been reported to cause any adverse skin reactions when applied in nail preparations.

ETHYL ACETATE is a colorless, flammable, fragrant liquid produced synthetically from acetic acid (vinegar) and ethyl alcohol (the alcohol of beverage). While it is slightly less effective, it is used in nail polishes and polish removers as a solvent alternative to acetone, since it is less harsh and does not whiten skin or nails. Several products use ethyl acetate, like *MAX FACTOR 'MAXI ENDLESS SHINE' NAIL ENAMEL*. Almost any nail product requiring a solvent vehicle is likely to use ethyl acetate to some degree. Ethyl acetate vapor is mildly irritating to eyes and skin. It can be absorbed through the skin and by inhalation, but amounts large enough to produce drowsiness or dizziness will not be encountered by proper use of nail products.

GLYCERIN is a syrupy, sweet, nontoxic, liquid which

may be synthesized from other chemicals or recovered as a by-product of soap manufacturing. It is used in nail formulations to absorb water, thus acting as a skin moisturizer in the product. Lotions that contain glycerin, such as *ESTEE LAUDER 'MAXIMUM CARE' BODY LOTION*, may also be recommended to moisturize the cuticle. When a chemical is used to hold water, it is referred to as a "humectant." Glycerin has not been reported to cause any adverse effects or allergic type reactions in humans.

GLYCERYL STEARATE is a fat prepared synthetically from other, natural fats. It is an emulsifier, keeping cosmetic chemicals dispersed throughout the nail formulation. Many nail products incorporate numerous skin softening ingredients into their formulations and use glyceryl stearate for this purpose. This chemical has not been reported to cause any adverse skin reactions. Even if ingested it is nontoxic and harmlessly digested like natural fats.

HYDROLYZED ANIMAL PROTEIN is derived from various animal sources in the butchering and packing process. The raw material is processed for incorporation into nail products. Many products use hydrolyzed animal protein, but one example is *CUTEX 'PERFECT CARE' CONDITIONING POLISH REMOVER*. Studies have shown that protein is absorbed by keratin in nails, thus proteins applied to the nails generally condition the nail, give body, and increase the resistance of the nail to cracking and splitting. It is completely non-poisonous, and in fact, is also used in food products. Hydrolyzed animal protein has not been reported to contribute to any adverse effects on skin.

ISOPROPYL ALCOHOL (rubbing alcohol) is a quick-drying vehicle used in nail conditioners to carry emollients and hydrolyzed animal protein. *SALLY HANSEN'S 'KWIK OFF' NAIL COLOR REMOVER* is a typical example of an alcohol-based remover, although many products use isopropyl alcohol. It is manufactured from several starting chemicals including propylene (a derivative of crude petroleum). Isopropyl alcohol can be absorbed through the skin and lungs, but amounts large enough to produce poisoning would not occur during the application of nail products. Long term effects have not been reported. Isopropyl alcohol can cause drying of the skin, but other additives in nail products usually compensate for this effect. Isopropyl alcohol may cause serious poisoning if ingested by mouth.

LACTIC ACID can be produced by fermenting starch, milk whey, potatoes and other food products, or it may be made synthetically from other starting chemicals. It is found naturally in the souring of milk, molasses, fruits, and numerous other foods, beverages and plants, due to the partial conversion of sugars during certain processes. It is used in nail products at a pH of about 4, which is significantly acid, working to dissolve the stratum corneum (the outermost layer of the skin, consisting of flat, packed, dead cells) and thus remove dead skin. In conjunction with a detergent in the product, which works to soften the skin, lactic acid is an effective cuticle remover. While it may cause stinging or burning if worked into cuts or scrapes in the surrounding skin, it is not dangerous at this concentration, and no long term, harmful effects have been reported.

LANOLIN or **HYDROUS WOOL FAT** is the fat removed from wool by washing with solvents with 25 to 30 percent water added. It is a yellowish-white, ointmentlike mass that has a characteristic odor. One of the chief constituents of lanolin is cholesterol, but numerous other fats are present. It is an ingredient in many creams and lotions, including nail products like *SALLY HANSEN'S CUTICLE MASSAGE CREAM* as a protectant and skin softener. Lanolin has not been associated with any health problems when used in nail products, but used in hand or face creams it is suspected of causing skin rashes after repeated use. It has also been reported to be associated with the production of blackheads (acne) when used in facial cosmetics.

NITROCELLULOSE is a cottonlike, pulpy, solid derived by treating wood pulp or other vegetable matter with mineral acids. Used to provide the decorative coating in nail lacquers, nitrocellulose requires other chemical "plasticizers" (see camphor above) and a solvent (see acetone and ethyl acetate, above) to produce the desired cosmetic effect. Nitrocellulose remains as a hardened resin on the nail to hold the colorants and finish of a nail product once the solvent evaporates. One of many brand names using nitrocellulose is *CHESEBROUGH-PONDS' CUTEX 'PERFECT COLOR FOR NAILS.'* Nitrocellulose has not been reported to cause any adverse effects on tissue when used in nail products and it has a long standing history of safety.

PARAFFIN helps hold moisture to the skin and nails when used in nail conditioning creams. It is a hard, white, waxy, solid material made synthetically from petroleum chemicals, and used in products like *REVLON'S CRYSTALLINE NAIL ENAMEL* line. It is completely inert and has not been reported to cause any adverse effects in nail products. Even when ingested in large quantity it is completely nonpoisonous.

POTASSIUM HYDROXIDE or **SODIUM HYDROXIDE** are alkaline-type chemicals prepared synthetically from other simpler potassium or sodium salts. They are extremely caustic chemicals used from 1 to 5 percent in moisturizing cream bases as cuticle removers. They may cause burning, particularly if they get into small cracks or cuts in the skin. Alkalies work in cuticle removers by causing swelling of the softened cuticle tissue, which aids in cuticle removal. Alkali hydroxides such as these pose no long term threat to health and are only dangerous due to their local irritant properties. Most cuticle remover products have abandoned these more irritating chemicals for safer, less irritating ones. For example, **TRISODIUM PHOSPHATE** (see below) is used for the same purpose as sodium and potassium hydroxide, but is less irritating to surrounding skin and nail.

PROPYLENE GLYCOL is a clear, colorless, liquid, made

synthetically. It is thick, has a characteristic taste, but is odorless. Since it absorbs moisture when exposed to the air and is soluble with most nail product ingredients, it is used as a moisturizing ingredient in nail and skin products. *REVLON'S NAIL STAIN REMOVER*, which claims to "moisturize and condition," includes propylene glycol to restore flexibility to the nail. The toxicity of this chemical is similar to glycerin (see above), thus it is practically nontoxic. The only adverse effects that have been reported with propylene glycol have been following injection into the blood stream, or following massive oral doses. Thus, it is completely safe as used in nail products. It has been used medicinally, following dilution with water, as an inhalation treatment in respiratory diseases for many years with few adverse effects. Problems related to this chemical when used in nail products have not been reported.

TEA LAURYL SULFATE is a synthetic detergent that helps to swell and soften dead skin, and for this reason may be used in cuticle removers. The "TEA" stands for **TRIETHANOLAMINE**. The detergent is of extremely low toxicity even when taken in very large doses orally. Minor skin irritation has been attributed to this detergent. However, in the concentrations used in nail products, it is not likely to produce adverse effects.

TOLUENE-SULFONAMIDE-FORMALDEHYDE or **TSF** is an artificially prepared resin that has become indispensable in nail lacquer technology. Typical brand name nail products that use TSF are *CUTEX NAIL CREAMS*, *REVLON 'SUPER NAILS NATURAL WONDER'* and *COVER GIRL'S 'OPULENCE'* by Noxell Corporation, although it can be found in virtually all enamel formulations. There is always a very small amount of free formaldehyde present in nail products containing this resin. Sensitization in humans has occurred due to formaldehyde and a condition known as onycholysis (loosening of the nails) has been reported in the medical literature. However, wide use in the general population is apparently tolerated very well and the FDA has released a statement "that potential formaldehyde exposure from FDA regulated products is very low and that no regulatory action against the use of formaldehyde . . . is necessary at this time." Thus the FDA concurs with several other government agencies that formaldehyde (in cosmetics) poses no significant health risk to humans. Persons sensitive to this chemical would most likely develop redness, itching and possibly swelling during the first few times the product is applied to the nails. Discontinuing use of the product with clearing of symptoms would be a clue to sensitivity due to formaldehyde.

TRISODIUM PHOSPHATE or **TSP** occurs as a crystalline chemical made artificially by a combination of minerals and caustics. It is very alkaline in solution, and for this reason it is used in cuticle eliminating products, like *REVLON'S PROFESSIONAL CUTICLE REMOVER* and *SALLY HANSEN'S GEL CUTICLE REMOVER*. Alkalies work in these products by causing swelling of the softened cuticle tissue, which aids in cuticle removal. Trisodium phosphate is capable of causing temporary burning or itching, especially when applied to diseased skin. If burning occurs following the use of this chemical it will usually subside within fifteen minutes. Permanent effects do not occur from TSP, but exaggerated redness and irritation should make one think twice about future use.

Powders

Powders are used to hide shine or greasiness in facial cosmetics, provide "slip" as in body talcs, provide absorbency, and also to impart a cooling sensation when used in other preparation powders. A face powder must impart a smooth finish to the skin, masking minor imperfections and shine due to moisture or grease, either from perspiration or other preparations used on the skin. The main function of body powder is to absorb moisture on skin and prevent abrasion by the clothing.

Because of their large surface area, it is believed that powders enhance radiation of heat from the skin and thus produce their cooling effect. Thus, powders find a substantial application in pharmaceuticals, such as foot powders which are secondarily used as vehicles for medications, as well as cosmetics. Powders applied to the face as cosmetics must perform a difficult task, making the skin look as though it would be pleasant to touch, giving a peach skin or "velvet" appearance and providing a pleasant scent released by fragrances which are absorbed to the powder. Talc and other powders do not plug sweat and oil gland openings as might be feared by some, even though the particles of powder are very small. Only the finest grades of talc and powders are used in cosmetic and pharmaceutical products. This is important since many fragrances are used with powders and the effectiveness of the fragrance depends on the quality of the powder.

An important health concern with the use of powders, particularly around and on the skin of infants, is that many of them are derived from minerals. This means they do not dissolve in water or saliva and they can be extremely hazardous if they get into the lungs by what is known as "aspiration." Coughing and choking, following an accidental ingestion of the powder by children, may cause some of the powder to lodge in the lungs, blocking the movement of air. This can be a life-threatening emergency. Any of these powders, including baby powders, should not be given to children to play with during diaper changes or at any other time.

Powder Ingredients

ALUMINUM SILICATE, HYDRATED good absorbent and adhesive properties. Derived naturally from numerous types of clay which contain varying proportions of aluminum oxide and silicon dioxide (see kaolin, below). For cosmetic purposes, it is made synthetically by heating aluminum fluoride with silica (sand) and water vapor.

ALUMINUM STEARATE or **ALUMINUM TRISTEARATE** is a nontoxic, white powder that is made synthetically from the reaction of aluminum salts with a naturally derived fatty acid, stearic acid.

BORIC ACID is used in body powders to keep the pH down below 7 and to neutralize free ammonia, important in minimizing diaper rash. It is made synthetically from **SODIUM BORATE (BORAX)** but occurs in nature as the mineral sassolite. Boric acid is dangerous when incorporated into body powders because it can be absorbed into the blood stream when applied to reddened or irritated skin. Application to intact skin does not result in absorption by the body. Boric acid is poisonous if swallowed and the symptoms of boric acid poisoning are well described in the medical literature. There are many safer alternatives to boric acid for use in dusting, body and baby powders.

CALCIUM CARBONATE is one of the most widely dispersed minerals in nature, found in surface deposits as aragonite, calcite, chalk limestone, dolomite and marble. It is also found in egg and oyster shells and in many other substances. It is used in body powders because it has excellent adhesive and absorbent properties and is completely nontoxic.

CALCIUM SILICATE or **CALCIUM METASILICATE** is found in *VASELINE INTENSIVE CARE BABY POWDER* as an absorbent. It is also widely used in the food and pharmaceutical industry. While calcium silicate has good adhesive and absorbent properties for use as a body powder, it is an irritating dust to the lungs and inhalation over long periods of time should be avoided. Calcium silicate is found in nature as the mineral wollastonite and is mined all over the world.

CETYL ALCOHOL and **STEARYL ALCOHOL** are white, waxy solid chemicals in powder or flake form that improve adhesion of powder to the skin. They are referred to as fatty alcohols and are prepared synthetically because they occur only rarely in nature. Cetyl alcohol is found in large amounts as a component of spermaceti, a wax made by sperm whales. Since sperm whale products are outlawed, natural cetyl alcohol is obtained by chemical alteration of tallow (animal fat).

KAOLIN, COLLOIDAL is a good absorbent and has excellent adhesive properties. It is used in baby powders like *VASELINE INTENSIVE CARE BABY POWDER* because of its purity and adsorbent properties. Kaolin is a high quality, naturally occurring clay, also known as **CHINA CLAY**, which consists mainly of **ALUMINUM OXIDE** and **SILICON DIOXIDE**, but also varying amounts of other minerals such as quartz and feldspar. It is mined in the United States. The term colloidal refers to the physical dispersion of the kaolin clay in the powder. Kaolin has many desirable properties, such as particle size, chemical inertness, whiteness, and its ability to absorb moisture. It is nontoxic when applied to the skin and is not known to produce contact allergy.

MAGNESIUM CARBONATE is an odorless, white powder for use in cosmetic or pharmaceutical powders, but occurs in nature as the mineral magnesite, an important source of the metal magnesium. Used in *DIAPARENE CORN STARCH BABY POWDER*, it is a good absorbent and has good adhesive properties. It is not known to cause allergic reactions and is virtually nontoxic when applied to the skin.

MAGNESIUM STEARATE is the best tolerated of the stearates on skin. It is a soft, white, light powder very suitable for body dusts. It is tasteless, odorless and nontoxic.

PRECIPITATED CHALK is merely **CALCIUM CARBONATE**, and "precipitated" refers to the synthetic process by which it is prepared from **CALCIUM CHLORIDE** and

SODIUM CARBONATE by precipitating it from a water solution. it is a white powder and is odorless, tasteless and nontoxic. Chalk is found in nature and is mined from surface deposits as are other minerals of calcium carbonate which include aragonite, oyster shells, and limestone. It has good absorbent and adhesive properties.

STARCH or **CORNSTARCH** has good absorbent and adhesive properties and it leaves the skin feeling very smooth. However, after it gets moist, it tends to cake. Because of this, if starch powders are left on the skin too long they can promote irritation and redness leading to infection.

SILICA, when powdered, exerts an effect of increasing fluffiness and helps the spreading property of powders. It is **SILICON DIOXIDE**, and occurs widely in nature as sand, quartz, flint and other minerals. The use of silica in body powders is not acceptable since it is toxic by inhalation. The inhalation over long periods of time causes the disease known as **SILICOSIS**.

TALC is a mineral, **MAGNESIUM SILICATE**. It is also known as soapstone. It does not readily absorb moisture, but it doesn't cake on the skin like starch. But when used in body powders it gives of feeling of slipperiness. Talc and other naturally occurring minerals are frequently contaminated with spore forming micro-organisms such as *Clostridium tetani*, the bacterium that causes tetanus. A highly refined and purified form of talc is used in *JOHNSON'S BABY POWDER* with only added fragrance. It is not good to breathe talc powder because silicates irritate the lungs and are known to cause long term problems.

TITANIUM DIOXIDE is a completely nontoxic powder which can vary in color depending on purity. When used in body powders only the purest, finest grades are used and the chemical is a white dust. It is prepared synthetically from minerals.

TRICALCIUM PHOSPHATE, found in *JOHNSON'S BABY CORNSTARCH POWDER*, is a white, odorless, tasteless powder probably employed in this formulation to prevent clumping. It occurs in nature in various minerals but is prepared synthetically for pharmaceutical and cosmetic applications.

ZINC OXIDE can improve the adhesion of powders and has mildly antiseptic properties. It is nontoxic. For these reasons, this white or grayish, odorless powder has been incorporated into many pharmaceutical and cosmetic preparations over the years. Zinc oxide is made artificially from zinc ores which occur in nature.

ZINC STEARATE is a white powder derived synthetically from zinc salts and the fatty acid, stearic acid. It is nontoxic.

5

Dental & Mouth Care

Although there are more than 162,000 dentists in the United States, dental disease is a very common health problem. The problem is consumers do not consider dental care a major health priority; usually we only go to a dentist in the event of an emergency, after the damage has been done. Teeth are made to last a lifetime provided proper care is taken.

Toothbrushes

There is an old dental maxim: If you want to keep your teeth, you have to keep them clean. The toothbrush is the first line of defense in keeping teeth free of plaque. The role played by plaque in the development of gingivitis (inflammation of the gums) was demonstrated in the early 1960s. Dental researchers had people stop brushing their teeth and let the plaque in their mouths build up. Within two to three weeks, signs of inflammation appeared—redness, swelling and an increased tendency to bleed. When they starting brushing again, the inflammation went away. **DENTAL PLAQUE** is defined as a thin, sticky, almost colorless film of food debris and other material that forms continuously on the teeth, providing a medium for bacterial growth. Studies show that plaque is directly linked to the development of **CAVITIES, GINGIVITIS** and to **PERIODONTITIS** (inflammation and infection of the bone that surrounds and supports the teeth). Both tooth decay and gum disease are things that can lead to tooth loss later in life. However, we used to think that most adult tooth loss was due to gum or bone disease. But newer studies show tooth decay is the reason for most tooth extractions later in life. Gum and bone inflammation and infection (gingivitis and periodontitis) cause only about one-tenth of all tooth loss in adults.

Brushing is important, but deciding among all the different types of toothbrushes that are available is often a source of confusion. Most dentists recommend a soft to medium nylon bristle. Studies show that soft bristles are better than hard in removing plaque. Brushing with too-hard bristles irritates the gum line and may cause bleeding, thereby keeping you from brushing thoroughly. The toothbrush needs to be replaced every two months, or sooner if there was a cold or other type of respiratory infection. It should be small, in order to reach all tooth surfaces and to fit in the rear of the mouth and on the tongue side of the teeth. Some people complain of gagging when brushing; in that case try using a child's size toothbrush. These considerations aside, virtually any toothbrush can be effective if properly used, and a choice can usually be made based on personal preference or a dentist's advise.

The Council on Dental Materials has so far not found that using a powered or **AUTOMATIC TOOTHBRUSH** produces better results than manual brushing. Therefore, use whatever one helps you to brush continuously and effectively. In some cases, as with small children and patients suffering from diseases (including multiple sclerosis or cerebral palsy), the powered toothbrush makes brushing the teeth much easier; in the case of children, the novelty may make it more interesting. Also, it should be pointed out that brushing alone cannot remove certain types of plaque, particularly that which occurs below the gums, called **SUBGINGIVAL PLAQUE**. A trip to the dentist is necessary for that. Nonetheless, controlling the buildup of plaque on the teeth above the gums, called **SUPRAGINGIVAL PLAQUE**, helps control both the quantity and harmful nature of plaque below the gum line. But no matter how good a toothbrush is, it will only do half the job unless a good toothpaste is used right along with it.

Toothpastes

Toothpastes are used with a toothbrush to clean the teeth. They are available in pastes, powders, and gels. They contain abrasives, flavoring, and foaming agents (detergents). These products help remove stains and plaque that occur above the gum line. But this is not because they have special "anti-plaque" ingredients. The abrasives and detergents in toothpastes aid in the mechanical removal of plaque that occurs during toothbrushing. If they taste good they encourage brushing more often. Some toothpastes are being marketed for preventing the buildup of "tartar." **TARTAR**, which is that white, brown or yellow-brown deposit of plaque that has calcified and hardened on the teeth at the gum line, was once thought to contribute to or even cause periodontal disease by physically irritating the gum tissues. It is now considered far less important, and, according to a recent issue of the Journal of the American Dental Association, tartar control toothpastes have a "cosmetic benefit" only. They have no effect on **GINGIVITIS** (inflammation or infection of the gums) or **PERIODONTITIS** (infection of bone).

Some toothpastes contain **FLUORIDE**, and when used regularly can help reduce the incidence of cavities. However, some dentists feel that fluoride toothpastes are more effective in children than in adults. Because of plaque build up on the teeth of an adult (see page 51), it is hard for the fluoride to penetrate through that barrier and protect the teeth. People often are confused about which toothpaste to buy. A good rule of thumb is to look at the package and see if it has been accepted by the American Dental Association (ADA). The ones that have been accepted have the least amount of abrasiveness, as well as the right amount of fluoride to adequately protect the teeth. ADA acceptance also means that the other claims made by the product label have been proved to the satisfaction of this professional group. That does not mean that the Food and Drug Administration agrees. An example is the anti-plaque claims made for mouthwashes (see page 58). Toothpastes that have been accepted by the Council on Dental Therapeutics are *AIM*, *CREST*, *AQUAFRESH*, *COLGATE*, and *CLOSE-UP*.

Sensitivity to Hot and Cold

The American Dental Association says that one out of four Americans has a problem with dental sensitivity at least once in his or her life. Dental sensitivity can cover the whole spectrum from a little discomfort to sharp and excruciating pain when teeth contact hot or cold liquids and foods. It can even occur from sucking in outside air on a cold, wintry day. Dental sensitivity is the result of damage or loss of enamel with exposure of the dentin, the ivory forming the largest part of the tooth. Sensitivity may also occur if the gum tissue recedes thereby exposing the root and allowing sensations through to the dentin below. The damage can be due to faulty brushing technique, gum recession caused by periodontal disease, or as a result of periodontal surgery. The research that has been done has looked at two methods of controlling tooth sensitivity. One way is to block off the small tubules that travel through the dentin. These tubelike openings in the dentin can transmit sensation to the nerve of the tooth. **STRONTIUM CHLORIDE,** a chemical found in *ORIGINAL FORMULA SENSODYNE-SC TOOTHPASTE* is a chemical that is thought to act in this way. The second theory is that some chemicals have a drug effect to reduce the excitability of the nerve. This would interrupt the signal that results in the sensation of pain. **POTASSIUM NITRATE** is one of these chemicals, used in products like *DENQUEL*, *FRESH MINT SENSODYNE*, *COOL GEL SENSODYNE*, and *PROMISE TOOTHPASTE*. Potassium nitrate seems to have the best track record and is supported by a number of scientific studies. Another chemical, **SODIUM CITRATE**, is used in at least one paste for sensitive teeth, *PROTECT*. But the way it works, if it really does, is not clear.

Many people but not everybody, do get relief from using these products. However, it is not clear why this benefit occurs. In any case, it is certainly worth a try. The manufacturers of these products say that, with regular use, there will be continued decrease in sensitivity occurring over the first two weeks of use.

Dental Floss and Tape

Dental floss is essential for removing plaque and debris in areas a toothbrush cannot reach. The crevices between the teeth and along the gum line attract bacteria, which can get to the tooth and destroy it. Dental floss should be inserted gently between the teeth. While grasping at both ends one should clean each tooth side with a back and forth motion as the floss hugs the tooth surface. Forcing it down between the teeth, may result in an injury to the gum. Dental floss is available in waxed and unwaxed varieties. Most dentists recommend the unwaxed floss, because the waxed floss sometimes leaves deposits of wax on the tooth. These in turn may cause plaque to stick to it and remain on the tooth. Waxed floss is usually used by people with tightly spaced teeth, because it moves more easily between the teeth. Dental tape or ribbon is another form available. There is no functional difference between floss, ribbon, or tape; choice is simply a matter of personal preference.

Brushing Aids

According to dental experts, most people do not brush their teeth properly and frequently miss some areas of their mouths, so it is a good idea to request instructions in effective brushing from a dentist or dental hygienist. To help people learn to brush properly, there is a type of dental product available in most drugstores known as a **DISCLOSING AGENT**. It is available in either liquid or tablet form. These products are very useful in teaching children, as well as adults, to brush their teeth properly. Disclosing agents contain one or more FDA approved dyes. Either in tablet or liquid form it is applied before brushing. Both forms stain or color the plaque and debris on the teeth; the next step is to brush off all the red color. Disclosing agents are effective for training children. The red dye in these products is **D&C RED No. 28** or other FDA approved dye.

Mouthwashes

Next to toothbrushes and toothpastes, the most commonly used over-the-counter dental products are mouthwashes. Mouthwashes have a long history. An ancient Chinese text contains the first known recommendation for the use of a mouthwash in the treatment of gum disease: rinse the mouth with urine. Strangely enough, in the 5000 years since that was written, urine (which from a healthy person is sterile) has been used as a mouthwash in cultures around the world. It seems that by keeping the acidity of the mouth low it may help reduce the formation of cavities. Admittedly it is an unpleasant approach and dentists agree that it is unlikely to be effective in preventing periodontal disease.

The modern era of mouthwashes began in the 1920s with the marketing of *LISTERINE MOUTHWASH*, which had already been sold for more than 40 years as a general antiseptic, as a remedy for bad breath. According to many of the advertisements "bad breath" is a major cause of social unpopularity. Listerine's advertising campaign introduced the American public to the term "**HALITOSIS**" and its social undesirability. The pitch was so successful that it is now considered a classic. **BAD BREATH** is generally caused by the presence of bacteria in the mouth. One's breath is usually at its worst upon waking; that is because bacteria grow in the mouth when it is inactive while we are sleeping. Usually within an hour or so after we wake up, the breath returns to normal. Bad breath is also sometimes caused by dyspepsia or other digestive disorders.

The ideal mouthwash should contain a high antiseptic concentration to rapidly kill bacteria in the mouth. Unfortunately, such a dose may be either very irritating to the tissues inside the mouth, or poisonous if swallowed. Additionally, it is probably not a good idea to try to completely kill all the bacteria in the mouth. There is a normal balance of bacteria in the mouth which if killed may allow for overgrowth of yeast which may result in oral thrush. So, needless to say, we don't yet have the "ideal" mouthwash.

Mouthwashes can be grouped into several types: those that are cosmetic, those that have ingredients to treat a sore throat and those that claim to prevent dental plaque. *SCOPE*, *LAVORIS*, and *LISTERMINT*, among others, are intended to freshen the breath temporarily. For example, if one eats a meal containing onions or garlic the mouthwash may remove the taste and odor for a few minutes. Thereafter the taste of garlic on the breath will be noticed again. That is because the garlic is in the stomach and not in the mouth. It is absorbed through the walls of the stomach into the bloodstream. As a result, every exhalation produces garlic breath. To mask the odor, try using a breath mint. It stays in the mouth and permeates the exhaled air to hide the odor. Some people use a spray, but except for the convenience of carrying it around, it is effective no longer than a mouthwash. What is more, a small pocket spray, can cost 4 or 5 times a pack of mints.

People sometimes use mouthwashes for the wrong reason. Gargling with the cosmetic mouthwashes for a **SORE THROAT** can actually cause the sore throat to become worse. The alcohol contained in these products evaporates from the throat, drying it out and causing further irritation. For a sore throat, gargle several times a day with lukewarm salt water: one teaspoonful of salt in an eight-ounce glass of warm water. (Too much salt will also irritate the throat.) If there is a fever along with the sore throat it may be a sign of infection. This warrants a call to the physician.

However, some mouthwashes are specifically intended to

treat a **SORE THROAT**. Products such as *CHLORASEPTIC* and *CEPASTAT* contain an ingredient called **PHENOL** which is a numbing ingredient, an anesthetic. These products numb the throat, mouth, and tongue. These mouthwashes can give relief, but only for about an hour. This may be very helpful if it allows enough time to fall asleep to get some needed rest during the course of the illness. Products that numb the throat are also available in pocket sprays and lozenges, but usually contain **BENZOCAINE** in this form. Using these products can be a problem when eating or drinking. Numbing the throat can make it dangerous to swallow. These products should be used at intervals between meals to be safe.

Anti-Plaque Mouthwashes

Mouthwash manufacturers frequently make claims about plaque control. They suggest that their products remove plaque from the teeth with **ANTI-MICROBIAL** or **CHEMICAL** agents. In the 1980s some scientific studies began to appear suggesting that some mouthwashes might really reduce plaque on the teeth above the gums (called **SUPRAGINGIVAL** plaque). A prescription product, *PERIDEX*, containing the antimicrobial **CHLORHEXIDINE** was approved by FDA in 1986 based on studies showing that it reduced gingivitis (inflammation or infection of the gums) by up to 41 percent by preventing plaque from forming on the teeth. Chlorhexidine mouthwashes have long been used in Europe, but this ingredient is not available over-the-counter in the United States. Shortly after Peridex was approved and even awarded the American Dental Association's "Seal of Acceptance," over-the-counter products, such as *LISTERINE*, also began making claims of plaque-fighting ability, although without the use of the ingredient chlorhexidine. The FDA has not yet approved Listerine, or any other nonprescription product, for this use. Nevertheless, some of the names imply that they are especially for plaque control, such as *PLAX* mouthwash. Those manufacturers claiming that their products prevent dental plaque and related conditions have been asked to submit scientific data to support such statements to FDA. According to the Federal Food, Drug, and Cosmetic Act, such statements as "for the reduction or prevention of plaque, tartar, calculus, film, sticky deposits, bacterial build-up, and gingivitis" are drug claims because they deal with treating or preventing disease and because they affect the structure or function of the body. It remains to be seen how the FDA panel will decide on these claims in the near future. If the FDA—using its panel of nongovernment, oral health care experts—finds that scientific data do not support the claims, the FDA would require manufacturers to drop the unsupported claims.

Denture Products

People who have not taken care of their teeth, or who have lost them through gum disease or an accident of some sort, can be fitted for dentures. Not surprisingly, there are now just about as many different products for use with dentures as for natural teeth.

Denture Adhesives

For example, there are just about as many brand name adhesives to keep dentures in place as there are toothpastes. Some of them are paste, others are powder. The adhesives in these products are gums made from naturally occurring **CELLULOSE** and **KARAYA** (see page 68). Some of the well known denture adhesive brands are *COREGA POWDER*, *EFFERGRIP* powder and cream, *FASTEETH*, *FIXODENT*, *ORAFIX*, *POLI-GRIP*, and *WERNET'S CREAM* and powder. Sometimes people who continually use adhesives cannot tell if their dentures are out of alignment and need an adjustment. If dentures do get out of alignment, they put pressure on various areas of the gum, creating painful sores and perhaps causing damage to the mouth itself. Prolonged use of adhesives, if dentures are not cleaned regularly, may stimulate the growth of bacteria, causing bad breath and infections in the mouth.

Denture Cleansers

To avoid permanent staining and bad breath, dentures must be brushed at least once daily. Any denture cleansers on the market are good to use, because they are compatible with the material that dentures are made from. Products like *POLIDENT CLEANSER* contain bleaching and disinfecting agents such as **SODIUM BORATE** and **SODIUM PERBORATE.** Soap and baking soda are also suitable cleansers for dentures, although they probably are not as effective as some of the prepared cleansers that can be purchased. No matter what denture cleanser is used, it is important to rinse the dentures thoroughly before placing them in the mouth. (Since some of these cleansing agents are corrosive, they should be kept well out of the reach of children. Every year there are a number of accidental poisonings as a result of children eating these and other over-the-counter products.) Sometimes soaking dentures in undiluted white vinegar will remove stubborn stains. Again, be sure to rinse them thoroughly before putting them back in the mouth.

Sonic and Ultrasonic Denture Cleaners

Sonic and ultrasonic denture-cleaning devices are relatively new products. They are electric. When they are plugged in they produce a vibration in the water, which, as it passes over the dentures, removes food particles and debris. Such a product makes a thoughtful gift, especially for the elderly, who have trouble cleaning their dentures. There are three distinct kinds to choose from. The **ULTRASONIC** is the most effective, the **MAGNETIC** stirrers second in effectiveness, and the **VIBRATOR** least effective. If help is needed in selecting the product ask your pharmacist or, better yet, call a dentist and see what he recommends.

Denture Reliners and Repair Kits

Dentures that do not fit properly may simply need a slight adjustment. However, poor fit may also indicate a change in the bone structure of the mouth. Many people think that using a reliner on dentures will solve the problem. These products can actually be dangerous, especially if used over a long period of time. They may change the shape of the denture or make it fit too tightly. This causes additional pressure on the gums and bone, as well as irritating the tongue and cheeks, causing sores that could lead to cancerous lesions. These products, like *EZO DENTURE CUSHIONS* and *DENTURITE* all warn that they are not to be used for more than a couple of weeks at the most. They should only be used in emergencies and for very short periods of time.

Occasionally people drop their dentures and break them and then may attempt to glue them back together, or use one of the denture repair kits. If the denture is not lined up exactly, it will once again put additional pressure on the gums, causing the same problems that the denture reliners cause. As a matter of fact, the FDA considers reliners and repair kits unsafe. Unfortunately, they are still on the market, and as long as there is a demand for them, they will remain in drugstores along with the other dental products.

Fever Blisters

This is one condition that makes people want to go around with their hand over their mouth. Many people think that fever blisters are caused by the sun, or a cold, or other conditions. Fever blisters are sometimes called "cold" sores. Actually they are caused by a virus, which may be triggered by sun exposure or illness. Specifically, the virus is herpes simplex virus type one or **HSV-1** (genital herpes is caused by a cousin known as **HSV-2**). About 40 percent of Americans have been infected by the virus by age 30, but it lies dormant in the body, flaring up from time to time with a cold or fever, exposure to excessive sunlight or during periods of stress. When we are out in the sun, the sun actually dries out the lips, and this dryness of the lips is a good environment for the virus to grow in. If fever blisters occur following sunlight exposure, coat the lips with a sun block.

Some people develop fever blisters when they have a cold. Nasal congestion often causes them to breathe through their mouths, which in turn dries out the lips. Also, the fever that sometimes accompanies a cold may cause the lips to dry out. Again, try coating the lips with a little *VASELINE* during the course of the illness.

Once a fever blister develops, as with most viruses, it must simply run its course, which is usually about seven to ten days. There is no complete cure. The few over-the-counter products are mixtures of soothing agents or simple astringents and there is limited evidence that they speed healing. One such product, *TANAC NO STING LIQUID*, uses a numbing agent, **BENZOCAINE**, and **TANNIC ACID** as an astringent. Astringents may cause the sores to form a hard scab on the lip, which then cracks when the mouth is opened, causing pain and discomfort.

Other products are intended to coat the fever blister and keep it soft, like *CHAPSTICK*, *BLISTIK*, and *VASELINE LIP THERAPY* lip balm, which work to simply cover and moisten the sore, so that it is not so painful. They also will sometimes include a sunblock chemical to prevent further drying of the area. Since they are in a tube similar to lipstick they are convenient to use. Some products like *BLISTEX* (containing **ALLANTOIN, CAMPHOR** and **PHENOL**), *COLGATE ORABASE LIP HEALER* (**BENZOCAINE, ALLANTOIN** and **MENTHOL**) and *VASELINE MEDICATED LIP THERAPY* (**ALLANTOIN**) are medicated and in cream form. When applying any of these products, be sure to cover the cold sore or fever blister completely, especially during the first two or three days when it is contagious and could spread.

Another product is *HERPECIN-L*, which may be used at the point of itching and burning of the lips. It contains **ALLANTOIN** and a sunscreen. This product is in the form of a lipstick.

Canker Sores

These differ from fever blisters in that they are ulcers that develop on the inside of the mouth. They usually appear in groups and most often are limited to the inside of the cheek and lips, though occasionally they form on the tongue and roof of the mouth. The sore is usually round or oval in shape and white in color; they can range in diameter from the size of a pinhead to the size of a quarter. Canker sores are not contagious. The cause of canker sores is not known, but it has been shown that people tend to develop them during times of physical and emotional stress. Also certain foods seem to trigger canker sores. Women tend to develop them more than men. One of two kinds of treatment is possible: Use one of the products for toothache or sore gums that contain a numbing ingredient, such as *ORAJEL*, or *ANBESOL GEL*, both of which contain **BENZOCAINE**, that may help stop the pain associated with a canker sore. Also one of the **PEROXIDE GELS** can be used such as *GLYOXIDE*, *PROXIGEL* or *CANKAID ORAL ANTISEPTIC*. They contain 10 percent **CARBAMIDE PEROXIDE** and they release oxygen at the site of the sore, which in turn helps to remove damaged tissue and promote healing. Avoid acidic foods because they will irritate the sore.

Toothache Medicines

Toothache drops are an old stand-by for a toothache. It always seems that toothaches develop on weekends, or in the evening when the dentist is not in his office. These products contain either **BENZOCAINE** or **EUGENOL** (the active ingredient in **OIL OF CLOVE**), which produces a local anesthetic action on the tooth or gum. Benzocaine is found in *LIQUID ORAJEL MAXIMUM STRENGTH LONG ACTING TOOTHACHE PAIN MEDICINE* and eugenol is in the brand name *RED CROSS TOOTHACHE MEDICATION.* Unfortunately, these products are not very effective and may sometimes injure the tooth further. **ASPIRIN**, as well as other over-the-counter pain relievers, may be useful for relieving the pain temporarily. However, under no circumstances should aspirin be applied directly to the teeth or gums. Aspirin will burn the tissue surrounding the tooth, as well as the tongue, causing sores that can take a long time to heal. It can also cause further damage to the tooth. Toothache is a local problem that should be treated by a dentist. Pain relievers treat only the symptom and not the cause.

So have a periodic check-up with a dentist, because more Americans lack dental care than have it. Those who take the proper preventative steps will have the fewest problems.

There are other products available in the drugstore such as an **ELECTRIC TOOTH BUFFER**, to help clean teeth more easily. A tooth buffer is similar to what the dentist uses to clean teeth. It consists of a handle with a round rubber end. The rubber tip spins and is used to buff or polish the teeth. We would like to point out, however, that even though it resembles the one a dentist uses, if used improperly, a tooth buffer can cause an injury to the tooth or gum.

Another product that has gained in popularity is the **WATER-PIK.** It squirts a pulsating stream of water to remove food particles and prevent the formation of bacteria between the teeth which may otherwise cause the loss of teeth due to gum disease. Some claim that this product works better than flossing. However, if you point the stream directly at the gum, it may cause the gum to pull away from the tooth. Adjust the force of water making sure it is neither too strong nor too weak to really clean between the teeth and at the gum line. When considering buying one, it would be a good idea to talk it over with a pharmacist, or with a dentist, to make sure that you know not only all the facts about the product but also how to use it properly.

Dental and Mouth Care Ingredients

As we have seen so far there are a lot of products on the market to help clean the teeth and keep breath fresh. Dental product ingredients may have cosmetic as well as therapeutic value. The products listed below are primarily those that are employed therapeutically to assist in the proper cleaning of teeth and are claimed to help control the buildup of dental plaque (see page 51). A few other miscellaneous products and ingredients are discussed and their purpose is explained as they are mentioned.

ALLANTOIN is an ingredient that comes from uric acid, a chemical found in urine. Certain animals, but not man, possess an enzyme that converts uric acid to allantoin. However, it is also found to occur in numerous plants. When purified, it is a white, crystalline powder which has no odor or taste. During World War I it was noticed that wounds which became infested with maggots healed with unexpected speed. Maggots are able to convert uric acid to allantoin and it was learned that the rapid healing was due to the presence of allantoin in their excretion. In spite of this, allantoin is banned by the FDA in products that claim to promote healing and prevent infection by application to the skin. The FDA just doesn't find enough hard scientific evidence that it works. But it is still allowed in over-the-counter aids to heal oral wounds, such as canker sores. This may not continue much longer, as the FDA has not found allantoin effective for this use either.

ALUMINA is **ALUMINUM OXIDE**, a chemical that occurs in nature as the mineral corundum. Commercially aluminum oxide can be made from other aluminum ores. It is considered safe and nontoxic and is used as a mild abrasive in such products as *PEPSODENT* and *ULTRA BRITE* toothpaste.

CALCIUM CARBONATE is a white, nontoxic, gritty powder and a naturally occurring mineral found in limestone, chalks and oyster shells. It is also made synthetically and purified and refined for use in dental products as an abrasive. *DENQUEL SENSITIVE TEETH TOOTHPASTE,* is one product that uses calcium carbonate for its polishing properties.

CALCIUM GLYCEROPHOSPHATE is a white, crystalline, odorless and tasteless powder that is used as a mild abrasive in tooth pastes. It is made artificially from mineral acids and glycerin, is nontoxic and recognized as safe for oral use.

CALCIUM PYROPHOSPHATE is a synthetically prepared abrasive which is made from naturally occurring starting minerals. It is a white powder used in toothpaste because it does not dissolve in water, maintaining its grittiness and is nontoxic.

DIATOMACEOUS EARTH is used as a mild abrasive in dental products. It is a gritty substance composed of the skeletons of small prehistoric aquatic plants related to algae (diatoms, hence the name) and having intricate geometric shapes. They are collected from the bottom of the ocean floor. It is found as an "inactive ingredient" in some toothpastes that claim to be "anti-stain," such as *CAFFREE.*

DICALCIUM PHOSPHATE DIHYDRATE, DICALCIUM PHOSPHATE or **CALCIUM PHOSPHATE DIBASIC** is a chemical made artificially from minerals that occur naturally in the earth. The white, tasteless, crystalline powder is used in toothpastes offering a more abrasive formulation, such as *TOPOL SMOKERS TOOTHPOLISH* and *COLGATE TOOTH POWDER*. As an abrasive it is nontoxic.

EUGENOL or **CLOVE OIL** is a pale yellow liquid which is a powerful germicide and antiseptic found in *RED CROSS*

TOOTHACHE DROPS. It is more frequently used in dental practice, in combination with zinc oxide and other chemicals as a temporary filling in caries and root canal work. It is the volatile oil distilled with steam from the dried flower buds of the plant, *Eugenia caryophyllus* which is grown in the West Indies and along the west coast of Africa. The active constituents of clove oil are chemicals similar to phenol. Eugenol is an effective numbing agent, but it is very harsh on the tissues in the mouth. It will burn sensitive areas that it comes into contact with, such as the skin around the lips.

FLUORIDES, such as **SODIUM FLUORIDE** are prepared synthetically for use in dental products. Sodium fluoride has been shown to prevent dental caries because the element fluoride is exchanged for a part of the tooth structure, making it more resistant to caries. Sodium fluoride is extremely poisonous in fairly small quantities, but the amounts incorporated into tooth products, like *GLEEM FLUORIDE TOOTHPASTE* and *ORAL-B ZENDIUM FLUORIDE TOOTHPASTE*, do not pose any poison hazard. Even so, children should be taught to spit out toothpastes, rather than swallowing after brushing. **SODIUM MONOFLUOROPHOSPHATE** or **MFP** is artificially prepared for use as tooth decay preventative in pastes and creams, like *PEARL DROPS TOOTH POLISH*, because it is a source of fluoride. Fluoride replaces the "hydroxy" part of hydroxyapatite, the major constituent of bone and tooth mineral, to form fluorapatite. Fluorapatite in the outer surface of dental enamel is harder and more resistant to acids than hydroxyapatite and therefore the enamel is less susceptible to tooth decay. Fluorine, the element, is present in small but widely varying concentrations in practically all soils, water supplies, plants and animals. Therefore, it is a constituent of all "normal" diets. Sodium monofluorophosphate is often used in smokers toothpastes such as *PEARL DROPS STAIN FIGHTING TOOTHPOLISH* and *TOPOL SMOKERS TOOTHPASTE*. However, it is also present in pastes like *AQUAFRESH* and *COLGATE*, thus one wonders what the "smokers" advantage is in the Pearl Drops product. These toothpastes offer no significant advantage over other pastes. If one really wants to get rid of smoking stains on teeth, stop smoking! **STANNOUS FLUORIDE, TINDIFLUORIDE** or **FLUORISTAN** is a white, lustrous, crystalline powder having a bitter, salty taste. It is only slightly soluble in water and is used in toothpastes as a source of fluoride for local application to the teeth. Fluoride replaces the "hydroxy" part of hydroxyapatite, a mineral which is the major constituent of bone and tooth mineral, to form fluorapatite. Fluorapatite in the outer surface of dental enamel is harder and more resistant to acids than hydroxyapatite and therefore the enamel is less susceptible to tooth decay. Since this chemical is applied locally it only affects the tooth substance in the outermost superficial layers and so must be applied periodically. Stannous fluoride also shows promise as an anti-plaque ingredient (see page 58).

KARAYA GUM is used as a glue for dentures (and also in ostomy products), and is found in products like *WERNET'S DENTURE ADHESIVE.* It is a gummy ooze from the plant *Sterculia urens* and other species of Sterculia, a type of tree native to Indian forests. The gum oozes from incisions made on the surface of the tree and hardens prior to collection. It is a pale yellow to pinkish-brown, shapeless substance prior to cleaning and is used in dentistry as a powder or paste.

MAGNESIUM OXIDE is an odorless, white, nontoxic powder practically insoluble in water. It is used in dental powders to keep them free flowing. It is prepared commercially by heating certain naturally occurring minerals such as magnesium carbonate to very high temperatures to obtain various grades.

MAGNESIUM SILICATE is used as an abrasive in dental powders to clean the teeth. It is a gritty, white powder that occurs naturally as the mineral talc, and is not absorbed and non-poisonous when swallowed.

POTASSIUM NITRATE occurs naturally as the mineral nitre or saltpeter as a white crust over the earth's surface on rocks and caves. For use in dentifrices it is a white, crystalline powder incorporated into dental pastes as a 5 percent concentration to reduce tooth hypersensitivity to heat and cold and pressure (tactile sensitivity) (see page 54). It is used in *COOL GEL SENSODYNE* and *FRESH MINT SENSODYNE* toothpastes for sensitive teeth and in *PROMISE TOOTHPASTE FOR SENSITIVE TEETH*. The current theory for the way potassium nitrate works in these products is that it has an effect on the nerve carrying the pain signal, interrupting it and preventing the feeling of pain. Research indicates that this effect can be achieved with many potassium salts, not just potassium nitrate.

SILICA, SILICA HYDRATED (meaning that more water is part of the molecule) or **SILICON DIOXIDE** is a white, powdered chemical when purified for use in dentifrices. It occurs in nature as sand, quartz and flint. It is made into gels for use as a mild abrasive substance in tooth cleaning products. Hydrated silica is found in Proctor and Gamble's *TARTAR CONTROL CREST* toothpaste.

SODIUM BICARBONATE (BAKING SODA, SODA ACID CARBONATE) is a white, crystalline powder with a salty and slightly bitter taste used alone or in combination with other products as an aid to oral hygiene. Sodium bicarbonate has been widely promoted as part of an oral hygiene program known as the **KEYES TECHNIQUE**. This program recommends that patients apply to their gums and brush their teeth with a mixture of salt, hydrogen peroxide, and baking soda. A four year study at the University of Minnesota, involving 171 patients, showed that while the baking soda mixture did help in the maintenance of oral health it was no more effective than ordinary toothpaste.

SODIUM PHOSPHATE or **SODIUM METAPHOSPHATE** or **SODIUM POLYPHOSPHATE** is a white powder that does not dissolve in water very well, so it makes a good dental polishing agent.

STANNOUS PYROPHOSPHATE is a white, free flowing, crystalline powder made synthetically from starting minerals and used as an anticaries agent in toothpastes.

STRONTIUM CHLORIDE is a white, crystalline powder with a sharp bitter taste made artificially in the chemical laboratory. It is claimed to reduce dental sensitivity to heat, cold and pressure. Running through the dentin of teeth are microscopic small "tubules" which, according to the experts, carry the pain impulses to the nerve of the tooth. Strontium chloride is believed to be deposited in the tubules where it blocks the pain. However, it is not considered by the American Dental Association to be as effective as products that use potassium nitrate in a concentration of 5 percent.

TETRAPOTASSIUM PYROPHOSPHATE or **TETRASODIUM PYROPHOSPHATE** is a white powder found in "tartar control" toothpastes, such as *COLGATE TARTAR CONTROL GEL.* They are somewhat alkaline and add mild abrasiveness and stain removal qualities to the paste. Dentists do not believe that these tartar control products offer anything more than cosmetic benefit (see page 53). But, "if it doesn't help at least it won't hurt." It is a nontoxic substance made synthetically from other minerals like sodium phosphate, mentioned earlier.

TRISODIUM PHOSPHATE is a white powder that does not dissolve in water. It is used as an abrasive or tooth polishing agent. It is similar to sodium phosphate, mentioned above, and is found in the product *CREST ADVANCED FORMULA TOOTHPASTE.*

6

Deodorants & Antiperspirants

Concern over perspiration is practically a national preoccupation. Worry about wetness and underarm odor prompts Americans to spend more than $750 million annually on over-the-counter deodorants, deodorant soaps, and antiperspirants. So understandably, these products are available in many different shapes and forms as well as in a wide variety of fragrances. While picking an antiperspirant sounds simple, it may not seem so after arriving at the drugstore to buy one only to find rows and rows of different brands. Which one to pick? What offers the best bargain? Which one will do the best job?

Two general approaches have been used in the battle against body odor 1) the application of antiseptics in **DEODORANTS** to slow down or stop the activity of bacteria on sweat and 2) the use of astringents, known as **ANTIPERSPIRANTS**, to inhibit the flow of perspiration from the skin. Many factors have come together to make **DEODORANTS** and **ANTIPERSPIRANTS** as popular as they are today. Better understanding of the function of sweat glands and the chemical composition of their secretions, new technology of easy-to-use devices (such as aerosols; thick liquids in lotions and rollers; and solid sticks) and finally the simple fact that soap and water are ineffective in preventing body odor have all contributed to the extensive use of these products.

Because **DEODORANTS** are not intended to affect a "bodily function," they are considered cosmetics by the FDA and their manufacturers may not make antiperspirant "drug" claims. Simple deodorants, usually those in stick form, are almost always a combination of a fragrance to mask body odor and the antibacterial ingredient, **TRICLOSAN**. For most people, deodorants alone are not enough to stop body odor, because they do not stop perspiration. Examples of simple cosmetic deodorants are *MENNEN SPEED STICK, OLD SPICE, BAN CLEAR, RIGHT GUARD SPORT STICK, SUAVE SUPER STICK DEODORANT,* and *BRUT DEODORANT STICK.*

ANTIPERSPIRANTS, on the other hand, work by irritating the skin to cause an inflammatory reaction accompanied by swelling and expansion of the cells around the sweat duct and its opening causing it to shrink. This reduces the amount of sweat that can get to the surface. As detrimental as this may sound, the FDA has found no evidence that antiperspirants harm sweat glands. Normal sweating will resume within a few days of completely stopping antiperspirant use. Both deodorants and antiperspirants try to control the breakdown of sweat by bacteria, which is the cause of body odor. But antiperspirants are much more effective since they both reduce perspiration and are antiseptic. This makes antiperspirants much more popular than plain deodorants. **ANTIPERSPIRANTS** are not only the most effective but also the most commonly available preparations for preventing body odor. Usually they contain **ALUMINUM CHLORIDE, ALUMINUM CHLOROHYDRATE**, or **ALUMINUM ZIRCONIUM TETRACHLOROHYDREX-GLY**, which stop perspiration.

Aerosol sprays used to apply deodorants and antiperspirants are still popular, but less so today. If inhaled on a daily basis they may be harmful. Since one normally sprays these products in a bathroom where the ventilation is minimal, a good rule of thumb is to limit applications to short sprays. A strong odor of the product is an indication of breathing too much of it in.

If you notice a rash or irritation of the area where you apply your deodorant or antiperspirant, stop using that particular kind. Some people are more sensitive than others to certain ingredients. If the rash is at all uncomfortable, applying one of the over-the-counter **HYDROCORTISONE** creams like *CORTAID* for a couple of days may help clear up the irritation. Be sure not to use another product with the same ingredient. There might be other ingredients in the deodorant or antiperspirant that could irritate the skin, so be sure to check the ingredients listed on the container, and through the process of elimination find the one causing the problem.

An important thing to think about when buying any underarm product is what the product is supposed to do. Since these products all contain very similar ingredients (within each class of deodorants and antiperspirants), it is difficult to know how any one can be much better than another. Consider the differences discussed later in the ingredient list, keep them in mind and buy the cheapest one.

Hyperhidrosis—Exaggerated Sweating

Some people suffer from an embarrassing problem of persistent and excessive sweating known as **HYPERHIDROSIS.** Their excessive sweating often causes severe embarrassment, restricted social activity and problems in performing their jobs. While different physical conditions are known to cause this condition, the most common cause of troublesome hyperhidrosis is emotion. The exact cause of this exaggerated emotional sweating is not known, but researchers think that a genetic factor may play a role. The interesting thing is that people with this problem in the underarm area seldom have underarm odor, most likely due to the amount of sweat they produce. In underarm emotional hyperhidrosis, sweating can be so profuse that a person's shirt or blouse and suitcoat may become soaked within 15 to 30 minutes. It is a good idea to see a physician if you have this problem. You can try one of the over-the-counter antiperspirants containing **ALUMINUM CHLORIDE**, like *CERTAIN DRI ANTIPERSPIRANT* by Numark Laboratories. But if that doesn't work, see a doctor. A prescription strength **ALUMINUM CHLORIDE HEXAHYDRATE** in **ALCOHOL** product is available, and it should be used, depending on a physicians advice, once or twice weekly at bedtime.

Deodorant and Antiperspirant Ingredients

ALUMINUM CHLORIDE is probably one of the most effective single ingredients to prevent perspiration. But aluminum chloride has its side effects. While very effective, it is irritating to many people when used as an antiperspirant. Aluminum chloride reacts with water in perspiration to form hydrochloric acid, causing irritation and reddened skin; and it will gradually fade or rot clothing. For this reason, other, better tolerated aluminum compounds have been developed. One product still employing aluminum chloride is *ARRID EXTRA DRY CREAM*. Prescription formulations containing high percentages of aluminum chloride are also available for persons suffering from hyperhidrosis, a medical condition of excessive and persistent sweating (see above).

ALUMINUM CHLOROHYDRATE, ALUMINUM HYDROXYCHLORIDE, ALUMINUM CHLORIDE HYDROXIDE or **ALUMINUM CHLOROHYDROXIDE** are all names for the same chemical which is a more refined version of aluminum chloride. It works the same way as aluminum chloride but creates fewer problems. Products that use this more refined ingredient usually have the names "dry," "dry formula," "extra dry," and "super dry." But do not go by the label alone. Pick up the product and read the ingredients yourself. Make sure it says aluminum chlorohydrate. This ingredient is available in sprays, roll-ons, and sticks. Among others, aluminum chlorohydrate is found in *MITCHUM CREAM*, *ARRID EXTRA DRY*, *REVLON HI & DRI*, and *SUAVE ROLL-ON*. Aluminum chlorohydrate is made synthetically from aluminum chloride by chemically changing the molecule to be less acid, thus less irritating to the skin and not as damaging to clothing. Because of the astringency effect of this chemical on the skin it is not thought to be absorbed into the blood stream to any significant extent. Contact allergy has not been reported following exposure to aluminum chlorohydrate. Another variation on this chemical process (reducing the amount of chlorine in the molecule to reduce irritation to skin and clothing) is **ALUMINUM SESQUICHLOROHYDRATE** found in *BAN ANTI-PERSPIRANT CREAM.*

ALUMINUM ZIRCONIUM TETRACHLOROHYDREX-GLY or **ZIRCONIUM ALUMINUM GLYCINE HYDROXYCHLORIDE** is a synthetic chemical known as a "coordination complex," and it is a compound containing the metals aluminum and zirconium with chlorine and glycine, to form an astringent, water soluble antiperspirant. The "GLY" is an accepted term for glycine, a naturally occurring amino acid found in gelatin and silk. Glycine replaces water in the molecule that would normally be attracted to the metals, thus reducing the tendency to produce irritation to the skin. At one time zirconium salts were used alone as antiperspirants but gained disfavor in the 1950s when they were implicated in the production of skin granulomas, lesions that are formed as a result of an inflammatory reaction caused by chemical or physical agents. Aluminum zirconium tetrachlorohydrex-gly is better tolerated by most people and no reports of contact allergy have been made on the aluminum zirconium combination to date. Manufacturers have switched to this better tolerated antiperspirant. *DIAL SOLID* and *MITCHUM SOLID* are just a couple of the many products that now employ this chemical as an antiperspirant.

TRICLOCARBAN or **TCC** is an antimicrobial agent made synthetically from urea and petroleum chemicals. It is used as a deodorant for application to the skin, but is presently still under review by the FDA's OTC Review Panel on Antimicrobials because of fears that it may not be safe for use on infants. This chemical was used to replace **HEXA-CHLOROPHENE** in bar soaps when hexachlorophene was taken off the market because of central nervous system poisoning following absorption by infants. Interestingly, there is suspicion, but inconclusive evidence, that this chemical can decompose under certain conditions to **ANILINE**, a toxic substance which can alter the oxygen carrying capacity of blood. Aniline is absorbed through the skin following application, but its toxic effects would only be significant in newborns, so the relevance of this in the use of an antiperspirant is unclear.

TRICLOSAN or **IRGASAN DP 300** is a synthetic antibacterial made from petroleum chemicals. It is probably the most common ingredient used to inhibit bacteria that decompose sweat, primarily from apocrine glands, to cause malodor. It has low toxicity and irritant properties when applied to the skin, making it an ideal antibacterial for this purpose. This ingredient is in *OLD SPICE CLASSIC DEODORANT* and many other deodorants (see introduction, above). However, the chemical is still under review by the FDA's OTC Review Panel because of fears that it may not be entirely safe, particularly in infants. Many deodorants which have been tried in the past are either too irritating for use on the skin or can be absorbed into the bloodstream to produce poisoning. While this does not appear to be the case with triclosan, it has not been ruled out entirely. It has not been reported to cause contact allergy.

7

Diet Aids & Stimulants

Diet Aids

Obesity is defined as a condition in which actual body weight is more than 20 percent higher than the ideal weight. A rule of thumb for determining the ideal weight is:

- Men five feet tall should weigh 106 pounds, with six additional pounds for every inch over five feet. Men five feet, eight inches tall, ideally would weigh 154 pounds.
- Women five feet tall should weigh 100 pounds, with an additional five pounds for every inch over five feet.

Based on this definition, it is estimated that 35 percent of Americans of all ages are obese, as is more than 50 percent of the adult population. People from every social and economic group are concerned about being overweight—especially women. But despite the risks, most of us continue to overeat.

A calorie is a measurement of the energy in foods and many people are concerned about the amount of calories they consume each day. But calories are only part of the story. Developed nations in the western world derive too much of their daily caloric intake from fat. This not only contributes to undesirable weight gain but is also related to a higher incidence of heart disease and other cardiovascular problems, such as high blood pressure and stroke. This is a book on nonprescription drugs, not obesity or weight loss, and there is no quick fix to be found among over-the-counter products for this problem. Any product available might only supplement an intelligent, disciplined, life-long program of weight control.

We must learn to think in terms of how people become overweight in the first place. Obesity is much easier to prevent than it is to cure. We always say that a fat baby is a healthy baby, but in fact parents often overfeed their children. Infancy and childhood are the times in our lives when fat cells are being formed. Overfeeding can cause excess fat cells to develop; these remain in the body throughout life, making it forever hard for that child to lose weight as he or she grows up.

Along with fat cells, habits and attitudes are also being formed in early life. Many parents use food as a bribe for good behavior, so that the child gets the idea that food is a reward. This attitude may carry over into later life. As an adult, every time the person feels frustrated, discouraged, or depressed he stuffs himself with food to feel better. Some parents instill in their children the idea that they have to eat everything on their plates, whether they want it or not, and then afterwards reward them with sweets such as ice cream.

Eating habits are very hard to change. That is why it is best to convey good eating habits to children when they are young. The older one gets the harder it is to change them.

American men and women tend to add both pounds and inches as the years go by. While becoming less active, the metabolism slows down, although eating habits may remain unchanged. Consequently, over-the-counter diet aids have become a multimillion-dollar industry.

Drugs as Diet Aids

Most diet brand name drug products sold today include **PHENYLPROPANOLAMINE** or **PPA** as an appetite suppressant. In 1979 a review panel for the Food and Drug Administration reported that **PPA** was both safe and effective for weight control. But as far back as the late 1960s evidence has been accumulating to question the effectivenss, and certainly the safety, of this drug as a long term aid to losing weight. Medical researchers have challenged the manufaturers of these products to advance any data that would conclusively show **PPA** superior to behavioral modification for long-term weight loss.

Chemically related to **EPHEDRINE**, and **AMPHETAMINE**, **PPA** is also found in many of the cold and sinus preparations as a decongestant (see decongestants, page 233). It does stimulate the central nervous system to some degree. However, experts say that the stimulation is not enough to suppress the appetite. While the precise mechanism for its effect is unknown, it is thought to suppress the appetite center in the brain.

Manufacturers continue to promote products such as *DIETAC, DEXATRIM MAXIMUM STRENGTH CAFFEINE-FREE CAPLETS*, and *ACUTRIM 16 HOUR STEADY CONTROL APPETITE SUPPRESSANT*. There are people who swear by these products because they used them and actually lost weight. That may be more a psychological result than anything else, since doubleblind studies, show that those who took a placebo (sugar pill) and those who took a capsule with **PPA** showed very little difference in weight loss.

Another problem with **PPA** is that people may not regard an over-the-counter drug with the same respect they tend to give prescription medicines. This could be dangerous because **PPA** is contraindicated for patients with hypertension, heart conditions, diabetes, or thyroid disease. Increased blood pressure appears to happen more often with doses greater than 75 mg daily, but it can occur with any dose. Other side effects occuring with these doses are nervousness, restlessness, insomnia, dizziness, tinnitus, headache, and nausea.

Poison centers are very familiar with overdoses of **PPA**, intentional or otherwise, because a high percentage of these patients end up in the emergency department of the local hospital. In one particular study one-third of all patients who had overdosed with **PPA** required hospitalization or emergency dapartment treatment and half of these had significant hypertension (high blood pressure) as a result of the overdose. A severe and sometimes life threatening elevation of blood pressure can occur if **PPA** is taken with other medicines, including **INDOMETHACIN** *(INDOCIN)* for arthritis, **METHYLDOPA** *(ALDOMET)* for high blood pressure and **MONOAMINE OXIDASE INHIBITOR ANTIDEPRESSANTS.** A person taking **PPA** should also avoid foods that contain caffeine to prevent the additive effect of these stimulants.

The bottom line is that indiscriminate use of over-the-counter weight control products containing **PHENYLPROPANOLAMINE** may result in serious complications in patients with heart disease, elevated blood pressure, diabetes and hyperthyroidism. This ingredient can produce less serious but uncomfortable symptoms in otherwise healthy people even when the labeled directions are followed.

BENZOCAINE is another drug approved by the FDA for use in diet products. We usually think of benzocaine as used to rub on the skin for its anesthetic effect. But diet products containing benzocaine are taken orally. Many of them are in the form of hard candy. The idea is to numb the inside of your mouth, thereby reducing the desire to eat, especially if you are a constant snacker. People chew or suck one of these candy products when they have the urge to eat. However, most of the products are in capsule and tablet form and the drug itself is swallowed before it comes into contact with the mouth, making it less effective. Benzocaine causes allergic reations in some people. A recent ban on weight control ingredients did not include benzocaine, but the FDA is reviewing safety and effectiveness studies for the drug. There is at least one product, *ADVANCED FORMULA DIET AYDS APPETITE CONTROL CUBES*, that still includes benzocaine, although most products have dropped it, perhaps seeing the handwriting on the wall for this ingredient's use in dieting.

Bulk-Producing Diet Aids

These diet aids contain ingredients such as **METHYLCELLULOSE, CARBOXYMETHYLCELLULOSE, PSYLLIUM, AGAR**, and **KARAYA GUM**, which are supposed to work by absorbing water. Water absorption causes them to swell, producing a sense of fullness, which in turn reduces the desire to eat. The problem is that these products have been shown to leave the stomach in about thirty minutes. When they reach the intestine they stimulate bowel movement. Thus, one is taking a product that reduces hunger for about 30 minutes, but also creates a laxative effect. The benefit of these diet aids is that they can help cut down on the intake of calories, but they are no more effective than a low-calorie diet alone. When using these products, they should always be used with water. If one uses a prescribed medicine for the stomach to slow intestinal movements, the possibility of intestinal blockage can occur if it is combined with a bulk-producing diet aid. The FDA has ruled most of these ingredients as having insufficient data to prove their effectiveness and is requiring more scientific studies before it makes a final ruling on whether or not manufacturers can continue to market them for weight loss. See the list at the end of this section.

At the very least, these ingredients have recently been affected by legislation that requires special labeling to warn consumers to take them with adequate fluid and to avoid them altogether if they have ever experienced difficulty in swallowing. The warning reads:

Take (or mix) this product with at least 8 ounces (a full glass) of water or other fluid. Taking this product without adequate fluid may cause it to swell and block the throat or esophagus and may cause choking. These products should not be used if there is difficulty in swallowing or in persons with any throat problems. If there is chest pain, vomiting, or difficulty in swallowing or breathing after taking this product, seek immediate medical attention.

FDA Banned Diet Ingredients

Ingredients classified as Category II nonprescription ingredients, that is, they have not been shown to be safe and effective, when promoted for use in diet products, are the following:

alcohol
alfalfa
anise oil
arginine
ascorbic acid
bearberry (uva ursi)
biotin
bone marrow-red
buchu
buchu-potassium extract
caffeine
caffeine citrate
calcium
calcium carbonate
calcium caseinate
calcium lactate
calcium pantothenate
cholecalciferol
choline
citric acid
cnicus benedictus
copper
copper gluconate
corn oil
corn syrup
corn silk-potassium extract
cupric sulfate
cyanocobalamin (bitamin B_{12})
cystine
dextrose
docusate sodium
ergocalciferol
ferric ammonium citrate
ferric pyrophosphate
ferrous fumarate
ferrous gluconate
ferrous sulfate
flax seed
folic acid
fructose
histidine
hydrastis canadensis
inositol
iodine
isoleucine
juniper-potassium extract
lactose
lecithin
leucine
liver concentrate
lysine
lysine hydrochloride
magnesium
magnesium oxide
malt
maltodextrin
manganese citrate
mannitol
methionine
mono- and diglycerides

niacinamide
organic vegetables
pancreatin
pantothenic acid
papain
papaya enzymes
pepsin
phenacetin
phenylalanine
phosphorus
phytolacca
pineapple enzymes
potassium citrate
pyridoxine-hydrochloride (vitamin B_6)
riboflavin (vitamin B_2)
rice polishings
saccharin
sea minerals
sesame seed
sodium
sodium caseinate
sodium chloride (table salt)
soybean protein
soy meal
sucrose
thiamine hydrochloride (vitamin B_1)
thiamine mononitrate (vitamin B_1 mononitrate)
threonine
tricalcium phosphate
tryptophan
tyrosine
uva ursi-potassium extract
valine
vitaline
vitamin A
vitamin A acetate
vitamin A palmitate
vitamin E
wheat germ
yeast

Some diet ingredients still lack proof that they are safe and effective. More studies are needed. You may continue to see these ingredients in products. They are still allowed until a ruling is made by the FDA. However, as mentioned above, some of these ingredients may require special labeling for the consumer (see page 81). The ingredients requiring more studies are:

alginic acid
carboxymethylcellulose-sodium
carrageenan
chondrus
guar gum
karaya gum
kelp
methylcellulose
plantago seed
sodium bicarbonate
xanthan gum

Low Calorie Balanced Foods

Canned diet products are used as substitutes for the usual diet. These products are available in powders, liquids, and granules, as well as cookies and soups. Dietary foods are low in sodium. Therefore weight loss in the first two weeks is probably caused by water loss from the tissues in the body. However, the long-term benefits of these products are questionable. If you are using the liquid form of food substitutes but you do not really care for the taste, try chilling it. It will taste a lot better.

Alternative Sweeteners

Sweeteners may be natural or artificial. While sugars sweeten foods they also add "empty" calories and contribute to dental caries. For this reason "artificial" alternatives have been developed.

TABLE SUGAR (SUCROSE) is the leading ingredient added to foods in the United States today. Sugars are added to foods and drugs in numerous forms, some of which are discussed below. The use of sugars in toothpaste and mouthwash, for example, is a problem because they do not dissolve well and contribute to dental caries. Like other carbohydrates, sugar is converted by the body into **GLUCOSE**, the primary fuel of the body. During digestion it is converted into equal parts of two simple sugars **GLUCOSE** (or **DEXTROSE**) and **FRUCTOSE**, or "fruit sugar." Fructose itself is eventually converted by the liver to glucose. Once sugars are in the bloodstream or the liver they are either used for energy or stored as **GLYCOGEN** until the body needs them. When more energy is needed the liver can convert glycogen to glucose.

Artificial sweeteners are not a source of energy for the body. While their use in food is every bit as controversial as sugar, several popular artificial sweeteners are widely used. Some of the artificial sweeteners listed below provide no calories and may aid in calorie reduction for certain people.

There are also sugar substitutes like **SORBITOL**, and **XYLITOL** which are really alcohols that are not as sweet as **SACCHARIN** or **ASPARTAME**, but they do have advantages. Neither of these products causes tooth decay, and some products containing **XYLITOL** have a more pleasant taste than those containing saccharin. There is some evidence that **XYLITOL** is implicated in the development of bladder tumors in mice, so its use is on the decline. Many of the dietetic gums and candies contain **SORBITOL** and **MANNITOL** as sweetening agents. But these ingredients can have a laxative effect, especially in children. Eating a whole package of mints can cause cramps and diarrhea. Parents often dismiss it by thinking it is just "something they ate." If a child develops intestinal distress every time he or she has a sugarless mint or gum, eliminate these products.

ASPARTAME is undoubtedly the most popular non-caloric sweetener approved by the Food and Drug Administration. It is marketed under the trade name *NUTRA-SWEET* and used in the product *EQUAL*. It is an alternative to **SACCHARIN**, which the FDA still considers to be unsafe. Aspartame is available in tablets and powder packets. It has also been approved for manufacturers' use in instant powdered drinks, cereals, sugarless gums and soft drinks.

One packet of *EQUAL* (4 calories) is equivalent in sweetness to two teaspoons of sugar (36 calories). The 4 calories in *EQUAL* comes from the carbohydrate filler powder the manufacturer uses just to give it some bulk. It also does not have the bitter aftertaste that saccharin has.

Sweetener Ingredients

ACESULFAME-K is obtained from **ACETOACETIC ACID**, a chemical that plays a role in the body's growth and development. It is 200 times sweeter than sucrose (table sugar). It is used in food and beverages in the United States, Britain, Germany, and Switzerland. It is not changed in the body to any other chemicals (unlike aspartame) and is eliminated unchanged by the kidneys in the urine. Studies have indicated that it is safe for long term use. This sweetener has promise as an additive to oral cosmetics and pharmaceuticals. Based on manufacturers testing, it is not known to be toxic, cancer-causing or to cause birth defects following long term use. **ACESULFAME-K** is marketed under the trade name *SUNETTE* brand sweetener and is found in products like *SWEET ONE*. Mixed with one gram of dextrose to give it some body, each packet provides 4 calories.

ASPARTAME, brand name *NUTRASWEET*, is a synthetic chemical sweetener that was discovered serendipitously by a G. D. Searle scientist in 1965. It exists as colorless needlelike crystals in solid form and has no bitter after taste. It is a "dipeptide," meaning that it is chemically composed of two amino acids (the building blocks of protein) and is a protein in all essential respects. Aspartame is 180 times sweeter on a weight basis than table sugar (sucrose) thus requiring much less per use. On a package of *EQUAL* the ingredients are **DEXTROSE** with **MALTODEXTRIN** and **ASPARTAME**. The 4 calories in each packet of *EQUAL* are from the carbohydrates dextrose and maltodextrin. The manufacturer has to add a filler just to make the aspartame usable. At first, the use of aspartame was controversial because of its metabolism in the human body to two other chemicals, both known to exert toxic effects. Aspartame as such is not absorbed into the blood stream. It is completely changed in the gastrointestinal tract to methanol (wood alcohol) and asperyl phenylalanine. While methanol is poisonous, the amounts produced by aspartame, are insignificant under normal circumstances. For example a liter (approximately one quart) of soft drink sweetened with aspartame would contain only one third the amount of methanol found in a normal fruit juice of this size (since fruits naturally contain small amounts of methanol). The other chemical, phenylalanine, is toxic to people with a genetic deficiency called **PKU (PHENYLKETONURIA)**. These people do not have an enzyme necessary to prevent the accumulation of phenylalanine and its breakdown products in the brain. This produces a syndrome of mental deficiency, epileptic seizures, muscular twitching, hyperactivity, brain wave abnormalities and growth retardation. However, the amount of phenylalanine produced by a quart of soft drink sweetened with aspartame is equivalent to the amount of phenylalanine found in a single egg or one ounce of cheddar cheese. Therefore, while there is a real and definite danger for persons with **PKU**, and it is agreed that these patients should entirely avoid consumption of aspartame just as they do other foods, the amounts required to produce serious toxicity, even in these individuals, is enormous considering expected levels of consumption. One last concern over aspartame is whether or not it produces brain tumors according to some early charges that the company's (G.D. Searle) animal studies were invalid. However these have since been repeated by an independent research firm and have convinced the FDA to rule out the possibility that aspartame causes brain tumors in long term use.

BROWN SUGAR consists of about 91 to 96 percent **SUCROSE** crystals contained in a molasses syrup with natural flavor and color. However, some refiners make brown sugar by simply adding syrup to refined white sugar in a mixer.

CORN SYRUPS are produced by the action of enzymes and/or starch acids on cornstarch from corn and result as the starch breaks down in the presence of water. These syrups usually contain fructose and dextrose.

CYCLAMATE, a synthetically prepared crystalline chemical, was discovered in 1937 by "accident." As a non-nutritive sweetener cyclamate was so popular over a twenty-year period that consumption ran as high as 18 million pounds a year. The sweetener was banned by the FDA in 1970 after cancer-causing potential of cyclamate surfaced. The manufacturer of cyclamate, Abbott Laboratories, petitioned the FDA over a ten year period with data and evidence in an attempt to refute the cancer causing claim. However, the FDA finally decided that Abbott had not shown conclusively that cyclamate "would not cause cancer and would not cause inheritable genetic damage." It is presently unavailable for popular use, but there is always a chance that this ingredient may make a comeback. Future changes in the way the cancer laws are applied could make it available again (see page 24, Delaney dilemma).

DEXTROSE or **GLUCOSE** is also called **CORN SUGAR**. It is made commercially from starch by the action of heat and acids or enzymes. It may be sold blended with regular sugar.

HONEY is an "invert" sugar formed by an enzyme from nectar gathered by the bees. Invert sugar is a mixture of the sugars fructose and glucose, but maltose and sucrose are also found in honey. Its composition and flavor vary with the source of the nectar.

INVERT SUGAR is a mixture of glucose and fructose formed by splitting sucrose in a process called "inversion," which occurs when acids or enzymes are added. Honey is an example of "invert" sugar.

LACTOSE or **MILK SUGAR** is a white, fluffy powder with a faintly sweet taste. It is made commercially as a byproduct of the cheese industry from whey and skim milk. It occurs in the milk of mammals, including humans.

MANNITOL is a white, crystalline or powdered sugar alcohol which is about half as sweet as table sugar. It occurs naturally in manna, which is the dried liquid which oozes from the plant *Fraxinus ornus*, a small tree which is native to southern Europe. For commercial use it may be prepared chemically from the sugar mannose.

RAW SUGAR is tan to brown in appearance and a coarse, granular solid prepared by evaporating sugarcane juice. The FDA regulations prohibit the sale of raw sugar unless impurities are removed.

SACCHARIN is a white crystalline powder made from petroleum chemicals. Presently a product of the Sherwin-Williams Paint Company, the sole U.S. producer, it was discovered in 1879 and originally used as an antiseptic and a food preservative. It is intensely sweet, said to be 500 times sweeter than table sugar (sucrose) in dilute solution. Saccharin is a non-nutritive artificial sweetener (no calories) and has been on the market longer than any other synthetic sweetener. While used in canned fruits, chewing gums, toothpaste, mouthwashes and other pharmaceuticals, its major uses are in soft drinks and as a table top sweetener. Following scientific studies in Canada and the U.S. in the 1970s which showed saccharin to be responsible for bladder tumors in test animals the FDA proposed banning saccharin in the U.S. However, in response to public outcry, Congress passed the Saccharin Study and Labeling Act in November of 1977. The law, in addition to requiring further study of the chemical, imposed a requirement for warning labels on foods containing saccharin and for the display of warning signs in establishments selling products with saccharin, which is still with us today.

SORBITOL is a sugar alcohol used as a sweetener in food products. It occurs naturally in some fruits and in plants of the rose family, but it is generally prepared from glucose by an electro-chemical process for commercial use. Sorbitol is about half as sweet as table sugar. It can be used as a substitute sweetener for diabetics because it is metabolized differently than table sugar.

TURBINADO SUGAR is sometimes labeled to suggest that it is "raw" sugar. Actually, it must go through a refining process to remove impurities and most of the molasses. It is produced by separating raw sugar crystals and washing them with steam. It is used by restaurants as a novelty condiment in addition to, or instead of, white sugar.

Group Therapy for Weight Loss

Group therapy has been proven very effective in treating obesity. Groups such as **TOPS** (Take Off Pounds Sensibly) have successful treatment records for obesity. Group pressure and support have proven to be a good deterrent to overeating for many persons. Also, eating more slowly causes you to feel satisfied more quickly, therefore eating less. These organizations have a lot of useful suggestions, as well as special weight reduction programs that can help you lose weight. They teach you how to eat for the rest of your life.

It remains that a change of dietary habits is critical to weight loss. Over-the-counter products will never take the place of proper diet and exercise.

Stimulants

How many of us remember staying up late cramming for final exams? It usually meant taking a product like *NODOZ* or *VIVARIN STIMULANT TABLETS* and *CAPLETS* to stay awake and alert. *NODOZ MAXIMUM STRENGTH CAPLETS* contain 200 mg of **CAFFEINE** per caplet. Some of these products contain the higher dose of caffeine, but in a sustained release form. *CAFFEDRINE* is one of these. While we do not recommend that these products be used as a substitute for sleep, it has been proven that these products do help increase mental alertness when sheer boredom and fatigue are the main causes. However, one can get the same effect by drinking a cup of coffee, because one 100 mg tablet of *NODOZ* is equal to about one cup of coffee in caffeine content. Or, if you do not like coffee, many soft drinks contain caffeine. In fact, excluding the caffeine that is naturally present in coffee, tea, cocoa and other products, the predominant use of caffeine as an added ingredient is in soft drinks, which accounts for the vast majority of the estimated 2 million-plus pounds of caffeine added to food annually in the United States. Caffeine is the only ingredient approved by the FDA for use in nonprescription stimulant products.

It is not a good idea to use any of the over-the-counter stimulant products regularly, because caffeine is a powerful central nervous system drug. It causes the heart rate to increase, promotes urination, and affects the stomach. It may even affect blood circulation. But even though caffeine can produce many unpleasant side effects, there are not many deaths reported from overdoses of caffeine. This is probably because the stomach irritation and vomiting it causes in overdoses prevents you from getting enough to be fatal. Many heavy coffee drinkers can attest to the stomach problems caffeine causes. Taking ten 100 mg caffeine tablets or more a day could cause you to become physically dependent on them. There is a definite withdrawal syndrome from caffeine that occurs if one is dependent on the tablets or caffeine-containing beverages. When deprived of caffeine (study subjects who were given a placebo) coffee drinkers complain of sleepiness, increased irritability and headaches. Administration of coffee causes increased alertness, less irritability and a feeling of contentedness. However, if you take caffeine tablets only occasionally, they should not cause problems. Patients with heart problems or circulatory diseases, should get clearance from a physician before taking any stimulant product.

CAFFEINE is a naturally occurring chemical which is found in more than sixty species of plants. Beverages that contain caffeine have been popular for hundreds of years. Uses of caffeine in medicine have included sexual function disorders, skin diseases, minimal brain dysfunction (hyperkinetic children), Parkinson's disease, cancer, as a stimulant agent in the treatment of poisoning by depressant drugs, use in babies born with respiratory disorders, inclusion in headache medicines to enhance pain relief, and its use as an aid in restoring mental alertness. Recent studies support only a few of these uses as valid medical applications for caffeine. However, any coffee drinker can tell about its effectiveness as a stimulant. Caffeine is a fine, white powder before it is added to medicines and soft drinks.

In 1980 the Food and Drug Administration was confronted with various studies that concerned them about the possible association of caffeine in the diet with several health problems. These problems ranged from the association of caffeine with birth defects, some forms of cancer, heart and blood vessel disease, behavioral problems, central nervous system disorders, reproductive problems and nonmalignant breast lumps (**FIBROCYSTIC DISEASE**) in women. One real concern was a study that demonstrated caffeine's potential for causing birth defects in animals. The agency said it did not know if there was a danger to people. It chose to lean on the side of caution by warning pregnant women and, at the same time, asking scientists to do more studies on caffeine's health effects. These have now been done, and they generally have produced less worrisome results. For that reason, and because the FDA determined that some of the earlier studies were faulty, the concern about caffeine has lessened.

But, while the FDA's concern over caffeine has moderated over the years, there are still unanswered questions. Caffeine is still a chemical stimulant that affects the central nervous system. It is a widely used food additive to which some people are more sensitive than others. It could have other, still unknown, effects. But determining what these effects are is not a simple matter, as some studies have shown, since other factors—such as smoking, alcohol consumption, poor diet, and drug use—also can affect health. While the FDA continues to look at caffeine, the old adage of doing things in moderation really applies here.

EXAMPLES OF CAFFEINE CONTENT OF DRUGS, BEVERAGES AND FOODS

Source	Average(mg)	Range(mg)
Coffee (5 ounce cup)		
Brewed, drip method	115	60-180
Brewed, percolator	80	40-170
Instant	65	30-120
Decaffeinated, brewed	3	2-5
Decaffeinated, instant	2	1-5
Tea (5 ounce cup)		
Brewed, major U.S brands	40	20-90
Brewed, imported brands	60	25-110
Instant	30	25-50
Iced (12 ounce glass)	70	67-76
Other Beverages		
Cocoa beverage (5 ounces)	4	2-20
Cola (6 ounces)		15-23
Chocolate milk beverage (8 oz)	5	2-7
Milk chocolate (1 oz.)	6	1-15
Food		
Semi-sweet chocolate (1 oz.)	20	5-35
Chocolate syrup (1 oz.)	4	
Chocolate pudding (1/2 cup)	5.5	
Chocolate ice cream (cup)	6.8	
Chocolate candy (1 oz.)	7.7	
Nonprescription Drugs:		
Alertness Tablets		
NoDoz	100	
Vivarin	200	
Pain Relief		
Anacin, Maximum Strength	32	
P-A-C Analgesic Tablets	32	
Vanquish Analgesic Caplets	33	
Excedrin Extra Strength	65	
Diuretics		
Aqua-Ban	100	

8

Drugs & Pregnancy

In the early 1960s worldwide attention was focused on a nonprescription sleep-aid drug marketed in West Germany. In the late 50s this drug was considered so safe that not only could it be sold without prescription, but you could take handfuls without hurting yourself, so said the drug companies. The understanding at that time was that in pregnancy the placenta was a marvelous protection for the developing baby. It was thought to completely protect the fetus from harmful substances in a mother's blood. Those popular perceptions were shattered when the much touted debut of **THALIDOMIDE** became a nightmare. At least six thousand grossly deformed babies were born of mothers who took the drug during pregnancy under brand names such as Contergan (West Germany) and Distaval (Scotland). These babies were born with a previously rare condition known as **PHOCOMELIA**, combining the Greek words for seal and limb. Malformed fingers or toes appeared at the ends of very foreshortened limbs—making them look like flippers. This tragedy was completely avoided in the United States because of the skepticism of an FDA physician, Dr. Frances Kelsey, who was not satisfied with the submitting drug company's proof of safety. The unusual deformities caused by thalidomide generated worldwide publicity and focused attention on the fact that certain drugs taken at a critical time in pregnancy had the potential for damaging the unborn baby.

This really should not have been such a surprise. In the second century after Christ, the Greek physician Soranus of Ephesus warned women not to take drugs at any time during pregnancy, but especially during the first trimester. He warned that when drugs taken to induce abortion did not work "... let no one assume that the fetus has not been injured at all ... for it has been harmed."

At a time when there are many prescription and over-the-counter drugs on the market, researchers are finding more and more scientific evidence that some drugs have a direct effect on fetuses.

Home Pregnancy Test Kits

It is therefore very important to detect pregnancy early and to take the right steps to safeguard health, as well as the health of the unborn child. One method of early detection is the do-it-yourself-at-home pregnancy test kit. These tests are now very accurate. Several kits are available on the market. *FIRST RESPONSE 1-STEP PREGNANCY TEST*, a one minute pregnancy test, *EPT*, Johnson & Johnson's *FACT PLUS*, and the *ANSWER QUICK & SIMPLE PREGNANCY TEST* are all good, quick tests for pregnancy. Many of the test kits available over-the-counter now are the same test procedures used by hospitals and doctors in their offices.

The benefits of establishing pregnancy within a few weeks after conception are boundless. Proper diet, exercise, and prenatal care can be started immediately to ensure a healthy baby. Before the test kits were available, if a woman missed a period she called her doctor. Usually he told her if she missed another period to make an appointment. By the time she got in to see her doctor she might already be three months pregnant. When a woman becomes pregnant, her body produces a special hormone known as **HCG (HUMAN CHORIONIC GONADOTROPIN)**, which appears in the urine. Most of the tests detect this hormone as early as the first day a period is missed.

Home pregnancy test kits have come a long way in the last few years. Many of the problems that plagued the early kits have been corrected. The tests used to be extremely delicate and adjustments had to be made for room temperature and so on. The slightest movement, such as children running through the room or the vibration of a refrigerator or air conditioner would change the reading. Where the results used to be available in hours, it now takes only one to five minutes, depending on the brand of the kit. It is no longer necessary to use the first urine in the morning. Any urine during the day can be used, but eating and drinking should be avoided for at least 3 hours before collecting urine with most of the kits. Most medicines should not affect the results of the kits. Most of the test kits advise repeating the test in one week if it is negative the first time. If it is negative a second time it is time to see a physician. There may be other reasons for missing a period that may need medical attention. The kits cost eight to fifteen dollars.

Drugs and Pregnancy

Many pregnant women take medication. Estimates indicate that pregnant women in this country take an average of four prescription or over-the-counter drugs, plus vitamin and mineral supplements, and have an undetermined exposure to potentially toxic substances in food, cosmetics, household chemicals, and the general environment.

According to the March of Dimes Foundation, each year more than a quarter of a million U.S. babies—or about 1 out of every 14—are born with birth defects. About one-third of the abnormalities are life-threatening, making birth defects —including low birth weight—the leading cause of infant mortality. A half million more potential lives are lost through miscarriage and stillbirth, usually because of faulty fetal development. About 1.2 million infants, children, and adults are hospitalized each year for treatment of birth defects. Birth defects contribute to the death of more than 60,000 Americans of all ages annually.

The causes of birth defects are unknown in about 65 percent to 70 percent of cases; about 20 percent of the defects are genetic, or inherited (a small percentage of these are due to infection during pregnancy, health problems of the mother and chromosomal defects). An estimated 2 to 3 percent of birth defects are due to chemicals or drugs, although it is suspected that the percentage may be higher since many women cannot remember all the drugs they took during pregnancy. Studies have concluded that prescription and over-the-counter drugs should be avoided whenever possible. Unfortunately, in many cases, pregnant women take as many, if not more, drugs than nonpregnant women. These drugs may have adverse affects on the mother and on the fetus.

Among all membrane systems of the body, the **PLACENTA** is unique; it separates two distinct individuals with differing genetic compositions, physiologic responses, and sensitivities to drugs. The fetus gets nutrients and eliminates waste through the placenta without having to depend on its own immature organs. However, when foreign substances appear in the mother's blood, the placenta does not form a true barrier between mother and fetus. In fact, most drugs that enter the mother's body will also enter the fetus.

A very important period is the first two weeks to 20 days after conception. During this period, there is no differentiation of cells in the embryo. If enough cells are harmed by a drug, then the embryo will die. No congenital malformations happen at this early stage; it is an "all-or-nothing" situation. If a chemical that can cause birth deformities, known as a **TERATOGEN**, is taken in this period it will either cause the death of the embryo and subsequent miscarriage, or not affect it at all. During the next one or two months, the organ systems are developing, and this time period is the most critical for the development of abnormalities. After the end of the eighth week, differentiation of the organs is completed. So, the first trimester of pregnancy is the most significant period for the occurrence of deformities and the survival of the fetus. If possible, during the first trimester no medicine of any kind should be taken unless advised by a doctor, including nonprescription drugs for pain, colds, coughs, nervousness, and insomnia.

ASPIRIN and aspirin-containing products should be avoided during pregnancy. For headache, try an ice pack on the head, lie quietly in a dark room, or simply take a walk and get away from the problem that caused the headache in the first place. If these treatments do not work use a pain reliever such as *TYLENOL* or *DATRIL*, (with a physician's approval), but stay away from the **SALICYLATES**.

For coughs and colds, be careful about the cough syrup used. Some have alcohol bases. Since alcohol should be avoided in pregnancy, it is obviously a good idea to avoid these cough syrups, such as *NYQUIL*, as well. Also avoid cough syrups containing **CODEINE**. The following are some of the possible adverse effects an unborn child may suffer if the mother takes drugs:

- **ANTIBIOTICS** of the **TETRACYCLINE** class, which are often prescribed for bacterial infections, may cause permanent discoloration of the child's teeth. This happens if they are taken during the second trimester when the fetus' teeth begin to calcify. **QUININE** and the antibiotic **STREPTOMYCIN**, even when taken at late stages in pregnancy, may cause hearing damage and deafness in the baby.
- **HORMONES,** such as **DIETHYLSTILBESTROL (DES),** a synthetic estrogen widely prescribed in the 1940s and 50s to prevent miscarriage and other problems, have been demonstrated to cause vaginal cancer in some young women, as a result of fetal exposure. This drug became a "time bomb" for the children of some 4 million to 6 million women who took it during pregnancy.
- Although consuming adequate vitamins during pregnancy is very important to both mother and fetus, excessive amounts can be dangerous. High levels of calcium in the blood and mental retardation may result from excessive amounts of **VITAMIN D**. High **VITAMIN A** intake during pregnancy also may cause birth defects, but it is not known at what level this can occur. A doctor is the best source of advice regarding vitamin intake during pregnancy.

- Large amounts of **VITAMIN B-6** and **VITAMIN C**, although not stored in the body, have been shown to cause withdrawal seizures in the newborn.
- **BARBITURATES**, taken throughout pregnancy or in the last three months, may cause the infant to be born with an addiction to barbiturates.
- **AMPHETAMINES**, taken by many women to aid in weight loss, has the potential to cause birth defects.
- Minor **TRANQUILIZERS**, such as *VALIUM*, *LIBRIUM*, *HALCION* and *DALMANE*, taken during early pregnancy, increase the chance that the baby will be born with a cleft lift or palate.
- **COCAINE** is a popular drug of abuse and is usually used in conjunction with many other drugs. Cocaine users do not have much appetite and can be malnourished. Babies have low birth weights. These mothers are so thin that they hardly look pregnant even at full term. Some do not make it to full term, because cocaine users are at high risk for premature delivery. While birth defects are not usually found in the form of structural changes in babies on cocaine from the mother, they can have brain damage, which is not always obvious at birth. Cocaine can cause the baby, while still in the womb, to have strokes (blood vessels that break in the brain due to high blood pressure) that lead to retardation.

  Infants born to mothers who abused cocaine may suffer from withdrawal symptoms such as restlessness, jitteriness and irritability. They may have small head size, poor eye contact and show poor organizational response to stimuli in their environment.
- **ASPIRIN** or drugs containing **SALICYLATES** may prolong pregnancy when taken in the last three months or cause excessive bleeding in the mother before and after delivery. A statement warning pregnant women not to take aspirin during the last three months of pregnancy without a physician's advice is required on all oral and rectal non-

prescription aspirin and drugs containing aspirin. A similar warning is required on **IBUPROFEN**, another pain reliever that has effects similar to aspirin (see page 182). These products also have a general pregnancy-nursing warning that reads: "As with any drug, if you are pregnant or nursing a baby, seek the advice of a health professional before using this product."

- **ALCOHOL** is a powerful drug and consuming even one to three ounces a day will probably harm the fetus. Studies show that stillbirths, premature birth, mental retardation, and physical and behavioral problems are found in children born to alcoholic mothers. Unfortunately, many expectant mothers do not even think of alcohol as a drug. One to three out of every 1,000 newborns, or about 5,000 babies per year, are born with **FETAL ALCOHOL SYNDROME (FAS)**. This is a collection of symptoms and characteristics that were first described in France by a physician who noticed that children of alcoholic mothers shared such well-defined characteristics that a diagnosis of maternal alcoholism could be made by just looking at them. **FAS** children may also have defects of the heart and genital and urinary organs and may have poor coordination, short attention span and behavioral problems. Women who drink the equivalent of three ounces of pure alcohol daily—six average mixed drinks or six cans of beer—frequently give birth to babies with the full range of **FAS** defects. They are also more likely to miscarry or have stillborn children or children who die in infancy.
- Smoking **TOBACCO**, especially daily, increases the chance that the baby will have a below-normal birth weight, averaging a half-pound less than babies born of nonsmokers. No specific malformations are connected with smoking, but low birth weight babies are 40 times more likely to die in infancy than those of normal weight. Nicotine, which constricts blood vessels, is believed to reduce blood flow to the baby. This means that the baby gets less nutri-

ents and oxygen. Smoking may also increase the risk of miscarriage, stillbirth and death in newborns.

- A final hazard is exposure to **X-RAYS** during pregnancy. The cells of the unborn child are dividing rapidly and forming into specialized cells and tissues which are sensitive to radiation. During the earliest weeks of pregnancy, especially avoid X-rays of the abdomen, lower back, pelvis, and hip.

Although a drug may be implicated in the occurrence of birth defects, it is difficult to determine if the drug is the primary culprit. In many instances, the pregnant woman has been exposed to other hazards, such as environmental pollution or diseases that may cause abnormalities. Before a drug is administered to a pregnant woman, the benefits to her must be carefully weighed against the possible harm to the fetus. The majority of drugs consumed by pregnant women are related to effects of pregnancy. These include prenatal vitamins, antacids, mild pain relievers, and laxatives. Most of the agents in these categories do not cause problems. However, there are several drugs in these groups as well as in many others that should be avoided during pregnancy.

If an over-the-counter product is used, pick one with a single ingredient and not a combination product, to avoid introducing unnecessary drugs into you and your child's body.

A pregnancy should always be disclosed before a prescription is written or any over the counter product is used.

Drugs and Breast-Feeding

Once the child is born, drugs can cause a problem if there is breast-feeding. In recent years there has been a marked upsurge in breast-feeding by American mothers. This trend should be welcomed by physicians as a contribution to infant health. There is strong evidence that breast milk contains **ANTIBODIES** that may help safeguard infants against infection while their own immune systems are maturing.

Despite the evident advantages of this natural method of infant nutrition, one should probably consider the fact that we are no longer living in a natural state. The lactating mother is, or may be, exposed to a host of unnatural substances, including drugs and other active chemicals that may be either ingested deliberately **(ALCOHOL, NICOTINE)** or absorbed passively from the environment. Some, though by no means all of these substances pass into the milk in large enough amounts to affect the metabolism of the baby nourished by it. Some, for example, most **ANTIHISTAMINES** inhibit lactation. Others may incapacitate the mother to properly care for the infant **(MARIJUANA, LSD)**.

Mild **ANALGESICS**, including **ASPIRIN**, **ACETAMINOPHEN**, and the prescription drug *DARVON*, are compatible with breast-feeding. **ERGOT** preparations, used to treat **MIGRAINES**, are not compatible, since they produce vomitting, diarrhea, and other toxic effects in the infant. The only time these drugs should not cause a problem is in the period immediately after birth, when they may be used to control uterine bleeding.

NARCOTIC PAIN RELIEVERS are safe when used in therapeutic doses. **TRANQUILIZERS** and **SEDATIVES** should, for the most part, be used with caution or not at all. **BARBITURATES** are very unpredictable. Some seem safe in therapeutic doses, and others probably should be avoided. Most anti-infective drugs are safe for the infant, with the exception of **TETRACYCLINE**, which can permanently stain the child's teeth.

HORMONES should be used with caution or not at all. This applies to **ORAL CONTRACEPTIVES**, the hormonal content of which can pass into the breast milk, with possible risk to the infant. Many physicians have the mother use an alternative contraceptive method during breast-feeding.

Most **LAXATIVES** are safe. Exceptions are preparations containing **CASCARA** and **ALOE**, which can give a baby diarrhea. Some **HERB TEAS** contain laxative substances that could produce diarrhea in the infant.

NICOTINE should be avoided. Maternal smoking can cause restlessness, diarrhea, and vomiting and can speed up a baby's heartbeat.

The important thing to keep in mind when breast-feeding is that when taking a drug, whether prescription or nonprescription, it can often be replaced with a drug that would be more compatible with the baby's system.

In either pregnancy or later breast-feeding an infant, the most sensible course is not to drink alcoholic beverages or smoke, and to take drugs only if necessary and with the knowledge and advice of a physician.

Morning Sickness

For centuries women have bemoaned morning sickness of pregnancy while doctors have stood by helpless. Remedies have ranged from applying caustic agents and salves to the cervix, to the consumption of whiskey, belladonna, popcorn, swamp dogwood, wild yams, wine of ipecac, and opium. Even in this age of high-tech medical care and bioengineering of drugs, treatment still relies on simple saltine crackers and sips of hot tea or iced liquids.

Described as early as 2,000 years before Christ, doctors still do not know exactly what causes it or how to cure it. Only one drug has ever been marketed for the treatment of morning sickness—Bendectin. FDA approved the drug in 1956 and approximately 900,000 women took the drug annually at the height of its use. But in 1983, Merrell Dow Pharmaceuticals, the drug's manufacturer, voluntarily took Bendectin off the market in the United States because of a number of lawsuits against the company from women who claimed that the drug caused birth defects. The company's insurance premium had soared so high because of the lawsuits that it was no longer profitable to sell the drug. It was never resolved whether Bendectin caused the birth defects or not. Bendectin contained an antihistamine, and some antihistamines have been shown to cause birth defects in animals. In 1980 an FDA panel reviewed the available data and found no association between the drug and birth defects. The panel did state that because it is nearly impossible to prove the absolute safety of any drug under every circumstance there remains a "residual uncertainty" about the drug's effects on the unborn child. We mention this because **DOXYLAMINE**, the antihistamine ingredient formerly in Bendectin, is still on the market in Europe. It is also still used in the United States in drugs approved by the FDA as sleep aids (see page 296). These sleep aids have a statement on them warning pregnant women to avoid the drug.

9

Ear Products

Ear disorders are very common, and in most cases cause a great deal of discomfort. However, before purchasing ear drops consider the symptoms and possible causes of the problem. The symptoms will play an important role in choosing the right product. For example, is there a cold or flu present? How long have the symptoms been present? Have they been swimming within the past several days? Is there a fever? Many disorders of the ear are minor and fairly easily resolved. But some untreated ear problems can result in hearing loss.

Doctors refer to inflammatory conditions of the outer ear as **OTITIS EXTERNA**. It can be caused by 1) infection from bacteria, fungi, or viruses 2) injury to the ear from excessive cleaning or scraping with homemade instruments, and 3) a skin reaction due to chemicals (hair spray, permanent wave lotion, perfume, etc.) or other skin conditions, such as seborrhea (see page 285) or psoriasis (see page 286).

Actually there are three different ways to treat ear problems without prescription drugs. The most common ear problems are caused by a build-up of **EARWAX**, which in turn causes pressure and pain in the ear. People sometimes stick different objects into the ear to try to break up the earwax and to clean the ear. They use things such as cotton swabs, hairpins, matchsticks, pencils, and fingers, among others. When using objects like these the eardrum can be scratched, forming an opening for infection.

If pain is caused by hardening of earwax, then use a product to soften it. One ingredient for that purpose is **CARBAMIDE PEROXIDE**, or the label may say **UREA PEROXIDE**, which is found in products such as *MURINE EAR WAX REMOVAL SYSTEM*, *DEBROX DROPS*, and *EAR DROPS BY MURINE.* Carbamide peroxide is the only safe and effective ingredient for removing excessive earwax, according to the FDA. This chemical is made from urea, and urea occurs naturally as a product of protein metabolism in animals.

Liquids that contain carbamide peroxide effervesce to release oxygen when placed in the ear, breaking up earwax and debris in the ear. The release of oxygen is also mildly antiseptic, which helps heal infected tissue. Pulling straight out ever-so-gently on the ear will straighten the ear canal and allow it to fill completely with the medicine. Hold this position for at least fifteen minutes, so that the drops have time to work. The next step is to remove the loosened earwax. Take a soft rubber syringe (usually this comes with the ear drops) and fill it with lukewarm water. Then, with the affected ear tilted down and over the sink, gently flush the ear with water. This process may be repeated a second time, if necessary. It should not be used on children under twelve years of age without checking with a doctor first.

Another substance that has been used for years to soften earwax is **OLIVE OIL**, also called **SWEET OIL**. The oil is first warmed by holding a container of it in a cup of hot tap water; it is then dropped into the ear. The heated oil melts some of the wax, or at least softens it, allowing easy removal by flushing out the ear with lukewarm water. Sweet oil is also very useful in relieving itching and burning in the ear. Olive oil has also been used to remove small **INSECTS** that get trapped in the ear. This can be frightening to small children because the insect cannot get out and continues to crawl frantically, exciting the child. Olive oil will smother the bug so it will stop crawling. It can then be irrigated out with warm water.

None of these agents above, including olive oil, should be placed in the ear canal if there is drainage (such as pus or blood) coming from the ear. This may be a sign that the eardrum has perforated (popped open). In this case, nothing should be placed in the ear unless prescribed by a physician.

Another cause of ear discomfort is seasonal; it occurs most often in the summer, when swimming is popular outdoors and the heat and humidity is high. **SWIMMER'S EAR** is the result of water being trapped in the ear, causing a severe earache. Loss of protective ear wax by excessive moisture trapped in the ear results in irritation of the skin lining the ear canal. Swimmer's ear is a condition that can eventually lead to infection, one of the types of **OTITIS EXTERNA**, mentioned previously. Even though it is called "swimmer's ear," other things can make you prone to the problem. For example, even persons who work in moist, warm environments have been known to have this condition frequently. Excessive bathing can also leave the ears constantly wet. If you have itching, burning, and mild to severe ear pain that is made worse by moving the ear around, pressing on the ear, or jaw movement, you may have **OTITIS EXTERNA**. If you think swimmer's ear is a contributing factor, try one of the over-the-counter drying agents mentioned below.

Products such as *SWIM EAR* contain **ANHYDROUS GLYCERIN** in **ISOPROPYL ALCOHOL**. The "anhydrous" means it does not contain any water, and isopropyl alcohol is plain rubbing alcohol. The alcohol works to kill bacteria and dry out the ear. Glycerin soothes the irritation somewhat. Some swimmer's ear products also contain **BORIC ACID**, usually in combination with alcohol, like *EAR-DRY* and *DRY/EAR DROPS*. Boric acid is a weak antiseptic and is nonirritating in the concentrations used. We don't like to recommend boric acid in the home because of its toxicity if swallowed accidentally by small children. However, in the concentrations in these preparations, it is generally safe.

These products can be used right after swimming each time to prevent swimmer's ear. However, they should not be used too often, because they can dry the ear to the point of causing other problems.

If the decision is made to use **EAR PLUGS** to prevent **EARACHES** that result from water in the ear, you will notice that there are two different kinds. One type is **RUBBER** and is used by people when they go swimming to keep water out of the ear. These can also be used in the shower. The other type of ear plug is made of **WAX**. It is not used to keep water out of the ear, but to eliminate noise. They do an excellent job of blocking out noise. They are also helpful with noisy jobs that cause headaches.

At one time nonprescription products were available that contained **ACETIC ACID**, the active ingredient in vinegar, which is antibacterial and antifungal. These products were used to treat minor infections, particularly when associated with "swimmer's ear." The FDA has banned this ingredient in such products because it is ineffective in the concentrations that were sold over the counter. Higher, more effective concentrations of acetic acid are still available with a prescription for the treatment of ear infections.

In summary, read the labels carefully when using eardrops, since the ingredients in the drops can make the difference between relieving earache and wasting money. Most over-the-counter ear products have been shown to be safe and effective and the choice of a specific product should be based on the symptoms. If there is no relief in one to two days or if there is a fever, drainage from the ear or hearing loss, there may be a more serious underlying condition for which you should seek the advice of a physician.

10

Eye Care

The seventeenth century poet George Herbert said that "diseases of the eye are to be cured with the elbow." Since the eye cannot be reached by the elbow, the idea, of course, is to leave your eyes alone. Until the development of modern surgery, disinfectants, and antibiotics this was probably true. Today there are many high-quality eye care products available to the consumer. The eyes may need assistance in protection from disease, adapting to vision problems as a result of heredity or aging, and protection from environmental factors such as contaminants and ultraviolet light.

While a pharmacist can help choose medicines to treat some of these simple problems, he or she is not a substitute for the eye specialists. Eye-care practitioners include ophthalmologists, optometrists, and opticians.

OPHTHALMOLOGISTS are physicians and surgeons who specialize in the diagnosis and treatment of eye disease. They also perform vision tests and prescribe glasses and contact lenses.

OPTOMETRISTS are state-licensed professionals who examine for visual defects and prescribe glasses and contact lenses. Optometrists can diagnose eye diseases, and in some states are licensed to prescribe medicines and manage certain eye diseases, but they do not perform surgery.

OPTICIANS fill prescriptions for eyeglasses, and in some states are licensed to fill prescriptions for contact lenses as well.

Eye Drops

There are a limited number of over-the-counter eye drops which are intended to "get the red out." These are basically safe and are effective in relieving minor eye symptoms such as burning, stinging, itching, tearing, tiredness, or eye strain.

None of these nonprescription medicines is intended to treat infection.

The simpler problems due to allergy, contaminants in the air, and fatigue are usually relatively painless and many of the over-the-counter eye drops for redness, irritation, and dry eye will help. If there is severe pain or blurred vision, eye drops will not help. Especially if these symptoms exist for 48 hours or more. The most common symptoms people experience are redness and irritation. These may be caused by a variety of conditions from eye strain to allergies.

Redness in the eye is caused by enlarged blood vessels. Most of the eye drops available contain a decongestant such as **PHENYLEPHRINE** found in *PREFRIN LIQUIFILM VASOCONSTRICTOR AND LUBRICANT EYE DROPS;* **NAPHAZOLINE** in products like *BAUSCH & LOMB ALLERGY DROPS;* and **TETRAHYDROZOLINE** in *MURINE PLUS LUBRICATING EYE REDNESS RELIEVER.* These ingredients constrict or tighten up the blood vessels, which in turn clears up the eye. Since most products do contain one of these ingredients, buy the cheapest one. In general, over-the-counter eye drops must be sterile while manufactured. They also have preservatives in them to keep them sterile. It is a good habit, before using an eye drop, to shake the bottle and hold it up to a light to make sure that the solution is perfectly clear and that no particles, such as filaments and fibers, are floating in it. All eye drops have expiration dates on the package, so be sure that the eye drops are not too old. A good, safe rule of thumb is not to use a bottle of eye drops after it has been opened for three months or more. **EYE WASHES**, accompanied by a small eye cup, are also available. Fill the eye cup with the eye wash solution, and hold it tightly over the eye. Open the eye and roll it around and from side to side. Eye washes are refreshing to the eye, and they are really useful if a foreign particle gets in the eye. But they are less convenient than the drops. Every home should have a fresh, sterile, unopened bottle of eye wash (not drops) and an eye cup for **EYE INJURY**

EMERGENCIES, particularly those involving chemicals and aerosol spray mishaps. If a chemical splashes in the eye, being able to rinse it quickly may save a trip to the emergency department of the local hospital. After rinsing, it may be helpful to call the regional poison center to be sure no other treatment is needed.

DRY EYE is not a single disease but a collection of symptoms that leads to abnormal tear flow and consistency in the eye. Tears are really a wonderfully complex solution produced by the lacrimal, sebaceous and mucous glands of the eye. Tears contain about 0.7 percent protein, mostly mucin and albumin, which form a protective, lubricating covering for the cornea. Most dry eye conditions are the result of abnormal tear production, that is, individual tear components are not present in healthy amounts. Menopausal or postmenopausal women are most often affected by dry eye. Diseases can also produce dry eye, including Sjogren's syndrome (a rheumatic condition which causes severe dryness of the mouth, swollen glands, and muscle pain and swelling) and vitamin A deficiency. Dry eye usually responds well to a physician's supervision and nonprescription tear substitutes, but in some cases may require surgical correction. Tear replacement products contain softening ingredients known as demulcents. Mucin is a natural demulcent and the artificial demulcents work similarly by coating the surface of irritated eyes and protecting underlying cells. The artificial coating provided by eye drops prevents drying of the eye due to environmental factors like heat or wind and this reduces irritation and dryness of the eye. Some of the ingredients found in eye drops to replace the natural mucin are **CELLULOSE DERIVATIVES**, **POLYVINYL ALCOHOL** (found in *HYPOTEARS* by Johnson & Johnson), **GLYCERIN**, **PROPYLENE GLYCOL**, **DEXTRAN 70** (in *TEARS NATURALE II* by Alcon), and **POVIDONE**. Eye ointments, such as *LACRILUBE S.O.P.*, are also available for the treatment of dry eye and these may contain lanolin, mineral oil, paraffin or similar nontoxic, sterile, oily materials. The ointments are more practical for bedtime use because they tend to blur vision temporarily.

Sometimes **PINK EYE**, may develop, in which the inner lining of the eye, the conjunctiva, becomes inflamed. Doctors refer to this as **CONJUNCTIVITIS**. It can usually be cleared up with any one of the over-the-counter eye drops, if it is not caused by microorganisms. But sometimes it is caused by bacteria or viruses and becomes contagious. This can be very dangerous and lead to complications and vision loss if not properly treated. When someone has a cold or a sinus infection they may rub their nose and then rub their eye. Actually what they are doing is spreading bacteria or viruses from the nose to the eye, resulting in classic pink eye. If a greenish discharge is noticed in the corner of the eye, there may be a contagious infection and will probably need an antibiotic eye drop, prescribed by a physician, to clear it up.

There are some over-the-counter eye drops and ointments purported to kill bacteria. They contain **BORIC ACID.** Since boric acid may be purchased as a bulk powder, a well meaning relative or neighbor may give advice to concoct an eye solution to treat an infection. However, we do not advise using any of these preparations—boric acid is very weak at killing bacteria, and it sometimes causes problems, especially in children. Sometimes kids can get into the contents of the bottle of eye drops. Every year there are a number of accidental poisonings in children who drink products like this. Also, since boric acid is a weak antiseptic, if an infection is present it may need an antibiotic. Continuing to use a boric acid solution while the infection is getting worse could permanently damage the eye. A **BORIC ACID OINTMENT** is available to treat **STYES**, the common term for a bacterial infection of an eyelash follicle, oil or sweat gland near the eye. **STYES** respond best to a hot compress and a sterile antibiotic product prescribed by a doctor. These promote drainage and healing.

Another thing to remember when using eye drops containing **DECONGESTANTS**, be careful; just as decongestants in nose sprays can cause a reaction (see Rebound Congestion, page 236 and Long Acting Nasal Decongestants page 240), so can those in eye drops. Decongestant eye drops constrict the blood vessels, getting rid of redness. Most of them are recommended by the manufacturer for "temporary relief of discomfort and redness due to minor eye irritations," these are in some cases the results of allergy. But prolonged use may cause the blood vessels to enlarge again in a shorter and shorter period of time. Also, remember that these eye drops are mainly used for cosmetic purposes, to clear the eyes. Prolonged use may actually mask the symptoms of a serious eye problem. For routine use, it is better to use a simple eye wash, such as *LAVOPTIK EYE WASH* or *BAUSCH & LOMB EYE WASH*. These products are simple, balanced salt solutions that do not contain any mercury preservatives or vessel-constricting drugs. We do not recommend any of the products that use **THIMEROSOL**, a mercury-containing ingredient used as a preservative, because many people are sensitive to it. Those people suffering from **GLAUCOMA** should not use any eye products without consulting a physician.

Contact Lenses

If you have never considered contact lenses or have not checked to see what has been going on in this area in the last few years, take another look (no pun intended). Today's contacts are not only better, but they offer some amazing options to wearers. Contact lenses are now available for all age groups, children to the elderly, and include improved materials that resist contaminants and allow more oxygen to pass through to nourish the eye. The term "contact" lens is really a misnomer. When properly positioned, the lens does not actually contact the surface of the eye. All lenses ride on a thin layer of tears over the cornea, the transparent covering at the front of the eyeball which covers the colored iris and pupil. There are more types and fits of lenses for problem eyes. New lenses are tolerated better by patients, last longer and accumulate fewer deposits. It is estimated that by the year 2000 there will be as many people using contact lenses as those who wear eyeglasses. To take advantage of these new developments, the patient must be conscientious about caring for the lenses. People sometimes regard contact lenses as cosmetic accessories rather than a medical device. If they are not careful about keeping them clean problems will result.

Recently there has been a proliferation of lens-care products, easily over 100 different brands and types to choose from on drug store shelves. However, the most important choice that will be made in choosing one of these products will probably be in selecting the right optometrist or ophthalmologist. He or she can make the selection based on your personal needs and fitting.

With over twenty million people wearing contact lenses this is an important aspect of eye care. Before handling the contact lenses or their case, be sure the wearer's hands are clean. There are three general rules or goals that are important for the person who wears any type of contact lens.

- Keep the lenses clean. This should be done on a daily basis to remove mucus from the lens surface. Daily use of a **CLEANING SOLUTION** may be the most important step in lens care. Studies show that deposits begin forming on a clean lens within minutes after its put in the eye. Tears contain some 60 different proteins and these are what stick to contact lenses.
- Contact lenses should be kept in a soaking solution when they are not in the eye. The **SOAKING** or **STORAGE SOLUTIONS** are different for the type of lens. Rigid lenses are stored in a soak containing a preservative. Soft lenses are stored in saline which is available in either preserved or preservative-free forms.

- A **WETTING AGENT** should be used to put the contact lens in the eye and rewetting solutions may be used throughout the day.

It is also important to clean the contact lens storage case on a regular basis—that is, every day or two. For hard contact lenses, use a mild soap or baking soda to clean the case, then let it air-dry. The soft lens storage case can be rinsed in hot tap water and then allowed to air-dry. Women may wear makeup with contacts, but should be careful if they wear soft lenses because these are easily penetrated by foreign substances. Mascara, makeup, and hair dyes can soak into the lens and ruin it. Foreign material on or under the lens will produce extreme discomfort. Care should be exercised by both the hard- and soft-lens wearer when using hair and deodorant sprays; these products should be used before the lenses are put in the eyes. Also, never administer eye medicine while the contacts are in place without checking with your physician or optometrist.

In the drugstore there are many products to use with contact lenses. The cleaning and wetting solutions are different for hard, rigid gas permeable and soft lenses. It is very important not to use a hard contact lens solution with the soft lenses, because hard lens solutions contain a preservative called **BENZALKONIUM CHLORIDE**. This ingredient binds into the soft plastic and causes a burning sensation when the soft lens is put in the eye. If this happens it is uncomfortable, but it will not cause permanent eye damage.

Hard Contact Lenses

The original hard Plexiglass-type **(POLYMETHYLMETHACRYLATE** or **PMMA)** contact lenses that became popular in the 1950s and 1960s are still worn by only about 1 percent of wearers, but are no longer recommended for first time users. Hard lenses do not permit oxygen to pass through. The cornea has no blood vessels in it and must receive its oxygen directly from the air. The hard contacts depend on that layer of tears between the lens and the cornea to supply oxygen. Too little oxygen can produce irritation, inflammation or even damage the cornea, especially if the lens is left in for more than 12 hours. Hard contact lenses usually last about five years. It is important to use the right solution on a hard contact lens. First of all there are the **CLEANING SOLUTIONS** such as *LENSINE EXTRA STRENGTH CLEANER, MIRAFLOW EXTRA STRENGTH* and *OPTI-CLEAN.* A cleansing solution should be used on a daily basis. It removes mucus and debris that could cloud or fog up the lens. The other type of solution is a **SOAKING SOLUTION** and is available in such products as *SOQUETTE, CONTIQUE SOAK TABS*, and *SOAKARE.* When not wearing contact lenses, be sure to use one of these solutions in the storage case; they contain an ingredient to kill bacteria that could cause eye infections. The third type of solution is the **WETTING SOLUTION**, such as *LIQUIFILM TEARS, VISALENS*, and *STAY-WET*. These products are used directly on the lenses just before putting them in the eyes. Their main purpose is to make the lens more compatible with the eye and to keep the lens from stinging the eye when it is applied. They also protect the lens from oily deposits on the fingers during insertion.

Rigid Gas-Permeable (RGP) Contact Lenses

Beginning in 1978, a new kind of hard lens was introduced. Known as a rigid gas-permeable lens, it was identical in appearance to a conventional hard lens, but with a crucial difference. Oxygen could penetrate its plastic. Like hard lenses **RGP**s are about the size of a very small, thin shirt button and cover only the pupil and a small part of the iris, the colored portion around the pupil. Made of slightly flexible plastics, including pure **PMMA** or combinations of **PMMA**, silicone, silicone/acrylate, cellulose acetate butyrate and fluorocarbons, they permit oxygen to pass through to the cornea. Like the old hard lenses, they correct most vision problems, including extreme astigmatism. They endure for years, can be polished to remove scratches, and are uncomfortable until one gets used to them. **RGPs** provide the most precise correction of all modern contact lenses, comparable to that achieved by eyeglasses. And like glasses, **RGPs** are custom ground to the doctor's prescription. Almost 20 percent of lens wearers use this type of lens.

EXTENDED-WEAR RIGID GAS-PERMEABLE lenses are also available. Enough oxygen passes through lenses to permit continuous wear for up to seven days and nights without removal, although few eye care practitioners recommend this. Some of the new extended wear rigid gas-permeable lenses are particularly resistant to the buildup of protein and other deposits on the lens and also are made from materials that protect the eye from 90 percent of ultraviolet radiation. Extended wear lenses are not for everyone. The FDA and The Contact Lens Institute warn that the longer a lens stays in the eye between cleanings and disinfection, the greater the possibility of infection. A study by the Contact Lens Institute showed that users of extended-wear lenses are more likely to develop **ULCERATIVE KERATITIS**, a disease of the cornea that can damage, even destroy, vision.

Soft Contact Lenses

In 1971 Bausch & Lomb introduced the first soft lens in the United States. Made of plastics that soak up water, the lenses are gelatinlike rather than hard. Over 60 brands are now available and some of these products absorb as much as 80 percent water. Eighty percent of people using contact lenses use the soft type. Soft contact lenses are a lot easier to get used to than hard ones—they are quite comfortable. A second advantage is that soft lenses help transmit oxygen to the cornea. Oxygen can dissolve in water and percolate through the lens to the eye. With proper care, which usually takes two to three minutes a day, these contacts will last about two years. Soft lenses are larger than hard lenses or **RGPs**, at least covering the entire pupil and iris, and they are very thin and flexible. Soft lenses are not custom-ground and they provide a softer focus than the more precise **RGPs**. **EXTENDED-WEAR SOFT LENSES** are similar to other soft lenses. They have either a higher water content or are thinner to permit more oxygen to pass through the lenses for continuous night and day wear. Ophthalmologists are still concerned about the extended-wear lenses because of the greater likelihood of eye problems, including infection. Remember that soft lenses are more easily penetrated by mascara and other eye makeup.

Soft contacts are stored in a solution that is similar to our own natural tears. At one time these solutions were prepared from a tablet. However, the FDA took the tablets off the market, because they were often prepared under conditions that were not sterile and a rare type of vision-threatening eye infection resulted. The FDA still does not condone the use of salt tablets. Now we have prepared solutions to store and disinfect the soft contact lenses. Products like *BOIL AND SOAK*, *LENSRINS*, and *LENS PLUS STERILE SALINE SOLUTION* are only intended to be used with the **HEAT OR THERMAL DISINFECTION METHOD**. A second method of disinfecting soft lenses is called the **CHEMICAL** or **"COLD TREATMENT,"** because no heat is used. Check with a doctor before using this method, because the chemicals in the treatment cause reactions in certain people. Do not switch back and forth between cold and hot methods of disinfecting, because it could ruin the lens. The third type of disinfection is also a chemical one. This is the use of **HYDROGEN PEROXIDE**. Lenses are placed in a purified hydrogen peroxide solution and the release of oxygen from peroxide kills microorganisms.

Never place contacts in the mouth to wet them, and never wipe them with a cloth or tissue that could scratch the lens. When you go to a doctor be sure to tell him that you wear contact lenses before he writes out a prescription for you, because some drugs can dry out the eye. It can be beneficial to wear some sort of medical alert necklace or bracelet if you wear contact lenses.

Contact lenses are great, convenient, attractive, and effective. But remember when getting a pair to be sure to get all the information available regarding the lenses. Read the literature thoroughly because knowing a lot about the lenses can prevent problems in the future. And if you are confused about which lens-care product to buy, ask an optometrist, ophthalmologist or pharmacist for help.

Disposable Contact Lenses

This idea in contact lenses takes the extended-wear concept one step further. They are designed to be worn night and day for a week or two and then discarded. Ideally, the concept would eliminate the need to clean and disinfect the lens, eye problems that result from improper cleaning, and reactions to lens cleaning solutions. Johnson & Johnson and Bausch & Lomb are both marketing versions of disposable lenses. In practice, however, optometrists recommend that even these lenses are removed and cleaned daily.

Contact Lens Solution Preservatives

BENZALKONIUM CHLORIDE is a detergent that has antimicrobial properties. It is a white or yellowish powder or gelatinous pieces with an aromatic odor and a very bitter taste. This chemical is referred to as a **QUATERNARY AMMONIUM COMPOUND** (which has importance only to the chemist, but it is a categorical term frequently used on product labels). An effective germicide and an extremely poisonous chemical when swallowed in quantity, it is used in minute concentrations in over-the-counter products as a preservative. It is too dangerous to be used routinely as a skin antiseptic because higher concentrations are required to be effective.

CHLORHEXIDINE is used in a few lens solution disinfectants. It is the same chemical used as an effective anti-plaque ingredient by dentists and can be found in one prescription mouthwash preparation. However when used in lens solutions, it has some unpleasant properties. It may be irritating to the eyes of some people and breakdown products of chlorhexidine can discolor solutions.

EDTA or **SODIUM EDETATE** is a chemical preservative used in many rigid and soft lens solution products. **EDTA** breaks down bacterial cell membranes, making it easier for other preservatives to work. For this reason **EDTA** is frequently used with other preservatives.

MERTHIOLATE is a cream colored, mercury-containing antiseptic developed in the fifties by Eli Lilly Co., brand named **THIMEROSOL**. It is non-irritating to the skin and mildly antibacterial and antifungal. Like other mercury-containing products for application to the skin, it poses an unnecessary risk of absorption of a dangerous, poisonous metal (mercury) and should no longer be used. Almost all manufacturers now use safer chemical preservatives.

PHENYLMERCURIC NITRATE is an organic mercury chemical that exists as a white, crystalline powder. It is used as an antiseptic in ointments for application to the skin, has been used in vaginal products as an antiseptic and preservative and in preparations for cleaning or wetting contact lenses. It is less effective than iodine, can produce mercury poisoning and is a very sensitizing chemical. Virtually all manufacturers have replaced it with preservatives less likely to cause irritation or an allergic reaction.

POTASSIUM SORBATE is the potassium salt of **SORBIC ACID** and both of these chemicals are becoming increasingly popular as preservatives in lens solutions. It is a safe alternative to thimerosal.

11

Feminine Hygiene

American society today is probably unsurpassed in its concern for cleanliness, personal hygiene, and elimination of body odor. Vaginal douches are not new, but feminine deodorant sprays are. They were introduced in the 1960s and since that time you can hardly pick up a magazine without seeing advertisements for them. According to the advertisements, you are not clean and refreshed unless you use one of these products. However, most gynecologists believe that the healthy vagina cleanses itself. Although some doctors seem to feel that douching, when done properly, promotes healthy vaginal tissues, the value of feminine deodorant sprays is very controversial. It has been found that the ingredients in douches and deodorants change the natural bacterial environment of the vagina, as do antibiotics. Their effectiveness, whether you use the spray or the powder, is questionable. Nevertheless, doctors are finding more and more women who have used these products and who subsequently develop irritation of the vagina. The deodorant sprays have also been known to cause allergic reactions in men after intercourse, resulting in irritation, itching, and pulling of the skin on the penis.

Douches

These are available in liquids, liquid concentrates (which are diluted with water before use), and powders (to be dissolved in water). No matter what product is used, be sure to follow the instructions on the package because of the possibility of local irritation.

Some douches like *MASSENGILL DOUCHE POWDER* contain astringents such as **AMMONIUM** and **POTASSIUM ALUMS** and are used to reduce local swelling and inflammation. Other douche products contain **BENZALKONIUM CHLORIDE** or an iodine product such as

BETADINE and are used to stop bacterial infections. If you notice signs of irritation and itching, try a douche with an ingredient to kill bacteria. If the infection is too far advanced, these products will not help much because of their low concentrations. It would be best to check with a doctor.

Special considerations when these products are used:

- Excessive pressure should never be used in giving douches. The force of gravity is sufficient to create a flow of the douche into the vagina if a bag, tube, and nozzle are used.
- Water used to dilute the powder or liquid concentrate should be lukewarm and not hot.
- Douching equipment should be cleaned thoroughly before and after use.
- Douches should not be used during pregnancy.
- A douche should not be used after using a contraceptive foam or suppository, because it will wash away some of the spermicide that serves as a protective barrier against impregnation.

Vaginal Anti-Infectives

CLOTRIMAZOLE and **MICONAZOLE** are approved as OTC anti-infective ingredients for self treatment of yeast infections. If you have been to your doctor at least once for a vaginal yeast infection, many physicians believe that you can safely diagnose it in the future on your own. Products now containing these ingredients are *GYNE-LOTRIMIN VAGINAL INSERTS* and *MONISTAT-7 DAY VAGINAL CREAM* and vaginal suppositories.

While most women note improvement within a few days, it is important to finish the seven-day treatment to make sure all of the problem fungus has been killed. Women who do not see rapid improvement of their symptoms are likely to have a problem other than a vaginal yeast infection.

In October 1992, the FDA required additions to the package insert in vaginal yeast infection products. They now include a notice that recurrent vaginal yeast infections, especially those that do not clear up easily with proper treatment, may also be the result of serious medical conditions, including HIV infection. The labeling also says: "If you experience vaginal yeast infections frequently (they recur within a two-month period) or if you have vaginal yeast infections that do not clear up easily with proper treatment, you should see your doctor promptly to determine the cause and to receive proper medical care."

In addition to the HIV notice, the following warnings also appear on information accompanying the products:

- Do not use if you have abdominal pain, fever, or foul-smelling vaginal discharge. You may have a condition that is more serious than a yeast infection. Contact your doctor immediately.
- Do not use if this is your first experience with vaginal itch and discomfort. See your doctor.
- If there is no improvement within three days, you may have a condition other than a yeast infection. Stop using this product and see your doctor.
- If symptoms recur within a two-month period, contact your doctor.
- Do not use during pregnancy except under the advice and supervision of a doctor.
- This medication is for vaginal yeast infections only. It is not for use in the mouth or the eyes. If accidentally swallowed, seek professional assistance or contact a Poison Control Center immediately.
- Keep this and all other drugs out of the reach of children. This product is not to be used in children less than 12 years of age.

In general, fungal infections like warm, moist places. A few simple steps can help reduce the number of infections women get.

Wear loose, natural-fiber clothing and underwear with a cotton crotch. As much as possible, avoid pantyhose, tights or leggings, nylon underwear, and tight jeans. Limit the use of deodorant tampons and feminine hygiene products if you feel an infection beginning, as they can interfere with beneficial bacteria in the vagina. Keep genitals dry after bathing or swimming (do not stay in a wet swimsuit for hours).

Feminine Deodorant Sprays

These are aerosol products intended to be used on the external genital area to reduce or mask objectionable odor.

They are available in mist or powder form. If these products are held too close to the skin while spraying, they can cause irritation and swelling of tissues. They should be held six to eight inches away from the body. We do not recommend these products. Good personal hygiene should make these things completely unnecessary.

Menstrual Pain Relievers

MENSTRUATION is a fact of life for women during their child-bearing years. At this point in a woman's cycle she may experience pain, fluid accumulation, backaches, breast tenderness, irritability, abnormal cramping, anxiety, and depression. It is therefore not surprising that many women are a little "on edge" during this period. The severity of the symptoms varies considerably from individual to individual.

However, a lot has been learned in recent years about the menstrual cycle and its associated production of body chemicals and hormones. Much of this knowledge has been used to treat the painful effects of menstruation, or menses. There are two kinds of painful menstruation, primary and secondary **DYSMENORRHEA**. It is very important to distinguish between them so both are treated properly. **PRIMARY DYSMENORRHEA** usually starts within three years of the onset of menstruation and lasts one or two days each month. This type of menstrual pain may lessen for some women as they grow older or after the birth of children, but it can also continue until menopause. **SECONDARY DYSMENORRHEA** is menstrual pain caused by disease such as pelvic inflammatory disease, **ENDOMETRIOSIS** (problems in the lining of the uterus), or nonmalignant growths in the uterus. Endometriosis is a major cause of secondary dysmenorrhea. Pain from it usually starts later in life and worsens with time. Another hint that disease might be the cause of menstrual pain is if pain also occurs during intercourse or other parts of the cycle.

Primary dysmenorrhea is a result of the normal production of **PROSTAGLANDIN**—chemical substances that are made by cells in the lining of the uterus and elsewhere throughout the body. The lining of the uterus, which has built up and thickened during the early stages of the menstrual cycle, breaks up and is sloughed off at the end of the cycle and releases prostaglandins. The prostaglandins, in turn, make the uterus contract more strongly than at any other time of the cycle. They can cause it to contract so much that the blood supply is cut off temporarily, depriving the uterine muscle of oxygen and causing pain. It is not clear whether women who suffer painful contractions are producing excessive amount of prostaglandins or that they are just more sensitive to them.

For many years women had little help for their symptoms. The use of aspirin, heating pads and hot baths helped only few women. There are now a number of over-the-counter products made specifically to treat these symptoms. The advent of pain relievers that reduce the production of prostaglandins has made it possible to directly treat the cause of the cramps. Known as **NSAIDs**, or **NON-STEROIDAL ANTI-INFLAMMATORY DRUGS**, these medications have proven remarkably effective for many women. Because **NSAIDs** inhibit the synthesis of prostaglandins, and thereby the contractions of the uterus, they may actually reduce menstrual flow. Make sure you take them as early as possible after the menstrual flow starts. Waiting too long may mean they will not be as effective. Pay attention to the label which advises taking with food or milk. This will reduce stomach upset. The active ingredient in several OTC nonsteroidal antiinflammatory brand products is **IBUPROFEN**, found in *ADVIL, NUPRIN, MOTRIN IB* and *MIDOL 200.* **NAPROXEN**, found in the brand name product *ALEVE*, is the most recent over-the-counter **NSAID. ASPIRIN** does work as a prostaglandin inhibitor, but not so powerfully as the specific inhibitors such as ibuprofen. Some products are simple pain-relievers and contain ingredients like **ACETAMINOPHEN**, found in *TYLENOL* and *DATRIL*. They probably do not work as well as the prostaglandin inhibitors, but doctors say that acetaminophen can successfully treat the headache and backache that often accompany menstrual cramps. Also, if there are chronic stomach problems present, or if there is stomach discomfort because of menstruation, one may want to alternate doses with one of these acetaminophen products. Some OTC menstrual pain medications, such as *MIDOL* and *PAMPRIN*, contain a mix of ingredients that includes a pain reliever, such as **ACETAMINOPHEN**, a diuretic such as **PAMABROM**, and an antihistamine, such as **PYRILAMINE MALEATE**. The newer formulations are switching to **IBUPROFEN**, such as *MIDOL 200 ADVANCED CRAMP FORMULA*. The antihistamine in these products may cause drowsiness, so if there are symptoms of nervousness and tension, these products might help to some degree.

Many misconceptions still exist regarding limitations in one's daily activities during menstruation. One of the most common misconceptions is that women should not bathe or wash themselves during this time. Good hygiene that includes routine showering or bathing is one of the most effective ways of reducing menstrual odors. Various feminine products including towelettes, sprays, and douches are marketed to assist the menstruating female in her personal hygiene. (See earlier discussion of the limitations of these products.)

PMS

PREMENSTRUAL SYNDROME or **PMS** is a complication of the normal menses that not all women have. The American College of Obstetrics and Gynecology (ACOG) says that from 20 to 40 percent of women suffer some symptoms of **PMS**, which it defines as "a recurring cycle of symptoms that are so severe as to affect lifestyle or work." **PMS** occurs in the last 7 to 10 days of the menstrual cycle—called the luteal phase. The time at which these symptoms occur is very important because it is what allows a doctor to track the cyclic nature of the condition and make a diagnosis.

Physicians at the FDA have stated that the variety and combination of symptoms of **PMS** are usually divided into four major groups. Breast tenderness, swelling, weight gain, and bloating make up one group of symptoms. The second group includes emotional changes such as depression, forgetfulness, crying, insomnia, and confusion. A third group involves headaches, food cravings (especially sweets), increased appetite, fatigue, and dizziness. The fourth group includes anxiety, nervous tension, mood swings and irritability.

PMS is alleviated by treating its symptoms. Some products mentioned above are marketed for **PMS**. Symptoms may be relieved by prostaglandin inhibitors such as **IBUPROFEN** or **NAPROXEN**, discussed earlier. Some women suffer swelling in the hands and feet during their periods. They may feel bloated. A product with a mild **DIURETIC** may help relieve this problem to some degree. The FDA has approved three OTC diuretics: **PAMABROM**, which is theophylline derivative, **CAFFEINE**, and **AMMONIUM CHLORIDE.** *AQUA-BAN* is one product containing ammonium chloride and caffeine. *TRI-AQUA* contains caffeine along with some herbs that are also mildly diuretic. However, these only help get rid of water in the body to a small degree, not as effectively as prescription diuretics would. Still, they may give enough relief to get through a period with the least amount of discomfort. If they are taken 5 to 6 days prior to the onset of menses these drugs may help to relieve symptoms related to **WATER RETENTION**. These include water weight, bloating, swelling, painful breasts, cramps and tension. On the other hand, too much caffeine may aggravate anxiety and tension, and some doctors think it may be associated with increased breast tenderness. It also helps to stay away from salt and salt-rich foods, such as pickles and snack chips, during a period. The antihistamine **PYRILAMINE MALEATE**, also included in OTC menstrual products, may be useful as a mild sedative, but it is not specifically approved by the FDA for this use in **PMS**.

Many women find they get relief by exercising, stopping smoking or changing their diets. Some doctors prescribe birth control pills for severe cases of **PMS**, because birth control pills prevent ovulation and therefore prevent the luteal phase from occurring.

Sanitary Napkins and Tampons

Years ago there were only two brands of sanitary napkins, *KOTEX* and *MODESS*. Pharmacists would wrap the boxes in plain paper because back then, women were embarrassed to be seen buying these products. For a long time, there was only one brand of tampon, *TAMPAX*, which received the same treatment. Nowadays we have all sorts of products, ranging from sanitary napkins and tampons to panty shields and liners.

Toxic Shock Syndrome (TSS)

One big concern with tampon use is toxic shock syndrome **(TSS)**. **TSS** was first described as a medical condition in 1978. Its flulike symptoms most frequently affected menstruating women under 30 who used tampons, particularly young women between the ages of 15 and 19. The FDA estimates that 1 to 17 per 100,000 menstruating women develop **TSS** each year. **TSS** also occurs in children, men and nonmenstruating women. These nonmenstrual cases can occur after such medical situations as surgery or a deep wound especially one with a foreign object in it. Toxic shock syndrome is believed to be caused by bacteria that get into the bloodstream, causing a bacterial infection. Reports of **TSS** associated with the use of tampons continue to decline. There have been no menstruation-related **TSS** deaths reported in the last couple of years, according to the U.S. Centers for Disease Control (CDC). The reports of **TSS** continue to decline from the high of 890 in 1980, when 38 women died of menstrual **TSS**. But according to CDC most cases of toxic shock syndrome are still menstruation-related. The Food and Drug Administration is concerned that teenagers just beginning to menstruate might not know about **TSS** or that, despite alerts on tampon packages, young women might believe **TSS** has gone away or is no longer serious. The symptoms of **TSS** are:

- sudden high fever—102°F or higher
- vomiting, diarrhea
- dizziness, fainting or near fainting when standing up
- a rash that looks like a sunburn

If symptoms appear during the menstrual period, the tampon should be removed and one should seek medical attention right away. Symptoms may not appear until the first few days after the end of the period. If there is a history of **TSS**, medical advice should be sought before using tampons. Toxic shock syndrome is rare, but it can be fatal.

The FDA has issued a new rule requiring that tampon packages labeled "junior," "regular," "super," or "super plus" conform to specific absorbencies and that these ranges be uniform from brand to brand. This will let women know the absorbency they are getting when they buy tampons, and to get the same absorbency when they switch brands. Manufacturers must use a test to measure absorbency developed with the help of the FDA.

It is important to compare tampon brands and choose the **LOWEST ABSORBENCY** needed to control menstrual flow because the risk of **TSS** increases with higher tampon absorbency. It may be desirable to use different tampon absorbencies for different days of the menstrual period. Absorbency of tampons has been lowered several times since 1980. New labeling requirements for tampons must appear on the insert or outer package and in easily understood terms explain:

- the risk of **TSS** to all women using tampons during their menstrual periods, especially the reported higher risks to women under 30
- the estimated incidence of **TSS** of 1 to 17 per 100,000 menstruating women per year
- the reduction of the risk of **TSS** by using tampons with the minimum absorbency needed to control menstrual flow
- the reduction of the risk of **TSS** by alternating tampon use with feminine pads during menstrual periods
- the avoidance of the risk of tampon associated **TSS** by not using tampons

The outer package must display one of the following terms representing the corresponding absorbency range of the tampons in the package:

Absorbency Range *(in grams)*	**Absorbency**
6 and under	Junior absorbency
6 to 9	Regular absorbency
9 to 12	Super absorbency
12 to 15	Super plus absorbency

This bacterial infection was found among women who used tampons, particularly a brand called *RELY*, which has since been removed from the market by the manufacturer. However, there are still many other brands of tampons on the market and a lot of women use them because of their comfort and convenience.

To reduce the risk of toxic shock syndrome read the package insert included with tampons carefully. Follow instructions closely, and regardless of which tampon absorbency chosen change the tampon every four to six hours, or more often if needed. Changing too frequently may cause some irritation.

To further reduce the risk of TSS alternate tampon use with feminine pads and use feminine pads at night. Products such as *STAYFREE ULTRA PLUS NIGHT SUPER PADS* are designed for this purpose.

If symptoms develop such as fever, chills, muscle aches, and nausea while wearing tampons, contact a physician immediately. If the symptoms are a sign of a bacterial infection due to wearing tampons, the longer the wait the more severe the infection can become, causing a serious hazard to health. Do not assume these symptoms are the flu if tampons are being used.

12

First Aid & Infection Care

Injuries have a way of happening when you least expect them. The incidence of minor cuts and scrapes increases when the kids are home, playing, running, or riding their bikes. This may send parents running to the corner drugstore (hopefully not the emergency department of the local hospital) to buy a supply of *BAND-AIDS* and other first aid supplies. First aid is everyone's responsibility. Being ready to give emergency care can make the critical difference in saving a life, relieving pain, or preventing further injury or infection. Mothers, fathers, and yes, even grandparents these days, are often home with the kids, and soon learn to become "household paramedics."

Here are a few first-aid tips on some of the most common minor injuries:

For minor partial thickness (first- or second-degree) **BURNS**, the first step is to run cold water over the area. Cold water is preferable to ice, but if ice is the only thing available, use it. Keep the burned area submerged as long as you feel pain. The sooner you get the area into cool water, the sooner you will get relief; it could also mean the difference between redness of the skin and a blister. For more serious burns, see a doctor.

To stop a **NOSE BLEED**, have the victim sit quietly and hold the nostrils pressed together. The site of bleeding is usually a blood vessel on the inside lining of the nose near the septum. This is at the level of the fleshy part of the nose, hence pinching the nostrils and holding pressure for 5 to 10 minutes usually stops the bleeding. Holding pressure on the bridge of the nose is not effective.

To give first aid for a **BRUISE**, apply ice or cold cloths as soon as the injury happens.

To give home treatment for a **BRUISE** a day or two after the injury, apply warm, wet cloths, or any other type of heat treatment.

A **FROSTBITTEN AREA** should be soaked first in water that is lukewarm, not hot, with the temperature very gradually increased. See a doctor as soon as possible.

If you are called upon to give first aid for **BLEEDING**, first apply direct pressure to the cut.

To remove a speck of **DIRT FROM SOMEONE'S EYE**, wash it with one of the sterile eye washes like *LAVOPTIK* (see page 113).

For a **MINOR CUT** or scratch the first thing to do is to wash it with soap and water. Remember, if the injury is severe, or if there is any doubt in your mind about how severe it is, call a physician or go to an emergency room.

A Homemade First Aid & Medicine Kit

You can buy first-aid kits in the drugstore, which have everything you will need to treat household emergencies. Unfortunately they often contain things you will never use as well. You can make your own first-aid kit to keep at home and carry in your car on trips. Find a plastic container with a lid, a good size one, preferably one that is airtight. The kit should include the following:

ADHESIVE TAPE AND SCISSORS: Use these with the gauze, although the scissors can be helpful for other things, like cutting clothing away from a wound.

ANTISEPTICS: Many antiseptics are fairly poisonous and are of very limited or questionable value. Dramatic healing from antiseptics applied to the skin is the exception and not the rule. So it is not a good idea to store the more poisonous antiseptics around the home. The best all-around household antiseptic is *BETADINE SOLUTION*. It kills bacteria and fungi, it forms a film that sticks to the wound, and because it is a brownish-purple color you can also see the area you are covering.

BAND-AIDS: Include an assortment. They are especially helpful in calming children when they suffer minor cuts and scrapes.

CHEMICAL ICE PACK: There may not be ice around when you need it for bumps, sprains and bruises. That is when this comes in handy. They are available under many trade names, but *INSTANT COLD PACK* by Truett is one. Your pharmacist can recommend others.

ELASTIC BANDAGES: Use them to wrap ankles and sore arms.

FIRST-AID BOOKLET: The AMERICAN RED CROSS has a good first-aid booklet which should be included in a home-made kit.

FLASHLIGHT: It is impossible to predict what time of day an injury will occur or what the weather will be like when it happens. A flashlight is also good for examining inside the mouth.

HAND TOWELS: These are useful for cleaning or as a compress to stop bleeding.

LIST OF EMERGENCY NUMBERS: Start with the official **EMERGENCY RESPONSE NUMBER** in your area, usually **911** and your **POISON CENTER**, listed in the front page of most phone books. By the way, poison centers are for adults as well as children. In many cities 24-hour health information telephone numbers, such as **ASK-A-NURSE**, are available when sponsored by local hospitals.

LOCK: A very important part of any first aid kit or medicine cabinet is a lock. Medications, drugs, and sharp instruments should be locked up to prevent more injuries, especially when there are kids around.

MAGNIFYING GLASS: This is important for examining areas close up and removing small splinters.

MEDICATED CREAMS, OINTMENTS: Products like *NEOSPORIN, NEOPOLYCIN,* and *MYCITRACIN* cream and ointment are useful for minor cuts and scratches. Since these products contain antibiotics to stop infection, the creams and ointments will have an expiration date on the package. Make sure the product is not outdated, and be sure to replace the old tube with a new supply. Other non-antibiotic first-aid creams that are available are mainly intended to soothe and coat the affected area, including *JOHNSON AND JOHNSON FIRST AID CREAM.* Johnson and Johnson even offers step-by-step directions for treating minor injuries on the back label of some of their products. In addition they provide a toll-free number on the boxes of certain bandages to provide answers to questions about their proper use.

MEDICATED SOAP: Use to clean surface wounds and scrapes.

PAIN RELIEVERS: These products, like *TYLENOL* and *LIQUIPRIN,* which contain **ACETAMINOPHEN** can be used for minor pain and fever in children and adults. ASPIRIN is generally acceptable in children for pain due to sprains and other physical injuries, but you must avoid it for illnesses associated with the flu or chicken pox (see page 177, Aspirin and Reye Syndrome).

SINGLE-EDGE RAZOR BLADE: This can be used to remove stingers caused by bees by a gentle scraping motion from side to side (see page 338). A sharp edge may also come in handy for other emergencies.

STERILE GAUZE: Various types are available. Pads, compresses, rolls and others. These are necessary for dressing larger wounds.

SYRUP OF IPECAC: This medication causes vomiting. It is good to have around in case of accidental poisoning, but do not use it unless instructed by the poison center (there are certain products that should not be vomited).

THERMOMETER: If a child is too young to check the temperature by mouth, try placing the thermometer under his or her closed arm for three to five minutes (normal temperature under the arm in children is 97.6°F). Using a **DIGITAL THERMOMETER** with an uncooperative child can reduce this time considerably, and they are inexpensive.

TWEEZERS: These can be used for splinters and "slivers" of glass and other foreign contaminants. Many scientific companies and surgical supply houses stock these medical tweezers.

These items will cover most minor injuries. It is also important to know what each of the items in the kit is used for, and when to use them. If you are going to be in an area where **SNAKES** are prevalent, then you should know how to contact the regional poison center in that area and where the nearest hospital emergency department is located. Or if you are highly **ALLERGIC TO BEE OR WASP STINGS** an *ANA KIT* should be included (see page 339). If you are a **DIABETIC** you may want to keep some sugar handy. It probably is a good idea to keep an extra bottle of **INSULIN** around in case one bottle is misplaced or accidentally broken. Just make sure that it is stored properly so it does not go bad or become outdated. If you keep an extra bottle of insulin in case of an accident with your regular supply, use your spare bottle next and then replace the spare bottle with a newly purchased bottle. In this manner you will keep the insulin as fresh as possible. Start with the basic items and add to the kit according to your own needs or the area you are going to.

Antimicrobial Ingredients

When people visit the drugstore to pick up Band-Aids, gauze, and tape to wrap wounds they often want to know what is good to put on the cut as a dressing. You might remember when you were a kid that products like **TINCTURE OF MERTHIOLATE** and **TINCTURE OF**

IODINE always brought their share of screams and yells when they were applied to a cut. Tincture means that alcohol is the base and it is alcohol that causes the burning. Solution means the ingredient is dissolved in water.

In most instances, washing with soap and water is adequate to treat a minor cut. However, the antibiotic ointments, creams, and solutions will keep small problems from turning into serious infections, especially if you have an active youngster.

The term antimicrobials is a general one that has lots of more specific subgroups. Medicines that are applied externally to an area of the body are often referred to as **ANTISEPTICS**. The same chemicals when used on an inanimate object, like false teeth, are called **DISINFECTANTS**. Antiseptics are still frequently used in feminine cleansing products such as douches, solutions for application to cuts and scratches, acne products, mouthwashes and dental preparations, and diaper rash creams and ointments.

ANTIBIOTIC is the term applied to chemicals produced by living organisms. For example a mold produces **PENICILLIN**, and bacteria are responsible for making **NEOMYCIN** and **BACITRACIN**. All of these chemicals are effective in treating infections in man.

ANTIFUNGAL drugs are also in the antimicrobial class and they are used to treat specific infections caused by mold and yeast, like athlete's foot, jock itch, and certain oral and vaginal infections. All antimicrobials kill or inhibit the growth of disease-causing organisms and help to treat and control infection.

Some of the antimicrobials discussed below have become much less important in modern times, particularly since the development of the more effective oral antibiotics, most of which are available only on prescription.

ACETIC ACID is the pungent smelling odor of household vinegar. This clear, liquid chemical is manufactured from several different sources including ethyl alcohol (the alcohol of beverages and spirits). A 5 percent solution (approximately the concentration of vinegar) is an effective antiseptic and will kill many types of microorganisms. Acetic acid has also been widely used as an antimicrobial for swimmer's ear, but the FDA has recently banned it from over-the-counter products for lack of conclusive proof of effectiveness at the nonprescription strengths. It is still available in prescription products for this purpose but at higher concentrations than it was available over-the-counter.

AMMONIATED MERCURY is prepared from ammonia gas and mercuric chloride and is a salt of the metal mercury. This white, odorless powder, incorporated as 5 percent into an ointment base, was popular at one time for psoriasis, impetigo and pinworm infestation. However, it is now banned by the FDA since newer drugs are much more effective and safer. Mercury can be absorbed through the skin and accumulate to produce systemic mercury poisoning. Of all the metals used as antiseptics, mercury is probably the oldest in history. It has never been demonstrated to kill bacteria, but only inhibit their harmful activity.

BACITRACIN is a polypeptide (a linked group of amino acids) produced by the growth of a bacteria known as *Bacillus subtilis*. It is a white to pale buff powder. The ability of this chemical to damage the kidneys when given systemically (injected into the bloodstream) is well known. Accordingly the use of it for any but life-threatening situations is inappropriate and dangerous. Its use is largely limited to infections which can be treated by application to the skin. For example, in combination with **NEOMYCIN** and **POLYMYXIN** as *MYCITRACIN* ointment.

BENZALKONIUM CHLORIDE is a detergent that has antimicrobial properties. It is a white or yellowish powder or jelly-like pieces with a pleasant odor but a very bitter taste. This chemical is referred to as a "quaternary ammonium compound" (which has importance in meaning only to the chemist, but it is a term frequently used on product labels). An effective germicide and an extremely poisonous chemical when swallowed in quantity, it is used in minute concentrations in over-the-counter products as a preservative. It is too dangerous to be used routinely as a skin antiseptic because higher concentrations are required to be effective.

BENZETHONIUM CHLORIDE is a detergent in the class of quaternary ammonium compounds, a chemical classification. A scaly solid which produces a clear soapy solution in water, it is a very effective antibacterial chemical used in low concentrations in mouthwashes, douches, acne products, baby wipes, diaper rash products and so on. Used primarily to preserve the product, it may be antiseptic to the surface where it is applied.

BORIC ACID is manufactured from **SODIUM BORATE** (*BORAX*) and occurs as white, odorless crystals, granules, or powder. It is present in nature as the mineral known as sassolite. Boric acid and its relative, **SODIUM PERBORATE**, are mild antiseptics. Boric acid is much too poisonous for any household medical uses. If misused or swallowed, it can produce serious poisoning and even death in children. Infants have died from the toxic effects of boric acid ointments applied to their reddened, sore, and irritated buttocks as a treatment for diaper rash over an extended period of time. Following application to reddened, irritated skin, the boric acid is absorbed into the blood.

CETYLPYRIDINIUM CHLORIDE is a synthetic detergent, white powder that has effective antibacterial properties and is frequently used in mouthwashes, douches, and diaper rash products. It may be used to impart its antibacterial effect to the skin or mucous membranes or as a preservative in the product. This type of detergent is known as a "cationic" detergent. It describes the part of the molecule which is responsible for the detergent effect. Many cationic detergents are good antimicrobials.

CRESOL is one of the main types of phenols obtained from creosote (which comes from wood tar). This oily liquid may be colorless, yellowish, brownish-yellow or pinkish and is similar to phenol. It is more effective as a disinfectant and about as poisonous. It has been sold as an additive for hot steam vaporizers to disinfectant humid air. In addition to being poisonous if ingested, it can produce serious burns if exposed to the skin and eyes. Products that contain cresol do not produce any significant medical benefit and are too poisonous to be kept in the home, especially since many safer alternatives are now available.

ETHYL ALCOHOL is the intoxicating alcohol of distilled beverages and fermentation. It may be manufactured by fermentation of starch, sugars, and other carbohydrates, or it is sometimes made synthetically from petroleum derivatives. It is widely used in medicines applied to the skin and other parts of the body, but is not a very effective antiseptic. Sometimes the alcohol in a product serves a dual function as an antiseptic and a vehicle (carrier for the drug, fragrance or other chemical which is dissolved in it). While most "rubbing" alcohols are isopropyl alcohol, there is at least one brand name product, *LAVACOL*, by Parke Davis, that is 70 percent ethyl alcohol. Ethyl alcohol is a more pleasant rubbing alcohol because it is naturally odorless, but it is more expensive.

HYDROGEN PEROXIDE is prepared synthetically and marketed as a 3 percent solution for medicinal antiseptic purposes. It is a very feeble antiseptic. This colorless liquid foams in the mouth or on a wound as its oxygen content is released on contact with mucous membranes or other tissue. If hydrogen peroxide is swallowed it is not poisonous, since it is merely changed to water and oxygen in the stomach. However, if a large amount is ingested it may induce unexpected vomiting and the victim might aspirate the liquid into their lungs. Because hydrogen peroxide foams or bubbles in contact with tissue it may be useful as a "mechanical" cleansing agent, the oxygen bubbles loosening and removing dirt, debris and dead tissue.

IODINE is used as an antiseptic and is an element which occurs in certain natural crystalline rock formations in the earth's crust. It is most often used as an effective antiseptic in the form of **TINCTURE OF IODINE**, which is a solution of iodine in 50 percent **ETHYL ALCOHOL**. Several other variations exist as **STRONG IODINE TINCTURE** and *LUGOL'S SOLUTION*, but are rarely used anymore. While iodine is an effective topical antiseptic, there is a safer (and less-staining) preparation available over-the-counter (see povidone-iodine later in this section).

ISOPROPYL ALCOHOL is the most common household medicinal alcohol and it is known as "rubbing" alcohol. Most rubbing alcohols are isopropyl. Isopropyl alcohol is manufactured from several starting chemicals including propylene (a derivative of crude petroleum). This alcohol is only slightly more effective than **ETHYL ALCOHOL** (see above) as an antiseptic, but about twice as poisonous if swallowed. It has an odor and is more irritating than **ETHYL ALCOHOL** when applied to the skin.

MERCUROCHROME is still used as an antiseptic and is the commercial name for chemically prepared, iridescent green scales or granules. As a 2 percent solution it was once a popular antiseptic, also known as MERBROMIN. It is a mercury-containing chemical, and with so many safer, modern antiseptics available, it has no place in the home medicine cabinet. While it is unlikely that occasional household use of Mercurochrome as an antiseptic would result in mercury poisoning, it is simply another source of a toxic metal to which the consumer is unnecessarily exposed.

MERTHIOLATE is a cream colored, mercury-containing antiseptic developed in the fifties by Eli Lilly Co., brand named *THIMEROSOL*. It is non-irritating to skin and is antibacterial and antifungal, but only mildly so. Like other mercury containing products for application to the skin, it poses an unnecessary risk of absorption of a dangerous, poisonous metal (mercury) and should no longer be used for household first-aid.

MERCURIC CHLORIDE or **BICHLORIDE OF MERCURY** is a highly toxic and corrosive salt of the metal mercury. It is a white powder or crystal. It is no longer available as an antiseptic chemical because of many deaths associated with its misuse. Any preparations in the home still containing this chemical should be destroyed. A regional poison center can advise on how to dispose of this extremely poisonous chemical.

MERCURIC OXIDE is prepared from other salts of the metal mercury. It is an orange-yellow powder and is incorporated into an ointment base for use as an antibacterial and antifungal salve, particularly for application to the eyelids. It is an "old-timer" and is poisonous if used for long periods of time or ingested. Safer alternatives are available for the treatment of infection.

NEOMYCIN is produced by a bacterium *Streptomyces fradiae* and is used to treat minor infections due to burns, wounds and simple sores. It is a popular antibiotic used in products like *NEOSPORIN OINTMENT*.

NITROMERSOL is also known as *METAPHEN* and is prepared by adding mercury (a toxic metal) to a petroleum based chemical to produce a yellow-brown powder or granules. It is a weak mercury-containing antiseptic and is not as effective as the safer iodine-containing products, such as *BETADINE*.

PHENOL also known as **CARBOLIC ACID** is a colorless, crystalline chemical at one time produced from coal tar, now produced synthetically from petroleum starting materials. In concentrated form it is corrosive and very poisonous.

In practice, few poisonings occur since it is used as a preservative, disinfectant, and antiseptic in various concentrations, usually 1 to 5 percent. It has very little use any longer as an antiseptic, except in a few patent medications, like *CAMPHO-PHENIQUE LIQUID* because it is effective as an antibacterial only when used in concentrations that are either too irritating or harmful. It is still used as a preservative in injectable medications. Historically, phenol was the standard against which all other disinfectants were compared. As useful skin antiseptics, the derivatives of phenol are much more likely to be encountered than phenol itself.

PHENYLMERCURIC ACETATE is a creamy white or crystalline powder that has been used as an antiseptic on the skin and incorporated into vaginal contraceptive jellies and foams. It is an organic mercury-containing chemical prepared from inorganic mercury and petroleum chemicals and can cause mercury poisoning. It also has a long history of producing irritation and sensitization when applied to skin and mucous membranes. Consequently, most manufacturers have removed it from their products.

PHENYLMERCURIC NITRATE is an organic mercury chemical that exists as a white, crystalline powder. It is used as an antiseptic in ointments for application to the skin, has been used in vaginal products as an antiseptic and preservative and is used in preparations for cleaning or wetting contact lenses. It is less effective than other antiseptics and can produce irritation and sensitization. Like other mercury-containing antiseptics and preservatives, its days are numbered. Most manufacturers have removed it from their products and substituted safer alternatives.

POLYMYXIN B is an antibiotic made by the bacterium *Bacillus polymyxa*. In combination with other antibiotics it works well to cure simple infections on the skin. It is found in *POLYSPORIN OINTMENT* and other "triple antibiotic" products.

POVIDONE-IODINE is a modern complex of iodine that reduces its toxicity while retaining its antiseptic properties. It is available as the brand name *BETADINE* in solution, ointments and aerosol sprays. Povidone is a synthetic polymer that slowly releases the iodine at the site where it is applied to provide a prolonged antibacterial effect. It is a good, effective, non-staining and safe household antiseptic. However, concern has been expressed about the use of povidone-iodine over long periods of time on certain areas of the body where absorption of drugs occurs easily, such as the vagina. Several povidone-iodine products suitable for vaginal use have been recently withdrawn from the market. Excessive use of these products may elevate the level of iodine in the blood to the point where it could produce hypothyroidism and goiter. This is especially true of fetal thyroid tissue. Thus, any iodine preparation should be used sparingly and with caution during pregnancy, if used at all. Lastly, prevent ingestion of iodine containing products by children and call a poison center if it occurs.

SODIUM BORATE or **BORAX** exists as a white powder, crystals or granules and is found naturally in immense quantities in California, particularly near Death Valley. It was used extensively as an oral antiseptic at one time, but its effectiveness is questionable and when taken by mouth it is poisonous. Safer alternatives are available for use in the mouth (see Chapter 5).

SODIUM PERBORATE is a white, odorless, crystalline powder with a salty taste. It is prepared from a boric acid salt by reaction with hydrogen peroxide and it is similar in toxicity to boric acid. It has been popular as an antiseptic mouthwash for oral infections, but is seldom used any longer.

Sports Injuries

Over 20 million sports-related injuries are reported yearly in the United States. The most frequently injurious sport was bicycling, followed by baseball, football, and basketball. However, roller blading, a recent sports fad, is rapidly gaining on the list of injury-prone sports. Wearing approved bicycle helmets is the single most important measure in preventing serious head injury. These should be worn by children and adults while bicycling as well as roller skating.

Since many schools have increased their emphasis on physical education, mom and dad are kept busy patching up those minor injuries the kids come home with. Many pharmacies have set up areas featuring various types of athletic supplies, including athletic supporters and braces for the knee, elbow, foot, or ankle. As a matter of fact, there is even a special kind of brace to prevent tennis elbow.

Since most sports injuries are strains, sprains, or bruises, here is a good rule of thumb for treating those injuries, based on the word ICE.

I	**C**	**E**
stands for **ICE.** Apply ice to the injured area as soon as possible after the injury happens.	is for **COMPRESSION.** After soaking the injured area in ice, wrap it with an elastic bandage.	is to remind you to keep the injured area **ELEVATED** as much as possible.

Today there are a wide variety of **ICE BAGS** to choose from. The most familiar and fittingly named one is the kind that you add ice cubes to. Another type has a gel in it and can be used as either a hot or a cold pack, by placing the package in the freezer or in warm water. The chemical ice pack is a package that has two separate chemicals in it. When the pack is needed, simply puncture the inner package and the two chemicals mix together, producing a cold pack.

Pain relievers may be used, such as **ASPIRIN** or **IBUPROFEN**, which will help relieve the **INFLAMMATION** causing the pain. But be careful about taking aspirin if you have been sick with the flu or other viral illness (see page 177 regarding Reye syndrome).

In order to cut down on the number of injuries, it is best to wear the proper type of equipment, such as helmets, braces, supporters, even goggles. Also, a good stretching program, both before and after exercise, is important to prevent sports injuries.

13

Foot Care

As the old saying goes, when your feet hurt you feel bad all over. Although foot conditions generally are not life threatening (except perhaps in diabetics), foot problems cause their share of pain and discomfort. Some common conditions that people suffer from are **CORNS, CALLUSES, BUNIONS,** and **WARTS**, simple **FOOT ODOR** and **ATHLETE'S FOOT**. See Chapter 25 on **SKIN MEDICINES** for the discussion on corns, calluses, bunions, and warts.

Foot Odor

Remember the television commercial in which the guy took off his shoes and the dog fell over! Well, no one is immune to foot odor, unless of course you do not wear any shoes at all. Foot odor is caused by the feet sweating inside one's shoes. Bacteria attack the perspiration, and the resulting decomposition of the sweat leads to foot odor. There are products in the foot care section of most drugstores to help you. These are usually available in aerosol cans. Some are nothing more than a fragrance, and these will not do an effective job. Other products, called "foot refreshers," contain **CAMPHOR** and **MENTHOL** and are intended to be sprayed on tired feet to give a cooling effect. To combat foot odor, look for the foot spray with the word "antiperspirant." Such a product works just like underarm deodorant and is intended to keep the feet from sweating, which in turn prevents odor.

Foot powders work to lessen foot odor by absorbing perspiration that develops. Alternatively, **BAKING SODA** works very well at eliminating odor.

Insoles that are available, such as *DR. SCHOLL'S ODOR ATTACKERS* contain **CHARCOAL**, which absorbs perspiration. They do have to be replaced periodically.

Chapter 13

Athlete's Foot

Everyone is becoming very exercise-minded nowadays. People are out jogging or playing tennis and racquetball. You come home, kick off your tennis shoes, rub your toes in the carpet, and suddenly you notice some itching or redness between the toes. Athlete's foot may occur at any age, but it is more common in adults. Athlete's foot is a **FUNGUS INFECTION** most often acquired by walking barefoot on infected floors in bathrooms, locker rooms, and camps. This fungus infection can spread to other members of the family via the bathroom floor, floor mats, or rugs. The main complaint of people suffering from athlete's foot is severe **ITCHING** although sometimes cracks develop between the toes that cause painful burning and stinging. There are many different products to treat athlete's foot, and they are available in many forms as well, including creams, ointments, liquids, powders and aerosol sprays. They contain one or more of the following ingredients:

ALUMINUM ACETATE is a white powder when dry but for use as an astringent on athlete's foot it is available as **BUROW'S SOLUTION**, which makes a clear and colorless or faintly yellow solution in water. You can buy a product called *DOMEBORO* in the pharmacy to make **BUROW'S SOLUTION**. It can be used as an astringent wash or as a wet dressing and reduces weeping and inflammation by injuring surface skin cells causing death of the cells and shrinkage. This shrinkage of the skin surface reduces the amount of fluid that can be lost, and results in drying. It is recommended in the wet, soggy type of athlete's foot, but only in conjunction with other antifungal agents like **CLOTRIMAZOLE, MICONAZOLE** and **TOLNAFTATE**.

ALUMINUM CHLORIDE is a white to yellowish crystalline chemical that is made from the elements chlorine and aluminum. It is a very irritating chemical and is toxic by mouth and inhalation. It is effective for applications to the skin in the treatment of certain soggy type conditions of athlete's foot in solutions of 20 to 30 percent. But just like Burow's solution above, it should only be used to produce drying of the wet, soggy type athlete's foot, and then additional antifungals should be used to really cure the disease.

CLOTRIMAZOLE is one of the newer FDA approved antifungal ingredients available in the product *LOTRIMIN AF ANTIFUNGAL* cream, lotion and solution, and *MYCELEX SOLUTION ANTIFUNGAL*. It is a synthetic "broad spectrum" antifungal agent, meaning it kills a wide range of different fungi and yeasts. Clotrimazole was first made available in over-the-counter products in 1990. Its main action is to kill fungus in the multiplying and growing stage of their development. It is very effective for athlete's foot infection with improvement usually occurring in the first week of treatment.

HALOPROGIN is considered as effective an antifungal agent as tolnaftate by doctors. While it is approved by the FDA for over-the-counter use, no manufacturer has chosen to put in on the market for OTC use. Perhaps they feel the competition is already too great in this area. It is available on prescription as a product known as *HALOTEX*.

IODOCHLORHYDROXYQUIN, found in *VIOFORM* is an antibacterial and antifungal, brownish-yellow, fluffy powder which is employed in creams and ointments usually at a 3 percent concentration. It is made synthetically by modifying a petroleum-derived chemical to incorporate the elements chlorine and iodine which contribute to the fungus- and bacteria-killing effect.

MICONAZOLE is another antifungal chemical that also has some antibacterial activity. This is an excellent property in an athlete's foot medication because some types of fungal infections are complicated by the presence of bacteria, especially the wet, soggy type of athletes foot, rather then the scaly, dry type. If you use this ingredient, found in *MICATIN* spray liquid, powder or cream, for the soggy type of athlete's foot and it does not clear up the problem in the time indicated on the label, consult a physician.

TOLNAFTATE is sold under the trade names of *TINACTIN* or *AFTATE*. Tolnaftate is one of the most effective antifungal agents that can be applied to the skin. It is available in aerosol, liquid, cream, and powder form and is applied twice a day. Usually one can see results in two to four weeks, but some cases may take four to six weeks, especially when lesions are present between the toes.

TRIACETIN is an oily, clear, straw-colored antifungal ingredient used to treat athletes foot and is available in the over-the-counter product *FUNGACETIN OINTMENT*. This chemical is kind of interesting in that it breaks down in the presence of moisture to release acetic acid, the active component of vinegar, to work as an antifungal. We do not recommend this ingredient because most people have the dry, scaly form of athlete's foot, where this drug will not be effective. There are too many other, very effective antifungal agents to waste time fooling around with ones that might work.

UNDECYLENIC ACID and **ZINC UNDECYLENATE** are the active ingredients in *DESENEX*, which is available in liquid, ointment, and powder. They are usually applied twice a day and you should notice improvement in two to four weeks. If there is no improvement, check with a doctor or pharmacist. The ingredient **UNDECYLENIC ACID** is a fatty acid that is prepared for commercial use by several methods, one of which includes derivation from castor oil. It is good for mild, chronic infections in athlete's foot. Occurring naturally as a component of sweat, it has the characteristic, but slight, odor of perspiration. **ZINC UNDECYLENATE** is made from undecylenic acid. The addition of the metal zinc to the chemical apparently adds astringency to reduce irritation and inflammation associated with fungal infections for which it is used.

There are other products available to treat athlete's foot, but they do not work quite as well to effectively kill the fungus that causes the problem. Since many of these products are available in powder form, it might be a good idea to use one of them after application of a liquid or cream to provide continuous release of medicine and to absorb moisture from the feet. However, be careful when using a powder as a primary treatment, especially on broken skin. Some powders contain boric acid, which should not be absorbed into the skin.

Jock Itch—A Close Relative of Athlete's Foot

That's right, jock itch and athlete's foot are related. In fact, all of the conditions described as jock itch, athlete's foot and ringworm (which, of course, is not a worm at all) on the body and the scalp, are caused by fungi in basically three main classes. The specific fungus and where it decides to grow on the body, will determine whether it is athlete's foot or jock itch. Different types of fungi will also produce different ways in which the disease will manifest itself. This is why the medicines used to treat jock itch are usually found in the same area of the pharmacy as athlete's foot medicine. **JOCK ITCH**, known by doctors as **TINEA CRURIS**, usually occurs in the groin area and on the inner folds of the legs, and results in severe itching. Sometimes the skin breaks open and on hot, sweaty days there can be additional irritation. The best thing to do is to wash the area thoroughly and as often as possible. After washing, apply one of the anti-fungal powders such as *TINACTIN* or *AFTATE*. It will kill the fungus and stop it from spreading. The powder also absorbs perspiration to prevent further irritation. Remember, you do not have to be a jock or even play sports to be bothered by this problem. The main thing is to know when you have it and how to effectively treat it.

Support Stockings

These products are usually found near the foot care products, but people do not know much about them. **VARICOSE VEINS** are a problem that many people, mostly women, suffer from. The condition may be aggravated sitting or standing too long in the same position. Blood flowing too slowly through an artery causes it to bulge out. Some people simply complain that their legs feel tired all the time. This could be caused by **POOR CIRCULATION**. In either case, wearing a support stocking may help. Do not be put off by this; support stockings are no longer ugly and unfashionable. In fact they are available in styles and colors to complement any wardrobe, including women's support panty hose. In order to get the right size, you need accurate measurements of the foot and the leg. Often their sizes are quite different than standard panty hose. If you have large calf muscles, you may get a pair that fits too tightly, which could cut off the circulation completely. This is especially important if you have a job where you sit or stand for long periods of time.

A product that has come on the market recently is an **ELECTRIC FOOT MASSAGER**. To operate, fill the unit with water, plug it in, then place feet in the water. Vibrations on the bottom of the feet help increase circulation in the feet, which results in their feeling refreshed. They work well for people who stand alot. It is not a good idea to add anything to the water in these machines, unless the manufacturer of the machine indicates that it is safe to do so. A build-up of chemicals could interfere with the proper working of the machine. An alternative is soaking feet in a tub of warm water and one or two ounces of **EPSOM SALTS**.

14

Infant Care

The birthrate in the U.S. continues to inch upward, 1–2 percent each year, after a decline in the late 70s and mid 1980s. The early 90s will continue to show an increase due to delayed childbearing—women who delayed childbearing when they were in their 20s are now having babies—but even so, fertility is slightly up among all age groups. More babies mean more diapers, wipes, formulas, bottles, humidifiers, vaporizers, and so on.

Since more and more women are returning to breast-feeding, preparing their own foods, and leaning away from prepared infant foods, new products have been developed for this market. Among them are nursing pads, breast pumps, nipple shields, breast creams, and specialized bottles and nipples.

BREAST PUMPS are available in different styles. One type is used to remove milk to reduce the pain and discomfort due to the buildup of milk in the breast. The other type has a bottle attached to it; as you remove the breast milk, it goes into the bottle to be fed to the infant later. This is helpful if nursing is really inconvenient. **AUTOMATIC BREAST PUMPS** are now available from home health care agencies and, in some cases, the local hospital.

Often women who are nursing develop sore nipples. There are special creams available to help relieve the irritation, such as *MASSE BREAST CREAM.* Also, when breast feeding, there are nursing pads that you place inside a bra to absorb any leakage.

Infant Formula

Even with the growing trend toward breast-feeding, the proportion of breast-fed infants throughout the population remains constant at about 20 percent. Therefore, infant formulas continue to serve a very large market, and you will find a number of different products to satisfy your infant's appetite and nutritional needs.

In evaluating an infant formula, remember that human milk is the standard to which all formulas are compared. Three basic nutritional principles should be considered: The formula should have enough nutrients, be easily digested, and have a balanced distribution of calories from **CARBOHYDRATES**, **PROTEINS**, and **FATS**. A pediatrician will be able to advise on a suitable formula. Some of the standard formulas commonly used are *ENFAMIL*, *IRON FORTIFIED ENFAMIL*, *SIMILAC*, *SIMILAC WITH IRON*, *SMA*, and *IRON FORTIFIED SMA*. Most of them use **LACTOSE** as a source of carbohydrates, cow's milk as a source of protein, and soy, corn and other vegetable oils as a source of fat. Some premature infants may develop an intolerance to the lactose, causing cramping and diarrhea or colic.

The digestibility of the product is important not only to the infant, but also to the parents, as it helps to eliminate wet shirts and blouses. Most commercial formulas have replaced **BUTTER FAT** with **VEGETABLE OILS**. Of these, **CORN** and **SOY** are easier to digest than **COCONUT OIL**, so refer to the list of ingredients on the container. Adequate fat in the diet ensures the absorption of the fat-soluble vitamins. Infants should not need additional vitamins if an infant formula with iron is used, unless they are being used to correct a deficiency.

Because of the prevalence of **MILK ALLERGIES**, there is some variations in the ingredients used in infant formulas.

Soy is often used instead of milk for protein; some formulas have a particular form of soy protein that is more palatable than others, such as *ISOMIL*, *PRO-SOBEE*, and *NURSOY*. Occasionally infants develop an allergy to the soy. In that case, there are other infant formulas that use different sources of protein (hydrolyzed casein) including *NUTRAMIGEN*, and *PREGESTIMIL*.

The important thing to keep in mind is that if the infant develops such symptoms as cramping, gas, and diarrhea while feeding on infant formula, the infant may not be able to tolerate that particular formula. At that point the doctor may recommend a different formula that does agree with the baby.

Feeding Equipment

There is a wide variety of equipment available to aid in feeding the infant. Among them are glass and plastic bottles in both four-ounce and eight-ounce sizes. *PLAYTEX*, *ANSA*, *EVENFLO* and *GERBER* all offer disposable bottles. There are specialized nipples; nipples for milk, juice, and medicine, and even orthodontic nipples. Some nipples resemble breast nipples. When using infant formula to feed a child, aside from bottles and nipples it is neceessary to have bottle brushes, bottle warmers, and nipple brushes. It is very important to keep the equipment used in preparing the infant formula as clean as possible. If bacteria builds up and comes into contact with the baby, it may cause such problems as diarrhea.

Diapers and Wipes

Diapers should be made of a soft material and loosely fitted to prevent rubbing. It is important to change diapers frequently to prevent **DIAPER RASH**. You should not use plastic pants routinely. They trap moisture in the diaper, so that if there is any irritation it does not heal properly.

The new disposable diapers are convenient and easy to use. Mothers have hailed them as a godsend. When you remove them, you simply throw them away. No washing diapers in special detergents and then drying and folding them. Although in many areas, particularly with concern over the environment and the use of landfills, disposable diaper services are making a comeback. Products like *KLEENEX HUGGIES*, *LUVS*, and *PAMPERS* have an absorbent layer of material covered by a thin layer of material designed to keep the wetness away from the child.

Disposable diapers are not the answer to diaper rash, because diaper rash is caused by ammonia, heat, and chemical irritants. These products may help keep an infant drier, but they also contain chemicals that can cause further irritation to the affected area. And since disposable diapers have a plastic outer covering, you may not notice that the child is wet as quickly as you would with a cloth diaper. Whether you are using disposable diapers or regular cloth diapers, the same rule applies: Change the infant as soon and as often as possible.

Diaper Rash

The best therapy for **DIAPER RASH** and **PRICKLY HEAT** is to keep the skin dry. Diaper rash is caused by ammonia, sweat retention, and mechanical and chemical irritants. Breast-fed infants tend to urinate less frequently and have a lower incidence of diaper rash.

Mild forms of diaper rash are best treated by changing diapers frequently and leaving them off during naps. It is also a good idea to apply a protective ointment, cream, or powder to the diapered area every time you change the child. If you do so, be sure to wipe away the excess cream from the time before, because bacteria can build up on the cream or powder.

After you remove the excess cream or powder, cleanse the area thoroughly before reapplying it, using one of the premoistened towelettes such as *WASH UP*, *WET ONES*, and *JOHNSON'S BABY WASH CLOTHS*. If these are not available, use plain soap and water. But be sure the soap is not irritating or drying to the skin. Your best bet would be to use a soap especially designed for infants' skin, such as *JOHNSON'S BABY BAR* or *IVORY SOAP*.

Teething Lotions and Gels

Babies cry for a variety of reasons. One of those reasons is teething, which can send mom off in a hurry to buy products such as *BABY NUMZIT GEL*, *BABY ORAJEL NIGHT-TIME FORMULA*, *ALCOHOL FREE ORAJEL* or *BABY ANBESOL GEL*. She doesn't usually know that these products have the same ingredients used in the toothache medicines and products for sore gums. Most of them will work a lot better if you apply these products directly to the sore gums and teeth. The only exception to this is teething pain, since the pain in that case is coming from within the gum itself. In cutting teeth the pain is actually caused by the cutting action of the tooth working its way to the surface of the gum. All of these products contain a deadening ingredient, **BENZOCAINE**. It will provide some temporary relief, but do not expect too much help from these products.

Use or overuse of these benzocaine-containing products has been associated with certain drug reactions in some infants. A condition known as methemoglobinemia in which the infant may turn a blue-brown color may be serious.

Usually in the infant area of the drugstore there will also be teething rings. Some contain a gel that you can place in the ice box and cool. When the baby chews on them, the cooling effect will often help to soothe his or her gums. The other kinds of teething rings are made of **RUBBER** or **LATEX** and they work pretty well too; by biting on these rings the child helps cut down on the pain associated with teething. Gently massaging the irritated gum area will also help.

If you do decide to use one of the gel types, and if the child has some teeth already, be sure he doesn't bite through the teething ring and swallow the gel. But if he or she does, do not worry. The gel is made with safe material, usually sterile water or glycerin, but if the seal is broken it could become unsanitary.

Teething lotions sometimes cause allergic reactions. If a

rash develops or the lotion seems to irritate the gums more, consult a physician. Teething children require time and patience, and that is something not found on a drugstore shelf.

15

Insulin & Diabetes Care

To say that diabetes is a significant health problem in the United States is an understatement. More and more people every year are diagnosed as being **DIABETIC**. In fact, the incidence of diabetes is increasing at an annual rate of 6 percent. You have **DIABETES MELLITUS**, or **SUGAR DIABETES**, when you do not make enough insulin on your own to meet your needs, or you aren't able to use what you make. The name for the disease is derived from the sweet taste of the urine that diabetics make (Latin mellis, "honey"). No wonder that the medical profession came up with a dip-stick method for testing the urine. **INSULIN** is a hormone that helps the body turn food we eat into energy. It makes little difference to the body whether we make our own in the pancreas gland or have to take it by injection.

Insulin

Some cases of diabetes can be controlled by diet alone. Others may require an oral prescription medicine, while still others must rely on daily injections of **INSULIN** for the rest of their lives. Approximately 10 percent of diabetics in the U.S. fall into this last group of what are called **TYPE I DIABETICS**, that is, they are **INSULIN DEPENDENT**. This type of diabetes can lead to blindness, gangrene of the extremities, kidney dysfunction, arteriosclerotic heart disease, and, if these complications are untreated, death.

All types of insulin must be injected because, when taken by mouth, insulin is broken down by the chemicals in the stomach and does not get absorbed into the blood stream. There are several different forms of insulin available, and each one works a little differently in the body. The different forms are usually indicated by differently coded boxes.

Insulin is commonly made from either beef or pork pancreas. **HUMAN INSULIN** is bio-engineered by a genetic cloning process that uses bacteria to make carbon copies of human insulin. Or, it can also be converted from **PORK INSULIN** by changing the make-up of the chemical linkages in such a way that it is identical to human insulin. This too, is done by bio-engineering and is referred to as semi-synthetic insulin. No matter how you look at it, the production of human insulin by bacteria is pretty amazing! **HUMAN INSULINS** are less likely to produce an allergic reaction than either **BEEF** or **PORK INSULIN**. So people who have a problem with **INSULIN ALLERGY**, **INSULIN RESISTANCE**, **PREGNANT PATIENTS WITH DIABETES**, and people who only use insulin intermittently will want to use human insulin.

Insulin is available in two strengths: U-40 and U-100. This means that there are, respectively, 40 units and 100 units of insulin in each cubic centimeter of fluid for injection. Eventually, only one strength may be available, the U-100. Syringes are specially marked for the strength of insulin used. These syringes come in 3 sizes: 30, 50, and 100 units.

Diabetics sometimes ask the pharmacist if there are syringes that are easier to read than others, since diabetics' eyesight is typically not very strong. Ask any pharmacist about a magnifying glass that is available from the Sherwood Company, the makers of *MONOJECT* syringes and needles, and that snaps right onto the syringe. It magnifies the numbers so that they are easy to read when you are drawing up your insulin. If your pharmacist can't order one for you, check with your local Diabetes Association and see if they can help you.

Self Monitoring Blood Glucose Kits

Diabetics also must check their **BLOOD SUGAR** regularly to make sure that the insulin is keeping the diabetes under control. Because diabetes is hereditary, it might be a good idea to include other members of your family in your blood sugar testing program. The **ELECTRONIC TESTING DEVICES** that measure blood sugar directly are the only acceptable kind for a diabetic with insulin-dependent diabetes to use. **URINE TEST STRIPS** (or some people call them "dip-stick" tests) that measure sugar in urine are inadequate and really do not tell you what is going on in your blood at the moment you take the urine test. With the urine test strips you are really measuring spill-over of sugar in the urine, so, generally speaking, only high glucose levels could be measured. Self monitoring of blood glucose is called SMBG for short. If you are an insulin-dependent diabetic, you will probably check your blood sugar four to seven times a day, since doing this is crucial to proper treatment of the potentially degenerative disease of diabetes. With SMBG you can modify the type of food you eat, vary the amount and time of exercise, and adjust medications. SMBG lets you and your doctor set up treatment goals and measure how effective your treatment is with a minimum disruption of daily life.

Blood glucose measurements were introduced for home use in the late 1960s so that diabetics could detect high and low blood sugar by looking at color changes on a chemical test strip from a single drop of blood. By the late 1970's the meters evolved to the point of being able to "read" the chemical strips. The blood glucose meters, sold in pharmacies (and even grocery stores), detect the glucose level in the blood on the strip and provide immediate warning about the onset of high or low blood sugar. Experts agree that measuring glucose in the blood is a more preferred method than measuring it in the urine. SMBG is also recommended for some diabetics who have **NON-INSULIN-DEPENDENT DIABETES** (known as **TYPE II**). **BLOOD GLUCOSE MONITORING METERS** include many features designed to make self-monitoring convenient. Many operate on batteries and are small enough to fit in a purse or shirt pocket and can be used almost anywhere. Some contain electronic memory, and more advanced models even have built-in modems for transmitting the test results to the diabetic's physician.

In the past there have been problems with the electronic blood glucose monitoring devices. The Food and Drug Administration's Center for Devices and Radiological Health claims that reports of inaccurate readings with the use of blood glucose meters, in the past, have been the largest medical device user problem reported to the FDA. They have been studying the problems for some time, and most of the bugs in the newer meters are getting worked out. User error seems to be involved in many complaints about inaccurate results. If you are thinking about using one of these meters, plan on spending time with your doctor or your pharmacist to make absolutely sure you get one that you can use easily. Your age or the physical problems from your diabetes may limit your ability to perform the steps for the use of the meter. According to the American Diabetes Association, about 27 percent of diabetics are visually impaired, and 25 percent have loss of sensation in hands or feet or problems in moving fingers. Some have below average reading skills. In addition, a substantial number of diabetic patients are Hispanics with a limited ability to speak English. Before using one of these meters, look at the steps:

1) The first step may be to calibrate the meter for the particular batch of test strips being used.
2) The user obtains a drop of blood by pricking a clean finger with a puncture device and places that drop of blood on the chemically treated pad of a testing strip.
3) Start the meter, which measures the exact time necessary for the chemicals in the pad to react to the blood.
4) Several seconds later, the meter alerts the user to blot or wipe the excess blood from the pad of the test strip. Many of the new meters eliminate this step.

5) At another signal from the machine, you insert the strip in the meter.
6) In a short time, the window shows the glucose level in the blood.

With different manufacturers and devices, of course, the procedure will change slightly, but these are the basic steps. You will want to make sure that you can quickly and easily perform all of the steps.

Blood glucose monitoring kits on the market include *ONE TOUCH II COMPLETE BLOOD GLUCOSE MONITORING KIT* by Johnson & Johnson, producing test results in 45 seconds, the *AMES GLUCOMETER ELITE*, the *ACCU-CHEK III DIABETES CARE KIT* by Boehringer Mannheim Diagnostics, and the *GLUCOMETER 3* by Ames. These products range in price from $49 to $175.

With any diabetes care products, always stay in close contact with a physician, and report any unusual problems that develop. Make sure when you are buying over-the-counter or other products that they do not contain sugar. Many of them do, to make the product taste better. Ask for your pharmacist's help in selecting a safe and effective product.

Foot care is also very important for diabetics since leg and foot circulation is often poor, increasing the chance of infection. Be extremely careful when using corn and callus removers, for example. This also means no bathroom surgery, such as cutting out ingrown toe nails, or trimming calluses. Check with a physician first. In these cases his or her help is very valuable.

16

Medical Devices and Home Health

Gadgets

We have all heard the expression "It is a hard pill to swallow." Well, some people do have a hard time taking tablet and capsule forms of medicines. In many drugstores, usually near the prescription counter, there are all kinds of gadgets to make taking medicine easier. For liquid medicines, there is a gadget composed of a calibrated tube with a spoon on one end. Simply pour the medicine into the tube up to the teaspoon mark, then place the other spoon end in the child's mouth to deliver the right amount of medicine each time. For people who have trouble swallowing tablets and capsules, there is the *DRINK-A-PILL*, manufactured by the Apex Medical Company. This gadget is a plastic cup with a ledge just inside the lip. Fill the cup with water, then place your pills on the ledge. You then drink the water and let nature take its course. As the water goes down, so do the pills. You will probably not even notice it.

For people who have difficulty remembering to take their medicine each day, there is a pill box with seven compartments, each one marked with the day of the week. This system helps you keep track of whether you have or have not taken your medicine on a particular day. Also available are the fancy little pill boxes that some people carry their medicine in. We do not advise using them because they do not provide an air-tight container, and medicines often lose their potency much faster when they are exposed to air. Also, since these containers do not have a prescription label, if any accident or emergency occurs, it will take doctors longer to find out what medicines you have been taking before they begin treatment on you. As a matter of fact, some people have had problems with the authorities when they found an unlabeled container of drugs in their possession. So if you do carry your medicine with you, do not take any chances. Also, leaving pills in an open container also poses a risk to small children who may mistake them for candy. Carry your medicine in its original bottle with the prescription label intact. It could be life-saving in an emergency situation.

In addition to the containers, there are other ways that a pharmacist can help a person take medicine properly, or perhaps help in taking care of someone else. **MEDICATION CALENDARS** have spaces for patients or professionals to mark off the amount of medicine to take and the time of day to take it. Space can also be provided for you to check off after the drug is taken. **INDIVIDUAL MEDICATION INSTRUCTION SHEETS** allow pharmacists to tape sample pills next to the dosage time on these sheets with complete instructions on how to take the specific medication. Using **COLOR-CODED BOTTLES**, a sticker with the same color as the pill is placed on the bottle to help patients remember which pills go with each bottle's information. **CLOCK FACES** with correct administration times can help patients who cannot read or have poor eyesight. Using **SELF SEALING PLASTIC BAGS**, all medicines to be taken at each dosing time are marked, put in small, individual bags, and sealed. The day's doses are all packed into one larger plastic bag, and the seven daily bags are sealed into a bag that holds a week's supply. **BLISTER CARDS**, a daily dose for a month is packed in a pop-out container marked or set for calendar days. The empty spaces help patients keep track of doses taken. A **CALENDAR TRAY**, a plastic box for a week's medications, has compartments to hold multiple medications for up to four doses per day. A **TIMER CAP** is a device that fits standard prescription bottles and can be programmed to flash and beep at the dose time. Some versions flash each time a dose is taken. **A TIMER DISPENSER** is a compartmentalized container that makes a sound, such as a beep or a buzz, when it is time for your dose. It also shows which compartment holds the appropriate medication.

Medical Alert Bracelets

You never know when an accident may happen. People often end up in an emergency room unconscious and unable to give vital information. People suffering from a chronic disease such as diabetes must be treated differently from other people. People who are taking certain prescription drugs may have a fatal reaction if they are given other drugs. A **MEDICAL ALERT BRACELET** gives doctors vital information about a medical background that will help them determine the fastest and safest treatment. Some bracelets show a phone number that can be called any time to obtain a person's complete medical background. The bracelets and necklaces also carry the medical alert symbol, which is recognized around the world. If a patient suffers from a chronic disease, is allergic to certain medicines, or takes certain prescription drugs, they should wear the medical alert bracelet.

Blood Pressure Kits

Drugstores carry a wide assortment of **HOME BLOOD PRESSURE KITS**, with a wide variety of prices as well. It is really not a bad idea to use one of these kits, especially if you have **HIGH BLOOD PRESSURE** and are taking medicine to keep it under control. Additionally, some people get what is known to doctors as "white coat hypertension." That is, they get nervous at the doctor's office and their blood pressure goes up! So an accurate record of daily blood pressure is maintained at home, show it to the doctor when he says your blood pressure is high in his office. Almost all of the popular kits now provide electronic monitoring of blood pressure.

Home blood pressure devices should be compared with a physician's equipment to confirm readings. Some stores and shopping malls have machines to measure blood pressure. All you do is place your money in the machine, put your arm in the designated place, and read off your blood pressure. These machines have been found to be inaccurate, since they are not serviced often enough. Do not think that a home blood pressure kit will take the place of a periodic checkup by a physician. A routine checkup also needs the experience that goes with it.

Home Health Services

In addition to these simple devices, many pharmacies and pharmacists have begun to provide comprehensive **HOME HEALTH SERVICES.** Recent advances in technology have reduced many types of bulky medical equipment to a more portable size, enabling a patient to leave the hospital more quickly following a major illness. And with a chronic ailment, **HOME MEDICAL EQUIPMENT** can also prevent a hospital stay. Community pharmacists have teamed up with local hospitals and physicians to provide ways for patients to care for themselves, or someone they love, at home.

Cardiac patients' heart rhythms can be monitored at home, for example, by portable devices consisting of an electrode placed on the chest and attached to a small electronic box worn in a pocket or pouch by the patient.

In some cases patients' lives have been saved in their own home by a **TELEPHONE DEFIBRILLATOR SYSTEM.** With symptoms such as chest pain, palpitations, or shortness of breath, you put a defibrillator pad containing electrodes on the patient's chest. The electrodes detect a heartbeat pattern, and an electrocardiogram **(EKG)** is sent to a base station through the telephone lines. Medical personnel at the base station evaluate the **EKG** and, if necessary, activate the defibrillator on the patient's chest so that it gives brief electric shocks. These shocks can help stabilize or restore a heartbeat until emergency medical personnel arrive on the scene.

There are also **PORTABLE OXYGEN SYSTEMS** that help ease the chronic shortness of breath characteristic of emphysema and chronic bronchitis. These chronic obstructive pulmonary diseases are second only to heart disease as a cause of disability.

Usually people with these respiratory conditions receive oxygen from large tanks or a device that concentrates the oxygen in room air. Oxygen is delivered to the patient through a tube that is either placed in the nose or surgically inserted into the neck (tracheostomy). When outside of the home you can sling a handbag-like sack of oxygen over your shoulders. This convenient oxygen container is filled from a tank of oxygen kept at home.

INTRAVENOUS (IV) CARE EQUIPMENT is also available for home use. Some people can receive cancer chemotherapy intravenously in their own home with the instruction and supervision of a home nurse, or in some cases the employees of pharmacies specializing in home care. IV equipment can also be used in the home to give antibiotics to people with infections such as pneumonia or osteomyelitis, a bone infection common in the elderly. Home use of IV antibiotics can allow an earlier hospital discharge of some patients with pneumonia.

TUBE FEEDINGS of nutritional supplements may be required in the elderly through a tube inserted through the nose and into the stomach, or in some cases surgically inserted directly into the stomach or small intestine. Stroke patients having difficulty swallowing may also need such tube feeding, as well as people with oral cancers or various stomach and intestinal disorders.

Some people who are suffering from diseases that interfere with their ability to digest and absorb nutrients need to be fed a nutritional solution by a **CATHETER** inserted surgically in a vein near the collar bone. This type of intravenous feeding, after training and help from various health professionals, can be done at home too. The products used to provide this home feeding are called **HOME TOTAL PARENTERAL NUTRITION (TPN)**. They are mixtures that are very specific for each patient and usually made by the home health pharmacy or hospital.

There are lots of other home devices that can be obtained through a pharmacy specializing in home health care. These pharmacies are also able to work closely with hospitals and your doctor to make sure that you get whatever you need for a speedy recovery or to take care of your chronic condition. Patients tend to do much better when they recover at home, or feel involved in, or in control of, the treatment of their own disabilities.

Do-It-Yourself Medical Testing

Medically trained or not, people are using the devices mentioned above, and many more, to test their eyesight, stools, urine, blood, and blood pressure in search of health clues related to vision problems, stomach disorders, infection, ovulation (see page 18), pregnancy (see page 95), diabetes (see page 163), hypertension, and other conditions. Even home testing for HIV is now possible.

The number of self tests that can be done in the home will increase in the future. All sorts of possibilities exist. Newborns in remote areas could be tested for genetic defects to ensure they get needed treatment early. Patients might take certain tests before medical appointments, parents could test children as part of each child's permanent health record, and members of retirement communities could monitor their health through self-testing. To make sure that you get the most from self-testing devices, here are some general precautions.

- If the test kit contains chemicals, note the expiration date. do not use the kit if the date is past, because chemicals may lose potency and affect results.

- Protect the product from heat or cold if necessary, even keeping it out of a sunny window on the trip home. Follow storage directions carefully.
- Study the package insert carefully before you start mixing or opening items.
- Use toll-free numbers. Almost every type of self-help device has one now. They are almost always listed somewhere on the package or the instructions. But if a number is not stated on a product, you can call toll-free "information" by dialing 1-800-555-1212 to find out if an "800" number is provided by the company.
- Learn what a test is intended to do and what its limitations are. Remember: The tests are not 100 percent accurate.
- Pay close attention to special precautions, such as avoiding physical activity or certain foods and drugs before testing.
- Follow instructions exactly. Perform the steps of the test or procedure in the exact sequence described in the manual or instructions.
- When collecting urine specimens use the container provided with the kit if possible. If you must use a different container, wash it first with distilled water, which is purer than tap or bottled water.
- When a step is timed, be precise. Use a stopwatch or, at least, a watch with a second hand.
- Write down what you should do if the results are positive, negative, or unclear.
- Keep accurate, written records of the results or your progress.
- Keep test kits that contain chemicals out of the reach of children, just like you would do with medicines. Promptly discard used test materials (generally by flushing them down the toilet) as directed.

If you have a specific problem with a test device you can call your local FDA district office listed in the telephone directory. Be prepared to describe the product completely, including product name, type, and serial and lot numbers (from the package or container), dosage strength and expiration date (if applicable).

17

Pain & Fever Medicines

Pain, ranging from headaches, to sore muscles, to arthritis, is something we all suffer from at one time or another. Unfortunately, there is no product on the market to prevent pain, only to treat the symptom once it begins. Before buying any sort of pain reliever, ask yourself some very important questions. For example, are there other symptoms accompanying the pain? Is there a **FEVER**? How high is it and how long has it existed? Could there be an **ALLERGY** to aspirin? Is **ASTHMA** or a stomach problem or an underlying medical condition present? Are prescription drugs to be used at the same time?

Even though pain is a common experience, some experts say it is a sensation that can be influenced by many factors, such as fatigue, anxiety, and fear. People may experience pain differently depending on their personalities. For example, studies show that introverts have a lower threshold for pain than extroverts. Still, whether an introvert or extrovert, black or white, male or female when pain is present, anyone wants to get rid of it quickly.

In deciding on an over-the-counter pain reliever, remember that just because they are available without a prescription does not mean that they are harmless. Anyone can safely self-medicate with nonprescription pain relievers if they stay within the dose limits given on the label. Be alert to overdosing with aspirin or similar drugs which may cause symptoms such as stomach irritation or ringing in the ears, at the very least; and even more serious symptoms, such as deafness, blood clotting problems and liver and kidney disease. **REYE SYNDROME**, a rare but life-threatening condition affecting children and young adults, has focused attention on the safe use of over-the-counter pain relievers that contain aspirin (see page 177). Overdoses of acetaminophen can also be poisonous. With acetaminophen, the person may not show symptoms or signs of overdose until after 24 hours when it is often too late for the antidote. And even though long term self-use of pain relievers at recommended doses may not cause symptoms, prolonged use without medical supervision may mask a serious illness.

To use OTC analgesics safely:

- Always read the label and follow instructions, cautions and warnings.
- Do not exceed the maximum dosages on the product's label.
- Adults should not take pain relievers for more than 10 days unless directed by a doctor, and for fever the limit is three days.
- Children and teenagers should limit use to five days for pain and three days for fever.
- Because of the danger of **REYE SYNDROME**, all children and young adults should not take aspirin for chicken pox, flu, or flulike symptoms. When in doubt, consult your doctor.
- Those allergic to aspirin should not take any medicine containing aspirinlike ingredients, such as **CARBASPIRIN CALCIUM, CHOLINE SALICYLATE, MAGNESIUM SALICYLATE**, and **SODIUM SALICYLATE.** Signs of a reaction are itching, hives, runny nose, swelling of the throat, chest pains and fainting.
- Pregnant women should not take aspirin, especially in the last three months of pregnancy unless instructed by a doctor. Aspirin taken near time of delivery can cause bleeding in both mother and child.
- When planning to have any kind of surgery avoid aspirin before the event, unless directed otherwise by a doctor. Too much aspirin at this time can cause prolonged bleeding.

Of all the products advertised, there really are only four pain-relieving ingredients approved for over-the-counter use: **ASPIRIN**, **ACETAMINOPHEN**, **IBUPROFEN**, and **NAPROXEN**. It is important to know something about each of these in order for you to choose the best one for your needs.

One often sees the words "extra strength" on the packages of pain relief products. Such products are usually combinations of several pain-relieving ingredients, or may include higher doses of **ASPIRIN** or **ACETAMINOPHEN**, such as 400mg of aspirin instead of 325 mg, or 500 mg **ACETAMINOPHEN** in *TYLENOL EXTRA STRENGTH* compared to 325 mg in the regular strength *TYLENOL*. Because the total of pain-relieving ingredients may be more than 325 mg the implication is that these products are stronger and more effective. Combinations of ingredients have not been proven to be more effective than an equal amount of an individual ingredient. If you are using one plain *TYLENOL* tablet and it gives you relief, why buy the more expensive extra-strength product? But if you normally take two tablets at a time, you might save money and get the same relief by taking one of the extra-strength tablets or capsules.

Aspirin Pain Relievers

Aspirin belongs to a group of drugs called **SALICYLATES,** which may appear on the package as **ASPIRIN, ACETYLSALICYLIC ACID, SODIUM SALICYLATE, MAGNESIUM SALICYLATE** as in *DOAN'S ANALGESIC CAPLETS*, and others. However, all of these "salicylates" are converted to the same ingredient in your blood stream, salicylic acid. Salicylic acid is found in the bark and leaves of willow trees, poplars, spirea, and other plants. Hippocrates, the "father of medicine," is said to have used willow to relieve pain. Even though aspirin was synthesized way back in 1853 it really did not come into widespread use until the early years of the 20th century. Today it is still probably the most popular nonprescription drug on the market. Some products marketed for over-the-counter pain relief contain other ingredients in addition to aspirin such as *ANACIN*, which also contains **CAFFEINE**; or *EXCEDRIN*, which adds **ACETAMINOPHEN** and **CAFFEINE**. But the most effective products in treating mild pain and in reducing **FEVER** and **INFLAMMATION** are those that contain only aspirin. In certain conditions such as **MUSCLE STRAIN** or **ARTHRITIS,** reducing inflammation can definitely relieve the pain. However, avoid taking aspirin products with the prescription drugs used to treat arthritis. Many of these drugs irritate the stomach; adding aspirin is asking for trouble. If you must use aspirin for additional relief, try to use it in between doses of a prescription drug. Aspirin is also very effective at lowering body temperature; that is why it is so frequently recommended for fever, aches, and pains associated with the **FLU** (but not in children or teenagers, see aspirin and Reye syndrome below).

For kids, it is better to use a non-aspirin pain reliever such as *TYLENOL* or *TEMPRA* to reduce fever or discomfort. However, note that non-aspirin over-the-counter pain relievers do not reduce inflammation; this is especially important for people to know who are suffering from arthritis, injuries and muscle strain.

If you get relief from aspirin for various problems, but it upsets the stomach, try a buffered aspirin product such as *BUFFERIN* or *ASCRIPTIN*, claimed to be less irritating to the stomach. Scientific evidence does not provide unqualified support for this claim. They contain ingredients that may protect the stomach lining while the aspirin is dissolving. People who suffer from chronic stomach problems like **ULCERS** may want to use an enteric-coated aspirin such as *ECOTRIN* or *A.S.A. ENSEALS* (enteric-coated means that they dissolve in the intestine rather than the stomach). But use caution with these products, too. If you have certain types of intestinal problem, these products should be avoided. Consult with a physician when in doubt.

Chapter 17

ASPIRIN is probably one of the best products on the market for relief from various forms of discomfort. Since most of us keep it on hand, it is important to know that aspirin can go bad. One way to judge is to take the cap off the bottle and smell the tablets. If they smell like vinegar, chances are that the product is no longer effective. Stale aspirin may also upset the stomach more, because one of the break down by-products of aspirin is **ACETIC ACID** (vinegar).

One question often asked is what brand of aspirin is best? If countless television commercials about different aspirin products are seen, it can become confusing. For example, one commercial shows us that most products contain only 325 mg of aspirin per tablet and concludes that the product with 400 mg of aspirin is stronger and better. However, both release aspirin into the bloodstream equally quickly, and for most people, 325 mg relieves discomfort as well as 400 mg. Our advice is to use the store brand; it is almost always less expensive. Many people assume that since it is so much cheaper and looks unfamiliar, it can not be as good as the highly advertised products.

No matter what brand of aspirin you buy, there are a few things to keep in mind. If you suffer from any type of stomach disorder, avoid it. Pregnant women also should avoid aspirin as much as possible, especially in the latter stages of pregnancy; because aspirin is an anticoagulant, it can cause excessive bleeding before and after delivery.

ASPIRIN also causes **ALLERGIC REACTIONS** in some people. One type causes shortness of breath or asthmalike symptoms. The other causes skin reactions, such as redness, swelling and hives. So if you suffer from **ASTHMA**, or chronic hives, you will want to be extremely careful when using aspirin products.

Aspirin also interacts with some prescription drugs. People taking other blood-thinning prescription drugs, such as *COUMADIN* and *DICUMAROL*, should avoid combining them with aspirin. The two together could thin the blood to the point of causing hemorrhaging. If both are being used and bruising is noticed, or reddish-colored urine, report to a physician immediately.

Aspirin may also counteract medicines containing **VITAMIN K**. Vitamin K is given to people to cause their blood to clot normally, while aspirin counteracts this effect.

Some people taking oral medicines for **DIABETES** should be careful about aspirin. Those taking *DIABINESE* and *ORINASE* along with aspirin may develop lower blood sugar levels. Report any unusual signs to your doctor.

Anti-inflammatory prescription drugs, such as *INDOCIN*, or the **NONSTEROIDAL ANTI-INFLAMMATORY DRUGS**, like *ADVIL*, *NUPRIN*, or *MOTRIN*, should not be combined with aspirin because in combination they can cause stomach ulcers.

Two prescription drugs used to treat **GOUT** are **PROBENECID** *(BENEMID)* and **SULFINPYRAZONE** *(ANTURANE)*. When combined with aspirin, they could precipitate a gouty attack, or **KIDNEY STONE** formation. So before taking aspirin with a prescription drug, check with a pharmacist or doctor to make sure it is safe.

Some of the common side effects of taking too much aspirin are dizziness, ringing in the ears, difficulty in hearing, nausea, vomiting, and diarrhea. Very high dosages may cause incoherent speech, delirium or hallucinations. Overdosages may result in fast and deep breathing **(TACHYPNEA)** and **ACIDOSIS** (too acidic) of the blood. And like any other drug, if enough is taken it will cause death. If you suspect an overdose or symptoms of poisoning, call your local poison center immediately.

Aspirin and Reye Syndrome

Health professionals have been successful in recent years in alerting the public to stay away from **ASPIRIN** in children when they have a viral illness like the flu or chicken pox. Following a Public Health Service study, the evidence is pretty clear now that there is an association between aspirin use by teenagers and children and the development of Reye syndrome. **REYE SYNDROME** is characterized by severe tiredness, belligerence and excessive vomiting just when a child or teenager seems to be recovering from the flu. The syndrome may progress into coma and seizures. It is fatal in about 20 percent of the cases. Some survivors suffer permanent brain damage. Current labeling for aspirin-containing products says "Warning: children and teenagers should not use this medicine for chicken pox or flu symptoms before a doctor is consulted about Reye syndrome, a rare but serious illness."

Two physicians, Douglas Reye of Australia and George Johnson of the United States reported multiple series of mysterious deaths in children that showed diseased brains, liver and kidneys. The syndrome was called Reye-Johnson syndrome, although it is now commonly called Reye syndrome. During the 1960s and 70s regional and then national surveillance of Reye syndrome was established by the Atlanta based Centers for Disease Control. Scientists observed that the syndrome occurred in association with out-breaks of the flu, especially influenza B. They also noted that it followed chicken pox, with children aged 5 to 15 most often affected. Although records show that Reye syndrome has affected an infant as young as 4 days old and has occurred in a 59-year-old man; more than 90 percent of reported cases are in children under 15. About 2 percent are in adults over 20. Less often it was associated with other viruses and acute respiratory and diarrheal illnesses.

Douglas Reye originally suspected that a poison or drug might have triggered the disease's development. It was in 1980 that surveillance specialists in the United States found that this connection between the disease and drugs was aspirin taken during flu or chicken pox. The public was quick to pick up on the association. Aspirin use in children under 10 declined by at least 50 percent from 1981 to 1988.

However, a lot of questions still remain about aspirin and

Reye syndrome. Even though the relationship is there (one study showed youngsters with Reye were 35 times more likely to have used aspirin than those in a control group), it is estimated that less than 0.1 percent of children having a viral infection and treated with aspirin develop the syndrome. So other factors are thought to be involved. Some children may be more susceptible than others. Cases have appeared among children in the same family and children have had more than one episode of the illness, indicating a genetic tendency to get the disease more easily.

Reye syndrome is difficult to diagnose in children under five and other disorders, like metabolism problems, can look like it. So remember, aspirin use during flu or chicken pox is asking for trouble. But there are times when aspirin use is, even in children, still appropriate. So check with a doctor in each instance where kids are involved.

New Uses for Aspirin

Aspirin is the original "wonder drug" and it seems to always be in the news for one reason or another. In 1980 aspirin was approved for use by doctors to prevent **SECOND TRANSIENT ISCHEMIC ATTACKS**—TIAs, or so-called mini-strokes—in some people. In 1985 it was again approved for doctors to recommend it to their patients for **SECOND HEART ATTACKS**. But in 1988 a study known as the Physician's Health Study—because the subjects were 22,071 male physicians—sponsored by the National Institutes of Health was reported in the New England Journal of Medicine and showed that an aspirin tablet every other day can reduce the risk of initial heart attacks by as much as 50 percent. Follow-up analysis of the results over a year later and presented in the same journal in July of 1989 confirmed the findings. Aspirin interferes with the process by which blood platelets clump together to form clots. This anti-clotting mechanism appears to help prevent heart attack and ischemic strokes in some cases. A blood clot that forms in a heart artery may block the vessel completely, cutting off blood flow to part of the heart muscle (in the case of a heart attack) or part of the brain (in the case of a stroke). Aspirin's role in anti-clotting activity is thought to reduce the risk of heart attacks and ischemic strokes by inhibiting formation of clots in the arteries.

Before you stock up on aspirin to prevent a heart attack or stroke, check with a physician. Aspirin is a potent drug that, taken over a long period of time, can cause serious side effects in some people, including stomach upset and bleeding, and injury to the kidneys and liver. The FDA warns of the pitfalls of human nature, stating that risks are always inherent when consumers latch onto promising news without being aware of the fine print. For example, one danger is the "more is better" assumption. Some might believe that if an aspirin every other day is good, then two aspirin a day must be four times as good. The FDA has not officially approved aspirin to prevent first heart attacks and strokes. It has an agreement with aspirin manufacturers to voluntarily refrain from promoting the study results until "appropriate physician's labeling is available." Currently the labeling that doctors get advises how the drug can be used to ward off second heart attacks and strokes only.

The FDA has proposed a new consumer label statement that will advise consumers to consult a physician before taking aspirin for new and long term uses. The statement reads, "Important: See your doctor before taking this product for your heart or for other new uses of aspirin, because serious side effects could occur with self-treatment."

Acetaminophen

Like aspirin, **ACETAMINOPHEN** dates back to the mid-1800s. But interestingly, it didn't become popular until the mid-1950s, when two American scientists discovered that it was the "active" breakdown product in the body when people took phenacetin. At that time phenacetin was used in over-the-counter pain relievers called **APC**, which stood for aspirin-phenacetin-caffeine. This combination has since been taken off the market because of a link to kidney disease. Acetaminophen, by itself, is much safer. When the ingredient was incorporated into *TYLENOL* and heavily marketed in the 1960s, it really took off. It is now found in many nonprescription drug products, alone or in combination, such as *TYLENOL, DATRIL*, and *TEMPRA*, as well as in generic store brands of pain relievers. This drug is effective against **NEURALGIA** and **PAIN** in the muscles or bones. It also reduces **FEVER**, usually in about one hour after it is taken, and produces its peak effect in two to four hours. The main advantage of the non-aspirin products over aspirin is that there is less irritation to the stomach and so they would be better suited for persons suffering from chronic stomach problems. However, they do not relieve **INFLAMMATION** as aspirin does, so the popular opinion is that they are not beneficial to the person suffering from **ARTHRITIS** or another inflammatory condition. However, this opinion may be challenged in the future. A recent study has shown that arthritis sufferers can get favorable results when the dose of acetaminophen is monitored closely and is high enough.

Because it lacks many side effects produced by aspirin, **ACETAMINOPHEN** is gaining popularity in this country as the common household pain reliever. However, there is concern about the public's lack of awareness of acetaminophen toxicity. In overdose, acetaminophen has been shown to be harmful to the liver, where the drug is broken down and destroyed. However, this problem only occurs when very high doses are taken. Eight 500 mg capsules or tablets taken daily in divided doses does not cause any apparent harm. However, poisoning can occur when more than fifteen 500 mg capsules or tablets are taken at one time. This usually only happens when someone is trying to hurt themselves, as in a suicide attempt. At this dose, toxic reactions can occur—

vomiting within a few hours, loss of appetite, nausea, and stomach pain within 24 hours. But be aware that some people may have minimal or no symptoms until 24 hours when they may seek medical attention. There is also evidence of liver damage and jaundice within two to four days. If you suspect a poisoning from acetaminophen, call your poison center immediately. Obviously, people with chronic liver conditions, or weakened livers from excessive drinking, must be careful when using acetaminophen.

Ibuprofen

Ibuprofen is sold under the trade names *ADVIL, NUPRIN, MOTRIN IB*, and many generic store brands. When introduced in 1984 it was the first new OTC painkiller in more than 30 years. Ibuprofen may be used for the temporary relief of minor aches and pains associated with the **COMMON COLD, HEADACHE, TOOTHACHE, MUSCULAR ACHES, BACKACHE, ARTHRITIS, FEVER** and **MENSTRUAL CRAMPS**. The drug is a lower dosage strength of the same **IBUPROFEN** used on prescription only in products like *MOTRIN*. Ibuprofen is an alternative to aspirin or acetaminophen; however, you should know that certain individuals who cannot take aspirin or other salicylate-containing products may not be able to take ibuprofen. A specific warning appears prominently on the label to remind you of this.

The single tablet strength of over-the-counter ibuprofen products is 200 milligrams. Prescription strengths are higher, 300, 400, and 600 mg. The recommended dose for self-medication by consumers is one tablet every four to six hours. If pain or fever does not respond to one tablet, two tablets may be used, but no more than six tablets should be taken in 24 hours, unless directed by a physician.

IBUPROFEN offers you the advantage of fewer stomach problems than aspirin (although some patients who cannot tolerate aspirin may also have serious gastrointestinal reactions to ibuprofen) and it is probably more effective for primary dysmenorrhea (painful menstrual cramps, see page 124).

Ibuprofen, like aspirin, belongs to the class of drugs called **NONSTEROIDAL ANTI-INFLAMMATORY DRUGS (NSAIDS)**. First developed in 1960 by a British firm, Boots Company, ibuprofen came on the market in Britain in 1969. In 1974 The Upjohn Company under a licensing agreement with Boots, introduced the prescription form of ibuprofen to American consumers as *MOTRIN*. It was initially used to treat the signs and symptoms of rheumatoid arthritis and osteoarthritis, but now has been expanded to include the indications mentioned earlier.

In spite of the huge variety of brand name products available to consumers there are really only a few pain relievers. Knowing how these ingredients work and what to avoid makes the choice a lot simpler.

Naproxen

NAPROXEN, another non-steroidal anti-inflammatory drug (NSAID), is marketed as *ALEVE*, the first nonprescription pain reliever containing a new analgesic ingredient in ten years. The drug is a nonprescription strength of the popular prescription drugs *NAPROSYN* and *ANAPROX*. Naproxen is approved for use in adults and children age 12 and over for the temporary relief of minor aches and pains associated with the common cold, headache, toothache, muscular aches, backache, minor arthritis pain, menstrual cramp pain and fever reduction.

As the first nonprescription pain reliever to contain naproxen, *ALEVE* offers consumers important benefits in over-the-counter pain relief. While other OTC pain relievers call for remedication, if needed every 4 to 6 hours or 6 to 8 hours, *ALEVE* provides pain relief that lasts 8 to 12 hours. In studies submitted to the FDA prior to approval, *ALEVE* provided pain relief in some people in as little as 20 minutes and for up to 12 hours with one dose. Naproxen is about as effective as **IBUPROFEN** but appears to be longer lasting with a single dose.

Patients who are allergic to **IBUPROFEN**, **ASPIRIN** or any pain-relieving drug are advised not to use this product, since they may also be allergic to naproxen. Naproxen should not be taken in combination with acetaminophen, ibuprofen, aspirin or any other naproxen-containing product without a doctor's approval.

Be especially careful to read the package insert with this product. There are warning and cautions about allergies, the use of alcohol, how the dose may be increased with experience, use during pregnancy, and when to consult a physician while taking naproxen. This drug is a very useful addition to over-the-counter analgesics. The FDA reviewed data from 32 clinical studies involving more than 7,000 patients and safety related information on naproxen, which has been available in 92 countries for the past 20 years and used by patients in more than 12.7 billion days of therapy. But like any drug, it has side effects and precautions that should be considered before you take it.

18

Pain & Soreness Relievers

It is said that physical exercise is good for the mind and the soul. However, a problem with strenuous physical activity is that it causes **SORE MUSCLES**. Soreness may also be due, not to strenuous physical activity, but simply doing something out of the ordinary or performing an activity incorrectly. As a matter of fact, since the physical fitness craze started, the sale of **LINIMENTS** has gone up, especially among people who started running for the first time.

It seems that each liniment or topical rub product, such as *ABSORBINE JR., MINERAL ICE, EUCALYPTAMINT,* and many more, has its version of the claim to give "temporary relief of minor muscular aches and pains resulting from over-exertion and fatigue." Some make the promotional claim that "It actually treats the cause of sore, tired muscles," or "penetrates deep into the skin." These claims usually cause confusion in the minds of the people using them.

MUSCLE RUBS are available in many forms: ointments, creams, liniments, and lotions. These products contain a variety of different ingredients, but they usually also contain the same few basic ones. The most common ingredients found in liniments are irritants to the skin, such as **METHYL SALICYLATE (OIL OF WINTERGREEN), MENTHOL** and **CAMPHOR** and are known as "counter-irritants." Counter-irritants are applied locally to produce a mild local reaction of redness and warmth due to increased circulation in the sore area. They are applied to the skin wherever the pain is experienced.

Pain is only as intense as it is perceived to be; therefore, when you apply a substance that produces irritation, that sensation crowds out the experience of the pain around it. So look at the ingredients in the liniments or rubs and know how they will work: **METHYL SALICYLATE** is probably the most widely used counter-irritant. When it is rubbed on the skin, it produces mild irritation, and it is absorbed into the skin to an appreciable extent. The range of effective concentrations of methyl salicylate is 10-60 percent. Methyl salicylate has a very pleasant odor and taste, similar to candy, which may attract children. Actually, as little as one teaspoonful of straight methyl salicylate may be fatal, so if you use products containing methyl salicylate, put them in a place completely out of the reach of children. **CAMPHOR** is found in many muscle rubs because it causes redness of skin. **MENTHOL** is used in muscle rubs because it has a mild anesthetic effect and produces a feeling of warmth. **TURPENTINE OIL** has been used for a number of years as a counter-irritant. It does work fairly well in a concentration of 10-50 percent. However, be careful if you do use this compound since it could cause blistering of the skin.

Muscle rubs are available in different forms. **LINIMENTS** have alcohol bases and penetrate deeper into the skin. **LOTIONS**, **CREAMS**, and **OINTMENTS** stay on the skin much longer, giving you a continuous release of medication. When applying a rub, keep the following in mind:

- Use only externally, on skin that is not broken.
- Do not apply to eyes, mucous membranes, abnormally sensitive skin, or skin that is already irritated.
- Discontinue using if excessive skin irritation develops.
- If pain persists longer than ten days or if extreme redness is present, contact a physician.
- Avoid using on children under twelve years of age.
- After applying these products, do not cover or tightly bind the treated area.
- If you are planning to use a heating pad or other form of heat treatment, do not use it in combination with a muscle rub. The two together could cause a severe burn to the skin.

Pain Reliever Ingredients

CAMPHOR is obtained naturally by steam distillation of parts of the camphor tree, *Cinnamomum camphora*, native to Taiwan and other parts of eastern Asia and naturalized in other parts of the world. It can also be made synthetically from a hydrocarbon obtained from oil of turpentine. It is used in ointments, lotions, liniments, rubs and other pharmaceuticals as a weak antiseptic, a mild anesthetic and as what is known as a rubefacient (meaning in Latin "to make red"). Application to the skin irritates the tissues slightly, causing the blood vessels to dilate the skin surface red. The dilated blood vessels in the skin bring additional blood and warmth to the surface and some relief to sore, aching muscles and other areas.

CAPSICUM or **CAPSICUM OLEORESIN** is the oil resin in Cayenne pepper, the dried ripe fruit of the plant *Capsicum frutescens* and other species of Capsicum. It is used as a rubefacient (in Latin meaning "to make red") since application to the skin irritates the tissues slightly, causing the blood vessels to dilate and thus making the surface red. The enlarged blood vessels in the skin bring additional blood and warmth to the surface to relieve sore muscles.

MENTHOL chemically is a type of alcohol obtained from different varieties of mint oils. It can be prepared from Japanese, Chinese, or American peppermint oil (from the plant, *Mentha piperita*) by refrigeration, during which the menthol crystallizes. It occurs as colorless, needle-like crystals, or as a crystalline powder and has a pleasant, peppermint odor. Historically, it has been used to stop itching and as a rubefacient (meaning from the Latin "to make red"). Application to the skin irritates the tissues slightly, causing the blood vessels to dilate. The dilated blood vessels in the skin bring more blood and warmth to the surface of the skin. Many times this will provide temporary relief of muscle ache.

METHYL SALICYLATE or **OIL OF WINTERGREEN** may be produced synthetically from petroleum chemicals, or naturally by steam distillation from the leaves of *Gaultheria procumbens*, an evergreen shrub which is native to North America. It occurs as a colorless, yellowish or reddish liquid and has the characteristic odor and taste of wintergreen. It is used as a rubefacient (meaning from the Latin "to make red"). Application to the skin irritates the tissues slightly, causing the blood vessels to dilate and thus making the surface red. The dilated blood vessels in the skin bring increased blood and warmth to the surface to relieve soreness and discomfort.

PHENOL also known as **CARBOLIC ACID** is a colorless, crystalline chemical at one time produced from coal tar, now produced synthetically from petroleum-starting materials. In concentrated form it is corrosive and very poisonous. In practice, few poisonings occur since it is used as a preservative, disinfectant and antiseptic in various concentrations, usually 1 to 5 percent. It has very little use any longer, except in a few patent medications, like *CAMPHO-PHENIQUE*. It has anesthetic and anti-itch properties and is still used in **PHENOLATED CALAMINE LOTION**.

Heat Lamps

Many people buy heat lamps to relieve muscle pain and soreness. Heat lamps provide warmth and can temporarily relieve aches and pains. However, do not be confused when you shop for them; they are usually found with the sunlamps and there is a difference (see sunlamps, page 348). Heat lamps generate infrared light. When using an infrared lamp, wear goggles during long sessions to prevent the moisture in the eyes from drying out.

Massage Products

There are now available in most drugstores a variety of appliances to massage sore muscles. Products such as **BACK**

MASSAGERS are actually pads that you unfold and place in a chair or lay out flat on your bed. When plugged in they vibrate, which increases circulation to the muscle and may help to heal it.

Some massagers are available in a Swedish design that attaches to the palm of your hand. Simply massage the sore muscles with the hand that holds the massager. Once again, the vibrating action will speed up healing by increasing the circulation. If you prefer a warm massage, these products are also made with heat elements, which produce warmth as you massage the muscles.

Massage products may be used with liniments and muscle rubs; they increase the penetration of the analgesics to help heal those sore, aching muscles. In addition to its other effects, a massage is likely to make you feel relaxed, especially if you are tense, causing the muscles to tighten up.

Dimethyl Sulfoxide (DMSO)

This is an industrial solvent that is a clear, colorless liquid. It was very popular and controversial in the early 1980s when it was seen as a cure-all for everything from muscle aches to arthritis. **DMSO** stands for **DIMETHYL SULFOXIDE**. It was first found to have medicinal properties when workers, using it to degrease the Alaskan pipeline, noticed that if they had bruises or aches or pains, DMSO coming into contact with the affected area seemed to help to make the pain go away. The FDA started testing DMSO, but the tests were halted because the chemical was found to cause eye problems. However, since these tests were done on non-primate animals, there was no proof that this would happen in humans. Tests on DMSO resumed, only this time they were done on healthy human volunteers in a controlled study. Simultaneously, companies all around the country began selling it to people, making claims that were not proven. Since the sale of DMSO is illegal in many states, people began going to border states to buy it, often getting inferior products. Some products contained traces of prescription drugs such as **CORTISONE.** Because of its ability to carry chemicals across the skin barrier, it can also carry contaminants and poisons. Using an unapproved form of this chemical can be dangerous. At present, the safest course of action is to avoid DMSO for any of its claims regarding arthritis. Testing by drug companies to determine if DMSO might be useful as a vehicle to get other beneficial medicines into the skin have been disappointing. Even people who have used DMSO after obtaining it illegally for the treatment of arthritis have not received the relief they expected. The only FDA approved use for DMSO is in interstitial cystitis, a bladder disorder. For this use it is administered by a physician directly into the bladder through a catheter.

19

Parasites

Lice Infestation

Lice are parasites that commonly affect humans. There are three types of lice: **HEAD LICE**, **BODY LICE**, and **PUBIC LICE**. Lice infestation is a condition that must be recognized and treated as soon as possible. It may exist in people of all ages and social levels; no one is immune. Lice are easily transmitted from person to person by sharing personal articles, such as hats, hair ribbons, combs, towels, and bedding, and by physical contact. The lice attach themselves to hair shafts and cloth fibers and lay their eggs. The adults and larvae bite their hosts to feed on blood. Extensive redness and itching can cause breaking and opening in the skin surface which can lead to other problems, like impetigo (a type of crusty bacterial infection) or boils.

Head Lice

Infestation by head lice is more common in children but may also occur in adults. As a matter of fact sometimes schools are closed because of an outbreak of lice that spreads in epidemic proportions. Any part of the scalp may be affected. The itching is often severe. You may notice pustules, bleeding areas on the scalp, and matting of the hair. It is important to check children's hair periodically; the lice can be seen on the scalp, or you may notice small, white sticky eggs on the hair itself. The tiny gray-white lice eggs are sometimes called nits. It is easier to spot the nits than the lice themselves. Because nits are dandruffy in appearance, they are easier to see on brunettes than on blondes. To distinguish them from dandruff or hair spray, pick up a strand of hair close to the scalp and pull your fingernail across the area where the whitish substance appears. If it is hairspray, lint, or dandruff it will come off easily, but nits will stay firmly attached to the hair. If you look closely, you may be able to see the bugs themselves on the back of the head and around the ears.

Body Lice

These organisms mainly live on the clothing and visit the skin only to feed. The eggs may also be found on the hairs of the affected region.

Pubic Lice

Pubic lice are more commonly called "crabs," because the organism has long tentacles and resembles a crab. These lice are very noticeable and attach themselves to the skin, usually at the point of emergence of a hair. Infestation is more common in men than in women. The lice are transmitted during sexual activity.

Treatment

Lice can be treated with a variety of over-the-counter products such as *RID LICE KILLING SHAMPOO, R & C SHAMPOO* or *A-200 SHAMPOO CONCENTRATE.* Virtually all of these products use the same ingredients, a combination of **PYRETHRINS** and **PIPERONYL BUTOXIDE**. Combining the chemical piperonyl butoxide with pyrethrins, the manufacturer can use less of the pyrethrin because piperonyl butoxide blocks the breakdown of the pyrethrins by the insect. The pyrethrins are based on **PYRETHRUMS** which are natural pesticides obtained from chrysanthemum plants. *NIX* is another brand product containing a synthetic pyrethrin known as **PERMETHRIN.** Permethrin is more effective than other pyrethrins and very safe for use in humans. Some physicians prefer the permethrin-containing products because it is more effective.

Liquid products like *NIX* are applied undiluted to the infested areas, such as hair and scalp, until entirely wet. Do not use on eye lashes or eyebrows. Allow the solution to remain on the area for ten minutes, no longer, since this is sufficient to kill lice and their eggs. Wash hair thoroughly with warm water and soap or shampoo, then dry the area. The shampoo products are used as directed on the label, but similar to a regular shampoo. After using, comb the hair thoroughly with a fine-tooth comb. Some products, such as *RID*, provide you with a comb. The combing removes dead lice and eggs. Many children who are treated for lice cannot go back to school because of nits that remain in the hair, even after combing. In these cases household vinegar may be applied to the hair and left on for several minutes, covering the head with a small towel. The vinegar dissolves the "chitin" or cement that the louse lays down on the hair shaft. Following the vinegar application, rinsing and combing again may be more successful. Do not exceed two consecutive applications in 24 hours, because the chemicals may irritate the skin. When using these products avoid getting them in the eyes. The products may be used on children. After getting rid of the lice, here are preventative steps to follow:

- Inspect all family members daily, for at least two weeks, and if they do become infested start the treatment again.
- Sterilize all personal clothing, bed clothes, and bedding of the infested person in hot water, at least 130°F, or by dry cleaning. Dry in a hot dryer for at least 20 minutes.
- Thoroughly wash all personal articles such as combs, brushes, etc., in hot water (130°F) for 20 minutes, or by soaking in a medicated shampoo, like *R & C*.
- If necessary, use one of the over-the-counter sprays for disinfecting furniture and bedding. They contain insecticides that are not suitable for humans or animals, so be careful not to confuse them with the products that are for human use. These are products like *RID LICE CONTROL SPRAY FOR BEDDING & FURNITURE* and *R & C SPRAY.* Since there really is no immunity from lice, per-

sonal cleanliness and avoiding infested persons and their bedding and clothes will aid in preventing infestation. These additional steps are important in order to cut down the chances of re-infestation:

- Completely change undergarments, clothes, and night wear daily. Wash them in hot water (130° F).
- Scrub toilet seats and vacuum upholstered furniture, rugs, and floors frequently.
- Tell children not to use borrowed combs or brushes or to wear anyone else's clothes.
- Inspect family members periodically for new lice infestation. If a new outbreak is spotted, do not waste time, begin treatment immediately.

Pinworms

There are many other kinds of worm infestations that can occur in people, but only pinworms can be treated with over-the-counter drugs.

The symptoms of pinworm infection are very irritating and can lead to some serious complications if not treated promptly and completely. For example, in girls the worms can enter the genital tract and become trapped within the uterus or fallopian tubules, or they can migrate into other body parts where they aggravate tissue and cause the development of granulomas, an abnormal growth of tissue. At first, pinworm infections result in irritation and itching in the rectal and groin area. The itching usually occurs at night when the female worm deposits her eggs in these areas. Nervousness, difficulty in concentrating, loss of appetite and a pallored look, including dark circles under the eyes frequently are observed in children having pinworms. This is most likely due to a lack of restful sleep.

Even though you can treat pinworms effectively with a nonprescription drug, it is still a good idea to see a physician if you suspect pinworms. You must get an accurate diagnosis of the problem. Other medical conditions and skin problems can act like pinworm infections. The best way to find out for sure is for a physician to use a test kit specifically for this purpose. Sticky tape is pressed to the rectum or adjacent area to collect eggs. The tape is them examined under a microscope to confirm pinworms.

The only ingredient approved by the FDA for self treatment of pinworms is **PYRANTEL PAMOATE.** This is available in the products *ANTIMINTH SUSPENSION* and *REESE'S PINWORM LIQUID.* Pyrantel pamoate is a chemical that paralyzes pinworms, causing them to lose their grip on the intestinal wall and be eliminated from the body in the stool. It may be necessary to have a physician choose a prescription medicine such as *VERMOX* **(MEBENDAZOLE).** There are many other prescription drugs available for treatment of pinworms and other worm infections.

Ticks

Ticks were described by Aristotle in the fourth century before Christ as "disgusting parasitic animals." It is funny, but they have not changed a bit. Ticks are found all over the world. As a significant means of transmitting human disease, they rank second only to the mosquito. Ticks are now known to pass on bacterial, viral, and protozoal diseases and also to cause disease through their own toxins. Two well-known diseases transmitted by ticks are **LYME DISEASE** and **ROCKY MOUNTAIN SPOTTED FEVER**. Lyme disease is named after Lyme, Connecticut, where it was first identified. After mothers of children in the area reported to the Connecticut health department what seemed to be a high incidence of juvenile rheumatoid arthritis, studies showed that a collection of symptoms was really due to a bacterium-like organism carried by **DEER TICKS**. Rocky Mountain spotted fever is caused by a bacterium that is carried by the **WOOD TICK** in the western United States and the **DOG TICK** is the primary carrier in the eastern United

States. Many other diseases are spread by ticks. Tularemia, Ehrlichiosis, Q Fever, relapsing fever, Colorado tick fever, Babesiosis, and tick paralysis are all known to be diseases caused by ticks.

Tick Removal

Ticks must be attached for several hours before they cause infection so check for them frequently. It is important to remove ticks early and completely. "Folk" methods of removing ticks by covering the tick for several minutes with petroleum jelly, fingernail polish, or rubbing alcohol do not work. Do not try using a hot match either, it does not work and will probably burn the victim. The important thing is to remove the tick with its mouth parts intact. Researchers have found that the best way to do this is the following:

- Apply an antiseptic like *BETADINE SOLUTION* to the area first.
- Use blunt, curved forceps or tweezers. If necessary, gloved fingers may be used. Bare fingers should never be used.
- Grasp the tick as close as possible to the skin surface and pull upwards with steady, even pressure.
- The tick should not be squeezed, crushed, or punctured, if possible.
- After removal of the tick, disinfect the attachment site with *BETADINE SOLUTION*. Wash hands thoroughly with soap and water. Secretions from the tick could be infective.
- Dispose of the tick in a container of alcohol or flush down the toilet.

You can prevent tick-borne disease by avoiding situations where tick bites are likely to occur. But if activities are planned in the woods wear protective clothing. There is really no effective, preventative measure for avoiding ticks completely. However, spraying one of the insect repellents (see page 336) around the open areas of clothing: pants cuffs, button holes, and other areas where the tick could get to the skin could be helpful. Carefully follow the directions of insect repellents for application to exposed body parts. Use them sparingly on children according to the directions on the label. Inspect your entire body, and those of children, several times a day. And do not forget to check the family pets.

The good news about ticks is that almost all of these tick diseases are treatable with antibiotics and a complete cure results if treated early.

20

Pets

Nowadays most drugstores have a section dedicated to pets. After all, most people love their pets almost as much as they love their children. Aside from giving him rawhide bones, flea collars, and shampoos, there are also things you can do at home to treat your pet during illness. Obviously, some of these tips are only temporary measures, until there is time to go to the veterinarian.

General Medicines

If a pet's eyes are **WATERY**, wash them with milk rather than water because milk is closer to their tearfilm. Or use any ordinary eye wash you have around the house.

ASPIRIN is safe to give to a dog occasionally. However, use **BUFFERED ASPIRIN**. Simple aspirin may cause irritation to the stomach and possibly cause your dog to vomit. Do not give your dog more than one adult 5-grain aspirin for 40 to 50 pounds of body weight every twelve hours, because it stays in their system longer than in humans. Generally speaking, it is not a good idea to give aspirin to cats. Because of the long excretion time, a toxic buildup in the body could occur. Although some veterinarians do recommend a dose they consider safe for their patients. In cats the dose is only given every 48 hours.

Pet Poisoning

It is no secret that people are unintentionally poisoned. But each year thousands of pets poison themselves as well—leaving their owners bereft and broken-hearted. Like little children, pets cannot read warning labels. They have no idea what might hurt them. Dogs and puppies, cats and kittens, gerbils, rabbits, and birds can ingest dangerous household products such as pesticides, rodent killers, cleaning fluids and powders, disinfectants, dishwasher detergent, cosmetics, drugs and medications, liquor, and car care products.

If a dog or cat has gotten into a poisonous product, be sure to save the container for the vet's information and call your local poison center. They possess the information needed to determine the severity of an exposure and to help you or your veterinarian treat an exposure. Poison centers possess complete, up-to-date product formulations. Without this vital knowledge, no exposure to a harmful product can be properly evaluated. If a visit to your veterinarian seems advisable, most poison centers will even call ahead and alert the veterinarian to the pet's problem. Precious time will be saved and the vet will be able to confer with the poison center about product formulations.

How do you know if a pet is poisoned? Vomiting, diarrhea, uncoordination could all be symptoms of a poison exposure. Any of these symptoms would warrant a call to the poison center if there is reason to suspect the pet could have been exposed to a harmful product. According to the National Animal Poison Control Center at the University of Illinois, pets are most likely to be poisoned by:

Rodenticides	17.2%
Pesticides	16.0%
Plants	12.7%
Human medications	10.0%
Household products	5.7%
Other chemicals	4.7%
Herbicides	4.1%
Paint, varnish, etc	3.8%

Rodenticides

Even though they are used to kill rats, mice, and other rodent pests, rodenticides can also be fatal to unsuspecting pets. Where are you most likely to place these poisons? On the floor, where animals can lap them up. If you must use rodenticides in the house, try to put them in the smallest possible crevice, away from a puppy's—or a child's—inquiring tongue. Be aware, too, that dogs and cats may eat rodents that have been poisoned, both indoors and outside. It really depends on how the rodent has been poisoned as to whether or not it will affect a pet. Call the poison center for help in this situation.

Pesticides

From a pet's position, pesticides are really bad news. Insect killers and weed killers may contain very toxic ingredients. Animals can be poisoned when they run across or play in a newly sprayed yard. Always keep a pet away from any recently sprayed lawn for several days. Do not allow a pet to run free in a garden where you have applied an insecticide or herbicide.

Plants

Some household pets—cats especially—seem to find decorative plants an irresistible "salad." These cats, however, are likely to find themselves sick if they eat dieffenbachia or hydrangea. Do not put these temptations in a cat's way. Notice, too, that people are most likely to have two of these plants—mistletoe and holly—around the December holiday season.

People Medicines

The best rule of thumb is do not give pets human medicine. Aspirin, as mentioned above, is not generally good for animals, and aspirin substitutes containing acetaminophen can be fatal, particularly to dogs. Never prescribe laxatives for animals; constipation should always be treated by a vet.

Paint, Varnish, etc.

An animal's super-sensitive sense of smell can be hurt by the powerful odors of paint and varnish and other household fix-up products. Use these chemically-based products only in a well-ventilated area.

Alcohol

Unknowing people sometimes find it funny to watch the puppy lap up beer and get dizzy. This would not be so funny if their favorite beagle died of an overdose of alcohol. Pets and alcohol just do not mix. Their small bodies (the same is true for children) simply cannot tolerate beer, wine, or liquor of any kind.

Antifreeze

Pets have been known to drink antifreeze. Most automobile antifreeze preparations are **ETHYLENE GLYCOL**, and ethylene glycol is sweet. So not only will animals drink it, they are attracted to it and may like it. If this happens, get the animal to a veterinarian as quickly as possible. Ethylene glycol will damage your pet's kidneys and cause death if not treated immediately. A vet will have to give the animal alcohol as an antidote for ethylene glycol. Alcohol prevents the ethylene glycol from breaking down into to the harmful byproducts that cause injury to the kidneys and brain. It is usually necessary to keep an animal intoxicated with alcohol long enough for the body to clear the antifreeze completely.

Chocolate

As delicious as it is, chocolate can be very toxic when ingested in large quantities by a dog or cat. Do not allow a pet to eat chocolate, especially the dark or baking chocolate. In some parts of the United States cocoa bean shells are used for mulch. If animals eat the shells they can also become poisoned.

If you need to make a pet vomit, you can do this by giving him **HYDROGEN PEROXIDE, SYRUP OF IPECAC**, or **SALT WATER**, unless the poison is an **ACID** or **ALKALI**. If it is an acid or alkali, offer milk but do not force it, and then get the animal to a veterinarian. Some pets, such as dogs, do not respond well to syrup of ipecac to induce vomiting. And too strong salt water may cause salt poisoning.

Check with a veterinarian regarding your particular animal and the safest way to induce vomiting in an emergency, or check with your regional poison center.

Miscellaneous Remedies

Suppose a pet gets paint, tar, or asphalt on his coat. Never use paint remover or kerosene! Trim away as much of the coating as possible and soak the remaining fur in vegetable oil for one hour or overnight, then shampoo it. If there is not any dog shampoo handy, use regular shampoo or a mild dishwashing detergent. If the pet has dry skin apply diluted *ALPHA KERI BATH OIL* from a spray bottle. Sometimes pets get sprayed by skunks during a romp in the woods. Use tomato juice to remove the smell.

Following are other common problems and treatments:

- Coughing: Use a children's cough syrup (without aspirin).
- Simple diarrhea: Give *KAOPECTATE, ADVANCED FORMULA*. Start with several tablespoonsful every few hours.
- Insect stings: Apply a paste of baking soda.
- Burns: Soak in cold water, then apply a bland first aid cream (see Chapter 12). Do not use butter.
- Mild constipation: check with your veterinarian and beware of **CASTOR OIL.** However, it is safe to place one drop of castor oil in the eye to prevent soap from getting into the animal's eyes while bathing.

These are a few of the home remedies for various problems a pet develops. Remember, though, to check with a veterinarian in a specific instance, just to be sure.

People often feel that pet products bought in the drugstore are safe. However, always read carefully the instructions on the product and follow them to the letter. Individuals (animal or human) may be allergic to certain ingredients, so watch for symptoms when administering a new product.

Three of the most common pet products are:

FLEA COLLARS: When putting one on a pet, allow two fingers between the collar and the neck. Do not leave the end long because the pet may chew on it. Before putting on the flea collar, leave it out in the air for 24 hours and try to keep it dry, although most collars now can tolerate getting wet. This varies from product to product.

WORM MEDICINE: Before using any of the worm medicines, have the stool of the pet checked by a veterinarian, because different worms require different treatments. A veterinarian can treat your pet to prevent the devastating results of heartworm infection. Never give worm medicine to a sick dog. Also, these products do not work prophylactically. Therefore, do not give once a month for prevention or "just in case."

PET SHAMPOOS: Many of these products are fine for normal use, but be sure to rinse the soap out thoroughly. Residues left behind could irritate the skin. Do not bathe the pet too often—in fact the less, the better, unless your pet has a condition for which your vet is treating him. If the pet has a skin condition be sure to check with your veterinarian first; he or she may advise you to use a special shampoo.

21

Poison Prevention & Treatment

Each year, emergency rooms around the country see thousands of children who unintentionally eat or drink a poisonous product around the house. If only parents had taken the necessary steps in advance, they might have prevented a serious, or even fatal, poisoning. In addition to the emergency room cases, poison centers take an estimated 2.2 million calls every year about children and adults. The combined databases of the American Association of Poison Control Centers and the National Safety Council report over 5,000 total fatalities every year (children and adults), and these do not include all deaths from poisonous animal bites; carbon monoxide deaths from fires; medical complications, such as drug reactions; and chronic exposure to toxic chemicals. All reports of poisoning deaths are underestimates of the real problem, since many poisoning occurrences, like drug abuse-related deaths and suicide due to drugs in older children, are frequently not listed as poisoning. The little bit of good news is that deaths in children under 6 have been going down every year since about 1962. This is due to increased awareness about childhood poisoning and better ways to treat it. But even though only a small number of children die, there are many thousands who are seriously injured every year. The tragedy is that these are preventable injuries, not accidents! Poison centers have the knowledge to predict and prevent these injuries. So, take advantage of this fantastic resource. Call your poison center for free prevention information, before you need it in an emergency.

Prevention

We want to talk about prevention first. All too often health professionals get so wrapped up in treating sick people that they forget to discuss how to prevent what made them ill in the first place. With poisoning, look around the house and correct any problem areas. It is often helpful to get down on your hands and knees and crawl around the living areas to get a "child's eye view" of what may be hidden dangers. Children will frequently find the pill that grandparents dropped on the carpet and could not find. Remember that poisonings can happen to adults as well as children. Label all products that have been removed from their original containers. Be careful with mixing chemicals and cleaning agents. Call your poison center when in doubt. These simple steps may prevent an unintentional poisoning from happening to you or any member of your family.

Many poison control centers across the country distribute **MR. YUK** stickers on request. The stickers show a picture of a scowling, green face. After instructing the children to stay away from those products that have the sticker on them, place them on all products that may be harmful. And most important, put one of the stickers with the poison center phone number on your phone.

Poisoning Facts

Children are poisoned most in the one- to five-year age group, with a peak at 18 months of age. This group of kids makes up about 65 percent of all incidents reported to poison centers in the United States. The most common time of the day in which poisonings happen is the late afternoon and early evening, between 5 and 8 P.M. The late morning is the next most common time and many of these exposures are mishaps in toddlers. The time of day when ingestions occur most frequently shows that children ingest poisons more often during family disorganization or disruption. The two peak times seem to correspond with times when the household is more chaotic. Also, when the status quo of the family is disturbed, such as by divorce, separation, death, or relocation, children tend to get into poisons more often.

So let us take a look at three areas of the home where most unintentional poisonings occur.

Basement or Garage

This is the area of the house where we store products such as **GASOLINE, CHARCOAL LIGHTER, ANTI-FREEZE, WINDSHIELD WASHER FLUID, TURPENTINE**, and **INSECTICIDES**. If there are such products on hand, always make sure to keep them in their original containers, tightly capped. If possible use a safety closure cap. When not using these products, keep them well out of the reach of children. Never keep them in soda bottles, cups, or glasses; children associate these things with eating and drinking. Lock things up, but remember that 75 percent of the time poisonings in children happen while the product is in use! So the user should never let them out of sight, even if that means carrying them. Kids act fast and so do poisons.

Under the Kitchen Sink

This is usually the area of the home where we store products such as drain openers, oven cleaners, and other household cleaners. Many of these products are corrosives, causing severe burns to the mouth and throat if swallowed. Unfortunately, this area is too easy for the child to reach. If you must store these products, be sure to store them in their original containers, since many products will be in a child-resistant package. It is safer to keep these products in a locked cabinet or in a high place out of the sight and reach of small children.

Bathroom Medicine Cabinet

A lot of poisonings occur in the bathroom and from kids getting into the bathroom medicine cabinet. As a matter of fact, we do not recommend keeping medicines in the "medicine" cabinet; a child may go into the bathroom and lock the door behind him or her, and you may have trouble getting to that child fast enough. In addition, many medicines are affected by heat and moisture, which often build up in a bathroom. Keep medicines in a locked drawer or cabinet and also use child-resistant containers. If there are medicines with the plain cap because they are easier to open pay particular attention to keep children away from the containers. Also, clean out medicine storage areas periodically and get rid of old or unused medicines. Do this by dumping the contents into the toilet and flushing them away. When administering drugs at night be sure to turn on the light so that you can see what you are using.

Symptoms and Treatment of Poisoning

Often people want to know how they can tell if their child has taken any of these products. Reactions vary depending on the product. The child may **VOMIT** for no apparent reason, or begin **COUGHING** or **CHOKING**. You may see a residue around the mouth and teeth of the child, or see that the contents of the package are drastically reduced. If medication or alcohol is involved the child may appear **SLUGGISH** or **TIRED** for no apparent reason.

The important thing is to act fast. For corrosives, like drain cleaners, and petroleum distillates, like gasoline, it is important to give milk or water right away. But do not give too much or force the fluid as this may cause vomiting and further injury from the poison. Then, check the container to see if there is a listing of ingredients on the package and bring it to the phone with you. Call the poison center and tell them what happened.

Be careful to avoid instructions on a product label that suggest complicated concoctions as antidotes like mixing egg whites, oatmeal or other foods to be given to "neutralize" the poison. Never use household vinegar to neutralize an alkaline corrosive chemical (like *DRANO* or *LIQUID PLUMR*) that someone may have drunk. By the same token, do not use baking soda for acids, such as toilet bowl cleaners. Even though this is sometimes recommended on product labels, doing this can cause a more serious burn than if you simply give milk or water. Use only water or milk to dilute poisons. Offer them, but do not force someone to drink if they do not want to. If serious burns have already occurred they aren't able to drink the liquids anyway. Forcing them to drink may cause them to cough and choke the chemical into the lungs. This could cause a chemical pneumonia, or worse, sudden death. If there are symptoms following an exposure to corrosives or petroleum distillates the poison center will probably send you directly to the emergency department.

For most ingestions of poisons nothing more than giving milk or water needs to be done. The poison center will reassure you and probably call you back to make sure that everything is fine.

For some products the poison center will tell you to cause vomiting. But it is easier said than done. Home remedies have included drinking a soap solution or sticking something down the throat to cause gagging and vomiting. These methods do not work and may be dangerous. The poison center may suggest that you induce vomiting with syrup of ipecac.

Syrup of Ipecac

After calling the poison center in an emergency, if instructed to cause vomiting there is really only one product in the pharmacy that is almost 100 percent effective in doing this. It is called *SYRUP OF IPECAC*. Syrup of ipecac is about as safe as any medicine can be, and it is effective. The dose is to give children one tablespoonful followed by approximately 8 ounces of water or *KOOL-AID* (or similar beverage as instructed by the poison center). Adults take two tablespoonsful followed by 8 ounces to a pint of water. If a child does not vomit in 20 minutes, the dose of one tablespoonful can be repeated up to the maximum dose of two tablespoonsful. Do not repeat the dose in adults because they have been given the maximum dose all at once. It is very important to drink water or *KOOL-AID* after a dose of ipecac, because it helps the medicine to be absorbed more quickly and adds some volume to the stomach which is necessary for vomiting to occur. Vomiting usually takes place in about 20 minutes. If it does not, repeat the dosage in children only as mentioned above. When instructed to give syrup of ipecac, pour it straight from the bottle into a spoon. Do not mix or stir it into any liquids. The water or *KOOL-AID* should be given separately, following the dose of ipecac.

Syrup of ipecac should be a permanent fixture in any home that has kids, and that includes grandparents' homes too! It could save a life.

Helping Your Poison Center Help You

Since the early 1950s poison control centers have demonstrated their importance in treating accidental ingestions and other types of poisonous exposures. At one time there were hundreds of poison control centers in the United States. The problem was that they really did not work closely with one another and they only served the local population of any city or town. As things got more complicated with the technology, and drug names got longer and harder to pronounce, it was necessary for poison centers to train doctors, nurses and pharmacists to answer emergency calls from a larger geographical area. This is because it is too expensive for every town and city to have the sophisticated computer technology it now takes to track down all the different drugs and chemicals found in hundreds of thousands of medicines, not to mention yard and garden and household products.

Modern poison centers are known as "regional" poison centers and usually will serve between 2 and 10 million people in a given area. A typical regional poison prevention and treatment program provides the following services:

1) Takes calls from the public and provides poison information and consultation in an emergency.
2) Is located in a major area hospital with an emergency department for providing emergency treatment.
3) Advertises free public access by a toll-free telephone system and direct link to 911 for:
   a. Information on poison exposures
   b. Treatment for poisoning
   c. Follow-up on cases managed at home
   d. Referral to emergency services if necessary
4) Teaches doctors, nurses, and other health professionals about toxicology, the science of poisons.
5) Coordination of hospital transport of poisoned patients. Sometimes a victim will need to be moved from an emergency department to a hospital that provides specialized care, such as dialysis.
6) Data collection and evaluation of the poisonings to determine trends and plan prevention programs.
7) Research on new antidotes and procedures to treat poisonings.
8) Public education and poison prevention teaching to all sorts of community groups, church organizations and so on.

In order to help the regional poison center help you following a potential poisoning, it is wise to be prepared. Advance knowledge can perhaps save a life. It makes a difference if the product is a liquid, powder, cream, tablet or capsule, or a solid, as seen below.

Swallowed Liquids

It is easy to exaggerate how much liquid has been swallowed, so the following may be useful.

1) Determine the quantity of the product in the container when it was purchased. From the original container, you can check the label for this information.
2) In most cases, at least a small portion had been used before the ingestion occurred. Was the container about three-fourths, one-half, or one-fourth full prior to ingestion. For a more accurate way, fill up the container to the level it was when the child got into it and then remove the amount suspected, using a measuring device to determine the quantity.
3) When children swallow liquids, particularly those with containers which are difficult to handle, they usually spill far more than they ingest. Explain circumstances like this to the poison center specialist.
4) On occasion, the smell of the product on the breath may be obvious. If there is no odor, however, that does not mean that the ingestion did not happen. So while this is helpful in determining that something probably has been swallowed, it should never be used to rule out a poisoning.

Swallowed Tablets or Capsules

Flavored, sweetened, or sugar coated tablets are among the most tasty and frequently eaten or swallowed drugs by children. It is entirely possible for most children to swallow large amounts of these medicines since they taste like candy. Drugs that are not flavored are eaten in much smaller amounts by children.

Some pills are not considered by adults to be as dangerous as they really are in overdose. Examples of these are **IRON** pills. Iron is good for you and pregnant women take them as a prenatal nutritional supplement. Right? In overdose, this can be dead wrong. Iron can cause bleeding and shock when taken in overdose by a child or adult. Another danger is a prescription class of drugs called **TRICYLCIC ANTIDEPRESSANTS** found in such products as *ELAVIL* and *TOFRANIL*. These pills are often very small, brightly colored and very potent, but these are good for you, right? After all they treat depression. Wrong, in overdose (just a few tablets or capsules), they can cause coma, seizures, and fatal rhythm irregularities. So keep these and all medications out of the reach of children.

In most situations, however, the amount of tablets or capsules swallowed is not easily known.

When the ingestion of tablets or capsules is involved, the following process is useful if a definite amount cannot be determined.

1) If an over-the-counter product is ingested and the original container is available, the number of tablets or capsules when purchased will be listed on the label. The number previously used and the number remaining can be estimated.

2) For prescription drugs if the original amount cannot be determined, the prescription number and name of the pharmacy will be on the label. Call the pharmacy to get the amount of the original prescription. After the original number has been obtained, you can calculate how many tablets or capsules were to be taken each day and for how many days have they been taken. With both over-the-counter and prescription drugs subtracting the number remaining from the amount estimated to be in the bottle before the poisoning will give the approximate number ingested.

3) Other things to think about regarding tablets and capsules include whether any may have fallen on the floor and whether the child possibly placed them somewhere out of sight. Many times, in haste, parents call a poison center only to find afterward that the drugs in question were simply misplaced. On more than one occasion, a child has fed the medicine to the family pet.

Chemical Eye Injuries

Following an eye splash from a cosmetic, household chemical or medicine, you will be advised to wash the eye as quickly as possible. Time is so important in washing the eye that you should not waste time looking for special solutions, just use tap water. However, it is a good idea to have an eye cup and eye wash solution in several areas of the home for just such an emergency. The poison center will advise you to irrigate injuries for different lengths of time, depending on the chemical involved. Oily, acid, and alkaline chemicals will require a longer time of rinsing. Water washable sprays and chemicals can usually be washed out in a few minutes. You do not want to do more harm than good by irrigating the eye to the point where it is irritated or injured. If simple rinsing does not do the job, you will probably need to be seen in an emergency department. If that is the case, the following will probably happen:

1) An anesthetic will often be used to numb the eye.
2) The doctor or nurse will irrigate the eye by using a large amount of special rinse solution dripped slowly into the eye.
3) A stain solution is used to color the eye so that any injured areas will stand out for the physician to see.
4) The physician may prescribe an antibiotic ointment.
5) A patch will be applied.
6) The physician will set up a specific follow-up with your regular doctor or an ophthalmologist.

Chemical Skin Injuries

1) Drench the skin with water. Use most readily available source (shower, hose, faucet, etc.).
2) Apply a steady stream of water while removing clothing.

3) Irrigate for 3 to 5 minutes for water washable chemicals and for at least 15 minutes for acids, alkalies, and other irritants and corrosives.
4) Any symptoms or signs of irritation that hang on after rinsing should be seen by a doctor. Some chemicals have numbing and deadening properties, like phenol, found in some disinfectants. So do not rely on the absence of pain as an indicator for stopping irrigation with these chemicals. Flush thoroughly for the full length of time the poison center tells you.

Inhaled Chemicals

1) Take whatever steps necessary to get the victim away from the exposure and to provide fresh ventilation. Do not expose yourself to the hazardous chemical!
2) Make sure the victim is breathing.
3) Call for help!

Food Poisoning

Be prepared to answer the following questions:

1) What signs and symptoms are you having; when did they start, how severe are they and for how long have you been ill?
2) What is the suspected food; the method of preparation, and the type of storage?
3) The poison center will use its resources to determine the most likely organism or substance to be responsible.
4) If signs and symptoms are considered to be minimal, they may advise a clear liquid diet with a gradual increase back to a regular diet.
5) If signs and symptoms are moderate to severe, they will refer you to a physician for treatment. Other things could be causing the problem and a physician is the one to decide.

6) Vomiting is not indicated unless a suspected poison has been eaten within a short period of time, usually 1/2 hour to 1 hour.
7) If botulism is highly suspect, you will be referred immediately for medical treatment.
8) The poison center may notify the local health department.

One final note on poisoning. Grandparents should be careful about where they leave their medications. One government survey shows that grandparents' medications, often not kept in child-resistant containers, accounted for almost one out of six cases in which small children swallowed prescription drugs. The findings of the study included information about where the poisonings took place and to whom the medication belonged. Most of the poisonings involving a grandparent's medicine happened when the child was visiting the grandparent, but in some cases, the grandparent lived with or was visiting the child. Poisonings involving a grandparent's medicines can be more dangerous than others. This is because they usually involve some of the more poisonous medications, such as heart drugs, blood pressure medicines and pain relievers. Just because your children are grown and gone does not mean you can let your guard down. Keeping the home poison-proof is a life long job, and could save a life!

22

Respiratory Medicines

Allergies

There are over 30 million Americans in the United States who suffer from **ALLERGIES**. As a matter of fact, some people suffer from allergic reactions and do not even know it. They have symptoms of allergies but either ignore them or blame them on other things, such as a cold or sinus problems. Upset stomachs, frequent headaches, and dry, itchy skin may all be symptoms of allergic reactions.

Allergy is actually an altered or exaggerated immune response. That is, a reaction in our bodies to fight off foreign invaders. When this happens our body releases a substance called **HISTAMINE**. It is this histamine that causes symptoms like itchy, watery eyes, congestion, swelling of the mucous membranes, and rashes. In order to prevent this reaction we take **ANTIHISTAMINES**.

Some products on the market, such as *CHLORTRIMETON* or *DIMETANE*, are straight antihistamines. These products work very well to relieve allergic symptoms. These products have a side effect of drowsiness and sleeplessness, so use them with caution if driving a car or if engaged in some other activity that requires mental alertness. Try to avoid mixing these products with prescription medicines like tranquilizers or sleeping pills. Avoid alcohol since it is a depressant and when combined with antihistamines will cause excessive drowsiness. Antihistamines may have the opposite effect in children and elderly people and cause them to become nervous and overexcited.

Some over-the-counter products, including *ALLEREST MAXIMUM STRENGTH TABLETS*, *ALLEREST 12 HOUR CAPLETS*, *CHLORTRIMETON DECONGESTANT TABLETS*, and *CORICIDIN D DECONGESTANT TABLETS* contain both an **ANTIHISTAMINE** and a

DECONGESTANT. While the antihistamine is working to relieve the itching and runny nose, it may cause the nose to become dry and clogged up; and the decongestant works very well to keep the nasal passages clear.

Some products, aside from having an antihistamine and decongestant in them, also have something for pain, such as **ASPIRIN** or **ACETAMINOPHEN**. Among these are *DRISTAN*, or *SINE-OFF MAXIMUM STRENGTH ALLERGY/SINUS FORMULA*. Other products, such as *SINUTAB MAXIMUM STRENGTH FORMULA*, *MAXIMUM STRENGTH TYLENOL ALLERGY SINUS MEDICATION*, and *SINAREST EXTRA STRENGTH TABLETS*, contain an antihistamine, decongestant, and nonaspirin pain reliever. Since these products all contain a pain reliever, obviously the only people who should take them are those with a headache or pain due to sinus pressure. As one can see, the terminology of these products has gotten very confusing. Usually, the "extra strength" means more pain reliever, but not always. Antihistamines usually found in these products are **CHLORPHENIRAMINE, PHENIRAMINE, BROMPHENIRAMINE**, and **PYRILAMINE**. Common decongestants are **PHENYLPROPANOLAMINE, PHENYLEPHRINE**, **EPHEDRINE**, and **PSEUDOEPHEDRINE**.

It is just a matter of selecting the right product to treat the symptoms, and after that of finding the least expensive one.

Hay Fever

People often develop "colds" in the late summer that seem to hang around forever. Allergies also develop in the spring when the mild temperatures cause the trees and grasses to start pollinating. We sometimes notice allergies after a long winter when we begin working around the yard or cutting the grass. Sneezing is a prominent symptom. If pollen is a cause of the allergy symptoms, many people feel better on rainy days, because the rain washes the pollen out of the air. Generally people suffering from these allergies feel worse during the morning hours. Actually "hay fever," or seasonal **ALLERGIC RHINITIS**, is the most common allergic disease. It is an inflammation of the membrane lining the nose caused by exposure to an allergen at specific times of the year. It is almost never caused by hay and fever is not one of its symptoms.

If someone enjoys working around the yard but does not enjoy the aggravation of sneezing and having **ITCHY, WATERY EYES**, try one of two things. Water plants or grass at night, when they are not pollinating, or wear a pollen mask, which is available at drugstores, to avoid breathing in the pollen.

Two other things that may cause allergic symptoms are mold and mildew, which grow outdoors on dead leaves and wet grass. Indoors, a damp basement, an unvented clothes dryer, and household plants are good places for them to grow. Mold and mildew can cause **NASAL CONGESTION** and even trigger an **ASTHMA ATTACK.** Allergic reactions to mold and mildew are most common in the evening hours, especially on damp evenings. They are not so common during the day because the sun dries the ground and grasses, thereby stopping mold growth.

Other Allergies

Physical contact with certain substances may cause an allergic reaction of the skin. These substances include just about everything and range from the chemicals found in jewelry and cosmetics to those found in detergents. A very common cause of allergic **RASHES** is contact with plants such as poison ivy, poison oak, and poison sumac (see page 331).

Dust, insects, foods, medications, cigarette smoke, animal fur, and feathers can all cause allergies by triggering various types of reactions in our bodies. Allergic reactions can even be fatal. Some appear on the skin in the form of **RASHES** or **HIVES**; some affect the respiratory tract, resulting in **ITCHY, WATERY EYES, SNEEZING**, and **NASAL**

CONGESTION. Many mild forms of allergy can be controlled by avoiding the irritating substance. The use of medicines containing antihistamines or decongestants offer relief from the symptoms. For more severe allergies, a series of desensitizing injections can reduce or even eliminate the allergic reaction.

Asthma

Asthma is a disease of the respiratory system, that system of passageways that carries air from the nose and mouth to the lungs. The chief feature of **ASTHMA** is difficult breathing, often accompanied by a wheeze or whistling sound during exhalation. Asthmatic attacks occur at varying intervals. Between attacks, asthmatics are usually free of respiratory symptoms.

During an asthmatic attack, the lining of the airways becomes congested and swollen and secretes excess mucus, which adds to the obstruction of the air flow. Spasm or constriction (narrowing) of the smooth muscles surrounding the airway leads to further reduction in air flow. Asthma is an over reaction of the respiratory system to any one or a combination of things, mainly

- allergy producing substances (allergens)
- respiratory infections
- emotional stress

Allergic asthma is seen most often in children. When it occurs, usually in the spring and summer, the cause of the allergy, and thus of the asthmatic attacks, is usually pollen or mold. When allergic asthma does not follow a seasonal pattern, it is usually caused by dust, animal dander, food, or drugs.

RESPIRATORY INFECTIONS are responsible for the development of asthmatic attacks in about 40 percent of asthmatics, usually middle aged or older people, although this is also true for many children. This type of asthma may also be seasonal, but often this occurs in winter, when the greatest number of respiratory infections occur.

EMOTIONAL STRESS, and no other detectable reason, appears to be the trigger for about one-third of all asthmatic attacks. In children the start of a new school term, the birth of a brother or sister, or a separation from the parents may be the emotional trigger. In adults, a wide variety of family or job related problems may provoke an attack.

Preventive measures are usually directed toward the specific cause of the asthmatic attacks, for example, eliminating the offending allergen from the environment of the asthmatic. If the cause of asthma is animal dander, get rid of feather or hair stuffed pillows, mattresses, quilts, etc. Occasionally, a family pet may be the cause. If this is so, it may be necessary to find a new home for the bird or animal.

If dust is the offender, there are many ways to make your home as dust free as possible. The center of attention in such cases should be the asthmatic's bedroom. After all, a child spends nearly half their life in the bedroom, while an adult normally passes about one-third of his time there.

Here are some useful suggestions:

- Use smooth, not fuzzy, washable blankets and bedspreads.
- Do not use upholstered furniture.
- Use light, washable cotton or synthetic fiber curtains rather than drapes.
- Use washable cotton throw rugs rather than wall-to-wall carpeting.
- Eliminate stuffed toys.
- Clean the room daily by damp dusting and damp mopping.
- Keep the door closed.

Vacuuming blows a great deal of dust into the air, so do not vacuum in the presence of an asthmatic person Also remember that the chemical irritants in many cleaning products used at home generally cause problems for asthmatics.

If pollen is the offender, an air conditioner with a filter should be installed in the asthmatic's room and sometimes the entire home. Obviously, long walks in the country are unadvisable during high pollen periods. Sometimes it is impossible to get away from an airborne allergen such as pollen. In these cases a physician may try a technique called **DESENSITIZATION**.

If a specific food is the cause, obviously it should not be eaten. Likewise, certain drugs are known to trigger asthmatic attacks in susceptible individuals. Among the most common offenders are aspirin and aspirin-containing compounds.

The following list of do's and do nots should prove very helpful:

- Do not smoke and do not stay in a room with people who do, whether it is at home, at a business, or in a public place.
- Do stay away if your home is being painted. Paint fumes are notorious for provoking asthmatic attacks.
- Do avoid sudden changes of temperature. Do not wander in and out of air conditioned stores on a hot summer's day.
- Do not go outside in extremely cold weather. If you must, a cold weather mask may be helpful.
- Do avoid people with respiratory infections whenever possible.
- Do try to avoid emotionally upsetting situations.
- Do get enough fluid in your diet, six to eight glasses of liquids a day.
- Do not over exert. But do not stay away from all exercise either. Be your own best guide as to how much activity you can tolerate. Schedule frequent rest periods if you know you are going to have a busy day.
- Do not take any prescription medicine without telling a physician. This includes simple remedies you can buy without a prescription. Remember that even aspirin can cause asthma.

- Do take all medications prescribed by a physician exactly as directed.
- Do not take sleeping pills or sedatives if you cannot sleep because of a mild asthma attack. These medications have a tendency to slow down the breathing and make breathing more difficult.
- Avoid inhalation of insecticides, deodorants and cleaning aids, etc.
- If a severe attack develops, get medical help immediately.

Some people who suffer from chronic lung problems like asthma use the portable aerosol products, such as *PRIMATENE MIST* or *BRONKAID MIST*. The active ingredient is **EPINEPHRINE**; which is intended to dilate the bronchioles making it easier to breathe.

There are some other over-the-counter medicines that have been used for years to treat people suffering from asthma. These products differ from the cold remedies in that they contain ingredients to open up the bronchioles. **EPHEDRINE** has been used for a number of years and is found in products like *BRONKAID* and *BRONKOTABS*.

Some products contain an additional ingredient called **THEOPHYLLINE**, which is found in *BRONKAID TABLETS*, *TEDRAL TABLETS* and *BRONKOTABS*. Theophylline causes relaxation of the muscles of the bronchioles. Theophylline and ephedrine can cause excessive stimulation of the central nervous system, which is why some manufacturers have added a sedative, such as phenobarbital to their products. Another main side effect of theophylline is that it causes irritation of the stomach.

Theophylline is still available in these OTC preparations but physicians do not recommend it any more for children and are getting away from recommending it altogether. It has too many side effects, is too difficult to regulate safe blood levels and can be fatal in overdose. Never use any of the OTC asthma products without a physician's specific instructions to do so. We include them here only because they are still available without a prescription. These products should not be used for self-medication of asthma without the specific advice and direction of a physician.

One thing to note about epinephrine, mentioned earlier, is that it is only effective when taken by injection or by inhalation, because it is destroyed by the gastric juices in the stomach. All over-the-counter aerosol products used for asthma contain epinephrine or one of its salt forms, including *ASTHMANEFRIN* (racepinephrine hydrochloride equivalent to 1 percent epinephrine base), *BRONKAID MIST SUSPENSION* (epinephrine bitartrate), and *PRIMATENE MIST SUSPENSION* (epinephrine bitartrate). Overuse of these products can produce side effects such as nervousness, tremors, restlessness, and palpitations. Sometimes people using these products develop a dry mouth and throat. There are many problems with these products. They sometimes cause further irritation to the bronchioles. Epinephrine, the active ingredient in these products, is readily destroyed by light or heat, so if you do use them on a physician's advice, store them in a cool, dark place.

Colds

In life two things are inevitable: taxes and colds. In reality though, a lot of symptoms mimic the common cold, including allergies, discussed above. Although symptoms for the common cold and allergies are similar, they are caused by different things. Nearly every company advertises the "right product to treat your problem"—one reason why cold remedies compose one of the largest areas of the pharmacy. Some of the products that are available contain a number of different ingredients, many of which we do not really need, and some of which can cause further complications. Some cold remedies are claimed to have ingredients to treat twenty cold symptoms. In fact, one of the main ingredients in these products is plain **ASPIRIN**, which will relieve much of the discomfort of a cold all by itself. Remember, however, to avoid aspirin-containing products in children with colds and the flu. See Reye syndrome (page 177).

Before recommending any cold remedy you should ask what are the symptoms: **RUNNY OR STUFFY NOSE, SORE THROAT, COUGH, FEVER, EARACHE**? Answering these questions will help you select the right product.

Also consider the duration of symptoms. Is there a history of allergies or of respiratory diseases such as **ASTHMA** or **BRONCHITIS**? Is there **DIABETES, GLAUCOMA, HEART DISEASE, THYROID** problems present, or **HIGH BLOOD PRESSURE** and use of prescription drugs? Then avoid certain over-the-counter medications. And finally, if a job requires mental alertness, certain over-the-counter medicines should be avoided because they cause drowsiness and may result in an accident or other dangerous situation.

The common cold is a mixture of symptoms affecting the upper respiratory tract. Usually the symptoms are caused by one of many viruses. The intensity of the symptoms may vary from hour to hour. Usually, a cold runs its course and leaves the body as quickly as it came. The only reasonable way to treat a cold is to alleviate the particular symptoms you have.

The common cold has been rated as the single most expensive illness in the United States. In fact, more time is lost from work and school because of the common cold than any other illness. Age is related to the incidence of the common cold. Children from one to five years old are most susceptible. For adults and children we spend approximately $500-700 million a year on over-the-counter cough, cold, and allergy products.

The table below is a list of single ingredient antihistamine and decongestant products that can be targeted to a specific symptom. It is best to stay with single ingredient products. This will avoid drugs that are not necessary and prevent undesirable side effects. The individual ingredients are discussed later in this chapter.

SINGLE INGREDIENT ANTIHISTAMINE PRODUCTS

(To relieve runny nose; watery, burning eyes; and sneezing)

Brompheniramine maleate	**Dimetane**, generics
Chlorpheniramine maleate	**Chlor-Trimeton**, generics
Diphenhydramine hydrochloride	**Benadryl, Nordryl** generics
Phenindamine tartrate	**Nolahist**
Pyrilamine maleate	**Nisaval**, generics
Triprolidine hydrochloride	**Actidil, Myidyl,** generics

SINGLE INGREDIENT DECONGESTANT PRODUCTS

(To relieve stuffy nose; congested head)

l-Desoxyephedrine	**Vicks Inhaler**
Ephedrine	**Vatronol Nose Drops, Ephedron Nasal**
Naphazoline	**Privine**
Oxymetazoline	**Afrin, Duration, Dristan Long Lasting,** generics

Phenylephrine hydrochloride	**Neo-synephrine** (nasal), **Alconefrin** (nasal), **Nostril,** generics
Propylhexadrine	**Benzedrex Inhaler**
Pseudoephedrine	**Sudafed, Novafed, Afrinol,** generics
Phenylpropanolamine	**Propagest, Rhindecon,** generics

Cough

What is a cold without a cough? Actually a cough is a natural reflex of the body to help clear mucus out of the bronchioles. **COUGH SUPPRESSANTS**, also known as **ANTITUSSIVES**, include drugs taken orally (tablets, capsules, and syrups) as well as locally applied medications, such as throat lozenges. Locally applied medicines can also include ointments to be rubbed on the chest or products to be used in a vaporizer. Both **CAMPHOR** and **MENTHOL** may be used in hot steam vaporizers and in ointments applied to the chest for a cough, relieving minor throat irritation. Caution should be exercised when using camphor-containing products, especially around children, as unintentional ingestions may be serious. Also, avoid hot steam vaporizers around children as serious burns have occurred. Drugs taken orally to stop the cough reflex, like **DEXTROMETHORPHAN** and **CODEINE**, act by working on the cough center in the brain. This is not always a good idea, since coughing is productive in bringing phlegm and mucus up from the lower respiratory tract so that it can be spit out or swallowed. But when that cough becomes an unproductive, aggravating tickle in the back of the throat, perhaps interrupting sleep, it is time to do something about it. This can be done in one of two ways. Usually the tickle is due to the throat being dried out from breathing through the mouth. A **COUGH DROP** or even a piece of hard candy will lubricate it and stop the tickle. If there is lot of head congestion, you may want to use a throat drop containing **MENTHOL** and **CAMPHOR**. While the throat drop moistens the throat, the menthol and camphor vapor help unclog the sinuses.

COUGH SYRUPS are more confusing. Many of them contain a mixture of antihistamines and decongestants. Antihistamines may be useful if cough is caused by post nasal drip. However, if you are already recommending a cold tablet, you could be getting a double dose of these drugs, bringing out their more serious side effects. Some cough syrups, such as *NYQUIL*, have alcoholic bases; as a matter of fact, *NYQUIL* is 25 percent alcohol, which makes it 50 proof. There may be reason to be concerned about the effect an alcohol-based cough syrup can have on a recovering alcoholic or others trying to avoid alcohol, such as diabetics. At one time cough products were labeled as either **SYRUPS** or **ELIXIRS**. Syrups had sugar bases, elixirs had alcohol bases. However, this convention is rapidly disappearing. Since either could have extremely dangerous consequences for a diabetic, one must become a label reader. A pharmacist will be able to help recommend a sugarless, nonalcoholic product if necessary.

Some of the cold remedies and hay fever products are available in long-acting forms. The ads for the time-release pills promise continuous relief for eight to twelve hours. But this may not be the case for everyone. No two individuals are alike, and many factors affect a person's ability to absorb medicines, including when they had their last meal. What lasts for one person for eight hours may only work for another for four hours. And if they take more than is recommended, additional problems may result. If the cold continues to get worse even while taking a favorite cold remedy, or a temperature begins, see a doctor for advice. The following ingredients are found in over-the-counter products.

Cough Suppressants

CODEINE PHOSPHATE and **CODEINE SULFATE** are prepared from opium and are very effective cough suppressants. They can be addicting, narcotic drugs and for this reason should not be used for more than a few days. Codeine containing products can be purchased over-the-counter, but in most states are "exempt" narcotics, meaning that you must ask the pharmacist to sell them from behind the counter as well as sign for them. Most physicians agree that when you really want to stop a nonproductive, nighttime cough . . . codeine is what is really needed.

DEXTROMETHORPHAN HYDROBROMIDE is the cough suppressant found in almost every over-the-counter cough formula. It is relatively safe and does not produce most of the side effects, such as drowsiness and stomach upset, that occur with codeine. There are long acting forms of this ingredient. *DELSYM* contains **DEXTROMETHORPHAN POLYSTIREX** and *EXTEND-12* is made with **DEXTROMETHORPHAN RESIN**. One should be careful with the long-acting forms in children because it is easier to give them too much. Pay close attention to the label for directions. They will differ from the regular strength formulas.

DIPHENHYDRAMINE is an antihistamine that has anti-cough activity. It is used in the popular *BENYLIN COUGH SYRUP*. While it is not clear how diphenhydramine works to stop a cough, it apparently works in the cough center of the brain.

GUAIFENESIN is an ingredient found in cough syrups that does not actually stop the cough reflex. In fact, it is not clear what guaifenesin does. Manufacturers claim that guaifenesin is able to clear thinned secretions from the respiratory tract, relieving chest congestion. If guaifenesin was effective in thinning and clearing secretions in the respiratory tract, you would not want to combine it with a cough suppressant. The cough reflex is necessary to eliminate the loosened phlegm. Guaifenesin's days as an OTC active ingredient should be numbered. There is no good evidence that it works as an expectorant, or what is now referred to as a "mucokinetic agent," that is, a drug that clears the respiratory tract of thickened phlegm. Guaifenesin is found in the products *ROBITUSSIN-DM, CHERACOL D*, or *PERTUSSIN COUGH SYRUP FOR CHILDREN*. The important thing to keep in mind, no matter what cough syrup you use, is this: If your cough persists for more than two or three days, check with a doctor. Respiratory infections are not things to be taken lightly.

Antihistamines

The term "antihistamine" is a very broad one describing this group of medicines' specific function in the body. Antihistamines (meaning literally to "oppose histamine") work against, or block, the action of histamine which is found in every body tissue. It is released from the tissues and into our system in allergies, causing **ITCHY**, **WATERY EYES**, **SNEEZING**, **RUNNY NOSE**, even **HIVES**. There is controversy about whether or not it is released during the common cold. Not all cold viruses kill tissue cells, but certainly some cells are killed by certain viruses and histamine is released. Antihistamines therefore prevent or relieve these allergy or cold symptoms. In addition, the traditional antihistamines have side effects that have been used to advantage, such as their drying effect on mucous membranes. Also, drowsiness is a common side effect of antihistamines like **DIPHENHYDRAMINE** and **DOXYLAMINE**. This side effect is taken advantage of in the over-the-counter sleep aid products like *NYTOL WITH DPH* **(DIPHENHYDRAMINE)** and *UNISOM NIGHTTIME SLEEP-AID* **(DOXYLAMINE).** It should be noted that the sedative effect of antihistamines in people is unpredictable and unreliable. Tolerance to the drowsiness can develop in a short time, so the use of antihistamines as sleep medicines is of questionable value, even though it is popular. It can even be dangerous due to unpleasant side effects that may develop, such as dry mouth, blurred vision, agitation, irritability and restlessness.

Since the early 1950s scores of various antihistamines have been available to choose from, most of them offering little or no advantage over each other, until recently. The introduction of **TERFENADINE** *(SELDANE)*, **ASTEMIZOLE** *(HISMANAL)* and **LORATADINE** *(CLARITIN)* represents new breakthroughs in antihistamine chemistry. These antihistamines give allergy sufferers new advantages not possible with the older antihistamines. The new antihistamines do not cause drowsiness, a common side effect of "traditional" antihistamines. Terfenadine is taken twice a day and astemizole only once daily. This is another advantage that makes it more convenient to get relief from symptoms. These three products are only available on prescription right now, but at least one of them may shortly be available over-the-counter. In the meantime, ask your doctor about them if you are not getting the relief expected from over-the-counter products. Some of the antihistamines most commonly found in over-the-counter products used for allergy and cold treatment are listed here:

BROMPHENIRAMINE MALEATE, found in *DIMETANE*, and **CHLORPHENIRAMINE MALEATE**, used in *CHLORTRIMETON*, are antihistamines with no important differences. Both have the advantage of producing minimal drowsiness. Many generic products use these two antihistamines under different product names.

DIPHENHYDRAMINE HYDROCHLORIDE (*BENADRYL* and others) is one of the oldest, most well known antihistamines. It causes more drowsiness than most other antihistamines. In addition to its use in colds and allergies, it has been used for the treatment of motion sickness, as a "sleeping pill," such as *NYTOL* (see page 296) and for Parkinsonism in the elderly (investigational). Diphenhydramine has been shown to have anti-cough activity and is presently used as a non-narcotic cough suppressant when coughs are due to cold or allergy (see page 228). Diphenhydramine can produce unpleasant side effects in addition to drowsiness, such as shakiness and irritability, and in children can produce a paradoxical reaction of hyperactivity and even hallucinations, however this is rare.

DOXYLAMINE SUCCINATE is a synthetic antihistamine more likely to produce a high degree of drowsiness. It is used in over-the-counter sleep aids (page 296). Doxylamine succinate was used in the once popular brand name prescription product, *BENDECTIN*, which was voluntarily withdrawn by the manufacturer due to lagging sales and litigation expenses related to alleged birth defects caused by the drug. However, later studies of women who have used the drug during pregnancy have produced conflicting findings. Some of the more recent studies apparently show that birth defects may not be due to the use of this drug. Its relationship to birth defects is still unclear at this time. In any case, no antihistamine should be used by a pregnant woman.

PHENINDAMINE TARTRATE is not one of the more popular antihistamines, but is still found in the product *NOLAHIST*. It differs a little in its chemistry but has no advantage over any of the more popular antihistamines.

PHENYLTOLOXAMINE CITRATE is an antihistamine included in over-the-counter pain relievers. It has no particular advantage over other similar antihistamines and may be included for its sedative effect. It is wise to avoid products that do not clearly explain why they add certain ingredients.

PYRILAMINE MALEATE is a bitter tasting chemical (which makes it hard to mask the taste in liquids) that produces minimal drowsiness compared to other antihistamines. Strangely enough, it was widely used in OTC sleeping medicines until recently (it is still found in the product *QUIET WORLD*, a combination of **PYRILAMINE MALEATE, ASPIRIN** and **ACETAMINOPHEN** made by Whitehall Labs). The manufacturer's intent was to take advantage of the side effect of drowsiness produced by this antihistamine (however minimal) to enhance sleepfulness.

TRIPROLIDINE HYDROCHLORIDE is found in the popular *ACTIFED* and is a virtually tasteless, white, crystalline powder, which has an advantage when used in liquid medicines. This drug produces minimal drowsiness but otherwise has no particular advantage over other antihistamines.

All these are antihistamines and relieve cold symptoms. But they are best suited for allergies. People who use antihistamines regularly sometimes find that they do not work as well as at first. This is because the presence of some antihistamines in the system causes the liver to produce enzymes at a faster rate to break down the antihistamines. That is, the body develops a tolerance for them.

Antihistamines may cause problems with a cold because they produce a drying effect. If there is congestion the antihistamine thickens and hardens the mucus, making it difficult to clear the upper respiratory passages. That is why many cold remedies contain both an antihistamine and decongestant; as the antihistamine dries, the decongestant keeps the sinuses open.

At recommended doses, most over-the-counter antihistamines are safe for use by children. However, an accidental overdose in children may lead to side effects of excitement and muscle-twitching. The package label should be consulted carefully for dosing instructions.

All of the over-the-counter antihistamines cause drowsiness, but the degree of drowsiness varies with the antihistamine. People should be careful not to combine them with tranquilizers or alcohol, which also cause drowsiness. The combination could be dangerous, especially if you have to operate any type of machinery or if a job requires alertness.

Antihistamines may also interact with birth control pills, because antihistamines cause the body to produce enzymes that break down certain chemicals in the body. One of the ingredients in birth control pills is a female hormone called **ESTRADIOL**, which is affected by the enzymes produced by antihistamines, causing the pill to be less effective. You may develop unusual bleeding or spotting; it may even cause frequent or irregular periods.

The point is, when just starting to take birth control pills, or after taking them for a while, watch for changes in the monthly cycle. It may be necessary to use a stronger birth control pill to counter the effects of the antihistamine, especially if they are used frequently.

Other common side effects of antihistamines are dry mouth, blurred vision, and urinary problems. People with **GLAUCOMA** should also try to avoid antihistamines, or use them under a doctor's supervision.

If you suffer from allergic reactions to plants, such as poison ivy, or insect bites, oral antihistamines will help relieve the itching and discomfort caused by these things. Some topical treatments for itching contain antihistamines, but since absorption is poor through the skin, you will find that oral products like *CHLORTRIMETON* and *DIMETANE* work much better.

Decongestants

Decongestants are probably the most useful ingredients in over-the-counter cold remedies. These products narrow or constrict the blood vessels, which in turn opens up the sinuses, so that we can breathe more easily. All of the drugs used as decongestants are similar as chemicals or in the way they act in the body. Popular decongestant drugs have some stimulant effects, and many drugs presently used as stimulants, for various reasons, were discovered while researchers looked for decongestants to treat the common cold.

Many products contain decongestants along with antihistamines or pain relievers; however, some products, like *SUDAFED* **(PSEUDOEPHEDRINE HYDROCHLORIDE)**, are just straight decongestants (see table on page 225).

There are several side effects of decongestants: Decongestants stimulate the central nervous system, which may result in sleeplessness. This side effect often helps offset the drowsiness caused by antihistamines. Because they make blood vessels smaller and stimulate the heart, decongestants may aggravate high blood pressure and cause the heart to race and beat irregularly. So be careful when using products containing these ingredients. Even though they can be purchased without a prescription, they should not be used if you experience any of these side effects. Check with a doctor about a safe alternative. The **DECONGESTANTS** listed below are commonly found in decongestant medicines.

EPHEDRINE, an oily feeling and almost colorless solid, occurs naturally in the plant Ma Huang, (Ma = astringent, Huang = yellow) from China. It can also be made artificially. **EPHEDRINE SULFATE** is a salt of the plant derivative ephedrine which occurs as a fine, white powder. It is used as an oral drug and a nasal decongestant in a solution or jelly. It should be used cautiously as it can cause central nervous system stimulation and should not be taken by people with high blood pressure. Ephedrine is effective in clearing the bronchioles to allow one to breathe easier. However, tolerance to the drug develops with frequently repeated doses, causing the body to need more and more of the drug in order for it to work properly. Overuse of products with ephedrine in them can cause nervousness, tremors, and insomnia. They can also cause the heart to speed up and even elevate the blood pressure. Products with ephedrine are slow in taking effect, but act for a long period of time. These products are mainly useful to people who have milder forms of asthma. Since they can affect sugar levels in the bloodstream, diabetics should monitor their urine sugar levels closely. Caution is advised for older male patients with prostate problems, because urinary retention may occur.

PHENYLEPHRINE HYDROCHLORIDE, the ingredient of *NEO-SYNEPHRINE*, is a drug used as a water solution in nose and eye decongestant medicines and as an oral decongestant. It is chemically similar to the body's own adrenalin and produces a similar but lessened effect to shrink mucous membranes in the nasal area in the treatment of colds and allergies. Phenylephrine is more popular for application to mucous membranes because it is not absorbed well from the stomach when its used by mouth.

PHENYLPROPANOLAMINE HYDROCHLORIDE or **PPA**, or **PROPADRINE**, is widely used as one of the most popular oral decongestant drugs. PPA has also been approved for use as an appetite suppressant and is the primary OTC drug used for this purpose.

PSEUDOEPHEDRINE HYDROCHLORIDE meaning "false" ephedrine, is a close chemical relative of **EPHEDRINE**. Like ephedrine, it occurs in plants of the genus Ephedra. It is an effective decongestant when taken orally but it may elevate blood pressure by causing blood vessels to become smaller. In sensitive individuals it may also cause insomnia, particularly if is taken in the form of the popular time-release preparation (such as *SUDAFED SA*).

Nasal Sprays, Drops, and Jellies

Reddened eyes and stuffy nasal passages are usually due to enlarged, irritated and inflamed blood vessels in these tissues. The common cold and allergies are the biggest culprits. Topical (meaning applied directly to the area) decongestants are available as drops, sprays, jellies, or inhaled vapors. They contain many of the same ingredients as the oral products but are applied directly into the nose or the eyes. Topically applied medicines used in the nose and eyes as decongestants work because they are able to shrink, or constrict, blood vessels on contact. They work well; after spraying, the nose opens up and we breathe freely. However, there is a danger because they work so well, one may begin using them all the time.

This tendency to get "hooked" on decongestant nose sprays is called **NASAL REBOUND** or **REBOUND CONGESTION** by doctors. In 1948 Clifford Lake, a physician on the staff of the Mayo Clinic, first described this condition. It occurs after using certain topical nasal decongestants. In rebound the nasal mucous membranes become even more congested as the drug's effect of narrowing the blood vessels wears off. It is not clear even to this day why this phenomenon occurs, but a couple of theories do exist. Some have argued that rebound happens because the chemicals in the decongestants themselves are irritating. However, while this may make the condition worse, it probably does not cause it. Another more acceptable theory is that while the decongestants narrow the blood vessels, they also starve the tissues of oxygen and thus cause the vessels to become fatigued and to lose tone. This causes the vessels to expand later, causing even worsened congestion. Continuing use of the drug will still shrink the vessels at first, but will not work as well. More and more it will be followed by an increase in the widening of the vessels to cause even greater nasal blockage. This finally forces one to seek a physician's help. If you have rebound congestion, you must stop using the decongestant immediately. You may find this very difficult. Some physicians have found it necessary to use steroids and sedatives to withdraw a patient from topical decongestant drugs. Rebound can be avoided if these drugs are not used for more than 3 days. Complications from the continued use of topical nasal decongestants could eventually lead to inflamed sinuses and even nasal polyps.

Excessive use of nose sprays also causes the nose to bleed

more easily. Their advantage is that, since they are not taken orally, they do not cause an increase in blood pressure and are less likely to produce jitteriness and other unpleasant side effects.

If someone has a bad cold and is taking a decongestant tablet but needs additional relief, it is reasonable to use a nose spray. However, it should not be used for more than three days; by then the cold should be better anyway.

Short Acting Nasal Decongestants

The short acting topical decongestants are **EPHEDRINE**, **EPINEPHRINE**, and **PHENYLEPHRINE**. They may be used every 3 to 4 hours as nose and eye medicines.

EPHEDRINE is an oily feeling, almost colorless solid which occurs naturally in the plant known as Ma Huang (*Ephedra sinica*). In Chinese characters "Ma" means astringent and "Huang" means yellow, probably referring to the taste and color of the drug. It has been used as a medicine in China for more than 5000 years. It is native to the southern coast of China and parts of the Middle East. It can be prepared synthetically. The salt, **EPHEDRINE SULFATE**, is a fine, white powder and is used as a decongestant in water solution or jelly form applied directly to the mucous membranes of the nose. It may be used every 4 hours for not more than 3 consecutive days. The drug causes blood vessels to constrict thus opening surrounding airways to allow the passage of air for normal breathing. **EPHEDRINE** is still used in *VICKS VATRONOL* in combination with cedarleaf oil and nutmeg oil. While this particular product contains an almost insignificant amount of oil (which is used only for proprietary reasons), the use of oil containing preparations in the nose is dangerous and should absolutely be avoided by very young and very old patients because of the danger of a what is known as "lipoid pneumonia." This can occur with long term use of oily medicines in the nose or mouth. They can eventually get into the lungs and cause a chronic pneumonialike condition.

Ephedrine is safe when used as directed on the label, but stay away from oily products. Overuse can cause effects to persist for some time and accumulate to cause increased heart rate and stimulation of the nervous system leading to restlessness, anxiety and sleeplessness. It should not be used in children under 6 years of age because absorption from mucous membranes into the body leads to similar effects of poisoning in children.

EPINEPHRINE or **ADRENALIN** is the principal stimulant hormone produced by the adrenal gland in most animals and man. It is important historically because it was the first hormone to be chemically copied in the laboratory. Thus, at first it was obtained from the adrenal glands of animals raised for food. Although synthetic epinephrine became available soon after the chemical structure had been discovered, the synthetic form was not widely used in medicine because the natural form was 15 times more active. With the increasing cost of animal by-products, it has become economically worthwhile to develop a method for synthetic manufacture of epinephrine. In the pure state the chemical forms white crystals that brown easily on exposure to air. **EPINEPHRINE** and several of its salts are approved as over-the-counter bronchodilators for use in asthma, such as *PRIMATENE MIST* and *BRONKAID MIST*, but only **EPINEPHRINE HYDROCHLORIDE** (*ADRENALIN CHLORIDE*, PARKE DAVIS) is approved for use in the nose and eyes as a decongestant. It is used in a very diluted solution of 1:1000 for this purpose, applied as drops or spray, or with a sterile swab in the nose, as required. This chemical has the same narrowing, or shrinking, effect on blood vessels as do all drugs in this group.

Never use epinephrine in the eyes while wearing soft contact lenses; discoloration of the lenses may occur. Epinephrine may cause temporary blurred vision when put directly in the eye. Patients should observe caution while driving, using machinery or performing other hazardous tasks.

PHENYLEPHRINE HYDROCHLORIDE is a popular ingredient in over-the-counter nasal drops and sprays, like *NEO-SYNEPHRINE*, for short term use as a decongestant. This is because the action on mucous membranes is of very short duration, and it has a good safety record. It is also used in eye drops to relieve congestion, itching and minor irritation and to "whiten" the eye ("get the red out"). Phenylephrine is available over-the-counter as a topical nasal decongestant in percentages ranging from 0.125 percent to 1 percent for the purpose of providing a dosage form for all age groups.

Phenylephrine is recommended in over-the-counter packaged products for children 2 years of age and older. Children under the age of 5 are likely to swallow some medication that is put into the nose by drops or spray. Accidental ingestion of small amounts of phenylephrine in this manner are not likely to produce toxicity by absorption into the blood stream, since it does not get absorbed well from the stomach. The danger of topically applied decongestants in infants is not always recognized, even by physicians. For example, phenylephrine is recommended in pediatric medical text books for application into the nostrils of infants under one year of age, but at least one case of potentially life-threatening nasal obstruction resulting from rebound congestion in a two-week-old infant has been reported. They should not be used in infants unless specifically prescribed by a physician for limited use over not longer than a day. (**SALINE NOSE DROPS** and **SUCTION** is a safer alternative). Phenylephrine as a 10 percent solution for the eyes has been associated with severe reactions following application into the eye. These have included extreme rises in blood pressure, heart irregularities and even episodes of bleeding in the brain. However, these are rare and most applications into the eye are safe if the strict instructions of a doctor are followed.

Long Acting Nasal Decongestants

Long acting decongestants are drugs that are chemically different from the shorter acting ones mentioned above. They affect both blood vessels which are thought to regulate blood flow to the mucous membranes as well as blood content of the membrane tissues of the nose, throat and sinuses. This double whammy effect is thought to be responsible for the extended duration of these chemicals. All four of the long acting decongestants listed here are in the same chemical class, therefore they share similar toxic effects. These drugs can produce profound side effects on the entire body if absorbed into the bloodstream from mucous membranes, particularly in children. Large doses of these long acting decongestants, even when applied only to the eye and nose, may have the whole body effects seen with similar drugs taken by mouth. For example, a similar drug in this class, **CLONIDINE**, was originally investigated for use as a nasal decongestant but was found to have significant blood pressure lowering activity. It is now marketed as a very effective prescription blood pressure drug.

NAPHAZOLINE HYDROCHLORIDE is found in *PRIVINE NASAL SPRAY* and also used in eye solutions as a decongestant. It has been evaluated by the FDA as a safe and effective product for use in treating the symptoms of the common cold and allergy. Naphazoline has been reported to cause drowsiness following use in the nose due to absorption into the bloodstream from the mucous membranes in some individuals. Dependence in adults and dangerous reactions of drowsiness and coma in children have been reported with naphazoline. It should not be used in children under 6 years of age or for longer than 3 days in older persons.

OXYMETAZOLINE HYDROCHLORIDE is popular as *AFRIN NASAL SPRAY*, the drug dissolved in water for use as a nasal decongestant. It is most popularly used in the nasal decongestants advertised as "long acting" because the effect persists over a 10 to 12 hour period.

Both "rebound" congestion, a worsening of congestion characterized by chronic redness, swelling and inflamed nasal passages, described above; and chronic irritation of nasal passages have been reported with prolonged use of oxymetazoline hydrochloride. It may also cause systemic effects such as high blood pressure, nervousness, insomnia and heart palpitation, but these are rare. It should not be used in children under 6 years of age since excessive drowsiness has been reported from swallowing the liquid that trickles down the throat when used in the nose. A case in the medical literature reports repeated use of oxymetazoline in the form of a nasal spray by a 20-year-old woman with an uncomplicated pregnancy which caused changes in the heart rate of the fetus. This use of oxymetazoline by a pregnant woman apparently resulted in constriction of blood vessels in the uterus, decreasing blood supply to the baby and resulting in the heart irregularities.

TETRAHYDROZOLINE is another ingredient used as a nasal decongestant and an eye drop to relieve redness and congestion. It is fairly long acting and is related to oxymetazoline (above). It is considered safe and effective by the FDA but is available OTC only for use in the eyes, such as *VISINE ORIGINAL FORMULA.* Nasal drops and sprays, such as *TYZINE*, are available only on prescription. Tetrahydrozoline has been reported by many poison centers to be a particular problem following accidental swallowing by children under the age of five. The drug causes mild drowsiness to profound coma with a fall in blood pressure. For this reason, it should never be used in children under six years of age and with caution even in older children. The drug is available only as eye drops over-the-counter. Tetrahydrozoline used as nose drops is available only on prescription because when excess solution trickles down the throat and is swallowed following application into the nose it has too much potential to cause serious side effects of drowsiness and lowered blood pressure in adults and children.

XYLOMETAZOLINE HYDROCHLORIDE is used in water solutions to relieve nasal congestion. It is promoted as a long acting decongestant which will relieve symptoms all day long. While it is considered safe and effective by the FDA the advantage over similar drugs, like oxymetazoline (see above), is not clear. Use in children under six may cause drowsiness and if accidentally swallowed can produce serious side effects of drowsiness and lowered blood pressure symptoms in relatively small amounts.

Decongestant Nasal Inhalers

In mankind's age old battle against the "runny nose" and nasal congestion, Smith, Kline & French Co. introduced the Benzedrine nasal inhaler in 1932. Made with amphetamine, when inhaled through the nose this chemical provided a potent blood vessel narrowing effect that produced shrinking of congested nasal mucous membranes. Because of its stimulating effect, the abuse of amphetamine that was to follow is now regrettable history. The existing inhalers contain chemical derivatives of amphetamine that still have the decongestant properties but are many times less likely to cause stimulation and have much less, if any, abuse potential.

DESOXYEPHEDRINE (l-DESOXYEPHEDRINE) or **LEVOMETHAMPHETAMINE** is the active ingredient in the *VICKS INHALER* used for nasal decongestion. The *VICKS INHALER* remains the only source of levomethamphetamine available in over-the-counter medicines. A crystalline substance with a bitter taste, it has occasionally been used by drug abusers who extract the amphetamine-like substance from the inhaler, concentrate and inject it intravenously. Thus its safety in over-the-counter preparations has been challenged. The Drug Enforcement Administration has gone on record stating that no national abuse of levomethamphetamine exists. As long as no hard evidence exists to challenge its designation as a nonprescription drug, it will remain available over-the-counter, according to the

U.S. Food and Drug Administration. The FDA OTC panel on Cold, Cough, Allergy, Bronchodilator, and Antiasthmatic Drug Products found that inhalers produce little or no significant blood vessel constricting side effects. This means that the FDA will not require warnings about using them with heart disease, high blood pressure, thyroid disease, diabetes or difficulty in urination due to enlargement of the prostate gland. The use of **l-DESOXYEPHEDRINE** as a topical nasal decongestant should be limited to not more than 7 days. The FDA has concluded that this drug when inhaled through the nose does not cause rebound congestion within a 7 day period.

PROPYLHEXEDRINE is a synthetic, clear liquid chemical related to amphetamine. It is used in the *BENZEDREX INHALER*, available from Smith Kline Consumer Products, as a decongestant. The drug is sealed in a fibrous material with other "aromatic" ingredients and inhaled through an inhaler cylinder. Introduced by Smith, Kline & French in 1949, they substituted it for amphetamine in the Benzedrine inhaler, reporting that propylhexedrine was an effective vessel constrictor (making blood vessels narrower) possessing only 1/12th the central nervous system stimulatory effect of amphetamine. The effect on mucous membranes is short, about 2 hours. Because the early inhaler actually contained amphetamine, it has had a long history of abuse, although the actual number of problems with this drug have been few. Propylhexedrine has far less stimulant activity than amphetamine. Nonetheless, the chemical has been extracted from the inhaler and injected by drug abusers, several times resulting in death from overdose and related side effects. In one study, the FDA acknowledges 21 cases of adverse reactions occurring over a 12-year period. All deaths known to have occurred with propylhexedrine occurred among individuals who had a history of drug abuse and knowingly abused the drug. The few isolated reports on the abuse of propylhexedrine do not indicate a widespread problem.

The FDA believes that propylhexedrine should continue to be available as an inhalant nasal decongestant because it is safe and effective when used as instructed in the package labeling.

Cool-Air Humidifiers

Another way to cope with a cold is to use a cool-air humidifier. However, caution is required because humidifiers may increase the presence of mold and mites. This may worsen the condition of people with asthma. Cool-air humidifiers may be useful even if you do not have a cold. Often times, especially during the cooler months when the heat is on, you may wake up in the morning with your nose and throat all dried out. This creates an environment receptive to viruses, which in turn causes colds.

When people go to a drugstore to buy a humidifier, they often are confused by all the different types. Remember that all cool-air humidifiers work the same way; the only difference is in the amount of water they hold, which in turn determines how long the unit will work without being refilled. If you use a cool-air humidifier, change the water each time you use it to avoid having mold develop. Also be sure to clean the humidifier periodically because the chemicals that are in the water can build up in the humidifier and hamper its performance.

Steam Vaporizers

Around the turn of the century, it was not uncommon in any home where a person was suffering from a respiratory disease, such as a cold or flu, to heat a pot or kettle of water with eucalyptus leaves in it. A towel was then placed over the pot and the vapors breathed in. The eucalyptus vapors helped open the sinuses. Later on companies came out with a more sophisticated form of this old folk remedy, which was called a "vaporizer" and it was electric. No longer was the water heated on a stove. The leaves were replaced by patented products, such as *KAS* (**EUCALYPTUS OIL, PEPPERMINT OIL, MENTHOL** and **CAMPHOR**), *VICKS VAPO STEAM* (**MENTHOL, CAMPHOR, EUCALYPTUS OIL, CEDARLEAF OIL** and **NUTMEG OIL**) and *VAPORIZER-IN-A-BOTTLE* (**CAMPHOR, MENTHOL** and **EUCALYPTUS OIL**), that you can now buy in a drugstore. But there was a potential hazard of a child or adult pulling over the vaporizer and causing a severe burn, or accidental poisoning if a child drank the vaporizer fluid. Hot air vaporizers are still being sold in drugstores, but they are a lot safer nowadays because they are available in units that cannot spill, even if they are accidentally knocked over. But the steam still can be dangerous to a small child or infant. Steam vaporizers are mainly used by adults in order to keep their noses open by breathing in inhalants. However, many doctors prefer the cool-air vaporizers. The moist cool air keeps the nose and throat passages coated so that mucus does not accumulate in one area, causing irritation.

Fever

FEVER is a rise of body temperature above normal. If you look carefully, most **THERMOMETERS** have an arrow pointing to the mark for **98.6**, for this is the normal oral temperature, measured on the Fahrenheit scale.

Since everyone is different, normal temperatures will vary; some children will have a slightly higher normal temperature, and some slightly lower. Oral temperatures range from 97.7 to 99.5°F. It is also important to know that the body temperature of a healthy child is continually changing, going up a little or down a little, depending on the time of day and the activity of the child.

However, when your child's temperature reaches 101°F. or more, it is probably due to illness. This does not mean that you should ignore temperatures lower than 101°F. A persistent low-grade fever or when a child's temperature is continually a degree or two above normal, may also indicate the presence of illness and the need for the advice of a physician. Here are some signs that will tell you when to take a child's temperature:

- Skin: hot, dry, excess sweating, rash
- Complexion: very pale or unusually flushed
- Cold Symptoms: runny nose, sneezing or coughing, hoarseness

It is also a good idea to check body temperature if the child tells you he or she does not feel well.

Taking a child's temperature is usually a lot easier said than done. There are two basic types of conventional glass thermometers, **ORAL** and **RECTAL**. The only difference is in the shape of the bulb on the end of each thermometer. The one on the rectal thermometer is round or oval. The bulb on the oral thermometer is slim and long. The markings on the two thermometers are the same.

RECTAL THERMOMETERS are most often recommended for infants. Apply a little *VASELINE* to the bulb end, then insert it into the **RECTUM** about one-third of its length. It should move easily; never force a thermometer. Hold the thermometer in the rectum for about two or three minutes, then gently pull it out. Wipe off the thermometer with a tissue. In good light, slowly rotate the thermometer until you see the mercury. The normal temperature rectally is **99.6°F**. After you have read the thermometer, wash it with cold or lukewarm, soapy water, wipe it with alcohol, and put it away in its container. Never use hot water.

When the child is one year or older, it is better to take the temperature with either type of thermometer in the **ARMPIT**, unless your doctor tells you otherwise. Place the bulb of the thermometer securely in the child's armpit and hold his arm across his chest. Allow the thermometer to remain there for three to four minutes. The normal temperature under the arm is **97.6°F**. If you call a doctor when a child is sick, always tell him or her not only what the child's temperature is, but also the way you took it, orally, rectally, or under the arm (axillary).

Nowadays there are easier ways to take a child's temperature. Instead of a thermometer, there are small **PATCHES** that can be attached to the child's forehead. They contain heat-sensitive colored crystals and, as the temperature changes, a different color shows up in the form of a number. A product that is available in the drugstore and that works in this way is called *DIGITEMP*. The advantage of using these products, besides avoiding the wrestling act with the kids, is that once you stick it to the child's head, you can leave it there as long as she or he is ill. It will give a constant read-out of the body temperature.

DIGITAL THERMOMETERS are also a very convenient way to get a quick, accurate temperature usually in less than a minute. This is important when your child is already uncomfortable from illness and has trouble cooperating. These are as accurate as glass thermometers and more accurate than the stick-on type. The price has come down on these electronic devices and they are available in drugstores for only six or seven dollars.

So if you have trouble taking your child's temperature, try using one of the digital thermometers. We think you will find them very useful. They are quite accurate and many hospitals are starting to use these kinds of fever thermometers.

Fever in itself is usually not dangerous, as long as it is not extremely high and lost body water is adequately replaced. In many instances, the best thing you can do for your child with a fever is to keep him cool. Here is how you can do this:

- Keep the child undressed in the house; the fewer the clothes, the faster the fever will go down.
- Do not cover the child with blankets or quilts in bed.
- Give lots of cool, clear liquids to the child. Do not give milk! Milk often upsets the stomach of a child with a fever.

- Give popsicles, ice water, sherbet or carbonated beverages.
- Give cool sponge baths. (If temperature is over 102°F set your child in a tub of tepid water.) Do not use alcohol. Sponge or pour water over the back and front for at least a half hour. Do not use cold water. It is best to administer a fever reducer such as **ACETAMINOPHEN** before sponging the child. The fever will be reduced more easily in this manner.
- Do not give the child an enema for fever. Enemas should be given only on a physician's orders.

You wouldn't think that taking a person's temperature is all that complicated. But you should consider these things when taking a body temperature. Dignity of the patient (rectal thermometers), contraindications (tissue injury in the mouth or throat), the potential for injury (bowel perforation), mouth breathing, uncooperative patient, complexity of thermometer operation, temperature recording time and the risk of infection from exposure to body fluids. All of these reasons are why the **TYMPANIC THERMOMETER** was developed for home use.

Studies for a long time have shown that the core body temperature is accurately determined by touching a heat sensor to the eardrum. The accuracy of this method is because of the eardrum's closeness to the body's temperature regulating gland in the head, the hypothalamus (providing the "core" temperature), and the carotid artery where both the eardrum and the hypothalamus get their blood supply.

However, when someone is sick at home, you can't stick a thermometer on their eardrum to measure their temperature (it is done with special thermometers during some types of surgery, but the patient is under anesthesia). Technological advances now make it possible to estimate the eardrum temperature by measurement of infrared emissions from the eardrum.

The infrared emission detection (or IRED) ear thermometer enables measurement of the eardrum temperature without directly contacting the eardrum. The thermometer is placed in the ear, like a doctor's otoscope and instantly measures the heat coming from the eardrum and ear canal. The IRED ear thermometer resembles a camera, it has a shutter, a reflective barrel (in place of a camera lens) and a passive infrared detector (in place of film). The thermometer takes a "picture" of the heat radiated and displays the temperature in only a second or two. The design and operation of IRED ear thermometers vary. Some IRED ear thermometers will convert the temperature of the ear to oral or rectal temperature equivalents. This is so you can report it to someone, like your family doctor, in a way they are used to measuring it. In the future, as we become accustomed to what a normal ear temperature is, this conversion will not be necessary.

The first available IRED ear thermometers were not reported as reliable in measuring temperature in infants and children under three years of age. This age group still needs more study until a recommendation can be made for home use. The newest devices do seem reliable in older children and adults. IRED ear thermometers offer the advantage of convenience, little patient cooperation, shorter time for measurement, less exposure to infectious body fluids when compared to glass or digital thermometers and no risk of mercury contamination or broken glass as sometimes occurs with glass thermometers. The downside of tympanic thermometers at present is their cost, around $100. If they become popular, you can expect the price to come down, just like it did with digital thermometers for use in the home.

IRED ear thermometers are a useful addition to the home arsenal of health care products. Some brand names are *FIRST-TEMP*, *GENIUS 3000A* and *THERMOSCAN PRO-1*.

23

Shampoos & Hair Products

SHAMPOOS and **CONDITIONERS** probably comprise the largest market in this group of items, both in consumer demand and economically. The first shampoos were based on true soaps until the mid 1940s when they began to be replaced by synthetic detergents. The basic ingredient in shampoos is the cleaning agent, a **DETERGENT** or **"SURFACTANT."** After all, the primary function of a shampoo is to clean the hair and scalp. Most detergents used in the manufacture of shampoos are synthetic and are derived from petroleum chemicals.

Normally the hair is 5 percent by weight "soil." Shampoos generally remove 80 percent or reduce the oily surface deposit on the hair to not more than 1 percent of its total weight. Levels higher than this may be objectionable. In addition to cleaning, added functions of shampoos include lubrication, conditioning (decreasing friction to improve the way the hair lays), body building (stiffening the hair fiber), prevention of static charge buildup, medication, and so on.

The shampoo section of the drugstore has grown by leaps and bounds. As a matter of fact, there are so many products available that you are likely to see not only shelves, but also baskets and barrels full of shampoos. These products all work to clean the hair.

Some shampoos say they make the hair shiny, others say they make it more manageable, and they all claim to make you beautiful. Many shampoos are "pH-balanced." But most people do not really know what that means. pH is the measurement of how acidic or alkaline a given thing is. Our skins, hair, scalps, and fingernails are all on the acid side. So you can run into real problems by using shampoos that have soapy bases. Soap is very alkaline. If you do not rinse it all off the scalp, you will get a build-up of alkalinity on the hair. Those deposits of alkalinity can eventually smother and destroy the hair follicle itself.

Therefore, it is probably a good idea to buy a **pH BALANCED SHAMPOO**, since it can actually work in harmony with the skin. Even if you fail to wash it completely out of your hair, you will not have serious problems. Pick the one that best suits your pocketbook, since most of the pH-balanced shampoos work in the same way.

Another group of shampoos are those containing **PROTEIN** and **CONDITIONERS**. These types of shampoos are generally good for the hair, but some people benefit more than others. You are likely to benefit if you are out in the sun a lot, because the sun bleaches the hair fibers and makes them brittle. If you have a job where chemicals or dust are in the air, these factors may damage the hair. If you have tinted or bleached hair, the natural protein may be stripped out of your hair. In these conditions, it may be best to use a shampoo with protein in it, to replace the protein in your hair. However, be very careful when choosing such a shampoo. Some do not work as well as others. Look for one containing **HYDROLYZED ANIMAL PROTEIN.** Protein from other sources does not do much for the hair. **CONDITIONERS** work hand-in-hand with the protein in shampoos. Because the conditioners work by coating the hair fibers, they prevent the hair from losing protein and moisture. They also give the hair more body and luster.

Some people prefer the use of a separate conditioner. **CONDITIONERS** are usually based on a **CATIONIC DETERGENT** and a fatty material. They are intended to make the hair more lustrous, easy to comb and free from static electricity when dry.

Most shampoo and conditioner formulations employ chemicals of very low toxicity, since daily use is anticipated, and the complete shampoo formulation must be medically safe for long term use.

Other personal cleansers include products for "problem skin" (see Chapter 25) and bath preparations (see Chapter 24).

Shampoo and Conditioner Ingredients

ALKYL DIMETHYL AMINE OXIDES, such as **COCAMINE, LAURAMINE, MYRISTAMINE, CETAMINE** and **STEARAMINE OXIDE**, are synthetic, water soluble wetting agents used as foam boosters and stabilizers in shampoos. Exerting mild detergency, they help to control thickness and flow of the final product. Most are pale yellow liquids in the concentrations used to formulate shampoos. These low toxicity, nonionic surfactants are compatible with most cosmetic ingredients and have not been reported to cause allergic dermatitis when used daily. At concentrations of use, they are completely harmless and non-irritating to skin.

AMMONIUM LAURETH SULFATE or **AMMONIUM LAURYL ETHER SULFATE (ALES)** is a synthetic, anionic surfactant or detergent that is considered mild and popular in shampoo formulations as a foaming and cleansing agent. Made from petroleum synthetic and inorganic chemicals, it is a thick, yellow or colorless liquid. **ALES** has not been reported to cause any adverse health effects when used in shampoo formulations. It is not an allergic sensitizer, nor a skin irritant in the concentrations used in shampoos.

AMMONIUM LAURYL SULFATE (ALS) is a synthetic, anionic detergent used in shampoos that are on the acid side, since ammonia would be liberated if the pH becomes alkaline. For formulation purposes, it is a colorless, clear liquid. It is an excellent foaming agent. This surfactant has been one of the industry standards since after World War II. It has a good safety record and is not known to produce adverse effects or allergic reactions when used daily.

AMMONIUM NONOXYNOL-4 SULFATE is a clear liquid used infrequently in shampoo formulations as a dispersing and wetting agent. It is added to make shampoos opaque. At shampoo concentrations it is not irritant and it has not been reported to cause allergic reactions.

AMMONIUM OLEATE is a yellowish-brown paste soap of low toxicity. It is not known to produce any allergic or toxic effects when used frequently.

AMPHOTERIC-2 is a yellow, synthetic, liquid surfactant used as a mild foaming and cleansing agent and conditioner. It is nontoxic and nonirritating to skin and eyes.

BENZALKONIUM CHLORIDE or *ZEPHIRAN* is a detergent that has many uses in products ranging from shampoos to contact lens solutions. Depending on the concentration, it can be used as a disinfectant, a preservative, or it can give special spreading qualities to shampoos. While it is not dangerous in most of these products due to the low concentration, it is extremely poisonous by ingestion in higher concentrations. It is corrosive to mucous membranes in concentrations greater than 10 percent, although severe irritation has been reported in the eyes at lesser concentrations. It has been reported to cause contact allergy in sensitive people.

BENZETHONIUM CHLORIDE or **HYAMINE 1622** is a colorless, odorless crystalline chemical made synthetically and is a cationic detergent. In its concentrated form it is extremely poisonous, but at concentrations of use as an antiseptic and preservative it is relatively safe. There may be cross sensitivity to this chemical from other similar cationic detergents, such as benzalkonium chloride (see above).

CETEARETH 5 is a white, waxy solid that is made from some naturally occurring fatty acid products and petroleum derived chemicals. It is a nonionic surfactant not reported to produce contact allergy. It serves as a thickener, opacifier and conditioner in shampoos, and is virtually nontoxic and nonirritating to skin and eyes.

CETEARETH 20 is a nonionic surfactant that has not been reported to cause contact allergy. This ingredient nas good foaming and cleansing properties. It is nontoxic and nonirritating to skin and eyes.

CETRIMONIUM BROMIDE or **CETAVLON** or **CETRIMIDE** is a synthetic, cationic detergent that has been reported to produce contact allergy. It is used in shampoos and other cosmetics as a preservative in very low concentrations. It is very poisonous in concentrated form, but reasonably safe at concentrations of use.

CHOLETH 24 is a pale yellow, waxy solid nonionic detergent not known to produce contact allergy. It is made synthetically from lanolin and contains about 25 percent cholesterol, making a useful ingredient in conditioning shampoos. It is used instead of cholesterol because it is cheaper. It is nontoxic in concentrations of use and is not irritating to skin or eyes.

COCAMIDE DIETHANOLAMINE or **COCAMIDE DEA** is a clear, pale, yellow liquid with a peculiar odor. It is a nonionic surfactant which is made by reacting a mixture of acids and coconut oil. It has been reported to produce contact allergy. This ingredient will stabilize the foam of most shampoos and greatly improve performance in the presence of sebum (body oil).

COCAMIDOPROPYL BETAINE or **LONZAINE** is a clear, pale yellow, thin liquid and a mild conditioning detergent which is added to shampoos to counteract the defatting action of other surfactants, that is, it tends to reduce the potential for skin irritation. It has the ability to thicken mildly acid formulations and it has become popular because it adds more than just detergency to a shampoo formulation, thus being a multi-functional ingredient. It is particularly mild regarding eye irritation and is nontoxic at concentrations of use in shampoos.

COCAMIDOPROPYL SULTAINE and **COCAMIDOPROPYL HYDROXY SULTAINE** are clear, synthetic amber liquids that are water soluble wetting agents which thicken certain shampoos. They are made synthetically from coconut oil derivatives and sulfur compounds. They have high tolerance for other ingredients, tending not to interact with them, therefore they are compatible with numerous cosmetic ingredients, which is important in modern day formulations. Cocamidopropyl sultaine is also used as a mild foaming and conditioning ingredient.

COCOBETAINE is a detergent or amphoteric surfactant made synthetically from coconut oil-starting products.

DIETHANOLAMINE LAURYL SULFATE or **DEA LAURYL SULFATE** is a clear yellow liquid used as an excellent detergent, foaming agent in shampoos, producing rich, thick suds and cleaning the hair well. While it may be slightly irritating to skin and eyes in concentrated form, at levels of use it is essentially nontoxic and nonirritating.

DIHYDROXYETHYL TALLOW GLYCINATE or **MIRATAINE** is a surfactant used as a conditioning agent. It occurs as a thick, amber liquid when used in shampoo formulations. It is made by chemical reactions with an amino acid, glycine, which occurs naturally in many proteins. It has not been reported to produce any adverse effects in contact with skin and is relatively nontoxic at concentrations of use.

DIOCTYL SODIUM SULFOSUCCINATE is a waxy solid made synthetically and used in low concentrations when found in shampoos. Used as a wetting agent, it is very safe, nontoxic by ingestion and nonirritating to skin and eyes.

HYDROLYZED ANIMAL PROTEIN is derived from various animal sources in meat processing. The raw material is processed for incorporation into cosmetic lotions. Studies have shown that proteins are absorbed by keratin (dead, flat cells of the outer layer of skin) and can contribute to body and elasticity, thus reducing cracking and tendency for infection.

LAURAMIDE DIETHANOLAMINE or **LAURAMIDE DEA** or **LAURIC ACID DIETHANOLAMIDE** is a nonionic detergent not known to produce contact allergy. This ingredient is a soft paste or solid which is made synthetically from the acids found in coconut oil. It is essentially nontoxic at concentrations of use in shampoos but it has been reported to be mildly irritating to skin and eyes. It is also suspect of liberating nitrosamines under certain conditions, chemicals which have been identified as causing cancer in laboratory animals.

LAURETH-4 is a nonionic detergent not known to produce contact allergy. It is a clear or slightly cloudy white or pale yellow liquid made from coconut oil acids and petroleum chemicals. It is nontoxic and not irritating to skin or eyes at concentrations of use in shampoo products. It is used to thicken products, stabilize foam and act as a "superfatting" conditioning agent.

LINOLEAMIDE DEA or **LINOLEIC ACID DIETHANOLAMIDE** is a nonionic conditioning ingredient added to shampoos at a concentration of 2 to 5 percent. It is a yellow, waxlike solid which can be prepared directly from oils like safflower or sunflower seed oil which have a high linoleic acid content. This ingredient may be a mild irritant to sensitive persons at a concentration of 5 percent or greater in the final product.

SARCOSINATES, such as **N-ACYL SARCOSINATE**, are highly lathering auxiliary surfactants. They are synthetically made from protein (amino acid) derivatives. This type of detergent has resistance to the delathering effects of natural hair oils and soil. They are obtained from sarcosine. Sarcosine is a crystalline chemical with a sweet taste, and low toxicity derived synthetically from creatinine (a metabolic waste product found in muscle, blood, and urine of mammals) or caffeine.

SODIUM C 14-16 OLEFIN SULFONATE or **SODIUM ALPHA OLEFIN SULFONATE** or **AOS** is a clear, thin yellow liquid made from petroleum products and employed in shampoos. It is an anionic surfactant used for its foaming and cleansing properties. Alpha olefin sulfonates are only slightly irritating and not very toxic even when inadvertently ingested.

SODIUM CETYL SULFATE or **SODIUM CETEARYL SULFATE** are closely related chemicals that appear as a thick, white paste prepared synthetically from fatty acids found in nature. It is used as a secondary surfactant in paste or cream shampoos to stiffen them and provide "body." It is not considered toxic at concentrations of use in shampoos.

SODIUM COCOYL SARCOSINATE is a yellow liquid or a thick paste. In addition to being a good cleansing, conditioning and foaming agent, it boosts lather in the presence of sebum (skin oil) and has some antibacterial activity. It is made synthetically from coconut oil and protein derivatives. It is relatively nontoxic and nonirritating to skin and eyes at normal levels of use in shampoos.

SODIUM LAURETH SULFATE (SLES) or **SODIUM LAURYL ETHER SULFATE** is a clear, colorless or pale yellow liquid. Used as a foaming and cleansing agent, it is an anionic detergent. Its low price and ability to be thickened easily have made this ingredient popular in very cheap shampoos.

SODIUM LAUROYL SARCOSINATE is a pale yellow liquid as it is added to shampoo formulations. It is made synthetically from coconut oil acids (or synthetics) and derivatives of amino acids and used as a mild foaming and cleansing agent which has conditioning and irritation reducing properties. It is nontoxic and nonirritating to skin and eyes.

SODIUM LAURYL SULFATE or **SLS** is an almost colorless, clear liquid, occasionally powder or flakes as added to shampoos at the formulation stage. It is an anionic detergent used in shampoos to provide foaming and cleansing action. It is only slightly toxic by ingestion, but long term use has shown it to be a safe shampoo ingredient. For many years **SLS** was the main shampoo surfactant, but it is used less often today in favor of milder detergents.

SODIUM MYRETH SULFATE is a pale yellow liquid which is made synthetically to perform as a mild foaming and cleansing agent. It is nontoxic and nonirritating to skin and eyes at levels of use in shampoos.

SODIUM OLEATE is a simple soap which is non-toxic.

SODIUM STEARATE is a white powder and a simple soap made synthetically and used as a thickener and detergent. It is completely nonpoisonous and nonirritating. Sodium stearate is not very water soluble and its function as a cleansing and foaming agent in shampoos is very limited. It is primarily added to shampoos to thicken them.

SODIUM TALLOWATE is the sodium salt of tallow, which is generally the fat of beef or mutton.

SULFATED CASTOR OIL or turkey red oil is an amber, thick liquid produced by treating castor oil with sulfuric acid and sodium hydroxide (lye). It is a poor foaming agent and cleansing agent but is mild and has good softening properties. It is probably used more for folkloric appeal on the label than for any functional qualities.

TRIETHANOLAMINE DODECYLBENZENE SULFONATE or **TEA DODECYLBENZENESULFONATE** or **LINEAR ALKYLBENZENESULFONATE, TEA SALT (LAS)** is a clear yellow liquid produced artificially from alkali and petroleum derivatives and used as a foaming and cleansing agent. It is thought to have a harsh or drying effect on hair and scalp.

TRIETHANOLAMINE LAURYL SULFATE or **TEA LAURYL SULFATE** is a colorless or pale yellow liquid used as a foaming and cleansing agent. It is produced synthetically from alkali and coconut oil acids. It is one of the surfactants that, along with sodium lauryl sulfate, has been the standard by which all other shampoo and cleanser surfactants are judged. TEA lauryl sulfate produces a good, rich foam on the hair, cleans and rinses out well and leaves the hair soft and manageable and with good appearance.

TRIETHANOLAMINE STEARATE is a cream colored, waxlike solid, anionic detergent used as an emulsifying agent for cosmetic ingredients. It has very low toxicity but it has been reported to induce contact allergic reactions in sensitive persons.

Baldness

The gradual but increasing loss of hair is called male pattern baldness and it affects many people. This form of baldness is hereditary and is usually caused by a build-up of the male hormone **TESTOSTERONE** in the scalp, causing an acidic condition that destroys the hair. The reason some hair stays in is because it is under different genetic control than other parts of the scalp. Men often come into the drugstore and ask for a vitamin or hair product to restore their hair. Unfortunately no product can do that. Some products are claimed to promote the growth of hair because they contain female hormones. The only problem is that the hair they produce is usually nothing more than white fuzz. Other products state that 80 percent of the people who use the product experience complete hair regrowth. The people who buy these products and find they do not work are simply told that they fall into the 20 percent failure category. Do not waste your money looking for a miracle. Ways of coping with baldness that do work include hair transplants or hair replacements. If you are losing your hair and you are concerned about it, you might want to check with a qualified hair expert for advice. There is one FDA approved prescription medication for baldness, *ROGAINE*. In many cases the active ingredient, **MINOXIDIL**, will grow hair on the crown of the head in male pattern baldness. It must be prescribed by a physician. It only works as long as the drug is applied to the head. Any new hair as a result of minoxidil will be lost within a few months of stopping treatment.

Hair Dyes

There are also a number of products on the market to color the hair. Some of these products can be rinsed out of the hair and others permanently color the hair. In order to get them out, you must wait until the hair grows out.

Always be careful when using hair dyes. They contain chemicals that can burn the eye. If this should happen, flush the eye immediately with water (see page 213). It might also be helpful to use an eye wash. Be sure to follow the instructions for the hair dye closely; if they tell you to wear rubber gloves, be sure you do. Some hair dyes may cause an allergic reaction of the skin, so it would be a good idea to test the product on a small area of the skin before using it. Also remember that these products are not intended to be used on the eyebrows because of the possibility of burning the eye. It is when you try to take short-cuts that needless accidents can happen. Before you buy a product read the instructions carefully. If it seems confusing, it would probably be to your advantage to have the dyeing done professionally by a hairdresser.

Other products that may be dangerous are those that gradually darken hair, such as *GRECIAN FORMULA*. They contain **LEAD ACETATE** to darken the hair. However, the FDA is now requiring the manufacturers of these products to put a warning on the label that they contain lead. This warning is not there just to decorate the package, even though these products contain only a small amount of lead and absorption through the scalp is poor. If you have any open wounds on the scalp or suffer from a scalp condition such as psoriasis, absorption would be higher.

Hair Brushes

People often want to know what brush to use. The natural bristle ones are best, as they help to distribute oil throughout the hair. Then again, with today's hair styles, most people want a dry, fluffy look. If you have long hair—that is, over the ears—use a wide bristle brush. For short hair use a natural bristle brush. If you notice the brush pulling your hair, it could mean that you need a wider bristle, or that you have damaged hair.

Hair Dryers

These are now available in many shapes, sizes, and colors, unlike many years ago when you put a plastic hat on your head and dried your hair while you polished your nails or read a magazine. Today's hair dryers are portable, compact, and easy to use. But they can burn or damage the hair.

Try to pick one with a low maximum temperature. A way to check is to turn it on using the hot setting and hold your hand about six inches away from it. If it burns you to the point that you have to pull your hand away, the dryer could hurt your hair. The wattage on the hair dryer does not mean a thing; it is the amount of heat given off that is important. When buying a hair dryer make sure it produces a lot of air movement. The higher the velocity of air it puts out, the better it will be for your hair.

Hair Removers

Hair has a mind of its own. It often does not grow in places, such as men's heads, where we want it to grow. Or it grows in places where we do not want it at all—for example, women's legs or underarms. The growth of hair is genetically determined. However, hair that is quite normal medically may be cosmetically unappealing. The options for removing unwanted hair are varied. There is no one best way to remove problem hair, and there are no drugs to effectively stop excess hair growth on otherwise healthy people. In general, there are two ways to get rid of hair: permanent or temporary. Temporary hair removal can be done in one of several ways.

Shaving

This can be done with either a blade and razor or an electric shaver. Shaving is the most popular way for both men and women to temporarily remove unwanted hair. But once you start removing hair by shaving, you are faced with the continuous task of avoiding the nubs of early growth. There is no medical reason why women troubled by excessive facial hair should not shave, yet few do. Most women turn to other forms of temporary hair removal, such as depilatories.

Depilatories

Depilatories are chemical agents that dissolve the hair so that it breaks off at the skin's surface. Several popular brands are *NEET, NEET BIKINI LINE CREAM* and *NAIR*, which are available in creams, foams, and lotions. Unfortunately, products that weaken the hair can also cause irritation, redness, and dryness of the skin. As a matter of fact if you have "detergent hands," or if you are sensitive to household cleaners with ammonia or strong soaps, you might well be allergic to depilatories. These products contain some pretty harsh chemicals, such as **THIOGLYCOLIC ACID** or other salts related to it like **SODIUM** or **CALCIUM THIOGLYCOLATE. CALCIUM HYDROXIDE** is frequently used also. If you do decide to try one of these products, it would probably be a good idea to first test it on a small area of the skin, before applying it to a large or prominent area. If you notice a reaction, do not use the product; it could create a problem worse than unsightly hair. These depilatories are only intended for the legs and arms and are too strong for the face. Serious face burns have occurred when, in particular, young women have used these on the face and above the lips to remove hair. There are some products that are intended strictly for the face such as *NUDIT* and *CREAM HAIR REMOVER FOR THE FACE* by Sally Hansen. These products are used two to three times a week. In order to cut down on unnecessary problems, follow the recommended limits closely. After use, wash the area thoroughly and apply any type of lubricating lotion or cream.

Waxes

These products are also available to get rid of hair. They are nothing more than **BEESWAX** or **PARAFFIN** that is treated and then left to cool until you can apply it to your skin without burning it. After the warm wax is applied to the skin it is allowed to further cool and set. When the cooled wax is stripped off quickly in the direction of hair growth, the embedded hairs are pulled out. This method is not very popular, because many people find the procedure painful. But there are a fair number of brands on the market, like *BETTER OFF* and *ZIPWAX HAIR REMOVER*. The advantage of the waxes over depilatories is that they remove hair for longer periods of time.

Bleaching

These products contain chemicals to bleach the hair white so that it is not noticeable. Most bleaches contain **PEROXIDE** to bleach the hair. This method is preferred by people who want to disguise rather than remove unwanted hair on their faces or arms. It is also the only method of dealing with unwanted hair that is generally recommended for children.

Electrolysis

There is one reasonably safe way of removing hair permanently. It is called electrolysis and actually destroys the hair germ cells by electric current. This procedure does have its drawbacks. First of all you must locate and treat each hair root individually, and that can be time-consuming. There is often some discomfort and reddening around the hair follicle, which may last several hours after the treatment. Permanent scarring of the skin sometimes occurs, and this can happen even with an experienced operator. The best way to find a competent electrologist is to ask your doctor or dermatologist whom they recommend. Be wary of any home electrolysis device. Do-it-yourself electrolysis carries a higher risk of scarring and infection.

24

Skin Care Products

For some people dry or chapped skin is an allergic condition that flares up now and then, usually with the change in seasons. Whatever the reason for dry skin, it is annoying and uncomfortable because of the constant itching and, in some cases, pain and inflammation. Dry skin is also more susceptible to bacterial infections than normal skin.

DRY SKIN is characterized by roughness, flaking, and tightness. As the word "dry" implies, dry skin results from a loss of moisture. The best way to treat dry skin is to replace the water that has been lost. However, adding water to the skin is useless unless the skin can retain it. If wet skin is not covered immediately with a substance like *VASELINE* or plastic, it will become dehydrated again quickly.

There are shelves and shelves of products to treat dry skin to be found in the drugstore. Various claims are made for these products, some say they "tone" the skin while others claim to lubricate, protect, or moisturize the surface of the skin.

ASTRINGENTS are products that are supposed to reduce oily skin and remove wrinkles by closing pores and "toning" the skin. Any product or chemical able to do either of these is, of course, only temporary. Oil glands are found in association with hair follicles over most of the body and closing the pore, or hair follicle, temporarily reduces the amount of oil excreted to the skin surface. **WRINKLES**, however, are a different story. They are caused by a loss of elasticity in the skin due to a degeneration of tissue at the cellular level and it is unlikely that any locally applied tonic or lotion will be successful in slowing down or preventing this process. Astringents are nothing more than weak antiperspirants (see Chapter 6). The types of chemicals used are the same used in antiperspirant preparations, that is, metal salts, particularly of the elements aluminum and zinc. A few naturally occurring substances are used as astringents because they possess

TANNINS or other chemicals that are naturally astringent. These will be described individually below. Alcohol is frequently included as part of the vehicle for astringents and this makes sense since it is important that any vehicle used to apply an astringent not leave a residue or film. Alcohol is volatile and evaporates quickly from the skin.

Although **COLD CREAMS** and **LOTIONS** date back to the first and second century A.D. there were no real changes in these products until the early twentieth century. It was not until about 1930 that the technology allowed for the development of products with a high water content to be formulated into the skin care items we take for granted today. Creams and lotions are usually oil-in-water emulsions with a high content of **EMOLLIENTS** (skin softeners) that leave a smooth protective film on the skin to maintain it in a hydrated and smooth condition. They combat dry skin by providing lubrication and preventing water loss by evaporation. While an exact definition of "emolliency" is very difficult to put into words, it is generally agreed that soft, supple skin results from the use of an emollient. Also under the category of lotions or creams are what the cosmetic chemist describes as "liquid pigmented lotions," known to the consumer as liquid makeup. Liquid makeup was originally developed as a base for face powder but it became popular as a multifunction cosmetic whose main purpose is to cover minor skin imperfections and to give a velvety finish to the skin by masking any shine due to secretions of the oil and sweat glands. The various chemicals employed in a skin care product will depend on what type of application is intended.

Lubricating Lotions

These products are mainly intended to lubricate the skin, causing it to feel smooth. In other words they are a strictly psychological approach to dry skin. Even though the skin feels smooth, it may not be back to normal. Most of the lubricating products are cosmetic. They are pretty effective at correcting the dry skin condition, but they do not get to the root of the problem of dry skin. Lubricating lotions contain ingredients like **MINERAL OIL, LANOLIN** and **VEGETABLE OIL. MINERAL OIL** and **LANOLIN** are found in products like *LUBRIDERM* lotion and *KERI* lotion. However, these ingredients do not produce lasting relief from dry skin.

No one likes to apply oil directly to his or her skin because it feels greasy. However, oils, found in products such as *LUBRIDERM LUBATH SKIN CONDITIONING OIL* and *ALPHA KERI MOISTURE RICH BODY OIL*, are prepared in oil dispersing "systems" and may be put into the bath water to help moisturize dry skin. These do help lubricate the skin, and they may be applied directly to the skin if you so choose. If you decide to use a bath oil, take some precautions such as putting a towel in the bottom of the bathtub; oily water can cause the bathtub to become extremely slippery and the towel will prevent you from falling. Do not use a bath mat, because it will become as slippery as the tub itself.

Many companies combine oil with water, resulting in a cloudy mixture, or lotion. Other ingredients are added to hold it in a lotion form. Most of the products found in the drugstore to treat dry skin are lotions containing oil and water: *VASELINE INTENSIVE LOTION, KERI LOTION, JERGENS*—the list is endless. The mineral-oil-in-water products might be a little better to use, because they are absorbed into the skin better. Using an oil-in-water lotion may help to relieve itching because of the cooling effect as the water evaporates from the skin surface. Most of these products do their best to reduce greasiness, but there is no getting away from the fact that they contain oils. If the oily feeling is bothersome, read the label and avoid products that contain **LIQUID PETROLATUM** or **MINERAL OIL** which is the ingredient most responsible for that oily feeling. Another alternative is to use them only at night, before going to bed.

Moisturizing Lotions and Creams

These products contain ingredients to replace the moisture your skin has lost. Some lotions contain **GLYCERIN** to treat dry skin; products such as *CORN HUSKERS* and *GLYCERIN AND ROSE WATER*, and *NEUTROGENA HAND CREAM* are very good at moisturizing the skin. Glycerin is said to act as a "magnet" to draw water from the atmosphere, holding it until the skin needs more water. Although lotions containing glycerin are somewhat effective in treating dry skin, glycerin does not penetrate the skin too well, and there must be enough water in the air for the glycerin to draw it to the skin. And if there were a lot of moisture in the air, one probably would not have the dry skin condition to begin with. Most of the products that you can buy contain only 50 percent glycerin. You can make your own glycerin lotion at home by mixing glycerin with an equal part water.

In addition to glycerin, many ingredients have been claimed to be effective moisturizers including **UREA, CARBOXYLIC ACIDS, LACTIC ACID**, and **PROPYLENE GLYCOL**. While manufacturers make exaggerated claims regarding these ingredients they really do not improve the effectiveness of the product very much.

Eczema

A problem that can affect both women and men, depending on what they do for a living, is something that used to be called in the TV commercials "dishpan hands." It has also been referred to as "housewife's eczema." It is a problem that affects a lot of people. It is a reaction caused by the ingredients in many household cleaners, such as dishwashing liquids, detergents, and various other cleaning products, when they come into contact with the skin. Nurses, doctors and other health care workers can develop this condition from frequent hand washing with disinfectant soaps and detergents. If you develop these skin problems after doing household chores, first wash your hands thoroughly and rinse them with cool water; while the hands are still wet apply any of the skin lotions we mentioned earlier, rub in well, then pat the hands dry with a clean towel. Also wear rubber gloves when doing the dishes or scrubbing the kitchen floor. By avoiding skin contact with these ingredients, the problems can be prevented. If you do develop very irritated skin on the hands, you might want to try one of the over-the-counter **HYDROCORTISONE** products. They work very well at relieving the itching and inflammation due to allergic reactions to various cleaners. If these simple remedies do not work, see your doctor for a diagnosis of your skin problem. Another type of eczema is known as **ATOPIC** or **ALLERGIC ECZEMA**, also referred to as **ATOPIC DERMATITIS**. This condition is a chronic, itching, inflammatory skin disease that occurs with greater frequency in persons with a personal or family history of allergy, including asthma or hay fever. In the case of allergic eczema, it is important to see a physician for a specific diagnosis. Prescription anti-inflammatory products are available and their effectiveness can be monitored over time. There are some excellent prescription products for skin care of allergic disorders.

Shaving Rash

Shaving rash is a problem that, obviously, affects more men than women. Often a man develops irritation along the neckline after he shaves. This manifests itself in redness and itching. Shaving rash sometimes happens when one tries to get an extra-close shave. There are some things you can do to prevent it.

First of all, it is always best to shave after showering. If you do not shower, be sure to wash your face thoroughly; or soak a washcloth in hot water, ring it out, then place it on the face and hold it there for a couple of minutes. The heat and water actually help soften the beard, making it easier to shave. Sometimes it helps to spread a thin layer of moisturizing cream on the face and neck before applying shaving cream over it.

Always try to shave in the direction of the beard. Shaving against the grain of the beard will likely cause a shaving rash and the irritation that goes along with it.

When finished, wash away the excess lather. It might also help to cleanse the face with an alcoholic astringent such as *WITCH HAZEL*. It will tighten up the pores and improve your skin tone. You are also wiping away any soapy residue of shaving, which can cause irritation. After drying the face, apply a non-greasy moisturizer to the skin.

After-shave lotions are nice, but some people get carried away with them. Most of them have alcohol bases that can irritate the skin.

Astringent, Lotion, and Cream Ingredients

ACETYLATED LANOLIN ALCOHOL is a thin fluid derived from lanolin and used as a penetrant, plasticizer and solvent for cosmetics incorporated into creams and lotions. Lanolin is a fatlike substance derived from the wool of sheep whose chief constituents are cholesterol and numerous fats. It is these constituents that are chemically treated (acetylated) to produce acetylated lanolin alcohols. Contact allergy has not been reported with this chemical, but it has been reported to cause blackheads (comedones) in test animals. Therefore acne-prone persons should probably avoid this substance.

ALCOHOL, SD (SPECIALLY DENATURED ALCOHOL) is a clear, volatile liquid used as a vehicle for astringents even though it has astringent properties itself. It is simply the same alcohol distilled for beverages and produced by fermentation except that it has been intentionally adulterated with one of many chemicals which are unpalatable, and even poisonous, to discourage ingestion and prevent its use from being diverted to the beverage market. Once specially denatured **(SD)**, the alcohol cannot be separated from the denaturant. The denaturant is identified by an alphanumeric code used ir. the industry and is available from a local poison center or the local office of the U.S. Bureau of Alcohol, Tobacco and Firearms. *REVLON 'MOON DROPS' MOISTURIZING SKIN TONER* is just one of hundreds of products that uses **SD** alcohol in its formulation.

ALOE VERA juice is from the plant that people may have in their homes, and which is called an aloe plant, *Aloe barbadensis*. The leaves of the plant are thick and fleshy and contain a jellylike substance called **ALOE VERA GEL.** Manufacturers use this natural moisturizer in various skin care products. It is an excellent nutrient for the skin, because it contains proteins, vitamins, and minerals, and helps remove dead skin and stimulate the growth of new skin. If you have used various lotions to treat dry skin but feel that you have not gotten results, you may want to try a product that contains aloe vera.

ALUMINUM CHLOROHYDRATE is an antiperspirant chemical, discussed in more detail earlier in this chapter, because it is an effective astringent. It is a white powder prepared synthetically from aluminum chloride and used in solution.

ARNICA (*Arnica montana*) claimed by manufacturers to have a stimulating effect on the epidermis when used in lotions. It is a perennial herb (*Arnica montana*) native to mountainous regions of Europe and cultivated in northern India. The dried flower heads are the parts used as they contain fatty acids and volatile oils which are responsible for its properties. It has been reported to cause contact allergy and irritant dermatitis, apparently due to specific chemical components (sesquiterpene lactones).

BALM OIL is derived from the plant *Melissa officinalis*, an aromatic, perennial herb growing in the Mediterranean area. An oil for use in cosmetic lotions is obtained by steam distillation of the leaves and flowering tops of the plant and used for its fragrance.

BIRCH or **BIRCH LEAF EXTRACT** is said to have a tonic and astringent effect on the skin, probably due to the presence of resinous acids in the extract. The wood and bark of the tree, *Betula alba*, the European white birch, is used to produce a tar oil. It has been used medicinally in creams, lotions and shampoos to treat psoriasis, eczema and other chronic skin diseases for which it may be effective in mild cases. However, it is unlikely that the small amount of this ingredient employed in the finished product has any real astringent value. More recently it is being used in simple cosmetic lotions.

BUTYL MYRISTATE a white oily liquid which is obtained synthetically from coconut oil. It is incorporated into lotions to soften skin.

BUTYL STEARATE is a colorless, skin softening liquid made synthetically from natural fats and used frequently in lotions, creams, lipsticks, hair and grooming preparations. It is completely nontoxic.

CARNAUBA WAX or **BRAZIL WAX,** from the leaves of the wax palm (*Copernicia cereferia*), one of the hardest of the waxes from plants. For this reason it is important economically. In food, it is used in the production of confections, such as glaze and polish on candy. Carnauba wax is not absorbed by the body and is completely inert when ingested. As used in food products, it is not known to produce any undesirable hypersensitivity or allergic reactions. Sometimes it is found in barrier creams as a skin protectant.

CASTOR OIL is prepared by extraction from castor seeds obtained from the plant *Ricinus communis*. While this plant contains extremely poisonous substances found in the seeds, they are destroyed in the extraction process. Castor oil is a pale yellow or almost colorless, transparent thick liquid with a nauseating taste. Castor oil has wide application in the pharmaceutical and cosmetic industries. It has emollient (skin softening) properties that are particularly taken advantage of when incorporated into lipsticks.

CETYL ALCOHOL is a white, waxy solid at room temperature. It is made synthetically from naturally occurring fatty acids and is used widely in face creams, lotions, lipsticks, etc., as an emollient and product softener. At least one case of dermatitis attributed to cetyl alcohol has been reported, although not in the recent scientific literature.

CETYL PALMITATE or **CETIN** at one time was obtained from **SPERMACETI**, a waxy substance obtained from the head of the sperm whale, and used as a principle ingredient in cold cream. Spermaceti consists almost entirely of cetyl palmitate. The sperm whale is presently an endangered species and production of cetyl palmitate from this source is illegal. Current production is synthetic from other naturally occurring fats. In recent years the use of jojoba oil has been used to replace the market for spermaceti in cosmetic lotions and creams. It has not been known to cause allergic reactions or to produce skin irritation.

COLLAGEN is employed in *EUROPEAN COLLAGEN COMPLEX EXCEPTIONAL BEAUTY LOTION*, by Revlon. Despite many claims, collagen-based cosmetics offer no benefits beyond softening and moisturizing the skin. It cannot smooth out or rid you of wrinkles because collagen's molecules are too large to get past the skin's outermost layer. Collagen, a protein, is the chief constituent of skin, connective tissue and bone. Most of the collagen used in cosmetics comes from cows.

DIMETHICONE, SIMETHICONE or **DIMETHYL POLYSILOXANE** is a synthetic, silicone-derived polymer patented by Corning Glass in 1948. It is a water-white, viscous, oil-like liquid used in creams and lotions as a skin protectant and a vehicle for other ingredients. It is also used orally as a popular antiflatulent (for stomach gas) in the over-the-counter pharmaceutical, *MYLICON* (see simethicone, page 307). It is considered completely nontoxic and is not known to produce any adverse reactions when used in cosmetics.

FENNEL EXTRACT, also called **FINOCCHIO**, is used in some dry skin formulations and is obtained from the perennial herb (*Anethum foeniculum*) native to the Mediterranean region but cultivated worldwide. The common, or bitter, fennel is used for its fragrance in lotions.

GLYCERYL DILAURATE or **GLYCEROL DILAURATE** is an emulsifier and emollient for creams and lotions. It is a combination of glycerin and lauric acid, a fatty acid which occurs in many vegetable fats, such as coconut and laurel oil.

GLYCERYL MONOOLEATE or **GLYCEROL MONOOLEATE** is a yellow oil or soft solid at room temperature and is a fat used in creams, lotions and other cosmetics as an emollient. It is a combination of glycerin and oleic acid, a component of almost all natural fats, like tallow or vegetable oil. It is nontoxic.

GLYCERYL MONORICINOLEATE, GLYCERYL RICINOLEATE or **GLYCEROL MONORICINOLEATE** is a yellow liquid oil used as a skin softener and emulsifier in lotions and creams. It is a combination of glycerin and ricinoleic acid, a fatty acid which composes 80 percent of the fatty acid content of castor oil.

GLYCERYL MONOSTEARATE or **GLYCEROL MONOSTEARATE** is a white- or cream-colored solid fat used as a thickener and emulsifier in creams and lotions. It it a combination of glycerin and stearic acid, which is the most common fatty acid occurring in natural animal and vegetable fats.

GLYCERYL STEARATE is a fat found in *NEUTROGENA MOISTURE NONCOMEDOGENIC FACIAL MOISTURIZER.*

HORSE CHESTNUT is the common name for the tree (*Aesculus hippocastanum*) whose derivatives are employed in lotions for the treatment of cellulitis and blotchiness. While manufacturers encourage the use of horsechestnut for these conditions it is difficult to substantiate effectiveness. The tree is native to eastern Europe.

HORSETAIL (sometimes called **SCOURING RUSH**) is claimed by manufacturers to have a tonic effect on the skin, thus it is incorporated into softening lotions. Claims for its tonic effect are unsubstantiated, but the plant (*Equisetum arvense*) has been used in folk medicine. It grows in rich, moist soils in most parts of the world.

HYDROLYZED ANIMAL PROTEIN is derived from various animal sources in meat processing. The raw material is processed for incorporation into cosmetic lotions. Studies have shown that proteins are absorbed by keratin (dead, flat cells of the epidermis) and can contribute to body and elasticity, thus reducing cracking and tendency for infection.

ISOPROPYL MYRISTATE is a colorless oil used in cosmetics for wetting and softening purposes. It is derived artificially from the distillation of coconut oil.

JOJOBA is the seed oil or liquid wax which has become a popular substitute for sperm whale oil or spermaceti. **JOJOBA** is processed from the seed or nuts of the jojoba shrub (*Simmondsia chinensis*), a shrub growing wild in the Southwestern desert, but more recently a cultivated crop. Its peanut sized seeds yield 50 percent oil by weight, a high content when compared to other oil yielding seed crops. Jojoba oil is not a true fat or oil, but a liquid wax. The difference is more important to chemists than the consumer, but jojoba is compared by cosmetic chemists to sperm whale oil in its ability to soften and protect the skin without greasiness.

LACTIC ACID is the acid found in the souring of milk as a result of the action of bacteria on lactose (milk sugar). It is also found naturally in numerous other foods and beverages like molasses, tomato juice, beer and wine. Many plants contain lactic acid as the result of the conversion of sugars at different times in their development. Commercially it is produced by fermentation of whey, cornstarch, potatoes and molasses. In low concentrations it is astringent and thus employed for this purpose in the cosmetic industry. In higher concentrations it is corrosive and is used pharmaceutically in the removal of warts.

LANOLIN or **HYDROUS WOOL FAT** is the fat removed from wool by washing with solvents with 25 to 30 percent water added. It is a yellowish-white, ointmentlike mass that has a characteristic odor. One of the chief constituents of lanolin is cholesterol, but numerous other fats are present. It is an ingredient in many creams and lotions as a protectant and skin softener.

LECITHIN is a waxy, colorless solid that may turn yellow or brown on exposure to light. Lecithin is found in relatively large quantities in egg yolk and liver and constitutes a certain small percentage of human plasma where it may function in important roles in the structure and function of cell membranes. It is prepared commercially from soybean oil, although it can also be prepared from corn and other vegetable seeds to form a a thick, semiliquid material with a characteristic odor. Used as an emulsifier in lotions and creams.

LINDENTREE or **LINDEN** extracts are used for their soothing properties in lotions and creams. It is from a fragrant tree (*Tilia cordata*) native to the temperate climates of the Northern Hemisphere.

MINERAL OIL or **LIQUID PETROLATUM** is a transparent, almost tasteless, odorless, oily liquid that is a mixture of hydrocarbons (the simplest of all organic compounds, being composed of just carbon and hydrogen). It is derived by distillation of high boiling point petroleum fractions. It is used as a substitute for natural fats and oils in cosmetics, but usually imparts a "greasy" feel to products. *OIL OF OLAY BEAUTY CREAM* and *OIL OF OLAY NIGHT CARE CREAM* both use mineral oil. It is nontoxic.

MINK OIL is one of the few animal (or vegetable) oils that is used to any substantial degree in cosmetics in its natural form. Color, odor, and stability of these oils preclude their use in any product with a reasonable shelf life expectancy. Mink oil is an exception to the rule and is a natural fat (triglyceride) obtained from the mink, a weasel-like animal (*Mustela vison*) of North America. The oil is nontoxic, has a luxurious non-oily feel, is absorbed readily by the skin, wets and spreads easily on the skin and is very stable when used in lotions and creams.

MYRISTYL ALCOHOL is a emollient used in creams and lotions and is prepared from myristic acid, a component of coconut oil.

PANAMAWOOD, PANAMABARK or **SOAPBARK** is used in skin products for its emulsifying and detergent properties. The dried inner bark of the tree (*Quillaja saponaria*) contains a high content of chemicals known as saponins which are responsible for this effect. It is also used in the food industry as a foaming agent.

POLYETHYLENE GLYCOLS (PEG) or **POLYOXYETHYLENES** or **POLYGLYCOLS** are synthetically prepared polymers. They range from clear, colorless, thick liquids to waxy solids and have many uses in the pharmaceutical and cosmetic industries. In lotions and creams they are frequently used as the major vehicle or "dispersant" for the other ingredients, that is, they provide the "body" to the cream or lotion. They are nontoxic and basically inert materials.

PROPYLENE GLYCOL or **1,2-PROPANEDIOL** is a thick liquid at room temperature and is made synthetically from propane, a petroleum chemical, or by heating glycerin with sodium hydroxide. It is used as a humectant (a water absorber) in cosmetic creams and lotions. Humectants keep water in the product to ensure smooth application and good shelf life. Propylene glycol is also used in shampoos and other cosmetics as a solvent, emollient, preservative, and agent to control thickness of the final product. It is considered safe when applied to the skin and has been time tested as an effective ingredient. Most people will tolerate propylene glycol with no adverse reactions. There is at least one report of delayed contact hypersensitivity. However, the large number of products in which it is found, for example *REVLON 'MOON DROPS' MOISTURE FILM*, attest to its relative safety when used on the skin.

ROMAN CHAMOMILE or **MATRICARIA** provides a cooling and protectant effect on skin. It is a strongly fragrant perennial plant (*Anthemis nobilis*) native to southern and western Europe, but naturalized in North America. The oils of this plant are used in lotions and are generally well tolerated, but cases of dermatitis from sensitivity to the plant have been reported.

ROSEMARY EXTRACT is said to have a stimulating astringent and deodorizing effect when incorporated into skin products. It also has folkloric appeal and (unproven) claims have been made that it stimulates hair growth. It is from the plant (*Rosemarinus officinalis*), a small evergreen shrub native to the Mediterranean region, but cultivated worldwide. An oil is obtained from the flowering tops of the plant by steam distillation. The oil found in the extract is irritating to the skin and may be toxic if ingested, however extremely small quantities are normally incorporated into lotions intended for applications to the skin.

SPERMACETI is the waxy substance once obtained from the head of sperm whales. It is almost completely composed of cetyl palmitate, a fat. The sperm whale is now a protected species and destruction for the purpose of obtaining the oil is prohibited. A white, somewhat translucent waxy-like substance with a pearly luster, it was used as the major emollient in skin softening preparations, including cold cream. It is completely nontoxic.

STEARIC ACID is the most common fatty acid occurring in natural animal and vegetable fats, although it can be made synthetically by hydrogenation (adding hydrogen artificially) of cottonseed and other vegetable oils. It can occur as white or slightly yellow crystals or powder. It is incorporated into lotions and creams to be reacted with an alkaline chemical, such as sodium hydroxide (or other milder salts), producing a soap which acts as an emulsifying agent in the final product. It is also used in shampoo products as a foaming and cleansing agent, thickener and conditioner in the final product. This ingredient is nontoxic and is not irritating to the skin or eyes.

TRIETHANOLAMINE is a liquid at room temperature prepared synthetically by the reaction of ammonia with petroleum chemicals to produce a neutralizing agent for fatty acids when they are incorporated into lotions and creams. Triethanolamine reacts with the fatty acids to make a soap that in turn acts as an emulsifying agent in the final product. In shampoos it may be used to adjust the final alkalinity of the product. It is of very low toxicity.

TRIETHANOLAMINE (TEA) STEARATE is a mixture of triethanolamine and stearic acid, which is the most common fatty acid occurring in natural animal and vegetable fats. It is a soap that acts as an emulsifying agent in creams and lotions and has been reported to be acceptable for use in cases where individuals were abnormally sensitive to sodium soaps. It appears to be very low in irritation to both intact and abraded skin and it is nontoxic when ingested.

WITCH HAZEL DISTILLED EXTRACT or **HAMAMELIS WATER** is prepared by steam distillation of the recently cut and partially dried leaves, bark and dormant twigs of *Hamamelis virginiana*, a small flowering tree native to North America, growing from Quebec to Georgia and west to Minnesota. Witch hazel distilled extract is claimed to have astringent properties but cosmetic scientists refute this, stating that the real astringent properties of witch hazel, tannins, remain in the residue and is absent from the distilled extract. **TINCTURE OF WITCH HAZEL**, a dark reddish brown liquid, is a powerful astringent because it contains the tannins, however it is not readily available to the consumer. The astringency associated with witch hazel distilled extract is probably due to the alcohol subsequently added to prevent decomposition of the solution.

ZINC CHLORIDE sometimes called **BUTTER OF ZINC** is composed of white, odorless granules and may be prepared artificially by the action of acid on zinc metal or it can be prepared from other zinc salts. It is mildly acid in water and thus has astringent properties when used in very weak cosmetic solutions. Higher concentrations can be very irritating to the skin and even corrosive.

ZINC SULFATE is a white, crystalline powder or granule that is prepared by the action of sulfuric acid on zinc metal. It also occurs in nature as the minerals, zinkosite and goslarite. A weak solution in water is acid and astringent. If ingested it is emetic (causes vomiting) and is moderately poisonous. Applied to the skin it is well tolerated and nontoxic.

ZINC PHENOLSULFONATE is an astringent chemical that exists as colorless, transparent crystals or a white granular powder which turns pink on exposure to air. It is made synthetically by reacting other zinc salts with petroleum chemicals. It is poisonous if swallowed but concentrations around 2 percent when applied to the skin are generally well tolerated.

25

Skin Medicines

Medicines used to treat **ACNE**, **DANDRUFF**, **SEBORRHEA** (overactivity of the oil glands), **PSORIASIS**, **BUNIONS**, **CALLUSES**, **CORNS** and **WARTS** have in common a property that earns them the fancy name of **"KERATOLYTIC"** (the word comes from "kerato," meaning the keratin or horny layer of the skin, and "lysis" meaning to loosen). The chemicals in this section are those that cause the loosening of the outermost layer of skin, causing it to slough or fall off. They can also be called sloughing agents. This is important in the treatment of acne, seborrhea and psoriasis because this process promotes new skin growth and healing and it removes the layer of dead skin that often harbors certain fungi and bacteria which cause infection. In the treatment of bunions, calluses, corns and warts chemicals are used in high enough concentrations to completely destroy the tissue, causing it to eventually drop off.

Acne

Acne is most common during the formative teenage years. Adolescence is a time for fun, friends, growing up, and, unfortunately, pimples. While acne affects virtually everyone between the ages of thirteen and twenty-three, it may begin in females, due to hormonal changes, as early as ten or as late as the twenties or thirties. As evidenced by the many commercials on radio and television, competition for this multimillion dollar market is keen among makers of acne medication. The large number of products, well over a hundred different ones available, attests to the fact that there is no cure for acne. Yet, one should not be discouraged from treating the symptoms. Acne occurs most commonly on the face, back, and chest. Although it does not pose a severe physical threat, it should not be ignored, since it may cause a great deal of emotional stress and anguish. Contrary to popular belief, acne is not caused by such things as bad eating habits or poor hygiene, even though the eating of certain foods, uncleanliness, undue stress, and premenstrual tension may cause a flare-up of acne. The tendency to develop acne runs in families, especially those in which one or both parents have oily skin.

This problem sends people into the drugstore in droves to find products to clear up their acne. But there are so many products to pick from that you may not know where to start. The truth is that treatment will vary according to the severity and the type of acne.

Acne itself cannot be cured. In most cases, however, with currently available treatments, symptoms may be reduced and permanent scarring minimized. The best treatment is to remove excess oil from the skin, and this can be done very effectively by washing. The affected areas should be washed thoroughly three times a day with warm water, soap, and a soft washcloth. Scrubbing should be gentle to avoid damage and should be done for several minutes to work the lather thoroughly into the skin. The purpose of the washing is to produce a mild drying of the skin. However, if washing produces a feeling of tautness in the skin, its intensity and frequency should be reduced.

Ordinary facial soaps usually produce satisfactory results. Some soaps contain ingredients such as **SULFUR** and **SALICYLIC ACID**, such as *AVEENO CLEANSING BAR FOR ACNE*, but it is doubtful that these soaps are better, since if the affected area is rinsed properly, these added medications are washed away. If it is inconvenient to wash during the day, a cleansing pad that contains **ALCOHOL** or **ACETONE** may be used.

Since these treatments are aimed mainly at removing excess oil from the skin, other topically applied fats and oils, including most cosmetics, should be eliminated. Excessive amounts of hair dressings that contain oils should be avoided. Try to keep your hair short, because oily hair that comes in contact with your skin could cause further irritation of your **ACNE** condition. Avoid any food or drink that you know triggers problems with your acne. And remember, while it is tempting to pick pimples and squeeze **BLACKHEADS**, this can injure the skin and underlying tissues. Physicians advise patients not to pick pimples. Instruments called **COMEDO EXTRACTORS** are used to remove blackheads. Some doctors may suggest that their patients use such instruments themselves. Usually, doctors would rather remove the blackheads in their office because of risk of scarring.

To clear up mild acne try the following:

- Get a nonprescription medicine and apply it regularly, according to the directions on the label. Over-the-counter products containing **BENZOYL PEROXIDE** and **SULFUR** are effective for treating mild acne.
- Use ordinary hygiene on affected areas, wash your face once or twice daily with your usual soap or cleanser.
- Avoid any food or drug you know to be a trigger to flare-ups.

If the above measures do not work, consult a dermatologist. Dermatologists can treat severe forms of acne with very effective prescription drugs.

The important thing to remember is that everyone goes through an acne period in their life. It is part of growing up. Unfortunately some people are affected more than others. There is no cure for acne. But adequate control can prevent permanent scarring, both physical and emotional. Dietary restriction is probably the most overemphasized and least effective of the more widely used treatments for acne. Chocolates, nuts, carbonated soft drinks, and fried foods may contribute only as a trigger to acne flare-up. It is suggested to avoid these foods for three weeks, then eat and drink them. If there is no change in the acne, then do not be concerned with the diet. If a particular food or drink causes acne to flare up, then simply avoid it.

Chapter 25

Dandruff

If itching and flaking occur on the scalp, there may be **DANDRUFF** present. Dandruff is not a disease but a normal condition like the growth of hair and nails, except that the end product is visible on the scalp as well as on clothing. It could have a cosmetic and social impact. Dandruff usually appears at puberty when many skin activities are altered, reaches a peak in early adulthood, levels off at middle age, and declines with advancing years. There is no cure for dandruff, only control of the condition. Of course, total removal of the hair will eliminate dandruff. However, that is a pretty drastic solution.

The best way to treat dandruff is by cleaning the hair and scalp frequently, perhaps daily. This should be sufficient to control dandruff, but you may also try one of the dandruff shampoos. One type, *SELSUN BLUE*, contains **SELENIUM SULFIDE**. This ingredient reduces the production of tissue on the scalp and is fairly effective at controlling dandruff. Some products, such as *SEBULEX*, contain **SALICYLIC ACID** and **SULPHUR** and are sold as antiseborrheic products. The sulphur helps cut down the production of oil on the scalp and the salicylic acid helps remove the built-up tissue from the scalp. These ingredients work very well in the treatment of dandruff. Before buying a dandruff shampoo, examine the scalp; there is no inflammation or redness of the scalp with dandruff. If you notice redness where the flaking is, check with a doctor before using an over-the-counter shampoo. There may be **SEBORRHEA** or **PSORIASIS** (see below), and in that case a physician will want to use a special medicated shampoo to treat the condition. Usually after shampooing the hair, leave the lather on the scalp for about five minutes so that the ingredients can work effectively. Rinse it out, and shampoo the hair with regular shampoo. But be sure to rinse the dandruff shampoo from the scalp thoroughly. If a residue remains on the hair, it will fall to the scalp and combine with the dandruff to form larger flakes which are even more noticeable.

Some shampoos contain **COAL TAR**, like *SEBUTONE*, which advertisers claim is a good treatment for dandruff, but tar is mainly used to treat psoriasis. Makers of some dandruff shampoos claim that you can feel your scalp tingle when the shampoo is working. Often these shampoos contain **MENTHOL** along with other ingredients, and the tingle you feel is nothing more than the cooling effect of the menthol on the scalp. In the future you will only find menthol included as an "inactive" ingredient in dandruff and psoriasis products because the FDA has banned it, claiming it ineffective in treating these conditions. There is no proof that it works for any of the scaling skin and hair conditions.

Seborrhea

Seborrhea is known officially as seborrheic dermatitis. It is a flaking skin disorder that causes patches of skin to appear as reddened and inflamed, sometimes oozing areas. Usually yellow, greasy scales are around hairy areas and parts of skin where there are a lot of oil glands, especially the middle of the face, fold between the nose and cheek, eyebrows, ear canals and folds of the ears. In some ways it is similar to dandruff, but dandruff is not accompanied by redness and inflammation. In severe cases of seborrhea the armpits and groin can be involved. This disease can occur in infants up to about 6 months of age and is what is commonly referred to as **CRADLE CAP**. Once you get through this early-in-life bout with the disease, you are not likely to see it again until after puberty. Seborrheic dermatitis, like many skin disorders, can be aggravated by emotional stress, strokes, Parkinson's disease and other nervous system problems. Doctors believe that the underlying cause of seborrhea is in the central nervous system, since it seems to be so very much aggravated by conditions which also affect this complex part of our bodies. It is very difficult to distinguish seborrhea from psoriasis, particularly when psoriasis occurs on the scalp, ears and face. A dermatologist can make the diagnosis and offer proper treatment. You can treat it with shampoo containing **TAR**, **SULFUR**, **SALICYLIC ACID**, **SELENIUM SULFIDE** or **ZINC PYRITHIONE**. Products containing selenium such as *SELSUN* should be avoided in infants as use has been associated with excess selenium absorption through the skin and resultant toxic effects. Found in products like, *SEBULEX*, *X-SEB SHAMPOO*, *HEAD AND SHOULDERS INTENSIVE TREATMENT*, and *ZINCON SHAMPOO*, these are all effective treatments which give a measure of relief, but unfortunately, do not cure the disease.

Psoriasis

This is a disease that affects every age group and seems to be due at least partly to heredity, since about one-fourth of people with this condition report a family history of it. Psoriasis is very common and may affect as much as 3 percent of the population of the United States. Psoriasis usually affects people in early adult life, but it may begin at any age. The lesions of psoriasis appear as reddened, elevated plaques that are topped with silvery, thick scales resembling mica. The scales are easily removed and tend to accumulate in clothing or bed. All parts of the body may become involved but particularly knees and elbows, trunk, buttocks and scalp. Palms and soles may be involved and, often time, the nails. One phenomenon of psoriasis is that if the skin is scratched or cut this will bring on more lesions and scaling. This may explain the high frequency with which psoriasis occurs on knees and elbows. There are many forms of psoriasis that physicians describe and you should certainly have a doctor diagnosed case before you decide to use any of the products mentioned here. There are many skin conditions that can be confused with psoriasis, so check with a physician. Unfortunately, there is no cure for psoriasis either, and treatment only controls the disease for as long as you are patient enough to continue it.

There are three types of skin therapy for **PSORIASIS** and a physician may use one or a combination of the following to treat: 1) High potency, prescription **STEROID** creams and ointments are applied to the skin; 2) **TAR**-containing over-the-counter products, either alone or in combination with **STEROIDS**; and lastly, 3) **ULTRAVIOLET LIGHT**, used under physician supervision, along with prescription ointments, creams and oral medications are used for severe cases. Some of the nonprescription products that contain tars and are useful in treating psoriasis are *T-DERM*, *PSORIGEL*, *MAZON* and *OXIPOR VHC*.

Bunions, Corns, Calluses and Warts

A **BUNION** is a swelling that occurs along the side of the big toe. They are usually caused by pressure from a tightly fitting shoe, but they may also be caused by pressure resulting from the way a person sits, stands, or walks. Treatment of **BUNIONS** often depends on the degree of discomfort. Bunions can become painful, swollen, and tender. **GOUT** can affect the great toe resulting in redness, swelling and exquisite tenderness. Check with a physician if you are not sure about the problem. Most over-the-counter products do not alter this condition at all. The only thing you can use is a **BUNION PAD**, which may give you relief. If it does not, surgery may be required. Remember, when using a bunion pad, use a slightly larger-sized shoe or slipper to avoid pressure.

A **CORN** is a raised, yellowish-gray area on the foot that has a central core. Corns are either hard or soft. Hard corns occur on the surfaces of the toes and appear very shiny. Soft corns are a thickening of the skin, usually found on the webs between the fourth and fifth toes.

The successful treatment of corns and calluses really depends on eliminating the causes, such as pressure and friction. One way of doing that is to buy well-fitted, binding footwear that distributes body weight evenly.

CORNS can also be treated by using medicated corn pads. The pads usually are available along with a medicated disc that is put directly on the corn itself. The disc contains **SALICYLIC ACID**, which is responsible for removing dead tissue. While the medicated disc works on the removal of the corn, the pad surrounds the corn, keeping the pressure off. Liquid corn removers also have salicylic acid as the main ingredient, such as *MOSCO CALLUS AND CORN REMOVER*, which is 40 percent salicylic acid. Simply apply a few drops to the corn itself. Avoid putting these products on healthy tissue nearby; it may cause irritation. Some corn and callus removers have an ingredient called **ZINC CHLORIDE**, which is even more irritating and caustic than salicylic acid. Be careful when using it and do not use it for long periods of time.

A **CALLUS** differs from a corn in that it has no central core and is much thicker. Calluses form on weight-bearing areas (such as the palms of the hands and the sides and soles of the feet).

Calluses can be handled in one of two ways: a pressure-relieving pad will stop the build-up of dead tissue, and products containing **SALICYLIC ACID** or **ZINC CHLORIDE** will remove some of the layers of tissue, which in turn will reduce pressure. When a person has a callus, the thickened skin can actually crack or split open, causing pain. One way to handle that is by reducing the callus with a file. Callus files may be found in the foot care section of the drugstore. They do the same job as the corn and callus removers, without chemicals. It is best to do your filing when the foot is dry. Afterwards apply a lotion (any type of moisturizing cream or lotion will do) to the area to reduce the irritation from filing.

An old home remedy for corns and calluses is **CASTOR OIL**. As a matter of fact it is still used in some of the products available today. Actually it does nothing to remove corns and calluses; it simply keeps the tissue soft and pliable. The oil is usually applied at bedtime; the foot is then covered with a sock to prevent the oil from staining the bed linens and to help the castor oil penetrate deeper. However, since castor oil does not remove the excess layers of skin that cause the problem, it is simply a treatment to give relief.

WARTS are caused by viruses. Warts are common in children and young adults and usually appear on exposed areas of the fingers, hands, face, and soles of the feet. Warts that appear on the soles of the feet are called **PLANTAR WARTS.** Sometimes they go unnoticed, but if they get large they can begin causing a great deal of discomfort. Since warts are caused by viruses they may, over a period of time, go away by themselves. Among the products that are available to treat warts are *COMPOUND W* and *DR. SCHOLL'S WART REMOVER SYSTEM*. Both of these products contain **SALICYLIC ACID**, either in solution or in a medicated disc, and they remove tissue. A word of warning: treatment of warts is extremely difficult. Warts may reappear several months after they supposedly have been cured no matter what procedure you use for removal.

When using any sort of over-the-counter product to remove **BUNIONS**, **CORNS**, **CALLUSES**, or **WARTS**, soak the affected area throughout the treatment period for at least five minutes a day in very warm (not hot) water to remove dead tissue. If you are using one of the liquid removers, an application of *VASELINE* or any **PETROLEUM JELLY** to the healthy skin surrounding the area, before applying the medicine, will protect the healthy skin.

Diabetes and Foot Care

Diabetics should be cautioned before using any foot product. Since their circulation in the feet and legs is usually not very good, any sort of foot sore may be very difficult to heal and may even cause severe bacterial infections. This very definitely means do not attempt "bathroom surgery" on the feet or toe nails using sharp knives or razor blades. In some cases diabetics have poor eyesight, which increases the chance of a serious mishap.

Skin Medicine Ingredients

ALLANTOIN is an ingredient that comes from uric acid, a chemical found in urine. Certain animals, but not man, possess an enzyme that converts uric acid to allantoin. However, it is also found to occur in numerous plants. It is a white, crystalline powder which has no odor or taste. During World War I it was noticed that wounds which became infested with maggots healed with unexpected speed. Maggots are able to convert uric acid to allantoin and it was learned that the rapid healing was due to the presence of allantoin in their excretion. At one time it was suggested for use orally to treat gastric ulcers. Allantoin is now used, usually in combination with other chemicals, to promote healing and prevent infection by application only to the skin. It is also used in some over-the-counter aids to heal oral wounds, such as canker sores, but the FDA has not found allantoin effective for this use. Allantoin is ineffective in dandruff, seborrhea and psoriasis drug products.

BENZOYL PEROXIDE is a frequent ingredient of acne products which is prepared synthetically from benzoic acid, a simple organic acid found naturally in Peruvian and tolu balsam. It is used to irritate the surface cells of the face and neck, causing an increased sloughing rate, which in turn peels away skin that blocks the pores that produce oil. This accommodates new growth and healing, opens the pores to let oil out and prevents the formation of pimples. This is a very popular ingredient in acne medicines, probably because it works. It is found in products such as *CLEAR BY DESIGN MEDICATED ACNE GEL*, *CLEARASIL MAXIMUM STRENGTH ACNE MEDICATION* and *OXY-5* and *-10*. Benzoyl peroxide is used in concentrations of five and ten percent. The lower concentration is best to use if you are beginning treatment. It is usually applied at night after the affected area has been washed with soap and water. Fair-skinned people may find it to their advantage to leave it on for only two hours at a time until the skin becomes conditioned to the treatment. Benzoyl peroxide produces a feeling of warmth and stinging when applied to the skin and can even cause the skin to turn red. If the stinging and burning sensation is too strong, remove the medicine immediately with soap and water and do not reapply it until the next day. Since this ingredient is highly irritating, avoid contact with the eyes, lips, and tender areas of the neck. If you are using other methods of treatment, such as sun lamps, do not use them together since either may irritate the skin, and in combination could cause serious damage. By the way, avoid getting any of these products on your clothes, carpets or other fabrics as they will bleach them. Just as a side note, the pure crystals of this chemical are explosive and for use in acne preparations contain at least 30 percent water to eliminate this hazard.

COAL TAR is the black, thick liquid with a moth-ball-like odor which is obtained by destructive distillation of wood. Amazingly, it takes a ton of coal to produce only 8.8 gallons of coal tar. Coal tar is used as the starting material for the production of many other chemicals that are used for medicine and industry. To mask the unpleasant odor, color, and staining properties of coal tar it has been incorporated into numerous kinds of pharmaceutical preparations such as creams, ointments, pastes, lotions, shampoos, and jellies. The mechanism for the action of coal tar is not known, but it appears to be antiseptic, anti-itch and photosensitizing. It is considered safe and effective by the FDA to treat dandruff, seborrheic dermatitis and psoriasis. Coal tar product labels should warn consumers to use caution when in the sun because the ingredient increases the risk of sunburn.

ICHTHYOL or **ICHTHAMMOL** literally means "fish oil" and it was first produced from the hydrocarbons of a shale found in Italy. This shale frequently bears impressions of fish, hence 'ichthy' which is derived from the Greek word for fish. Ichthyol is obtained by distilling bituminous schists. The process of preparing Ichthyol includes the addition of sulfur. It is a reddish-brown to brownish-black, thick fluid with a strong characteristic odor. An irritant chemical which has only mild antibacterial properties, it is used much less now than in past years. We do not recommend this ingredient and the FDA does not consider ichthyol an effective treatment for problem skin conditions. We include it here because some products still contain this ingredient or its derivatives, usually listed as inactive.

JUNIPER TAR or **CADE OIL** has been banned by the FDA for use as an active ingredient in over-the-counter products for dandruff, seborrhea and psoriasis because it is ineffective in treating these diseases. It is the volatile oil obtained from woody parts of *Juniperus oxycedrus*. It is a dark brown, clear, thick liquid having a tarry odor and a faintly bitter taste. It is a mildly irritating oil that was used as a topical anti-itch preparation in several different, chronic dermatologic disorders like psoriasis, atopic dermatitis and generalized itching. This ingredient may appear for some time on labels. The tar can produce injury to the eyes and should be kept clear of that area. It may still be found in ointments, shampoos and even bath preparations.

PINE TAR is another ingredient banned by the FDA for use in nonprescription dandruff, psoriasis and seborrhea drugs because of lack of evidence that it works. It is similar to other tars in that it is obtained from the destruction of wood. This tar is obtained from *Pinus palustris* or other species of the Pinus genus (family Pinaceae). Pine tar is usually obtained as a by-product in the manufacture of charcoal or other chemicals from this wood. It is a complicated mixture of phenol-like chemicals. It is a very thick, black to brown liquid and was used externally as a mild irritant. It has weak antibacterial properties and was used in chronic skin diseases, particularly those that produce eczema. To what extent the FDA will allow it as an "inactive" ingredient remains to be seen. In some cases these ingredients are considered "proprietary," that is, included for some characteristic, such as scent, the manufacturer considers essential in distinguishing its product in the marketplace.

RESORCINOL exists as white, or nearly white, needle shaped crystals or powder. It has a faint characteristic sweet odor and slightly bitter taste. It is synthetically prepared from petroleum chemicals. Resorcinol has mild antibacterial and antifungal properties but was primarily used in acne preparations because it is irritating to the skin, causing it to slough. The FDA is not convinced that it is effective by itself for acne and they do not permit it in acne medications unless combined with sulfur. It is still used for psoriasis, seborrhea and eczema and works by lifting and dispersing the scales of psoriasis so they can be removed for new tissue growth. A word of warning, African Americans should try to avoid using products containing resorcinol, because it may produce a dark brown scale on the skin.

SALICYLIC ACID is produced artificially by a chemical process, although there are numerous relatives of salicylic acid found in natural plants and oils. Salicylic acid prepared from natural sources may have an **OIL OF WINTERGREEN** odor. It is used in the treatment of warts and corns because it is irritating and causes tissue cells to swell, soften and ultimately fall off when it is used in sufficiently high concentrations. **SALICYLIC ACID** was extensively used to treat athlete's foot (tinea pedis, a fungal infection) at one time until the less toxic, better products came along, such as **TOLNAFTATE** (*TINACTIN*), **MICONAZOLE** (*MICATIN*) and **CLOTRIMAZOLE** (*LOTRIMIN*), (see page 148), athlete's foot. The "old timer" *WHITFIELD'S OINTMENT* **(BENZOIC AND SALICYLIC ACID OINTMENT)**, which contains it for use in athlete's foot is still available in drugstores. Salicylic acid is approved by the FDA as safe and effective for use in products advertised to treat dandruff, seborrheic dermatitis and psoriasis at varying concentrations. *X-SEB SHAMPOO* is a 4 percent salicylic acid product indicated for dandruff. *MG 217 PSORIASIS MEDI-*

CATION is 1.5 percent **SALICYLIC ACID** and a 2 percent seborrhea product to relieve skin flaking is *P&S SHAMPOO*. In acne medications salicylic acid is only approved for use in concentrations up to 2 percent, such as the *AVEENO CLEANSING BAR FOR ACNE* (2 percent), *OXY CLEAN MEDICATED CLEANSER* (0.5 percent) and *CLEAR BY DESIGN MEDICATED CLEANSING PADS* (1 percent). In products to treat corns and calluses, like *FREEZONE SOLUTION* (13.6 percent), salicylic acid is present in a much higher concentration. Warts can also be removed with salicylic acid in concentrations as high as 17 percent, in products like *COMPOUND W* solution and gel. Be very careful with these high percentage salicylic acid products because they can burn. Do not use these products if you are a diabetic, or have poor blood circulation.

SELENIUM SULFIDE or **SELENIUM DISULFIDE** is a combination of the metal selenium and sulfur. A reddish-brown to bright orange powder prepared by a synthetic chemical reaction, it is the active ingredient in *SELSUN BLUE SHAMPOO*. As dandruff is the condition of accelerated shedding of skin cells from the scalp, selenium sulfide is claimed to reduce the turnover rate of these epidermal cells thus keeping the loss of these skin cells at a more normal rate. This improves appearance of the hair by reducing the amount of skin and the size of the flakes shedding at any particular time. Selenium sulfide is also mildly antibacterial and antifungal. However, the FDA has ruled that selenium sulfide may only be used in over-the-counter products to treat dandruff and seborrheic dermatitis safely and effectively. It is very toxic orally and care should be taken to avoid ingestion during use.

SULFUR is found in both Sicily and the United States. In its elemental form it is mined from these native deposits. It is frequently found in combination with metals (ores) and widely distributed in nature. Pure elemental sulfur has been applied in numerous dosage forms, such as creams, ointments, dusting powders, lotions and so on because it is germicidal, antifungal and irritating enough to cause skin to slough when used in higher percentages. The main purpose of sulfur is to cut down the production of oil by the oil-producing glands. Sulfur is still accepted by the FDA as being an effective agent for improving the condition of acne. Products containing sulfur include *CLEARASIL ADULT CARE MEDICATED BLEMISH CREAM*, and *ACNOMEL CREAM*. Sulfur is also approved by the FDA as safe and effective for the treatment of dandruff.

ZINC CHLORIDE is a white, granular powder prepared from metallic zinc and chlorine gas that is weakly antiseptic and very water soluble. It is used in over-the-counter products to remove corns and calluses because it is a caustic that destroys cells by precipitating protein, causing the cells to fall off.

ZINC PYRITHIONE is a chemical mixture of zinc, a metal, and pyrithione, a derivative of pyridine which is a chemical found in coal tar (now synthesized from petroleum) and used as a starting chemical for numerous drugs. When applied to the scalp it is mildly antibacterial and antifungal and, like selenium sulfide (see above), is supposed to reduce the turnover rate of shedded surface skin cells from the scalp. This shedding is accelerated in persons with dandruff. Shampoos that contain zinc pyrithione, like *ZINCON DANDRUFF SHAMPOO*, have shown success in improving the condition when used at a concentration of 1 percent. Products with this ingredient can relieve the itching, irritation and scalp flaking associated with dandruff and seborrhea. Because of the success of zinc pyrithione, two compounds chemically related have been patented. They are **ZINC MERCAPTOQUINOLINE-1-OXIDE** and **ZINC 2-MERCAPTOQUIN OXALINE-1-OXIDE**. In most respects they are similar to zinc pyrithione. The FDA has ruled that zinc pyrithione is both safe and effective when used to treat dandruff and seborrheic dermatitis.

26

Sleep Aids & Tranquilizers

Antihistamines

Nothing is as restful as a good night's sleep, but almost half the American population fail to achieve this seemingly simple goal. Some people have trouble falling asleep, others awaken in the middle of the night and cannot go back to sleep. In those situations, it seems that the more one looks at the alarm clock on the night stand, the more one panics, making it almost impossible to get to sleep.

Even though almost half the population has trouble falling asleep, the selection of sleeping aids in the drugstores is rather limited. Scientific review of all over-the-counter sleep aids has shown that only two antihistamines are safe and effective sleep inducers, **DIPHENHYDRAMINE** and **DOXYLAMINE**. The antihistamines **DIPHENHYDRAMINE HYDROCHLORIDE** and **DIPHENHYDRAMINE CITRATE** are ingredients in *COMPOZ, NERVINE, NYTOL, SLEEP-EZE-3, SLEEPINAL, SOMINEX*, and *SOMINEX-2*. **DOXYLAMINE SUCCINATE** is the ingredient in *UNISOM, DOXYSOM* and *ULTRA SLEEP*. Ingredients that have been banned as sleep inducers include: pyrilamine maleate, potassium bromide, sodium bromide and scopolamine hydrobromide.

The FDA standards for over-the-counter sleep aids state that approved products must include the following warnings on labels:

- Do not give to children under 12.
- If sleeplessness persists continuously for more than two weeks, consult a doctor. Insomnia may be a symptom of serious underlying medical illness.

- Do not take this product if there is asthma, glaucoma, emphysema, chronic pulmonary disease, shortness of breath, difficulty in breathing, or difficulty in urination due to enlargement of the prostate gland, unless directed by a doctor.
- Avoid alcoholic beverages while taking this product.
- If one is using sedatives or tranquilizers, do not use this product without first consulting a doctor.

What is an antihistamine doing in a product supposed to induce sleep? Remember that antihistamines have the side effect of causing drowsiness, exactly what one needs to sleep. But the problem with these drugs is that the drowsiness is short lived, occasionally very mild; and some people are tolerant to the drowsiness effect in the first place.

Other products contain both an antihistamine and a pain reliever: for example, *SOMINEX PAIN RELIEF FORMULA*. These products may be effective if pain is what is keeping them awake in the first place.

Although these products are promoted as being safe and non-habit forming, antihistamines do have side effects, which include dizziness, ringing in the ears, blurred vision, and dryness of the mouth and throat. Even mild overdose symptoms from antihistamines are very uncomfortable. They can produce nervousness, nausea, headache, heart palpitations, increased irritability and even hallucinations. Large doses of antihistamines stimulate the central nervous system, resulting in possible seizures. However, the antihistamines used in these products do have a margin of safety if you follow the dosage instruction on the package. If you decide to use these products and they do not work for you, check with a physician. **INSOMNIA** may be a sign of serious underlying illness, such as anxiety or depression.

L-Tryptophan and Blood Disorder

L-TRYPTOPHAN is an over-the counter dietary supplement that has been used by individuals for sleeping difficulties and many other conditions such as premenstrual syndrome, stress, depression and alcohol and drug abuse. The FDA has not approved L-tryptophan for these or any other drug uses.

The FDA has recalled this drug after reports linked consumption of the amino acid tablets or capsules with **EOSINOPHILIA-MYALGIA SYNDROME**, a potentially fatal blood disorder. Eosinophilia-myalgia syndrome can cause a high fever, muscle and joint pain, weakness, skin rash, and swelling of the arms and legs. By December of 1989, state health departments had reported 707 cases of this syndrome to the U.S. Centers for Disease control, and one death had been linked directly to tryptophan use. The FDA has concluded that there is a "strong, virtually unequivocal link between consumption of L-tryptophan tablets or capsules and the syndrome."

Nonchemical Ways to Get to Sleep

If people who have difficulty falling asleep would take the time to figure out what is keeping them awake, they might cure their insomnia without taking anything at all. If you wake up during the night, get out of bed and walk around for a while before trying to go back to sleep. If you have trouble falling asleep, try watching television or reading a book; these activities tire the eyes, often to the point of causing them to close. Some people drink a glass of warm milk, which helps relax them so that they can get to sleep. But avoid big meals at bedtime, these can keep you awake and cause indigestion and gastroesophageal reflux, a condition where acid from the stomach manages to work its way past the stomach-esophagus junction, which normally protects the esophagus. The stomach acid causes burning in the esophagus and will keep you painfully awake.

Another way of relaxing the body is to soak in a tub of water, as warm as you can stand it. The warm water helps relax the muscles and releases the tension that has built up in them all day. Some people find that a hot shower will cause them to feel tired and sleepy. Exercise will help, but exercise at least 4 hours before retiring for the night. If you exercise too close to bedtime, the stimulation will keep you awake.

Finally if you wake up during the night to void, and afterwards cannot get back to sleep, limit the intake of fluids in the evening from about nine o'clock on. If these suggestions sound too simple, remember that it is often the simple methods that work best.

27

Stomach Medicines

Antacids

One area of the drugstore that we all have visited at one time or another is the area that contains the antacids. Every year Americans spend millions of dollars on antacid products to relieve **ACID INDIGESTION** and **HEARTBURN** from periodic bouts of overeating or drinking. It seems that you can hardly watch television or pick up a magazine without seeing an ad of some kind for an antacid product that claims to do wonders for indigestion. With lifestyles the way they are, eating on the run is a part of everyday living, and indigestion is the unwelcome "fringe benefit." Medical statistics show that over twenty million Americans suffer daily from heartburn and these are the heaviest antacid users. Another one third of the population experiences occasional symptoms. And among pregnant women, 25 percent have daily heartburn and about half suffer distress at various times during pregnancy.

Trend watchers of the over-the-counter market report that in spite of the introduction of new prescription drugs like **PRILOSEC** to treat gastric ulcer, antacid sales continue to show a healthy increase in sales, about five percent a year. That amounts to hundreds of millions of dollars annually, making antacids the fourth largest OTC category.

But before taking an over-the-counter antacid, there are some things to consider: How long has there been acid indigestion? Where is the pain located and when does it occur? Is it immediately, or several hours, after a meal? Is the pain relieved by food? Is it aggravated by coffee, carbonated beverages, or smoking? Are other medications taken, or has a doctor prescribed a salt-free diet or treatment for high blood pressure? Answering these questions will help in selecting the right antacid and avoid additional problems. So, antacids should only be taken regularly after checking with a physician. This way he or she can regulate the amount to take and how often to take it. This is very important in getting an antacid to work. Also, diet, stress, smoking and alcohol use should all be modified first, before going on a long-term antacid course of therapy. Just changing these things alone may solve the problem.

ANTACIDS are medicines used to reduce the amount of acid in the stomach and to relieve the symptoms of irritation and heartburn that too much acid produces. Antacids are also a mainstay in the treatment of peptic ulcer and are often used in conjunction with prescription drugs. New research shows that **ANTACIDS** probably work in a combination of three ways: First, they stimulate a group of natural body chemicals known as prostaglandins; second they cause an increase in the production of mucus in the stomach, which is protective; and third, they increase blood flow to the lining of the stomach. All of these things reduce acid production and help a sore stomach heal.

No matter what brand of antacid you use, it is usually available in tablet and liquid form. Do both work equally well? The liquids generally work faster. But the tablets are more convenient to carry around. If you want them to work as fast as the liquid, be sure to chew them up well and follow with water. Oftentimes people suck on them. Of course, this is not wrong, but they do not work as quickly that way. The problem is not in the mouth, it is in the stomach; so get the medicine down as quickly as you can.

The effervescent antacids work very rapidly to give relief, but should not be used for chronic stomach problems. The **EFFERVESCENT** antacid that we are all familiar with is *ALKA SELTZER*, which is available in two varieties. What is the difference? *ALKA SELTZER* in the blue package contains a standard dose of aspirin in addition to the antacid. *ALKA SELTZER* in the gold package contains no aspirin. When *ALKA SELTZER* (blue) is mixed with water, the antacid formed is sodium citrate; *ALKA SELTZER* (gold) is a combination of sodium and potassium citrate. The FDA considers these safe and effective antacids for short term use. So if there is a headache along with an upset stomach, the blue may be effective. An added advantage of effervescent antacid/headache combinations is that when mixed with water they convert the aspirin to a salt of aspirin that is less irritating to the stomach. This may be an advantage when used to treat a problem like hangover (see page 4) or food overindulgence. If there is just an occasional upset stomach, try the *ALKA SELTZER* in the gold package.

A big problem with over-the-counter antacids is their possible interaction with prescription drugs. Antacids containing **ALUMINUM, CALCIUM,** and **MAGNESIUM** should not be combined with a certain group of antibiotics called the **TETRACYCLINES**. These chemicals combine with the tetracycline and cause it not to be absorbed properly. If you must take the two together, ask a doctor if you should space the doses, taking, for example, the tetracycline one hour before the antacid. **IRON** products should not be given with antacids because they decrease the body's ability to absorb the iron properly. Also, certain heart medications such as **DIGOXIN** and **DIGITOXIN** may be absorbed into the antacid that has coated the stomach, preventing it from being released into the blood.

Some people who suffer from **PARKINSON'S DISEASE** take a drug called **LEVODOPA**. Unlike the other drug interactions, antacids may cause increased absorption of levodopa when the two are taken together. In general, since antacids work by either affecting stomach secretions coating the stomach or neutralizing the acid in the stomach, taking any other medication—especially simultaneously could be dangerous.

No matter what type of antacid you use, here are some things to keep in mind: When using antacids to relieve indigestion, do not take them for longer than two weeks. If you do not get relief in this period of time, check with a doctor. When taking antacids, you should be aware they may cause diarrhea or constipation. Patients on **SALT-FREE DIETS** should choose those antacids specifically marked as no or low sodium. These days, there are lots of choices in this category. All antacids are not the same, and the failure of an antacid to treat your condition could be due to poor selection, taking it at the wrong time, or not taking the proper dose.

Antacids for Diabetics

Some of the well-known and widely used antacids, both liquids and tablets, contain sugar. Sugar is an "inactive" ingredient and almost all manufacturers now list it on the label either as inactive or under the heading, "also contains:". So look for it along with other ingredients you want to avoid. Many sugar-free products are now available, such as: *AMPHOJEL, CAMALOX, GELUSIL, MAALOX TC* (Therapeutic Concentrate), *MAALOX PLUS*, and *RIOPAN* and *RIOPAN PLUS*. Most of these contain **SACCHARIN**, or a combination of saccharin and **SORBITOL**, a sweet alcohol that occurs naturally in fruit and is used to mask the after taste of saccharin. Both saccharin and sorbitol are safe for diabetics. Some products, like *MAALOX TC*, are free of both sugar and saccharin and contain only sorbitol as the sweetener. While most antacids have been reformulated to remove sugar, some still contain it, so check the label.

Antacid Ingredients

Choosing the right antacid product depends on knowing what the various ingredients do. The information below should help you make an intelligent choice based on the symptoms.

ALGINIC ACID is not an antacid, but is found with sodium bicarbonate in some antacid combination products like *GAVISCON*. It is a component of the cell wall of certain seaweeds (giant or horsetail kelp) and in the presence of saliva it reacts with sodium bicarbonate to form sodium alginate. The protective effect is supposedly due to foaming and thickening of the stomach contents due to the presence of sodium alginate. It is safe, but the FDA doubts its effectiveness. That is why you will find it listed as an "inactive" ingredient on the label. If you give this ingredient a try, it makes the most sense when used for a condition a doctor will describe as gastroesophageal reflux. This is where acid from the stomach manages to work its way past the stomach-esophagus junction, which normally protects the esophagus.

ALUMINUM SALTS are usually found in antacid products as either **ALUMINUM HYDROXIDE, ALUMINUM CARBONATE** or **ALUMINUM PHOSPHATE**. Of the three, aluminum hydroxide has the greatest neutralizing capacity. Aluminum hydroxide is also sometimes described on the label as **ALUMINA TRIHYDRATE, ALUMINUM HYDRATE** or **HYDRATED ALUMINA**. It is a white powder that is part aluminum oxide (a naturally occurring mineral known as corundum) and may contain varying amounts of aluminum carbonate and bicarbonate. It is obtained from bauxite ore found in North and South America and the Carribean. Since it is practically insoluble in water, little gets into the bloodstream. However, routine ingestion of aluminum salts have been controversial for years. The FDA has considered evidence that some investigators claim links them to Alzheimer's disease. However, at the present time the FDA claims there is no substantial evidence that this is true. Aluminum hydroxide is found in products like *AMPHOJEL*, which is an **ALUMINUM HYDROXIDE GEL. ALUMINUM CARBONATE** is found in *BASALGEL* and **ALUMINUM PHOSPHATE** is found in *PHOSPHALJEL*, although *PHOSPHALJEL* is no longer labeled as an antacid. It is used to control certain electrolyte conditions of the bowel. The main side effect of aluminum antacids is constipation. Sometimes in elderly persons, since their intestinal movements are slower anyway, intestinal obstructions may develop. This constipating effect may be avoided by combining aluminum and magnesium salts in one product (see page 306), or by administering laxatives and stool softeners.

CALCIUM CARBONATE occurs in nature as chalk, oyster shells, limestone and other minerals. Even though it is found abundantly in nature, pharmaceutical companies make it artificially from other starting chemicals into a fine, white, microcrystalline powder for use in antacids as a neutralizing agent. It has uses in other pharmaceuticals as an abrasive, and the same salt may be used as a dietary supplement for calcium, but in much lower doses than as an antacid. As an antacid it produces rapid neutralization of stomach acid. Calcium carbonate is found in *TITRALAC LIQUID* and *TABLETS* and *TUMS CHEWABLE TABLETS*, to name just a couple of products. The primary side effect of calcium antacids is constipation. Also, too much calcium usage may result in the formation of kidney stones. Calcium antacids therefore should not be used for chronic stomach problems like ulcers. If consumed for more than a week or so, calcium may also cause **ACID REBOUND**, or the production of excess stomach acid, which could further irritate an ulcer.

ESSENTIAL OILS are "inactive" ingredients found in many antacids to flavor them. They are worthy of mention because in the "old days" carminatives, as they were called, or stomach "sweeteners" were simply mixed with water. They are called "essential" because they give the flower or leaf of the plant they come from its fragrance. They are naturally occurring oils, although many of them have been prepared synthetically due to shortages of the natural product. Essential oils are used in extremely small quantities as odor or flavoring agents in antacids and other pharmaceuticals. Examples are **PEPPERMINT OIL** and **OIL OF WINTERGREEN**.

MAGNESIUM SALTS that are commonly used in antacids are **MAGNESIUM OXIDE, MAGNESIUM CARBONATE, MAGNESIUM HYDROXIDE** and **MAGNESIUM TRISILICATE**; of these the first three are the most potent. **MAGNESIUM OXIDE**, is also known as **MAGNESIA** (as in **MILK OF MAGNESIA**). While this chemical is used to neutralize stomach acid in pharmaceutical antacids it has wide use in industry as well. It occurs naturally as a mineral known as periclase, but it is a fine, white, odorless powder made from magnesium hydroxide (see below) for use in antacids. **MAGNESIUM CARBONATE** is found in nature also, as a substance called magnesite. For use in antacids it is a synthetically prepared, purer variety, white, bulky light powder which neutralizes stomach acidity nicely; it is also widely used in the food and cosmetic industry. **MAGNESIUM HYDROXIDE** is also a naturally occurring chemical, found in the mineral brucite, but is prepared from simpler chemicals in a purified form when used in medicines as an antacid. Finally, **MAGNESIUM TRISILICATE** is a neutralizing agent which is actually a mixture of magnesium oxide (see above) and silicon dioxide. It occurs in nature as several minerals but is commercially prepared from other mineral salts which are commonly found in sea water. Magnesium salts are found in *PHILLIPS' MILK OF MAGNESIA*. Usually one teaspoonful is suitable for an antacid, but one tablespoonful is a laxative dose. Not surprisingly the most common side effect of magnesium is diarrhea. Probably the best antacids on the market are combinations of **ALUMINUM** and **MAGNESIUM**, such as *ALUDROX, GELUSIL, EXTRA STRENGTH MAALOX WHIP, KOLANTYL GEL, MYLANTA*, and *MAALOX* and *MAALOX TC*. Both aluminum and magnesium are very good neutralizers of stomach acid, and aluminum offsets the side effects of magnesium, while magnesium offsets the side effects of aluminum.

MAGALDRATE is a white powder which is a mixture of magnesium and aluminum hydroxides (see individually above). Magaldrate is a separate chemical and not just a physical mixture of the two powders. Magaldrate is found in *RIOPAN PLUS TABLETS*. The term is a contraction of these chemical names. As mentioned above, magnesium tends to cause diarrhea and aluminum can produce constipation.

Thus, in combination they are balanced to disturb normal bowel function as little as possible. However this combination produces a lower amount of stomach acid neutralization than other available preparations on the market.

SIMETHICONE is found in many over-the-counter antacid products advertised as "gas-relieving" or "anti-gas." *MYLANTA II* tablets, *EXTRA STRENGTH MAALOX PLUS* and *DIGEL LIQUID* all contain simethicone in addition to an antacid. It is a "defoaming" agent which is a mixture of practically inert, synthetic polymers (90-99 percent polydimethylsiloxane) and refined, naturally occurring silicon dioxide (the main component of sand) used with acid neutralizing antacids in antacid preparations. It has no antacid activity itself, but it is used with antacids because simethicone breaks down gas bubbles in the stomach so that they can be eliminated by belching or passing gas. This is a little confusing, since it is advertised as a gas preventative. What simethicone actually does is prevent or reduce pain that an accumulation of gas can cause. But, the gas is still there, it just doesn't form in large bubbles as much. Some scientists who are critical of simethicone's use in over-the-counter products say that it has an anti-gas effect in test tubes but does not seem to relieve the symptoms of gas in most people. Simethicone might be helpful in some people who have the problem of cramping and discomfort, sometimes following certain types of surgery. But remember, if simethicone works, there will be reduced pain and cramping, but more gas and belching, not less. If the problem is strictly discomfort caused by gas, look for simethicone in products such as *MYLICON CHEWABLE TABLETS*, *MYLICON DROPS*, *GAS-X CHEWABLE TABLETS* and *PHAZYME SOFTGELS*.

SODIUM BICARBONATE (BAKING SODA, SODA ACID CARBONATE) is an ingredient that every cook and homemaker is familiar with. The same white, crystalline powder with a salty and slightly bitter taste is found in some of the oldest and most popular antacids on the market such as *ALKA SELTZER, BELL/ANS, SODA MINT*, and *BROMO SELTZER*. It is made from sodium carbonate which occurs naturally near salt lakes as a mineral called thermonatrite. Sodium bicarbonate is a potent antacid effective mainly for the relief of symptoms of occasional overeating or indigestion. Products containing sodium bicarbonate are not intended to be used for long periods of time, because they can eventually overload the system with **SODIUM**. This is extremely important for people who suffer from high blood pressure, since sodium may be a contributing factor in hypertension. It is for this reason that doctors prescribe salt-free diets for patients with high blood pressure (salt is the chemical compound **SODIUM CHLORIDE)**.

Remember that not all antacids are equal, so you must know what you want the antacid to do. Large chain stores may carry their own brands of antacid. Compare their ingredients with the ingredients in the product you normally buy and you will probably notice that the only difference is in the price.

Anti-Diarrheals

A condition that is the source of much humor is no joking matter for the person who has it. Diarrhea can be caused by a variety of different agents, such as a virus, drugs of various kinds, and certain foods. Diarrhea in infants and young children is common. About 50 percent of the time its incidence is often attributed to a viral infection of the intestinal tract. Diarrhea caused by bacteria and viruses is infectious and has been a major problem in day care centers and nursing homes in recent years.

Viral diarrhea usually develops rapidly without any warning signals, lasts about one to two days, and produces a low grade fever. However, diarrhea in small infants and the elderly can be dangerous. The loss of water and salts in a short period of time may cause severe **DEHYDRATION**, which could develop into serious complications.

When **DIARRHEA** strikes it is important to keep the person you're caring for, especially children from becoming dehydrated. This can be done simply by giving fluids that contain **WATER, ELECTROLYTES** and a limited amount of **SUGAR.** Diarrhea not only drains fluids from our system but also restricts liquids from being absorbed through the intestinal wall. So simply drinking fluids is ineffective, they just pass straight through. In the 1960s, almost by accident, an important discovery was made. Medical scientists working with oral rehydration methods added sugar to salt solutions to make them more pleasant to drink. By doing this they discovered that the sugar was the key to getting electrolytes absorbed. Commercial rehydration fluids are available, particularly for infants, like *PEDIALYTE ORAL ELECTROLYTE REHYDRATION SOLUTION*. You can make a home preparation by mixing **one level teaspoonful of table salt and eight level teaspoonsful of table sugar, mixed in a quart of water.** In third world countries mixtures like this have been hailed by world health organizations as lifesaving. We recommend the commercial preparations which you can find in most drug stores in the United States.

The characteristics of the stool can be helpful in determining the cause of diarrhea. For example, undigested food particles in the stool indicate small-intestine irritation. Black, tarry stool can mean upper intestinal bleeding or bleeding from the stomach. Red stool may indicate large intestine bleeding, or perhaps simply eating a food containing a red dye, such as beets, or the skin of red vegetables, like tomatoes. At this point it would be a good idea to check with a doctor before using over-the-counter products.

Diarrhea is a symptom of a problem; therefore, treatment should be aimed at the problem causing the diarrhea and not just at stopping the mad dashes to the bathroom, unpleasant though these may be.

ADSORBENTS are the type of ingredient most frequently found in over-the-counter anti-diarrhea products such as *KAOLIN, PECTIN, ATTAPULGITE* and *BISMUTH SUBSALICYLATE.* They work by adsorbing (holding on their surfaces) nutrients, toxins, and bacteria from the intestinal tract. Because they are generally taken in large doses, most of them are flavored to taste good. Adsorbents are generally used in the treatment of minor diarrhea, because they are relatively safe and have the ability to adsorb ingested materials as well as bacteria and other irritating matter when taken orally. In most cases these products are not themselves absorbed into the body. They act like a sponge in the intestines, and they sometimes cause constipation because of the water they absorb. In infants, however, the symptom of fluid loss must be controlled immediately to prevent dehydration and its severe consequences.

However, people using an adsorbent diarrhea product should be careful if they are taking any other type of medicine, because it may interfere with the body's ability to absorb the medicine properly. Before buying this or any product, it would be wise to talk it over with a physician, pharmacist or nurse first.

Adsorbents are usually taken after each loose bowel movement until the diarrhea is controlled. Some of the products that fall into this class are: *KAOPECTATE, ADVANCED FORMULA, RHEABAN* and *PEPTO-BISMOL LIQUID* and *TABLETS*. Remember to check with a physician before giving *PEPTO-BISMOL* to children because it contains a salicylate (see Reye Syndrome, page 177).

OTC products to treat diarrhea used to contain additional ingredients, such as the **BELLADONNA ALKALOIDS**. When diarrhea is due to increased intestinal activity, these ingredients are claimed to slow it down. However, the belladonna alkaloids, atropine, scopolamine and hyoscyamine were found in over the counter antidiarrheal products in too low a dose to be effective and have been banned by the FDA in OTC products. If the manufacturer were to include them at higher amounts they would be too toxic and would have too many side effects. These products may remain on the market until existing supplies are used up or until manufacturers can reformulate them. If these products are still around the house, they should not be used in children without the consent of a doctor, and people who have glaucoma or pressure in the eyes should avoid them completely. Side effects include blurring of vision, rapid pulse, or dizziness. These products are not intended for long use.

Years ago **PAREGORIC** was used to treat diarrhea. Aside from the horrible taste, it worked well to stop diarrhea. Paregoric contains an opium derivative, morphine, which works directly on the small intestine and colon to slow them down, thereby slowing passage of intestinal contents as well. This in turn allows us to reabsorb water and salts from the intestines and stops diarrhea.

At the present time, straight paregoric is available only on a physician's prescription. Because of its narcotic content, people began to abuse the drug. Some people became hooked on it and went from drugstore to drugstore to buy bottles of it. Pharmacists could only sell a maximum of two ounces in a 48-hour period to a single individual, so at the time of the sale each person signed his or her name and address in a record book.

Paregoric has been recently banned by the FDA in products not requiring a prescription, like *PAREPECTOLIN* or *KAPECTOLIN WITH PAREGORIC*. Other products contain powdered opium in amounts similar to paregoric, like *DONNAGEL-PG* or *KAPECTOLIN-PG*. These products until recently could be purchased in some states without a prescription, but you had to ask the pharmacist and sign for them. The FDA no longer considers them safe and effective at the doses found in the over-the-counter strengths.

A new safe and effective alternative to paregoric is the ingredient **LOPERAMIDE** found in the product *IMODIUM AD* caplets and liquid and other brand name products. This drug is very effective and much safer than paregoric or powdered opium in relieving diarrhea (also see page 315). **LOPERAMIDE** slows down the movement of the intestines and reduces water loss.

Sometimes people develop diarrhea when they take certain kinds of prescription medicines, such as antibiotics. Since these are made to kill bacteria, they may kill the beneficial bacteria in the intestines that are responsible for proper intestinal and bowel functions, resulting in diarrhea. There are some products that restore normal intestinal bacteria, such as *BACID CAPSULES* and *LACTINEX TABLETS* and *GRANULES*. The FDA has recently banned these sources of bacteria for use as a cure for diarrhea.

Even for loose stools related to the use of antibiotics, the FDA says its effective to drink buttermilk or eat yogurt. Be sure first that it is alright to drink it while taking the antibiotic, since milk can interact with the **TETRACYCLINE** antibiotics. Drink it one hour before or two hours after a dose of medicine.

Although people joke about diarrhea, it can cause serious problems. If we lose too much fluid, we become dehydrated. This is especially dangerous in infants, because it happens so fast. If a child has diarrhea, keep a close eye on him or her. It might help to take their temperature often, to make sure it is not getting too high from the loss of fluids. If a child develops a fever, call a doctor and have the patient drink plenty of fluids. If there is blood in the stool, or if the stool becomes very slimy, call a doctor; diarrhea may not be the only problem.

Antidiarrheal drug products banned by the FDA are: glycine, scopolamine hydrobromide, aluminum hydroxide, atropine sulfate, calcium carbonate, carboxymethylcellulose, homatropine methylbromide, hyoscyamine sulfate, lactobacillus acidophilus, lactobacillus bulgaricus, opium-powdered, opium tincture, paregoric, phenyl salicylate, zinc phenolsulfonate.

Below is a listing of ingredients used to treat diarrhea.

A study of these can help you find one for the immediate problem.

Anti-diarrheal Ingredients

ATROPINE SULFATE is no longer considered safe and effective by the FDA in over-the-counter products for the reasons discussed above (see page 310). But it may be on the market for awhile until manufacturers can reformulate their products, so we include it here for your information. It is prepared from an intensely bitter drug found in the plant *Atropa belladonna*. It was used in antidiarrheal medicines because it slows the normal rhythmic movement of the gastrointestinal spasms. It is prescribed to treat "spastic colon," "irritable bowel syndrome," and related disorders when diarrhea may be caused by an undesirable or abnormal increase in intestinal muscle tone. The drug causes its effect by paralyzing muscles involved in certain functions, like movement of the intestines The problem is that this effect is not very specific and side effects involve the salivary glands, the urinary bladder and blood vessels in the skin, causing dry mouth, difficulty in urination and flushing of the skin, to name a few. Atropine is safe in small doses, but is available on prescription only for good reasons, as the side effects listed above occur with great frequency. It is poisonous in overdose and can cause potentially fatal heart rhythm disturbance. Any use of atropine should be only on the advice or prescription of a physician.

ATTAPULGITE is a clay mineral composed of magnesium and aluminum silicate. It occurs in sediments from lakes and salt deposits and desert soils. The refined preparation is used as an adsorbent in treating diarrhea. Attapulgite is found in *KAOPECTATE, ADVANCED FORMULA*.

BISMUTH SUBSALICYLATE, an ingredient of *PEPTO-BISMOL*, is a white, odorless, powdered salt of the naturally occurring metal, bismuth. It has antacid, adsorbent and astringent actions. Care should be taken as this preparation is similar to aspirin and should be avoided by persons sensitive to aspirin or by children because of concern for Reye Syndrome (see page 177). Also, bismuth poisoning can occur if the drug is taken for long periods of time. This ingredient is for short term use only (also see Traveler's Diarrhea, Chapter 30).

HYOSCINE HYDROBROMIDE (or scopolamine) is a powdered or crystalline derivative from various plants such as belladonna (*Atropa belladonna*) or jimson (*Datura stramonium*). It produces virtually the same effect on the body as atropine, described above.

HYOSCYAMINE SULFATE is essentially the same drug as atropine (see above). It is found in many of the same plants as atropine. In antidiarrheal preparations it is used for the identical purpose and no advantage over atropine exists.

KAOLIN is a high quality clay which consists of aluminum oxide and silicon dioxide. It is widely used for pharmaceuticals because of its purity and adsorbent properties, for which it is incorporated into antidiarrheal preparations. An FDA panel evaluating antidiarrheal drugs recognized that this and other popular adsorbent clays are safe but added that there is not enough proof to determine that these agents really work. Clays are not selective and adsorb nutrients and digestive enzymes as well as bacteria and poisons when they are taken by mouth. An added concern about aluminum salts in particular is that aluminum in the diet is claimed by some to be a link to Alzheimer's Disease or presenile dementia (premature senility). The FDA has officially stated that there is not enough evidence to substantiate this claim. Even though some of these salts are claimed not to be absorbed from the bowel, some absorption is possible and when used over long periods of time can increase the net amount of aluminum in the body.

LACTOBACILLUS ACIDOPHILUS and another bacteria, *Lactobacillus bulgaricus*, are used to "seed" the gastrointestinal tract with favorable bacteria in the belief that diarrhea may sometimes be caused by an upset in the normal bacteria resident in the bowel. It is thought that these bacteria keep down the growth of other disease-producing bacteria. However, review panels for the FDA have stated that there is probably no advantage over a simple diet which includes 240 to 400 grams of lactose (milk sugar) or dextrin (starch gum) which can be obtained from milk or buttermilk. However, the use of tablets is a less fattening way to promote growth of these beneficial bacteria. As of May 1991 the FDA has banned the use of this bacteria as an anti-diarrheal in over-the-counter products.

LOPERAMIDE is a synthetic chemical similar to morphine. It acts as an antidiarrheal drug by slowing intestinal movement and by reducing the loss of water and electrolytes rectally. Unlike the narcotics, your body does not develop a tolerance to loperamide. This means that the drug will continue to work as an anti-diarrheal even if taken for long periods of time. However, you should not use loperamide for anything more than controlling temporary diarrhea. Loperamide is a relative newcomer to the over-the-counter market and is a safe, effective alternative to the older paregoric-containing products.

PECTIN a naturally occurring carbohydrate found in cell walls and tissues of plants and especially in fruit, in the same chemical family of starch and cellulose. Pectin has a tendency to absorb water and thicken, thus providing bulk in diarrheal illnesses.

Hemorrhoid Medicines

Hemorrhoids are another condition that many people joke about. But hemorrhoids are no laughing matter; it is one of the most annoying and uncomfortable of disorders. However, many of the symptoms can be self-treated. There are a number of over-the-counter products for relief of the burning, pain, itching and bleeding of hemorrhoids.

Some of the causes of hemorrhoids are constipation and diarrhea, coughing, sneezing, vomiting, pregnancy, and physical exertion. Thus we are all prime candidates for hemorrhoids.

Pregnancy is by far the most common cause of hemorrhoids in young women. Some of the signs and symptoms are itching, burning, pain, inflammation, irritation, swelling, and a lot of discomfort. All of these symptoms can be relieved by self-medication. Bleeding, seepage and protrusion are more serious symptoms that should not be self-medicated.

Over-the-counter preparations are available in creams, ointments, suppositories, and towelettes. Some contain a local anesthetic such as **BENZOCAINE**, found in *PAZO HEMORRHOIDAL SUPPOSITORIES;* **PRAMOXINE HYDROCHLORIDE**, used in *ANUSOL HEMORRHOIDAL OINTMENT* and *TRONOLANE ANESTHETIC CREAM*; or *DIBUCAINE* employed in *NUPERCAINAL HEMORRHOIDAL ANESTHETIC OINTMENT*. Make sure these tubes containing anesthetic are not within children's reach as they can be very poisonous or fatal if eaten. These products are effective at relieving pain, burning, itching, and irritation. Also remember that local anesthetics produce allergic reactions in some people. Some products also have an ingredient that constricts or tightens the blood vessels. One ingredient that works in this way is **EPHEDRINE**, also found in *PAZO SUPPOSITORIES* mentioned above. This product is most effective at relieving itching due to the swelling of the rectal blood vessels.

Other products contain protectants. These cover the affected area and act to prevent irritation and water loss from the tissues. They also help protect tissue from additional irritation from fecal matter and air. For example, *PREPARATION H OINTMENT* and *SUPPOSITORY* have shark liver oil as the protectant. Other ingredients used for protecting the irritated area are **LANOLIN, PETROLATUM**

(VASELINE), **COCOA BUTTER, CALAMINE**, and **MINERAL OIL.** All of these protectants are recommended for both internal and external use, with the exception of **GLYCERIN**, which is recommended for external use only. Of the recommended protectants, petrolatum is probably the most effective.

Some of the hemorrhoidal products contain an astringent such as **HAMAMELIS WATER (WITCH HAZEL)**. This is found in *TUCKS PADS* and *PREPARATION H CLEANSING PADS*. These products are easy to use to cleanse the area, and since they contain an astringent (see page 265), will help shrink swollen tissues. As a matter of fact, some women use these pads to tighten up wrinkles on the face. Use them mainly to cleanse the area, prior to applying a cream or ointment.

Hemorrhoidal suppositories are also available and have been used for many years. A suppository helps ease straining at the stool by its lubricating effect. However, suppositories work slowly because they must melt in order to release the active ingredient. *PREPARATION H SUPPOSITORIES* are very popular. The active ingredient is shark liver oil, which mainly works by protecting the irritated tissue. Other products like *PAZO* and *RECTAL MEDICONE SUPPOSITORIES* have a deadening ingredient such as **BENZOCAINE.** They also have astringents to shrink swollen tissue.

No matter what type of product you use to treat your hemorrhoids, there are a few things to keep in mind: It is a good idea to soak yourself in a tub of hot water for about fifteen to thirty minutes before applying your cream or ointment. The hot water will not only help to relieve the itching and irritation, but also to open the pores of the skin so medicine is absorbed faster. Also watch what you eat; some foods may aggravate the symptoms, especially those delicious spicy dishes. It also helps to take a stool softener like *COLACE* periodically. This keeps the stool soft to eliminate strain and reduce further irritation.

A good rule of thumb is to select a product with as few ingredients as possible. Do not mix hemorrhoid products with a harsh stimulant laxative; it will only cause further irritation. Select a product that is a plain stool softener, or ask your pharmacist or doctor.

Intestinal Gas (flatulence)

The most common cause of intestinal gas is swallowing air. In fact, most of the gas inside us is composed of oxygen and nitrogen, the same gases that the atmosphere is made of. Swallowing air is hard to avoid—a little goes down with each mouthful of food. Eating too fast can increase the amount of air we swallow. Even ill-fitting dentures and chewing gum can be the cause of taking in too much air. Other intestinal gases include hydrogen, carbon dioxide and methane. These are produced in the large intestine when undigested food is fermented by bacteria that live in the colon. All five of these gases are odorless and make up about 99 percent of all intestinal gas. The foul odor associated with flatus (the medical name for gas when it is passed rectally) comes from gases that result from the fermentation process. Some of these gases can be detected by smell in very low concentrations.

Some people swallow more air than others, and some people produce more gas than others. Researchers have found that it is not the amount of gas that causes the discomfort (both stomach and social) but the movement of the gas. Slow transit time of food in the intestinal tract contributes to the problem. People who swallow more air and drink lots of beer and carbonated soft drinks may have trouble with belching. Foods that get into the stomach in an undigested state and are fermented by bacteria result in more flatus production.

Gas production is best controlled by diet. Foods like beans, bagels, bran, broccoli, Brussels sprouts, cabbage, cauliflower, onions, and milk and milk products for those who are lactose intolerant (see below) can be a real problem.

Unfortunately, modern medicine doesn't have any good answers for a person with a gas problem. The FDA has approved only one ingredient, **SIMETHICONE**, as safe and effective for relief of flatulence and gas (see page 307). But the FDA advisory panels, made up of independent scientists, disagree with the FDA and say that no ingredient has been proven effective in treating gas and flatulence. Simethicone is safe enough, it just isn't a cure-all for a real gas problem (see page 307).

Relieving gas in a socially acceptable manner still remains elusive to many people. The best advice seems to be: Watch your diet, eat more slowly, chew your food well, and relax, since some researchers believe that stress may contribute to that gassy feeling.

Lactose Intolerance

A common complaint among kids is a stomachache in the morning before getting onto the school bus. Recently doctors found that one cause of such recurring stomachaches in children is their inability to digest the sugar in milk. **LACTOSE INTOLERANCE** sometimes occurs in adults as well. As a matter of fact, people who have drunk milk all their lives without a problem may suddenly notice that they develop cramps, gas, and even diarrhea when they drink milk or eat other dairy products containing lactose. However, because we rely on milk for its calcium, we can not just cut it out of our diets without making adjustments to get it from other sources. Fortunately, there are products on the market that make the milk easier to digest by supplying the lactase enzyme. *LACTAID* and *DAIRY EASE* are two products that do what your own body should do, which is to "split" the lactose into its normal digestible form, without interfering with the taste of the milk.

These products are available in liquid, caplet and powder form. You can add them to a quart of fresh milk and leave it in the refrigerator for about 24 hours. After this period of time, about 70 percent of the sugars in the milk are broken down. *LACTAID* works quite well in fresh skim or whole milk, powdered milk, or canned milk. The milk may be homogenized or not. It is not recommended for use in chocolate milk, although chocolate may be added after treatment. Be sure if you use whole milk that it is fresh, as the enzyme in this product does not work in buttermilk or other cultured products. Some forms of these products, like *DAIRY EASE*, are intended to be taken orally right at the time you eat or drink the products you normally can not tolerate. You are to take it with the "first bite of any lactose content food." The tablet forms can be swallowed, chewed or crushed and sprinkled on food.

Many children and elderly adults develop this "allergy" to milk. If you are not sure whether you have this problem, it is very easy to find out. If you notice cramping, gas, or diarrhea after you drink milk, discontinue the use of all dairy products for 24 to 48 hours. If the symptoms disappear and then reappear with repeated use of the product, there is a good chance that there is a lactose intolerance to milk.

Laxatives

Everyone has needed a laxative at one time or another. But if you reach for a laxative every time the bowels refuse to move, you could be headed for trouble. The Food and Drug Administration warns that laxatives are, after all, drugs. And like other drugs, they pose the risk of side effects and habituation. Moreover, use of a laxative at the onset of constipation could delay treatment for a serious underlying problem that is causing the irregularity. We want to emphasize at the outset of this section that it is very important to see a physician if there is a persistent change of bowel habits.

LAXATIVES work by stimulating movement of the intestine, which forces out waste material. The most frequent users of laxatives are elderly people because, unfortunately, the older we get the less active we become. Bodily functions slow down. As the saying goes, you can tell you are getting older when you start listening to laxative commercials. Laxatives are used by people to give them regularity in their bowel movements. The problem is, regularity is vaguely defined. One study showed that the range of bowel movement frequency in humans is from three times per day to three times per week. So constipation cannot be defined solely in terms of the number of bowel movements in any given period.

Constipation can be caused by a variety of conditions:

- environmental changes
- failure to acquire a regular habit
- faulty eating habits
- mental stress
- taking certain prescription drugs
- laxative abuse

If there is constipation, try to figure out what might be causing the problem. Taking laxatives routinely, for instance, may cause laxative dependency. Constipation can often be relieved by eating a high fiber diet, plentiful liquid consumption, and regular exercise, or simply altering one's daily routine to allow more time on the commode to relax and let nature take its course.

The FDA Advisory Panel on Over-the-Counter Laxatives, Antidiarrheal, Emetic, and Anti-emetic Drugs in 1975 analyzed the ingredients in most over-the-counter oral and rectal laxatives available in the United States. It approved some ingredients as safe and effective for temporary use (category I), some as unsafe and ineffective (category II), and some as lacking sufficient data on safety and effectiveness, needing further testing (category III). A key finding of the advisory panel was that overuse of laxatives was common. This continues to be a problem. So when considering the choices below, make sure to follow instructions carefully and do not overuse them. Overuse can lead to a worsening of the condition.

Stimulant Laxatives

Stimulant laxatives work by irritating the lining of the intestines, which in turn irritates the nerves that cause the intestinal muscles to move and thus cause a bowel movement. Stimulant laxatives are contraindicated with abdominal pain, nausea or vomiting; these may be symptoms of appendicitis. Stimulant laxatives are effective but should be used cautiously and are not recommended for routine use by people with simple constipation. They should never be used for longer than one week of regular treatment, nor should you exceed the recommended dosage. Among the ingredients most commonly used in stimulant laxatives is **BISACODYL**, which is available in tablets and suppository form. The tablets usually work in six to ten hours. The rectal suppositories work in 15 to 60 minutes. It is an ingredient found in *DULCOLAX*. **PHENOLPHTHALEIN** is another ingredient found in some stimulant laxatives such as *EXLAX, FEEN-A-MINT, MODANE* and *ALOPHEN* and usually works in six to eight hours. **ALOE, CASCARA**, and **SENNA** usually work in eight to twelve hours, or sometimes may require up to 24 hours to work. **ALOE** and **CASCARA** can be found in *NATURE'S REMEDY; SENNA* is available in *FLETCHER'S CASTORIA, SENOKOT* and *BLACK DRAUGHT*.

In choosing any one of these ingredients be aware that it is a stimulant laxative and how soon to expect relief.

The FDA has banned the following stimulant-laxative ingredients beginning in May 1991: calomel, colocynth, elasterin resin, gamboge, ipomea, jalap, podophyllum resin, aloin, bile salts, bile acids, calcium pantothenate, frangula, ox bile, prune concentrate, prune powder, rhubarb-Chinese, and sodium oleate.

Lubricants and Stool Softeners

MINERAL OIL and certain digestible plant oils, for example, **OLIVE OIL**, soften fecal contents by coating them with oil, making it easier to pass them. Using mineral oil as a laxative can cause absorption of the oil-soluble vitamins A and D from our bodies. If taking oil-soluble vitamins such as A, D, E, and K at the same time as mineral oil, the vitamins will not be absorbed into the body. They will instead be absorbed into the oil, and then eliminated from the body. Prolonged use of these products may cause deficiencies in these vitamins. Mineral oil should not be taken with meals because it may delay the emptying of the stomach. If large doses are taken, it may lubricate the intestine to the point of causing anal leakage, which could lead to anal itching or hemorrhoids. Some products combine mineral oil and other ingredients into emulsions. *KONDREMUL* is one of these which is mineral oil, Irish moss and flavors. Another product is *AGORAL* which is marshmallow or raspberry flavored mineral oil.

These products are mainly designed to soften stools. It is probably better to use an ingredient called **SODIUM DOCUSATE**, found in the product called *COLACE*, if you are looking for a stool softener rather than a laxative. Occasionally, stool softeners are combined with laxatives. *DOXIDAN* and *PERI-COLACE* are products like this. *DOXIDAN LIQUIGELS* contain docusate and phenolphthalein, while *PERI-COLACE* is docusate and **CASANTHRANOL.** The FDA has recently banned one ingredient, Poloxamer 188, as a stool softener ingredient.

Saline Laxatives

Saline laxatives are mainly used for immediate evacuation of the bowel before X-rays, tests, or surgery. These products should never by used for long-term treatment of constipation. The active ingredient in saline laxatives either **MAGNESIUM SULFATE (EPSOM SALTS)** or **MAGNESIUM CITRATE**. They usually work in about three to five hours. Products containing magnesium should not be used by people with kidney disease.

Enemas

Enemas are normally used to prepare patients for surgery, child delivery, and X-ray examination. But occasionally they are used in cases of constipation. An enema works in two to fifteen minutes. One of the most commonly used is *FLEET ENEMA*. Care should be taken when administering enemas, since a misdirected or inadequately lubricated nozzle could cause severe irritation to the anal canal. *FLEET ENEMA* and the like contain phosphate compounds and overuse in children may lead to toxic levels of phosphorus in the blood. They should not be used in children unless directed by a physician.

Suppositories

GLYCERIN SUPPOSITORIES have been an old standby for infants and adults for years. Inserted rectally, they have an irritant effect and usually produce results in 15 to 60 minutes. Aside from the inconvenience of using a suppository, side effects are minimal.

Bulk-Producing Laxatives

These laxatives are probably the best choice for simple constipation. *CITRUCEL* contains an ingredient called **METHYLCELLULOSE** and is available in powder form. A similar product is *UNIFIBER* which contains a close relative, **CELLULOSE**. When these products get into the intestine, they absorb water and swell. This gives the intestine a natural feeling of fullness, which in turn stimulates movement. They are usually effective in 12 to 24 hours, but sometimes may require as long as three days. If there is a need for a laxative that works fast, these products will not do the job. Bulk-producing laxatives may combine with certain drugs, such as the salicylates found in some pain relievers, and should not be taken together, because they could cause these drugs not to be absorbed into the body properly. Some bulk-producing laxatives (like *METAMUCIL*, *SERUTAN* and *KON-*

SYL) contain **PSYLLIUM**, which in combination with the salicylates speeds up movement in the gut, causing the drugs to be passed out more quickly and decreasing absorption.

Bulk-producing laxatives have recently been affected by legislation that now requires special labeling to warn users to take them with adequate fluid and to avoid them altogether if they have ever experienced difficulty in swallowing. The warning reads:

"Take (or mix) this product with at least 8 ounces (a full glass) of water or other fluid. Taking this product without adequate fluid may cause it to swell and block your throat or esophagus and may cause choking. Do not take this product if you have ever had difficulty in swallowing or have any throat problems. If you experience chest pain, vomiting, or difficulty in swallowing or breathing after taking this product, seek immediate medical attention."

In addition, certain bulk-producing laxatives are entirely banned by the FDA. They are carrageenan (degraded), agar, carrageenan (native) and guar gum. The agency has said that these have not been proven effective and guar gum presents a safety hazard in laxative products.

Remember, regular use of most laxatives, especially the stimulant type, can cause laxative dependency. Excessive use can cause diarrhea and vomiting, which could lead to serious problems.

Laxative Ingredients

Consider the following ingredients carefully when making your choice:

ALOE the aloe used as a drug in laxatives should not be confused with the aloe vera frequently used in lotions and gels (see aloe vera) although they both come from the same plant, *Aloe barbadensis*. Aloe comes from the yellow, bitter juice found in specialized cells of the leaf and is an irritating drug. This irritation causes movement of the intestinal tract which leads to evacuation of the bowel. However, the use of aloe as a laxative is to be discouraged. It is too irritating and there are other, safer alternatives.

BISACODYL occurs as a white to off-white crystalline powder considered a stimulant laxative which irritates the bowel to make a movement easier.

CASANTHRANOL is an irritant cathartic ingredient that is very similar to **CASCARA SAGRADA** in its action. In fact it is a chemically treated derivative of **CASCARA.**

CASCARA SAGRADA is the dried bark of the tree *Rhamnus purshiana*. For medicinal use it occurs as a yellow brown to yellow orange powder. It contains a number of chemicals to produce irritation of the intestinal tract and evacuation of the bowel.

CASTOR OIL is the oil squeezed from the seed of the plant *Ricinus communis*. While the seeds are extremely poisonous the oil that is squeezed from the kernel of the seed is relatively free of toxins. Any remaining poison in the oil is destroyed by steaming during manufacture. Castor oil contains at least two chemicals that are the cathartic principles.

DANTHRON is a synthetic drug that chemically resembles the active ingredients in aloe, senna and cascara. It is an orange, crystalline powder which acts to irritate and thus stimulate the bowel to catharsis.

DIBASIC SODIUM PHOSPHATE exists as colorless, translucent crystals or white powder with a salty taste prepared from simpler, naturally occurring chemicals. It is used in laxatives and enemas to induce the accumulation of fluid in the bowel to produce evacuation. Effectiveness of these chemicals is contested and may simply be due to the additional fluid introduced orally or rectally.

CALCIUM DOCUSATE is synthetic and is prepared as a white granular chemical in the dry form having a characteristic odor. Derived from sodium docusate it is claimed to be more effective as a stool softener.

SODIUM DOCUSATE occurs as a white, waxlike, plastic solid when dry. Solutions are usually made and marketed in soft gelatin capsules. The solution has a bitter taste and characteristic odor. This chemically is really a detergent or surfactant, and it is this property that makes it effective as a stool softener.

MAGNESIUM CITRATE or **CITRATE OF MAGNESIA** is a white, odorless crystalline chemical or powder when dry but is usually sold as a solution which is a colorless to slightly yellow, clear, effervescent liquid having a sweet, acid taste and a lemon flavor. It is prepared by combining magnesium carbonate, citric acid and sodium or potassium bicarbonate in solution. The citric acid combined with sodium or potassium bicarbonate enables the solution to effervesce or bubble.

MAGNESIUM SULFATE or **EPSOM SALT** is an odorless, white or colorless, needlelike, bitter tasting salt that has been popular as a saline cathartic for many years. The term Epsom is the name of an English spa at a natural spring of the same name, thus it is a naturally occurring mineral. It is also extracted from salt water brines. The salt, which is poorly absorbed, causes the accumulation of water from the surrounding tissues to occur in the bowel. This bulk of fluid facilitates the production of a stool.

METHYLCELLULOSE occurs as a white, fibrous powder or granules which when mixed with water swells to produce a clear, thick suspension which provides bulk to permit a bowel movement. It is prepared by a chemical reaction from cellulose, which is the fundamental constituent of all vegetable tissue and is a natural carbohydrate.

MINERAL OIL is a complex mixture of hydrocarbons (the simplest of organic chemicals) derived from crude petroleum and used as a lubricant laxative.

MONOBASIC SODIUM PHOSPHATE, prepared synthetically from basic starting chemicals, it is a crystalline powder used in enemas to produce evacuation of the colon within 2 to 5 minutes.

PLANTAGO or **PSYLLIUM** preparations are obtained from the seeds of a variety of species of plantago plant. The coating of the dried, ripe plantago seed has a high content of mucilages which provide bulk to enhance bowel movement.

SENNA is unground or powdered dried leaflet of the plant *Cassia actifolia* or *Cassia angustifolia*. These are low branching shrubs growing wild in Somalia, Arabia and India. Senna may be prepared as powders, granules, tablets, syrups or extracts, but all rely on the intestinal irritant effect of active principles found in senna which is considered to be one of the milder irritant cathartics.

PHENOLPHTHALEIN is a white or faintly yellowish white crystalline powder which irritates or stimulates the intestinal lining to produce a bowel movement. Recent studies indicate that this chemical changes fluid absorption in the intestines to produce collection of fluid in the bowel. Additional fluid will cause the stool to move and be eliminated.

28

Summer Ailments

Heat

Everyone enjoys being outdoors enjoying nature, playing sports, and going on picnics in the summertime. But there is a danger of developing **HEAT EXHAUSTION** or possibly **HEATSTROKE**, which may be life-threatening. Most epidemics of heat-related illness happen when the temperature is above 90°F with relative humidity above 50 percent.

It is important to know the difference between heat exhaustion and heat stroke. With **HEAT EXHAUSTION** body temperature is usually normal or only slightly elevated. The victim usually develops cramps in the muscles, nausea and even vomiting. The signs and symptoms are primarily due to water depletion. Cramps are due primarily to loss of salt from exertion or heavy sweating where there is high temperature. The skin becomes pale and clammy, and the victim may become faint. If the person is conscious they may complain of headache, fatigue, and weakness. They may be irritable and confused. The best first aid is to get the person to a cool area and sponge down the skin with a cold, wet cloth. Once they regain consciousness, give them fluids to drink. Be careful, because heat exhaustion can turn into heat stroke.

With **HEATSTROKE**, on the other hand, matters are much more serious. Body temperature is usually over 104°F and the person has stopped sweating. Heat stroke is the least common overheating emergency, but the most serious form. Emergency medical people report that as many as 3 out of 4 persons who suffer true heatstroke die. The body's temperature regulating system becomes overwhelmed and begins to malfunction. The **CLASSIC HEATSTROKE** victim is an elderly person or an infant. It usually develops over a few days, such as during a heat wave, in those who are unable to obtain enough fluids and keep themselves cool. Because it develops over a period of time, dehydration occurs and these persons will stop sweating, so they appear very dry. There is also what is called **EXERTIONAL HEATSTROKE** which occurs in young, fit people who have not adjusted to a change in climate before they are involved in heavy exercise. This happens frequently in athletes, outdoor workers and military recruits. This type of heatstroke develops over a few hours, so you do not get dehydrated. That means that you can be sweating heavily and still suffer from exertional heatstroke.

The person suffering from **HEATSTROKE** faints and the skin appears red and fiery hot. The number of persons who die from heat stroke is high, so you have to act fast to help someone. Call for professional help immediately, or have someone else do it while you get the person into the shade, and try to lower the body temperature with either cold water or ice. The victim must get to a hospital emergency department for proper treatment. There is one case of heat stroke on record in a 52-year-old man where the body temperature rose to 116°F! With emergency treatment and aggressive care over a several-day period he survived with no permanent effects. It is the highest human body temperature reported with eventual recovery.

The best thing to do during hot weather is to keep as cool as possible. Wear loose-fitting clothing in light colors rather than dark ones, because dark colors absorb more heat. If you perspire a lot, you want to take a salt tablet to replenish the salt your body is losing. Usually this should not be done unless you consult a physician. In most cases, the dramatic loss of salt only occurs in highly stressful conditions such as a marathon. The normal diet is typically overloaded with salt. Be careful when taking these tablets; they can cause irritation to the stomach leading to nausea and vomiting.

When perspiration evaporates, the body cools down. But perspiration has **SALT** in it, and if too much salt is lost, illness results. If you must be in the heat, especially if you have a job where you are outside exercising or doing strenuous work: Always drink lots of liquids, plain water is the best, but you can use products such as *GATORADE*; they contain salts dissolved in the liquid to replace those the body is losing. If you do not have *GATORADE* handy, try dissolving a teaspoonful of salt in a quart of lemonade or *KOOL-AID* and carry that with you. If you are affected by the heat, it would be a good idea to stay indoors or in the shade on very humid days, when there is a lot of moisture in the air and sweat cannot evaporate fast enough to cool the body properly. Taking the necessary precautions can prevent serious effects of heat.

Some drugs that can make people more susceptible to heat illness are:

- heat stimulants (decongestants, diet aids, caffeine)
- antidepressants
- antipsychotic drugs
- salicylates (see page 174)
- thyroid medicines
- alcohol

Poison Ivy (Oak, Sumac)

No one is immune to poison ivy. Some people say that they can rub it all over them and they do not develop a rash. That might be true for a while. But as your body chemistry changes, so could its ability to resist effects of poison ivy. Usually a poison ivy rash is the result of direct contact with the plant. But you can come into contact with it indirectly. For example, if a dog or cat runs into some bushes and the substance on the leaves of the plant gets on the pet's fur, when you touch the pet you get poison ivy rash. If a neighbor burns some weeds to get rid of them, the poison from the plant can be carried in the smoke, and if the smoke comes into contact with the skin, a poison ivy reaction may be the result.

How do you know if you have a poison ivy rash? If you have been in the woods or some other place where there are weeds, and if three days later you develop itching, swelling, and a streaky rash on the skin, you are doubtless the proud owner of a poison ivy reaction.

POISON IVY poisoning usually runs its course in about ten to fourteen days, and there is really very little one can do to stop it. However over-the-counter medications can treat the symptoms, usually severe itching and a rash accompanied by little blisters that ooze a liquid when you scratch them. Years ago it was thought that the liquid caused the rash to spread. Let us set the record straight right now. The liquid that flows from the rash does not spread poison ivy rash on the skin. It is the poisonous substance from the plant that causes the rash. Scratching gets the substance under your fingernails and then everything you touch will cause an outbreak of the rash. If you come home from being outdoors and think you might have brushed against the plant, wash your clothing right away. Otherwise, the next time you put on that favorite pair of jeans you will get poison ivy. If you have been all day in the woods and get home late, do not just take off your clothes and go to bed without a shower. If you have the substance on your skin it will rub off on the sheets, and the next time you climb into bed you could cause a new outbreak of poison ivy reaction.

There are many products available to treat the poisoning. Some of them are intended to help dry up the rash. *IVY DRY* contains **TANNIC ACID**, which helps stop the oozing of the blisters. Other products like *CALADRYL* and *ZIRADRYL* have the antihistamine **DIPHENHYDRAMINE** in them along with varying astringents. **DIPHENHYDRAMINE** and **TRIPELENNAMINE** are two antihistamines that have been found to be effective as anti-itch ingredients by the FDA Advisory Review Panel on OTC Topical Analgesic, Antirheumatic, Otic, Burn, and Sunburn Prevention and Treatment Drug Products. Antihistamines do help stop itching because they are local numbing agents, or anesthetics. Some products contain the anesthetic ingredient **BENZOCAINE** in combination with other ingredients, products like *IVAREST, IVY DRY*, or *CALAMYCIN.* **BENZOCAINE** has also shown to be safe and effective by the same advisory review panel, but people should be careful when using these products. If the skin is broken, products containing **BENZOCAINE** could themselves cause allergic reactions. Also, antihistamines, like diphenhydramine, applied to the skin and given orally at the same time to children, have resulted in hallucinations and bizarre reactions. Do not use an antihistamine on the skin and by mouth at the same time in children.

When all is said and done, the simplest treatment is still the best. Mild cases of poison ivy may require no more than wet compresses or soaking in cool water to relieve the itching. Dilute **ALUMINUM ACETATE,** or **BUROW'S SOLUTION, SALT WATER** or **SODIUM BICARBONATE (BAKING SODA) SOLUTIONS** can work well to dry up oozing blisters. *DOMEBORO TABLETS* are available in drugstores to make **BUROW'S SOLUTION.** An old stand-by for your recovery period is **CALAMINE** lotion. It is inexpensive, simple, and when it dries on the skin it forms a protective coating to prevent scratching and possible skin infection, which can spread rapidly. Other FDA approved protectants are **ALUMINUM HYDROXIDE GEL, KAOLIN, ZINC ACETATE, ZINC CARBONATE**, and **ZINC OXIDE**, and these are found in numerous creams that can be applied to the skin. They all work reasonably well.

Another way of stopping the itching is to soak fifteen to twenty minutes in a tub of room temperature water and *AVEENO COLLOIDAL OATMEAL.* Pat dry afterwards; do not rub dry, or the itching will start all over again. Then apply **HYDROCORTISONE CREAM** (not ointment) and lightly rub it in. Or, you can even make your own oatmeal preparation by tying up about half a cupful of uncooked oatmeal in a clean cloth, such as a large handerchief, and soaking it in water. Squeezing releases an oatmeally solution that will help dry up oozing blisters. When using oatmeal in any of the ways we just mentioned, be careful because it is a little messy and can make the tub extra slippery.

Remember, no matter what method you try, a poison ivy condition usually runs its course in ten to fourteen days, the first five of which are usually the most uncomfortable.

If you are affected by a severe case of poison ivy on or near the eyes or genitals, do not experiment with over-the-counter products. See a physician instead. A prescription for oral **PREDNISONE** or **DEXAMETHASONE**, both steroids, may be warranted in some cases.The swelling could prevent urination if it is near the genitals and impaired vision if it is near the eyes.

If extremely allergic to poison ivy, it would be wise to check with an allergist. He or she may be able to reduce your sensitivity to the plant by giving allergy injections. If you are going to be outdoors, taking a weekend camping trip or vacation, you may want to make sure your first-aid kit has some of the items mentioned above in it to give you relief.

Anti-inflammatory and Astringent Ingredients

Inflammation and itching and weeping are conditions of the skin frequently symptomatic of many underlying disorders. **ECZEMA,** (see page 268) a noninfectious condition of the skin defined by inflammation, itching and sometimes weeping is the general name sometimes used to describe this condition. Occasionally itching may become significantly irritating and even painful. At these times the use of medications may be necessary. Drugs used to treat inflammation and itching do nothing more than reduce the severity of symptoms. Anti-inflammatory drugs may be astringents or steroids. Anti-itching chemicals may be astringents, steroids, lubricants and anesthetics as well.

ALUMINUM ACETATE is a white powder when dry but in use as an astringent occurs only as a solution (known as **BUROW'S SOLUTION**) which is clear and colorless or faintly yellow. It can be used as an astringent wash or as a wet dressing and reduces weeping and inflammation by injuring surface skin cells causing death of the cells and shrinkage. Look for this in the drugstore as *DOMEBORO TABLETS* for solution or powder. This shrinkage of the skin surface reduces the amount of fluid that can be lost.

CALAMINE also known as **PREPARED CALAMINE** has been used for many years to make a pharmaceutical lotion which is still popular as an astringent and protectant for the skin in conditions of inflammation and itching. The powder used to make the lotion is actually a combination of zinc oxide, at least 98 percent, and from 0.5 percent to 2 percent ferric oxide which gives the powder its pink coloration. While its effectiveness has been questioned calamine lotion appears to toughen the skin and reduce inflammation and weeping when used to treat certain skin conditions.

DIPHENHYDRAMINE is a white, crystalline powder with a bitter taste. It is used widely as an oral antihistamine for the treatment of allergy and cold symptoms but it has numbing properties when applied to the skin and mucous membranes. It is used as an anti-itch ingredient in *CALADRYL LOTION*.

HYDROCORTISONE is an effective anti-inflammatory steroid drug. It is considered the standard by which all other anti-inflammatory steroids are measured. It can be extracted from the adrenal glands of animals but for commercial use it is made synthetically from other steroids. Steroid anti-inflammatory chemicals will suppress local heat, redness, swelling and tenderness by which inflammation is recognized. They do this by a complicated series of steps at the microscopic and cellular level. The only topically applied steroid approved for over-the-counter use is hydrocortisone as a 0.5 percent and 1 percent cream and ointment by numerous brand names, such as *CORTAID*, *CORTIZONE 5*, and *LANACORT 5*. Always buy a generic cortisone cream if possible, they are all the same and the store brand is much cheaper.

POTASSIUM ALUMINUM SULFATE, ALUMINUM POTASSIUM SULFATE or **ALUM** is a white, odorless, crystalline powder that occurs in several minerals in nature and is also made artificially from aluminum and potassium salts. Aluminum salts are astringent. You can find it in the drugstore in a four or eight ounce container to mix your own solution. Generally the directions will tell you to add one teaspoonful to a pint of warm water. This will make a one percent solution. It can be used as an astringent wash or as a wet dressing on the skin and reduces weeping and inflammation by injuring surface skin cells causing death of the cells and shrinkage. This shrinkage of the skin surface reduces the amount of fluid that can be lost.

ZINC OXIDE occurs in nature as the mineral zincite. For commercial use it is more practical and economical to prepare it artificially from metallic zinc. Zinc oxide is most often used as a 25 percent paste on the skin to serve as a protection from moisture and abrasion. it is approved by the FDA for poison ivy, and also for diaper rash and prickly heat. it is mildly astringent and a weak antiseptic. Zinc oxide is the main ingredient in **CALAMINE LOTION**.

Insect Repellents

What's a picnic in the park, or a romp in the woods, without insect bites? Thanks to modern science, we now have insect repellents with which to spray ourselves. The problem with these products is that people usually spray only their arms and legs and end up with mosquito bites on their heads. Obviously, it is not very safe to spray your face or head, but products like *6-12 PLUS*, *OFF* and *OFF DEEP WOODS FORMULA* are available in liquid form and towelettes which you can rub on areas of the face, head, and neck. Always avoid getting the repellent in the eyes or mouth. Some repellents are good to spray on clothing if one is going to a wooded area with ticks and chiggers. In any case, make sure to apply the repellent to all the areas exposed to **MOSQUITOES**. When using aerosols, always hold them at least six inches away from the body when spraying. Be sure to read the information on the repellent thoroughly before use.

The most common and probably best all-purpose personal insect repellent, found in the products mentioned above, is known as **DEET (N,N-DIETHYLMETA-TOLUAMIDE)**. But **DEET** is controversial because as much as 50 percent of an application gets absorbed into the blood stream through the skin. Poisoning can occur from misuse of products containing it. There are several cases that have been reported in the medical literature where poisoning has been the result of applying this ingredient nightly for 2 weeks to 3 months to infants. Overuse can result in injury to the central nervous system. Also, some accidental swallowings of **DEET** have resulted in seizures and coma, which can occur as rapidly as 30 minutes to one hour. But these are problems that happen as a result of misuse. Using these insect repellants according to the way they are labeled appears to be safe.

In the past products have been promoted to repel mosquitoes by taking an oral medication, products like *SKEETER GO AWAY* and *SKEETER TABS*. The FDA has ruled that these drugs are not effective and that they are misbranded. There is no scientific evidence that they work. The companies that sold them also charged excessive prices for nothing more than plain old vitamin b1, or thiamine, which you can buy in the vitamin section of your drugstore at around one-third the price of the insect repellent tablets.

When hiking in a wooded area spray repellants around pants cuffs, socks, and openings in outer clothing. **CHIGGERS** are insects that can cause unbearable aggravation, and in the worst possible places. They usually go to the tight-fitting clothing areas, such as the socks and belt line, because of the build-up of the blood supply. Chiggers actually eat their way into the skin, and the saliva they release causes severe itching. Sprinkling sulfur powder around clothing that fits tightly will work to repel chiggers, but products like *OFF* work better. There are products on the market to treat chigger bites. They dry on the skin and are supposed to eventually smother the bug. However, these generally do not work, because the chigger may have fallen off due to friction from clothing or scratching. But even though the chigger is gone, the secretions left behind continue to irritate the skin for several days. First soak yourself in a tub of warm water to get clean and relieve the itching. You may try *AVEENO COLLOIDAL OATMEAL* added to the bath water. Pat yourself dry. Products like *CHIGGEREX*, *SKEETER STIX*, or *STINGKILL* contain numbing ingredients, such as **BENZOCAINE** or **LIDOCAINE**, and can be spot applied to relieve itching. An oral **ANTIHISTAMINE** can be used at bedtime to relieve the itching and cause drowsiness.

Bee and Wasp Stings

Bee and wasp stings are painful, to say the least. Many people also run a risk of severe allergic reaction to the sting. Take simple precautions to avoid being stung. Always wear shoes when walking in grass. Wear gloves when gardening and moving bushes and plants. Wasps, in particular, like to build nests in the protection of certain shrubs. Wear tight fitting, long-sleeved, light colored shirts when gardening, and be extra cautious around flowers. If you feel something "light" on you, ask someone else to observe it before attempting to swat it or remove it. Do not leave opened beverage cans around outside. They attract insects, and stings inside the mouth near the throat opening can be extremely dangerous.

Wasps and bees are different in that **WASPS** are predators, they use their stingers to kill other animals. That means they do not leave it behind when they sting. On the other hand, **BEES** are vegetarians, so to speak, they use their stinger to protect themselves and the nest. When a bee stings, it generally loses its stinger with some attached parts of its body, including the poison sac. So, if stung by a bee, first remove the stinger from the bite and do not squeeze the stinger and the attached poison sac. If you do, you will be injecting yourself with more of the poison. Remove it by a gentle scraping action, back and forth, with a knife edge or other object, like a credit card. After the stinger has been removed, apply ice to the bite; that will reduce the pain and actually slow the venom's entry into the system. Apply the ice on and off for 10 to 15 minute periods for several hours. For most stings, this is all that will be necessary. An oral pain reliever may help. Some home remedies have been advised in the past, like baking soda, but it is doubtful that it is any more helpful than just applying ice. Some people report consistent relief by applying a paste of powdered meat tenderizer that contains the enzyme **PAPAIN**. But again, it is hard to prove or disprove the value of some of these remedies.

If the reaction seems to continue to get worse, get to an emergency room. Some people are highly **ALLERGIC** to bee and wasp stings, to the point that a single sting may cause respiratory distress, shock or even result in death. If that is the case for you or your family, carry an emergency bee and wasp sting kit with you. One such kit is called *ANA KIT*. This is a prescription item, but it contains all the emergency items needed in the event of a bee or wasp sting, such as a ready-to-use syringe containing **EPINEPHRINE**, a tourniquet, and antihistamine tablets, along with complete instructions on how to use the kit properly. Make sure the epinephrine is always fresh and ready to use; the product has an expiration date. Watch it very closely. Also, if it begins turning an amber or brown color, get a fresh supply regardless of the date. Epinephrine opens the bronchial airways so that you can breath more easily. Store the *ANA KIT* in a cool dark place to keep it fresh longer.

29

Sunburn & Tanning Agents

Have you ever closely noticed the skin under your arms or on your buttocks? Aside from the normal thinning due to age, it is usually wrinkle-free and soft. You should do this from time to time to convince yourself of the sun's damaging effects on the skin. For this reason, the Food and Drug Administration, the American Academy of Dermatology, the National Cancer Institute, and the American Cancer Society have been delivering a consistent message to the public on sun exposure. Because of increasing skin cancer, the experts are warning of repeated exposure to the sun's ultraviolet radiation, **UV-A** and **UV-B** wavelengths of light. It is well known now that these imperil all sun worshippers, regardless of skin color. Dermatologists attribute the dramatic rise in skin cancers (the rate of melanomas has doubled in less than a decade, and melanoma is the number one cancer in young women under age 35) to our love affair with the sun and to changed lifestyles that put people outdoors for longer periods, for more months of the year, and often in skimpier outfits that leave more skin exposed. It is especially important for parents, coaches, camp counsellors, and so on to protect small children from sun exposure. There is evidence that shows that people who have had severe sunburns at an early age are also at higher risk for melanomas. Fifty to eighty percent of a persons lifetime exposure to the sun occurs during childhood, by the age of 18. Studies show that a history of painful or blistering sunburn during the first 10 to 20 years of life doubles the risk of skin cancer. For children, dermatologists even recommend that putting on a sunscreen should be as everyday an occurrence as brushing their teeth.

Even tanning slowly and carefully is dangerous, but every person whose aim is to have fun in the sun here and abroad has probably experienced a **SUNBURN**. The painful redness, swelling, and tenderness of the skin are the results of being exposed too long to the sun's ultraviolet rays. Initially, sun causes the blood vessels in skin to dilate, and that is why you turn red after the exposure. The sunbathing process eventually kills skin cells and alters the function of collagen and elastin, the connective tissue in the skin. That why you "peel" several days later, loosing that layer of skin.

Cancer aside, sun exposure also ages the skin. Long-term exposure, even without burning, causes skin to age prematurely, resulting in a loss of elasticity, thinning, wrinkling, and drying. Cumulative exposure from childhood to adulthood may cause precancerous skin conditions, and skin cancer may ensue. There really is no such thing as a "safe tan," according to dermatologists. The tanning is really the body's response to cell damage, it is producing a dark pigment, called melanin, that skin cells make to block out damaging rays. While the immediate harm of sun exposure, burning, blistering and peeling, is painful, it is the long-term effects that you should really be concerned about. However, if you decide to stay in the sun, there are plenty of products on which to spend money.

Suntan lotions and oils may be products with pretty exotic names, like *TROPICAL BLEND* or *HAWAIIAN TROPIC*. It is true that **OILS** will give a very lustrous tan. However, the oil actually magnifies the sun's rays, causing the sun to penetrate the skin more deeply. This in turn could cause a pretty severe burn, especially if you are in the sun for the first time in the season, or if you have sensitive skin.

Some suntan products have a sunscreen added to prevent sunburn. Sunscreen is an especially good idea if you are going out for the first time, or if you have sensitive skin. But some sunscreening agents are better than others.

Of course since these products do block out some of the harmful burning rays of the sun, suntanning will take a lot longer. If the tanning process takes longer, you will avoid the peeling and itching that goes with a sunburn. Many of these products have alcohol bases, which makes them easy to apply. Make sure to apply them evenly, which will in turn give an even tan. However they wash off the skin easily, so if you perspire a lot, or go swimming, be sure to reapply them if you continue to be out in the sun. Products in cream and lotion form stay on the skin longer than the products with alcohol bases. Some people develop a rash when using a product containing **PABA**, one sunscreen agent, because they are allergic to it. In that case, pick a different sunscreen, which the pharmacist can help select. For areas, such as the nose, ears, and lips, that are especially sensitive, coat them with an ointment such as **ZINC OXIDE**, which will block out the sun completely.

After beginning a tan using a sunscreen, it may be a good idea to change to a suntan lotion or oil, which will enrich the tan without burning. Some systems offer a suntanning process that consists of four or five different lotions. They start with the first bottle for a couple of days, then use the other lotions in succession. By the time you get to the last bottle, you are supposed to have a luxurious tan. This method is fine if your vacation lasts three to four weeks. But you can cut down the time and expense by using a good sunscreening lotion first, then an oil after the tanning process begins.

Sunburn

Normally the healing process for sunburn takes two to three days. But those two or three days can be misery, especially if you are on vacation to enjoy yourself. Among the products available to releive the pain of a sunburn are *SOLARCAINE AEROSOL SPRAY*, and *AMERICAINE TOPICAL ANESTHETIC SPRAY*; these products contain the ingredient **BENZOCAINE**, in fairly high concentration, 20 percent. They are also available in creams and lotions which may contain another effective numbing agent, **LIDOCAINE**. Sprays are easier to use. After all, when you have a severe sunburn you can hardly touch the skin, much less use a lotion on it. Be careful when using these products, especially if you have blisters or broken skin; spraying them on broken skin can cause allergic reactions or further irritation to the skin. Another good treatment is to fill the bathtub with cool water, then submerge the sunburned area in the cool water for about thirty minutes. It will soothe the sunburn and relieve the pain temporarily, probably just as much as the anesthetic sprays. Also, you could take an oral pain reliever like **ASPIRIN**, which helps relieve inflammation, and so gives some relief for sunburn. If you cannot take aspirin, try one of the nonaspirin pain relievers, such as *TYLENOL.*

There are a few additional things to keep in mind if you are going to be out in the sun. If you shower before going out, avoid using deodorant. It dries out the skin and washes away the skin's protective coating, making the skin more susceptible to the sun. Certain medications may cause the skin to become super-sensitive to the sun, resulting in more severe sunburn. Some drugs that cause this are the **TETRACYCLINE** antibiotics, certain tranquilizers, such as *VALIUM* and **BARBITURATES**, and **THIAZIDE** diuretics. The best advice pertaining to medications is to tell your pharmacist or doctor what drugs you are presently taking. If taking one that reacts with the sun, take the appropriate steps by using a sunscreen or avoid long exposure to the sun.

Sunscreens

Few people can totally avoid sun exposure. As a precaution, a sunscreen is needed regularly, particularly if there are plans to spend any extended time in the sun. A panel of scientific experts was used by the FDA to study the over-the-counter sunscreens. The panel's report said that liberal, regular use of sunscreen products may help reduce the high incidence of skin cancer and help protect susceptible persons from sunburn. The experts recommended that the labels of such products warn that overexposure to the sun may cause premature aging of the skin and skin cancer, and state that sunscreens may provide possible protection against these harmful effects. This panel agreed that 21 chemical ingredients marketed in over-the-counter sunscreens are safe and effective in the prevention of sunburn when properly used. The experts warned that sunscreens merely extend the time it takes for the sun to cause a burn and there is no total protection from sunburn. Sunscreens use the following numerical system, the **SUN PROTECTION FACTOR (SPF)** to designate the relative effectiveness of a product:

- **SPF 2 to 4:** Minimal protection from sunburning, permits suntanning, recommended for people who rarely burn and tan easily and deeply.
- **SPF 4 to 6:** Moderate protection from sunburning, permits some suntanning, recommended for people who tan well with minimal burning.
- **SPF 6 to 8:** Extra protection from sunburning, permits limited suntanning, recommended for people who burn moderately and tan gradually.
- **SPF 8 to under 15:** maximal protection from sunburning, permits little or no suntanning, recommended for people who always burn easily and tan minimally.
- **SPF 15 or greater:** ultra protection from sunburn, offers most protection, permits no suntanning, recommended for people who burn easily and never tan.

Remember that sunscreens will not work as effectively, or perhaps not at all, if they are washed off by swimming or diluted by sweating. They should be reapplied frequently to insure protection. The American Academy of Dermatology and the National Institutes of Health agree that people should wear a sunscreen with an SPF of 15 or higher. The FDA claims that sunscreens with an SPF higher than 30 probably do not make sense. Since the number 15 means that you can stay out in the sun 15 times longer than if you were wearing no sunscreen, and still get the same amount of redness. But whatever SPF number is decided upon, they are all safe. Just select a formulation that feels comfortable, a solution, lotion or cream, and apply it each time before you go out in the sun.

The different chemicals used as sunscreens are used because they absorb ultraviolet light from the sun in different wavelengths. They are formulated to give the protection described in the numerical system mentioned above and discussed individually below.

Sunscreen Ingredients

AMINOBENZOIC ACID, PARA-AMINOBENZOIC ACID or **PABA** is a naturally occurring essential nutrient for a number of living organisms. It is a white or yellowish crystalline chemical when pure, and is one of the first modern sunscreens that was incorporated into numerous types of lotions and creams as an effective sunburn preventative. PABA absorbs light mostly of wavelength 290 nanometers, which is within the range to which the skin is particularly sensitive, making it an excellent sunscreen. However, it rarely shows up in current formulations since it dissolves in water, washing off easily, and it stains clothes.

CINOXATE is an almost odorless, thick, slightly yellow liquid prepared from cinnamic acid, a naturally occurring chemical in certain plant balsams, oil of cinnamon and coca leaves. It absorbs light mostly at about the wavelength of 310 nanometers, which is within the range to which the skin is particularly sensitive, making it an excellent sunscreen.

DIETHANOLAMINE p-METHOXYCINNAMATE is a derivative of cinnamic acid, an acid found naturally in cinnamon, plant balsams and coca leaves. It absorbs light at about the wavelength of 290 nanometers, which is within the range to which the skin is sensitive. It is an excellent sunscreen.

DIGALLOYL TRIOLEATE is a chemical derivative of two naturally occurring chemicals, oleic acid which is present in animal and vegetable fats and tannic acid which is found in the bark and fruit of many plants, particularly the oak species. It is a clear, thick liquid with a slight odor that absorbs light at about wavelength 305-310, the range to which the skin is sensitive, thus it is a good sunscreening agent.

DIHYDROXYACETONE is often included in sunscreen preparations. It is prepared from glycerin by the action of a microorganism. When applied to skin it reacts with certain components of the epidermis, the top layer of skin, to produce a color which forms very quickly and simulates a natural suntan. Because this color formation has no ultraviolet screening properties, it is considered a cosmetic and not a sunscreen product. Therefore, it may be included in any sunscreen product without concern for regulatory limitations, as long as sunscreening claims are not made for the dihydroxyacetone itself. It is apparently safe, and is a "bronzer" or tanning agent approved by the FDA's Division of Colors and Cosmetics.

DIOXYBENZONE is an off-white to yellow powder and is prepared synthetically form petroleum chemicals. Light is absorbed in the 280-290 nanometer range, the part of the ultraviolet spectrum which produces burning, making it a good sunscreen. Dioxybenzone is more expensive than other sunscreens.

ETHYL-4-bis-(HYDROXYPROPYL)-1-AMINOBENZOATE is a derivative of aminobenzoic acid (see above) and provides protection from ultraviolet radiation by absorbing light mostly at about wavelength 310 nanometers. It is an effective sunscreen but does not have the adhesiveness for the skin that other sunscreens possess. However, it is free of undesirable side effects such as stinging of tender facial skin.

GLYCERYL AMINOBENZOATE is a synthetically made chemical derivative of **PABA**. It is a pale yellow or amber, waxy stuff that has a sweet odor. Absorbance of UV light is greatest at about wavelength 295 nanometers, making it a useful sunscreen, however it has the disadvantage of having a tendency to discolor fabrics.

HOMOSALATE is a drug that is a clear, colorless to yellow oily liquid at room temperature and is chemically related to aspirin. It absorbs light in the ultraviolet range of about 305 nanometers, thus it is an effective sunscreen. It is among the most popular of the sunscreens and is good for quick tanning products where a moderate SPF value is desired.

METHYL ANTHRANILATE or **MENTHYL ANTHRANILATE** is a relative of **PABA**. It occurs naturally in numerous essential oils, e.g. bergamot and jasmine and also in grape juice. For commercial use it may be prepared synthetically. At room temperature it is an amber, thick liquid and absorbs UV sunlight at about 310 nanometers which is within the range that will produce skin burning, thus it is an effective sunscreen.

OCTYL METHOXYCINNAMATE is a practically odorless, pale yellow, oily liquid that is a derivative of cinnamic acid, a chemical which occurs naturally in cinnamon and coca leaves. It absorbs UV light in the 310 nanometer wavelength.

OXYBENZONE is a synthetic off-white to yellow powder at room temperature made from petroleum chemicals and used as a sunscreen. Maximum absorbance of UV light occurs at 280-290 nanometers.

PADIMATE O is a synthetically prepared yellow, oily liquid derived from aminobenzoic acid (see PABA). Absorbance of UV is at about 310 nanometers. It is particularly good with regard to adhering to skin following application and resists water removal. This ingredient is intended for the person who wishes to tan quickly, but does not burn easily.

RED PETROLATUM is an oily substance obtained from crude petroleum and paraffin wax and has an inherent red coloration. It is referred to as an "opaque" sunscreen because it physically screens the skin from the sun, scattering light and preventing the rays of the sun from reaching the skin.

TITANIUM DIOXIDE is a white powder that is found in nature as several naturally occurring minerals or it can be made synthetically by the direct combination of titanium (a metal) and oxygen. Applied to the skin in cream form it provides a physical screen from the sun, however it is usually used in combination with one of the chemical sunscreens.

TRIETHANOLAMINE SALICYLATE is a waxy synthetic, solid derivative of salicylic acid, a chemical which occurs in nature in numerous plants. It absorbs UV light in the 300 to 305 nanometer wavelength to perform well as a sunscreen.

Sunlamps

Sunlamps can give off both Ultraviolet A (**UV-A**) and ultraviolet B **(UV-B)** radiation. Indoor tanning booths and beds use UV-A, a form of radiation just beyond visible light on the radiation spectrum. Its wavelengths are shorter than visible light but longer than UV-B, the radiation emitted by older sunlamps. Sunlamps are mainly used by people who want to look tan all year long. We do not recommend the use of sunlamps for any reason, but if you insist on using one, remember never to use a sunlamp without a timer. If the timer does not have an automatic shut-off device, make sure it has an alarm loud enough to wake you in case you fall asleep. Always use ultraviolet-filtering goggles to protect the eyes when using a sunlamp. Be aware also that a hot shower or sauna session just before using a sunlamp can leave you more sensitive than usual to ultraviolet light. If you have sensitive skin to begin with, be sure to protect your lips, because the light may make them dry and crack. A lip sunscreen will also minimize the risk of developing lip cancer or sores (see page 61) from repeated exposure to ultraviolet light.

All of the experts now agree that all sunlight—including artificial sunlight beamed out of the sunlamps and other popular tanning devices, has the potential to damage human skin.

UV-B radiation is far more likely to cause burns and is believed to be the most cancer-causing component of sunlight. But new studies show that UV-A also may cause problems. Cells taken from mice and exposed to levels of UV-A radiation comparable to those from tanning devices showed an increased rate of mutation, indicating the possibility of cancer-causing effects.

Wavelengths in UV-A radiation penetrate the skin more deeply than UV-B radiation, producing a deeper tan but perhaps long-term damage such as premature aging of the skin and cancer, as well. UV-A tanning devices can cause serious burns in people who have sensitive skin, are photosensitive because of drugs or food, have cold sores, or have had certain kinds of eye surgery.

Sunglasses

Ultraviolet radiation can damage the eyes as well. There is a study on Chesapeake Bay watermen who spend large amounts of time on the water that shows those who wore sun protection developed fewer cataracts. Additionally, glare from the sun causes unnecessary squinting and eye strain perhaps resulting in a headache. Obviously, the best thing to do to prevent these problems is to wear a good pair of sunglasses. But not just any sunglasses will protect, no matter how expensive or glamorous they are. Of course, the best sunglasses are those obtained from an optical store. Such stores not only specialize in glasses of all kinds, but you can be assured of getting the most finely ground lenses available to suit your particular eyes. Unfortunately, there is a higher price for these glasses. This usually sends people into the drugstore to buy sunglasses off the bargain rack. The price will definitely meet the requirements of your pocketbook, but the glasses may not meet the requirements of your eyes. Often the sunglasses found on the bargain racks have actual flaws in the lenses. They may appear as scratches or bubbles in the lenses. These may cause unnecessary eye strain, which could result in a severe headache, or even nausea and vomiting. Interestingly, cost is not a factor in protecting your eyes from ultraviolet radiation, because even some of the least expensive sunglasses can offer good protection. Just look for labels that indicate the American National Standards Institute **(ANSI)** classification discussed below.

There are other things to look for when recommending sunglasses. Examine both lenses carefully; make sure they are the same color and shade. Hold them away from your face and look at a straight line somewhere through each lens. You can use a line in the ceiling of the store or a corner of the building. Make sure that the line is perfectly straight. If the lens causes the straight line to appear wavy, the lens contains an optical defect. This may cause unnecessary eye strain and the annoying problems that go along with it.

Selecting the right color lens is sometimes just as important as making sure that the lenses have no flaws. The amount of visible light, or glare, blocked by sunglasses depends on the darkness of the lenses. The darker shades of special-purpose sunglasses are intended for a high level of brightness, while the lighter shades can be used for less bright situations like skiing on a cloudy day. The best way to select the color of the lenses is to know what you want them to do for you. Dark gray lenses are most effective at blocking out glare. They also give a true lifelike color to objects. Another effective color for blocking out glare is a brown lens. Brown lenses appear to brighten up objects. This could be important to a fisherman, for example. Yellow lenses do not do a thing to block out glare, but they brighten everything. They give a definite outline to the objects you see. As far as rose-colored lenses go, life does not look rosier through these lenses. They are mainly used for cosmetic purposes along with green and blue lenses. However, rose-colored lenses do help to some degree to reduce the glare of fluorescent lights. So if you work in an office, where the fluorescent lights cause a glare on your work, maybe even resulting in periodic headaches, you might want to try working with rose-colored lenses. People also seem to like photo-sensitive lenses, which darken as they are exposed to increased light. These are fine for some conditions, but if you are going to be on the beach or in the snow, where the sun is very bright, most photo-sensitive lenses do not get dark enough to block out glare effectively. Polarized glasses are also good for cutting down on glare. No matter what color lenses you end up buying, make sure the lenses are free from flaws.

One thing to remember in all of this is that there is a big difference in cutting down on glare and blocking out the harmful ultraviolet radiation of the sun. In fact, the darkness of any lens, regardless of color, does not mean much about UV blockage. The FDA and the Sunglass Association of America have agreed that manufacturers may voluntarily label sunglasses according to the performance standards set by the American National Standards Institute **(ANSI)** in New York. According to ANSI, sunglasses fall into three categories:

- **COSMETIC USE**—lightly tinted for non-harsh sunlight and around town uses such as shopping. These will block at least 70 percent of UV-B and 20 percent of UVA, and less than 60 percent of visible light (glare)
- **GENERAL PURPOSE**—medium-dark tinted for most outdoor use such as boating, flying, hiking, picnicking, and beach outings. They also can be used for snow settings. They block at least 95 percent of UV-B and at least 60 percent of UVA, and from 60 to 92 percent of visible light.
- **SPECIAL PURPOSE**—dark-tinted glasses for intense sunlight such as tropical beaches and ski slopes and for activities like mountain climbing. They will block at least 99 percent of UV-B and 60 percent of UVA, in addition to from 20 to 97 percent of visible light.

Some people, for medical reasons, need maximum eye protection from both UVA and UV-B radiation. You will need sunglasses that ensure 95 to 100 percent blockage of both wavelengths. Check with an ophthalmologist on this. Also, if you need complete protection, pick glass frames that wrap around. The small stylish frames let lots of light seep in from the sides.

30

Travel & Vacation

Vacations are supposed to be a time for relaxation and enjoyment, but sometimes in their haste to get away from it all, people overlook certain aspects of travel that can prove hazardous to their health.

Travelers' Diarrhea

This problem goes under many names such as "Montezuma's revenge," "runs," "Delhi belly," the "skitters" or, in Spanish-speaking countries, "turista." Whatever one calls it, it is a villain that terrorizes many travelers every year. The most common cause is bacteria in the water, which produces a sudden onset of nausea, bloating, cramps, sometimes fever, and that general out-of-sorts feeling known as malaise; all of this along with diarrhea. Some experts say that not only the water but also environmental changes and unfamiliar foods and beverages can alter the intestinal flora, causing diarrhea.

Travelers' diarrhea generally disappears in three or four days, and one recommended treatment consists of rest, lots of fluids (especially for children), and simply letting it run its course. Antibiotics are effective in treating travelers diarrhea and in preventing it. But all of these are prescription drugs. You might want to call a physician before traveling to certain areas of the world where this is known to be a problem. He can prescribe an antibiotic to use prophylactically, or one to have available in case of problems. The first line of defense now for early treatment of travelers' diarrhea is the antibiotic **TRIMETHOPRIM / SULFAMETHOXAZOLE** (*BACTRIM* or *SEPTRA*). A prescription drug long used for other illnesses, it is the only antibiotic approved by the Food and Drug Administration for travelers' diarrhea. This drug is ninety percent effective against the organisms that cause the disease. It usually shortens the illness and makes it less severe. Travelers can ask their physician about other prescription drugs that may be effective in preventing travelers' diarrhea such as **NORFLOXACIN**.

The use of a couple of over-the-counter ingredients, **BISMUTH SUBSALICYLATE** found in *PEPTO-BISMOL*, and **LOPERAMIDE** in the brand name *IMODIUM AD*, are effective in treating travelers' diarrhea. Many scientific studies have been published on the effectiveness of these products in treating travelers' diarrhea. And several additional studies recommend the use of *PEPTO-BISMOL TABLETS* taken daily to prevent diarrhea before it occurs. One of these studies recommends taking 8 tablets of *PEPTO-BISMOL* daily in 4 divided doses, or 2 tablets 4 times a day in adults. This is probably a safe recommendation as long as you do not continue it for longer than three weeks.

A dose of liquid *PEPTO-BISMOL* to actually treat a case of travelers' diarrhea in adults is two tablespoonsful (one ounce) every 30 minutes for eight doses only, or four tablespoonsful (two ounces) four times daily. If you are really concerned about encountering travelers' diarrhea it is a good idea to discuss it with a physician before using these products and doses. As mentioned above, there are very effective and safe prescription alternatives available.

The FDA reminds people that both of the nonprescription drugs used for diarrhea only treat the symptoms of diarrhea, rather than kill the bacteria that cause the illness. *PEPTO-BISMOL* may take a few hours to work and cannot stop severe diarrhea. You should not use it if you are taking aspirin or other blood thinners, if you are pregnant, or have a seizure disorder like epilepsy. Products containing bismuth subsalicylate also should be avoided by children and teenagers recovering from flu, chicken pox, or other viral infections, because of the risk of Reye syndrome (see page 177).

However, taking the right precautions will avoid the problem of travelers' diarrhea in the first place.

You have heard the expression "do not drink the water"; remember that this applies to ice cubes as well. Always boil water you are not sure about, and this includes tap water even in good hotels. Use this for brushing your teeth or drinking in your hotel room. Avoid bottled water unless it is carbonated. The carbonation process inhibits bacterial growth. It is also smart to skip milk and other dairy products unless certain they have been pasteurized. Use water purification tablets, such as *HALAZONE*, and out-doors people and campers can purify water by placing five drops of **TINCTURE OF IODINE** from a first-aid kit in a quart of water and letting it stand for about fifteen minutes before using. Eat hot, thoroughly cooked meals if possible, and avoid fresh fruit and vegetables unless peeled and washed by trusted hands, namely your own.

If you do get sick and the diarrhea lasts more than four days or is accompanied by severe cramps, bloody stools, or foul-smelling gas, contact a physician. More rarely, some people may develop constipation while traveling because of sudden changes in their eating habits. This can usually be remedied by taking a stool softener like *COLACE* or simply using **MILK OF MAGNESIA**.

Most other diseases or medical conditions to which American travelers are likely to be exposed to are rare and easily avoided. If you are thinking about a trip and want to learn more about travelers' illnesses, the Centers for Disease Control (CDC) publishes an annual "Health Information for International Travel." Copies are available for $5 from the U.S. Government Printing Office by writing the Superintendent of Documents, Washington, D.C. 20402. The CDC also maintains a recorded telephone message system with general and geographic-specific information on travelers' diseases. The number is (404) 332-4559.

Motion Sickness

Many people get motion sickness while traveling by sea, air, or land. The main symptoms of motion sickness are nausea and vomiting and sometimes dizziness. For people who suffer from motion sickness every time they travel, prevention is much easier than treatment after the symptoms have appeared. Some steps can be taken to avoid motion sickness. One is to sit in a position least likely to have exposure to ascending motion. For example, if you often develop motion sickness when traveling by airplane, try sitting in a seat between the wings of the plane. Sitting in a semi-reclined position will also help. Reading or unusual visual stimulation should be avoided.

People who usually develop motion sickness should avoid eating or drinking too much before leaving on a trip. While on the trip, only fluids and simple foods should be consumed.

There are products available for motion sickness, such as *BONINE*, *DRAMAMINE*, and *MAREZINE*, which are antihistamines; and *EMETROL*, which is a mixture of sugars. These antinauseants should be taken 30 minutes to an hour before the trip. All of the antihistamines are considered safe and effective by the FDA and do work well at preventing motion sickness. Some are available in liquid form for children. Unfortunately, the antihistamines cause excessive drowsiness and sleepiness, which is an unwanted side effect in travelers of any age. So if you decide to take one of these products, let someone else do the driving.

If these nonprescription products do not give you relief from motion sickness, try the newer transdermal patches containing **SCOPOLAMINE** that can be easily applied behind the ear prior to travel. Of course, these have some minor side effects too. These are prescription products, such as *TRANSDERM-SCOP TRANSDERMAL THERAPEUTIC SYSTEM* manufactured by Ciba.

Antinauseant Ingredients

The antinausea medicines work by several mechanisms in the body to reduce nausea, vertigo and motion sickness. Antihistamines are used as antinauseants to reduce the sensitivity of the inner ear where some disorders of this type are believed to originate. Additionally an area of the brain known as the chemoreceptor trigger zone (CTZ) is thought to be affected by antihistamines used to treat nausea. Other mechanisms are described below after each drug.

CYCLIZINE HYDROCHLORIDE is a drug that has antihistamine properties and is used exclusively for nausea of motion sickness. It has been shown to produce birth defects in animals and therefore should not be used during pregnancy or child-bearing age women.

DIMENHYDRINATE, found in *DRAMAMINE* is a synthetic compound of two drugs, theophylline and diphenhydramine, chemically combined to produce an effective motion sickness medicine.

MECLIZINE is a central nervous system acting drug and is an antihistamine. It is found in *BONINE* and is effective for nausea, vomiting and dizziness associated with motion sickness. This ingredient should not be used if you have asthma, glaucoma, emphysema, chronic pulmonary disease, shortness of breath, difficulty in breathing, or difficulty in urination due to enlargement of the prostate gland, unless directed by a doctor.

SUGARS or **CARBOHYDRATES** such as **FRUCTOSE** (fruit sugar) or **GLUCOSE** (corn or grape sugar) usually combined with **PHOSPHORIC ACID** are said to relieve nausea and vomiting by reducing or eliminating muscle contractions in the stomach wall. A popular over-the-counter product known as *EMETROL* uses this combination to relieve nausea and vomiting. It is supposed to work by relaxing and slowing the emptying time of the stomach. But the FDA isn't convinced that it works just yet. They have classified this combination of sugars in Category III (insufficient evidence to establish effectiveness) in their OTC review process.

Storing Medicine While Traveling

People who take medicines routinely for various problems, such as high blood pressure, diabetes, etc., must be sure to pack their medicines along with all the other items they take on vacation or business trips. Be sure to keep the medicine in its original prescription bottle with the label on it. People sometimes want to put their pills in smaller containers to carry them. If you are going to do this, ask the pharmacist to use a smaller bottle with a prescription label on it. You never know when an emergency might happen. If you need treatment, a doctor can easily look at your prescription bottle to get the name of the medicines and know what treatment would be best.

Another good reason to keep medicines in their original bottles with the label on them is in the event that you are stopped by the local authorities. If they find an unmarked bottle of medicine, it could cause some unnecessary harassment. When traveling, avoid putting the medicines into a suitcase and throwing them in the trunk of the car. Excessive heat causes some medicines to deteriorate. If you are going to carry medicines with you and you are traveling in an air-conditioned car, keep the medicine in the glove compartment. As an added safety precaution, keep the glove compartment locked, especially if there are small children traveling along.

If traveling by airplane, bus, or train, it is a good idea not to pack medicine in a suitcase that will be placed in the luggage compartment, but to keep it in a case that is a carry-on. Luggage sometimes gets lost, but if you carry an overnight case, you will not be without your medicine.

Some people develop congestion in the ears due to changes in pressure when traveling by airplane. Usually yawning or chewing gum opens them up. But some people have a difficult time keeping them open. Try a decongestant inhaler, such as *BENZEDREX INHALER. AFRIN NASAL SPRAY* is another effective decongestant for this purpose. These decongestants keep the sinuses open, which helps to keep the ears open as well. The nasal decongestant inhalers are good because they can be used just before a flight and they begin to work almost immediately. *BENZEDREX* is short acting, an hour to two at most. *AFRIN*, on the other hand, can last up to 12 hours. So pick the one that suits your travel agenda. If sprays do not help, try taking a decongestant tablet such as *SUDAFED* a couple of hours before your trip.

As a precaution against losing medicine or leaving it sitting at home, have the physician write a new prescription for all the medicines. Keep those written prescriptions handy, or in some other safe place, so that you can have them filled at a nearby pharmacy should you need them.

DIABETICS sometimes have problems with medicine while traveling, especially if they have to inject themselves with **INSULIN**. Although insulin should be refrigerated, it can be kept in a car; it will stay fresh as long as air conditioning keeps the inside of the car cool and close to normal room temperature. If there is not an air conditioner, fill a small plastic bag with ice. Then put the insulin in another plastic bag and place that in the bag of ice. As long as you can keep replenishing the ice supply, the insulin will be cool and ready for use.

31

Vitamins, Minerals, & Trace Elements

Americans spend hundreds of millions of dollars each year on vitamin and mineral supplements. It is impossible to discuss vitamins and minerals without mentioning food. After all, that is where all of our vitamins and minerals should come from. However, there are many medical reasons why people may not be able to derive the nutrition they need from food. That is why vitamin and mineral supplements are available over-the-counter.

There is a lot going on with regard to standardizing the optimal intake of vitamins, minerals and other nutrients these days. The Food and Drug Administration has proposed a major overhaul of the food label, and one of its principal changes would revise the way nutrient content is expressed. The FDA has proposed a "Daily Values" method of calculating how much of a vitamin or mineral is healthy to derive from a daily intake of food.

The FDA is leaning toward recommending vitamins and minerals in amounts that could be reached by eating a variety of foods such as fruits, vegetables and whole grains.

When the FDA created its U.S. Recommended Daily Allowances for vitamins and minerals in 1973, the agency elected to base them on the highest National Academy of Science's Recommended Dietary Allowances for each nutrient (excluding values for pregnant and nursing women). Essentially, that was the nutrition level that young adult males require. This approach is being modified because the highest value concept now conflicts with dietary guidelines from other agencies regarding children, women and the elderly. In order to meet the higher value levels, these groups, because of their lower caloric intakes, would have to eat either more food or more fortified foods and fewer fresh fruits and vegetables.

The new approach will use adjusted average levels for vitamins, minerals, and protein recommended for various age/sex groups in the most recent National Academy's Recommended Dietary Allowances, instead of the highest recommended values.

The vitamins and minerals in this chapter are discussed in the way they are found in pharmaceutical supplements. In otherwise healthy people, vitamins and minerals in the form of tablets and capsules should be taken as supplements to a well rounded diet. Always check with a physician before taking these supplements. The term RDA, when used in this chapter, refers to the National Academy of Science's Recommended Dietary Allowances.

A vitamin, according to the United States Government is:

- in natural food, but is distinct from fat, protein or carbohydrate (starches and sugars).
- found in foods in extremely small concentration.
- essential for normal human growth and development.
- something our bodies do not produce enough of on their own, so we have to get it from what we eat.
- something that when we do not get it in our diet causes a vitamin deficiency disease that can only be corrected by adding the vitamin to the diet.

So everybody needs vitamins. However, in many cases the average American diet does not need additional vitamin supplements. Vitamin supplements are useful to some individuals, such as growing children, the elderly who, due to a medical condition, often cannot properly absorb certain vitamins from the foods they eat, or the person recuperating from an illness. But for the average person, the healthiest way for us to get our needed vitamins is to eat a variety of foods. If we are as vitamin-deficient as some people claim, why are vitamin deficiency illnesses not reported by physicians in the United States?

Marketing practices have confused the issue further with the words "organic" or "natural" on vitamin supplements.

Is there a difference in these products? Yes: The natural vitamins are more expensive than the synthetic. The reason the natural or organic product is more expensive is that it is extracted from foods or plants without being made in the chemical laboratory. But, our bodies breakdown the laboratory made synthetic vitamins and use them in exactly the same way as the natural or organic vitamins.

It has also been found that "natural" vitamins frequently are supplemented by the synthetic vitamin. For example, the amount of **ASCORBIC ACID** extracted from rose hips is relatively small, and sometimes synthetic vitamin C is added to bring it up to the strength it is supposed to be. This addition is not shown on the label, and such products always cost a lot more than the synthetic and equally effective vitamin.

Once again it is not wrong to take supplemental vitamins. Take the multiple vitamin and mineral combination to get enough vitamins and minerals, but not too much of any one vitamin. Problems can develop if you start taking individual vitamins without consulting a physician. Some are fat-soluble, which means that what the body does not use it stores in the fat cells. These vitamins can reach a very high level and produce side effects, some of them serious. Certain vitamins are needed to help each other work properly. **VITAMIN D**, for instance, helps the body use **CALCIUM**, and **VITAMIN C** helps us use **IRON** more effectively.

Many parents choose to give their children chewable vitamins regularly. Nowadays there are a wide variety of brands to choose from: *FLINTSTONES* and *BUGS BUNNY CHILDREN'S CHEWABLE*, *POLY-VI-SOL*, and *CENTRUM, JR.*, to name a few. They are pleasant-tasting and come in the shapes of various cartoon or other characters. Since vitamins are important to growing children, for strong bones and teeth, it would not hurt to give them one of these chewable vitamins each day, especially if they do not always eat properly. Check with a pediatrician on this. When giving vitamins to children, always refer to them as medicine and not candy. If children associate the vitamins with candy, someday when an adult is out of the room they may eat the contents of an entire bottle, thinking it is nothing more than candy. And there can be serious side effects from too much of certain vitamins, such as **VITAMINS A, D, E**, and **K**. And some of these vitamins add **IRON**, which can cause additional problems.

Some vitamins may seem less expensive because you get more tablets in the bottle. But when you realize that you need to take two, three, or more tablets a day to get a daily dose then fewer tablets with greater potentcy are a better buy. Check the label on each bottle of vitamins for the Recommended Daily Dietary Allowance. Some are measured in milligrams and some are given in a term known as **IU**, which stands for **INTERNATIONAL UNITS**. Your pharmacist can help with this. Many stores have their own brands, which are just as good quality, just as effective, and will save money. Always be sure that the vitamins are fresh. Check the package for an expiration date.

Fat-Soluble Vitamins

The fat-soluble vitamins available as nonprescription items are **VITAMINS A, D**, and **E**. Severe deficiencies of any of these vitamins may result in conditions as serious as blindness or bone deformity, and excessive doses may be harmful. Do not exceed the recommended dosage on the label for a particular age or sex or during pregnancy.

Vitamin A

Vitamin A has a number of important functions in the human body. It is essential for growth and for keeping skin and other tissues healthy, it helps eyes adapt to dim light and perceive colors, and is essential for normal tooth development. The vitamin is also required for the growth of bone, reproduction and development of the embryo. While rare in the United States, deficiency in the diet has long been known to produce numerous visual disorders, including night blindness. Vitamin A deficiency does occur in developing countries. Other symptoms are skin changes, stunted growth, and serious eye problems, such as drying, thickening, wrinkling, and other effects on the eye.

Vitamin A is present in eggs, whole milk, butter, meat and oily salt water fish. These foods contain a slightly different variation of the vitamin than when it is in green and yellow vegetables and fruits. In the latter, the vitamin is present as **CAROTENES**, substances that are formed into vitamin A chiefly in the small intestines.

A more complete list of foods with vitamin A are beef, chicken and pork livers; whole and vitamin A fortified milk; cheddar cheese; margarine; egg yolk; deep green, yellow or orange vegetables and fruits (including carrots, spinach, collards, broccoli, kale, nectarines, apricots, mangoes, cantaloupe, pumpkins, winter squash, turnip greens, sweet potatoes, and watermelon).

Problems with Too Much Vitamin A

Many articles in the medical literature have shown that vitamin A is very poisonous when we get too much. Reports have been occurring ever since 1857 when Arctic explorers developed a syndrome of headache, dizziness, and diarrhea after eating too much bear liver. Problems from too much vitamin A are more common in the United States than vitamin A deficiency. While small amounts of vitamin A are essential to health it is clear that large amounts over a period of time produce serious illness. Damage to red blood cells, liver, eyes, bone and other organs has been well documented. Also vitamin A produces birth defects when administered to pregnant rats over long periods of time, suggesting the possibility in humans. There are more reports of overdoses in children than adults. Infants may develop increased pressure in the head ("pseudotumor cerebri" and hydrocephalus) when only ten times the RDA is administered for several weeks. Older children may have symptoms of head pressure and pain that mimics a brain tumor, such as headache, nausea, vomiting, dizziness, lethargy, ringing in the ears and double vision.

Most multiple vitamins include vitamin A both in children's and adult preparations. *POLY VI SOL CHEWABLE VITAMINS* by Mead Johnson is a typical multivitamin that contains vitamin A for children 2 to 4 years of age. *MYADEC* by Parke Davis is one for adults and children over 4 years of age.

Vitamin D

Vitamin D, **VITAMIN D3 OR CHOLECALCIFEROL**, is the "sunshine vitamin" and is needed to help the body absorb and use calcium and phosphorous, which is needed for strong bones and teeth. Vitamin D's role in the regulation of calcium balance in the body is important in three main ways: 1) it helps produce a protein that is needed to get calcium from the intestinal tract into the blood stream, 2) it helps move calcium from the bones into the blood whenever it is needed, and 3) it helps to reabsorb calcium in the kidney, preventing too much calcium from being urinated out of our body. Lack of vitamin D, which results in a loss of calcium and phosphorus, is the cause of softening of the bones in infants and children (rickets) and adults (osteomalacia).

Sometimes vitamin D deficiencies are caused by kidney disease. Sources of vitamin D include sunlight (which stimulates vitamin D production in the skin), fatty fish, fish liver oils, vitamin D-fortified milk, egg yolk, and butter. Some foods are artificially fortified with vitamin D, including milk and cereals.

Problems with Too Much Vitamin D

Excess intake of vitamin D can result in serious poisoning. Since this vitamin can be stored in the body, excessive amounts produce side effects such as loss of appetite, nausea, weakness, weight loss, frequent urination, and high levels of calcium in the blood, which could cause kidney stones. Doctors will sometimes prescribe liquid vitamin D for infants. If you use this product, be sure to measure the amount you give the child very carefully. There are many reports of poisoning resulting from too much vitamin D when people take vitamin supplements. This is unfortunate because no healthy person needs more than 400 international units per day of vitamin D. Use of highly concentrated vitamin D preparations is only required by a few people with specific diseases who require unusual doses of the vitamin. One of the "fat-soluble vitamins," it is stored in the fatty tissues of the body and is present in the circulating blood. Since vitamin D promotes absorption of calcium from the intestines, too much stored vitamin D can cause excess calcium in the blood. Thus, calcification of body organs may result, especially damaging the kidneys. This results in accompanying weakness, lack of energy, loss of appetite and constipation. It is hard to determine minimum toxic doses because individual requirements for the vitamin are so varied. For those with special needs there is vitamin D alone or in combination with calcium supplements, such as *POSTURE-D HIGH POTENCY CALCIUM SUPPLEMENT WITH VITAMIN D.*

Vitamin E

Vitamin E is naturally found in food as **ALPHA**, **BETA** and **GAMMA TOCOPHEROLS**. The richest sources are green leaves and vegetable oils such as wheat germ oil. Some common everyday sources are: nuts; vegetable oils; fortified ready-to-eat cereals; green leafy vegetables; margarines made from vegetable oils; shrimp and other seafood (including clams, salmon, and scallops); some fruits, such as apples, apricots and peaches. Vitamin E is a light yellow, thick, oily substance. In animals, the lack of this vitamin produces harmful effects on the reproductive system, heart, blood vessels, muscles and blood and because the vitamin prevents sterility in rats it has been dubbed the "antisterility vitamin."

However, use in humans for reproductive disorders has been disappointing. The nutritional role of vitamin E in man is still controversial. Probably no vitamin has received as much lay publicity or serious interest by scientific researchers as vitamin E. It has been suggested as a cure for impotence, muscle and nerve disorders, heart and circulatory problems, a protection against aging and the ingestion of "toxins" in the diet, as well as a way to grow hair to name just a few. There is almost more information on the possible beneficial effects of vitamin E in the scientific literature than there is anything else. One study of 28 adults taking doses between 100 to 800 international units for 3 years showed no apparent harmful effects (it also showed no apparent benefits either). However, caution is advised since there are many reports of toxicity in animals even though the doses have been much higher proportionately. Also, an allergic reaction to a vitamin E aerosol deodorant has been reported. Vitamin E has been reported to increase the need for vitamin A and D but it is not clear how important this is. Some recent studies suggest that large intakes of vitamin E may cause increased levels of blood cholesterol and lipids, but more studies are needed. Make sure a product or diet includes the daily values recommended for vitamin E on the label to meet 100 percent of needs for your sex and age.

Water-Soluble Vitamins

The water-soluble vitamins are **ASCORBIC ACID, THIAMINE HYDROCHLORIDE, RIBOFLAVIN, NIACIN, PYRIDOXINE HYDROCHLORIDE, CYANOCOBALAMIN, FOLIC ACID, PANTOTHENIC ACID, BIOTIN, RIBOFLAVINOIDS, CHOLINE**, and **INOSITOL**. Water soluble means that what our body does not use is excreted in the urine. One water-soluble vitamin, **RIBOFLAVIN**, is the reason that urine turns bright yellow after taking a multiple vitamin. Our system is flushing the excess out. Even when we take too much, these vitamins are less likely to produce poisoning since the body has a way to get rid of the excess.

Ascorbic Acid (Vitamin C)

Ascorbic acid or **VITAMIN C** is a tart tasting, white, powder. It is responsible for healthy teeth and gums. Vitamin C also promotes wound healing and helps the body use iron properly. If we are deficient in vitamin C, the gums may become swollen and bleed easily (scurvy). Wounds heal slowly or old ones reopen. If not treated, all of these symptoms can result in death. The most common early symptom of vitamin C deficiency is rough skin, which is experienced most often in the winter when fresh fruits and vegetables are not plentiful. A more serious symptom is easy bruising.

Probably the widest held current belief about this vitamin is that it helps to prevent the common cold. Ascorbic acid has become a sort of super folk-hero vitamin in this regard. According to a leading medical journal a study was conducted at West Point in which one group of cadets were given placebos (sugar pills), the other group, vitamin C. The results of the study showed that the group that took vitamin C had more colds than the other group. There is still research being done on vitamin C and the common cold. While it still hasn't been shown to be helpful, it is a fact that very little poisoning occurs from this vitamin considering the large amounts that are taken for whatever reason.

The best source of vitamin C is to eat several servings of fresh citrus fruits and several servings of fresh vegetables each day. The daily dose of vitamin C should be based on the food or product label to meet 100 percent of dietary requirements. Except for smokers, higher doses probably will not do any good. People who smoke should take additional vitamin C, because smokers show a decreased level of vitamin C in the blood. The National Research Council recommends that smokers consume at least 100 mg of vitamin C per day.

However, larger doses of vitamin C, greater than 1000 mg

(1 gram) per day may cause nausea, abdominal cramps and diarrhea and, since it makes the urine more acid, the formation of kidney stones. Also, because vitamin C is an acid, it may alter the normal acidity of blood in extreme doses and cause interactions with other drugs that may be taken at the same time, such as aspirin. Still, some proponents advocate from 5 to 15 grams of vitamin C daily.

While problems reported with very large doses of vitamin C are minimal, large doses of vitamin C during pregnancy could cause the child to be born with rebound scurvy. Since vitamin C is a water-soluble vitamin, it enters the systems of both mother and child, resulting in the infant requiring higher doses of vitamin C than normal after birth. If normal doses are then given, the infant may develop the vitamin C deficiency disease called **SCURVY**. However this is quite rare.

Diabetics should be careful when taking vitamin C, especially if they are using the old urine dip sticks periodically to make sure that their diabetes is under control (see page 160). Vitamin C can alter these readings. Vitamin C should be avoided when taking blood-thinning drugs like *COUMADIN* and **DICUMAROL**. Vitamin C also helps the body use iron properly.

If you choose to supplement the diet with vitamin C tablets just buy the cheapest one possible. The body doesn't know the difference between the natural and the synthetic vitamin C. The commercially available vitamin C, which must be produced in quantity, is almost all made by synthetic methods. Common methods modify simple sugars like glucose since vitamin C is a glucose-like molecule. What people call "natural" is really a small amount of the vitamin from citrus fruit, rose hips or acerola combined with mostly synthetic vitamin anyway. Again, buy the cheapest.

Biotin

Biotin is considered part of the vitamin B complex of vitamins and has a role in the body's ability to make protein,

DNA, and carbohydrates. It occurs naturally in most animals and plants. Normally, bacteria in the intestine make enough biotin. Large amounts of this chemical have been given to animals and man with no reported harmful effects.

Folic Acid

Folic Acid is also known as **PTEROGLUTAMIC ACID** and is a bright yellow powder. It is widely found in nature in several forms and is abundant in deep green, leafy vegetables (the word folic comes from folium which literally means "a leaf"), liver, kidney, and yeast. Vitamin labels may list folic acid as **FOLACIN**. Or sometimes the term **FOLATE** is used. Folic acid is necessary for normal cell development and red and white blood cell production in the body. Folic acid deficiency is a common cause of anemia. Without folic acid humans grow slowly, are lethargic and develop blood cell disorders. The main reasons for folic acid deficiency are pregnancy, alcoholism, interference with medicine you may be taking, and an inability to absorb the right amount of folic acid from the intestines. The need for folacin is greater during pregnancy, since folacin is important to rapidly growing cells. Prenatal multivitamin tablets include additional amounts of this vitamin to provide the extra you need during pregnancy and nursing. The Food and Drug Administration proposes that all bread and grain products be fortified with folic acid. Just 0.4 milligrams of the nutrient every day in a pregnant woman can greatly reduce the risk of neural tube defects in unborn babies, which affect the brain and spinal cord. Neural tube defects occur in an embryo before a woman may realize she is pregnant. Since more than half of all pregnancies are unplanned, FDA has taken steps to fortify food so that all women of childbearing age get a daily dose of folic acid in their regular diet.

You can buy folic acid tablets over-the-counter in doses of 0.1mg per tablet, but these should only be taken on your doctor's advice. Taking too much folic acid on your own can mask a certain type of anemia, called pernicious anemia.

Pantothenic Acid

Pantothenic Acid is a pale yellow, thick oil which is distributed in practically all living cells, thus the root name "pan", meaning all or universal. It is important for the release of carbohydrates, production and storage of glucose, and in the manufacture and breakdown of fatty acids. It is also important in the synthesis of other vital components, such as the steroid hormones. Pantothenic acid is found in foods like whole grain cereals and legumes, vegetables and fruit. It is apparently of low toxicity—even with very massive doses the only problems are apparently diarrhea and water retention.

Vitamin B1 (thiamine)

Vitamin B1 or thiamine is responsible for breaking down fats and carbohydrates into energy. This in turn keeps the vital organs, such as the heart, muscles, and nervous systems, functioning well. A good source of vitamin B1 is the hull of rice grains. Other good sources are pork, beef, fresh peas, and beans. Thiamine deficiencies occur in **ALCOHOLICS** or in anyone who has been vomiting for a long period of time. Thiamine's toxicity is relatively mild because it is a water-soluble vitamin, and our body gets rid of what it does not need in the urine. Thiamine is mainly used to supplement the diets of alcoholics because they have poor dietary habits.

Vitamin B2 (Riboflavin)

Vitamin B2 or Riboflavin is the familiar vitamin that turns the urine visibly bright yellow. Found in milk, eggs, malted barley, leafy vegetables, and yeast, the absence of this vitamin in the diet causes the condition known as ariboflavinosis which causes lip, tongue, eye and skin lesions. If you become deficient in riboflavin, you may develop a crack in the corner of the mouth or the lip. Taking riboflavin or the B-complex for a couple of days will usually clear it up. Minute amounts of riboflavin are found in all plant and animal cells. It has demonstrated little toxicity and appears very safe.

Vitamin B6 (pyridoxine)

Vitamin B6 is part of the vitamin B complex that is really three related compounds that may appear on the label as **PYRIDOXINE, PYRIDOXAL** and **PYRIDOXAMINE**. The most commonly used salt in vitamin preparations and supplements is **PYRIDOXINE HYDROCHLORIDE. PYRIDOXINE** is essential in nutrition and is especially important in infants and children, as well as in pregnant or lactating women. The symptoms of pyridoxine deficiency are convulsions which lead to unconsciousness, with uncontrollable tremors or shaking and irritability.

Foods rich in pyridoxine are meats, cereals, lentils, nuts, and some fruits and vegetables, such as bananas, avocados, and potatoes. Cooking destroys some of the vitamin, and artificial infant formulas are required to contain pyridoxine. Several drugs reduce pyridoxine's use by the body, including the antitubercular drugs **ISONIAZID** and **CYCLOSERINE** (*SEROMYCIN*), as well as the drug **HYDRALAZINE** for high blood pressure. Women taking **ESTROGEN** in birth control pills will also lose too much pyridoxine. If you are taking any of these drugs you may want to supplement your diet with vitamin B6. On the other hand, pyridoxine may block the effects of a prescription drug known as **LEVODOPA**, used for **PARKINSON'S DISEASE**. In that case, you should avoid **PYRIDOXINE** supplements as much as possible.

Vitamin B12

Vitamin B12 may show on a label as its chemical name, **CYANOCOBALAMIN**. Deficiency of vitamin B12 is also known as pernicious anemia, so called because it was inevitably fatal before the discovery of liver therapy. Animal liver is rich in this vitamin. Vitamin B12 works with other vitamins in the formation of blood and is necessary for normal functioning of cells. It also plays a big role in breaking down fats and carbohydrates for energy. Sources include animal organs, particularly liver, kidney, muscle and foods derived from milk. Certain microorganisms also form vitamin B12. There are almost no reports connecting vitamin B12 with toxicity.

Vegetarians may need to supplement their diets with additional cyanocobalamin, since it is important in cell production. If you are deficient in this vitamin, you develop stomach problems, inflammation of the tongue, sore mouth, and diarrhea. However, vitamin B12 deficiency is rare, and more than 95 percent of cases seen in the United States are related to the body's inability to absorb the vitamin. Some prescription drugs may cause cyanocobalamin not to be absorbed properly, so check with your doctor or pharmacist about vitamin supplementation when you are on medication for long periods of time.

Niacin

Niacin or **NICOTINIC ACID** is considered part of the vitamin B complex and is present in all cells. It helps many body processes; it releases energy from glucose (blood sugar), helps produce needed fat in the body and helps the cells use oxygen. Minute amounts occur in all living cells. It is found in significant amounts in liver, yeast, milk, alfalfa, legumes and whole cereals. **NIACINAMIDE** is a form of niacin that is interchangeable with niacin, as far as the body is concerned. A deficiency of this chemical produces the condition known as pellagra (which causes lesions in and around the mouth and other mucous membranes), insomnia, weakness, irritability, abdominal pain, vertigo and numerous other symptoms. Since the mid 1970s it has been recognized that niacin has an apparent beneficial effect by lowering the liver's production of blood fats (blood cholesterol and triglycerides). However, the amounts of niacin shown by research to lower blood cholesterol and triglycerides are very large, from one to three grams daily. This is a dose that produces annoying side effects in most people. Niacin is available either as niacin (nicotinic acid) or as niacinamide. Both work the same way, but niacin causes flushing of the skin and niacinamide does not. Foods rich in niacin are beef, cow's milk, and whole eggs. Deficiencies of niacin are evident as a thickening of the skin on the face, which may look like a severe burn. Niacin should not be taken by people suffering from ulcers or other chronic stomach problems. Sometimes niacin can trigger asthma attacks.

Many vitamin products sold today consist of a combination of many of the B vitamins, such as **THIAMINE (B1), RIBOFLAVIN (B2), NIACIN, PYRIDOXINE (B6)**, and **CYANOCOBALAMIN (B12)**. Rather than using any of the B vitamins individually, you might be better off with the B complex, because it is often difficult to pinpoint the exact B vitamin that you are lacking. But check with your doctor before you spend a lot of money on something you may not need.

Minerals and Trace Elements

A mineral is literally a substance that is "mined", or extracted from the earth, since they have been formed naturally. In nutrition they stand in contrast to the organic nutrients, such as vitamins, proteins, carbohydrates and fats. The terms "macro-minerals" and "trace elements" are used by the Food and Nutrition Board of the National Academy of Sciences.

MACRO-MINERALS include calcium, phosphorus, magnesium, sodium, potassium and chlorine. The last three, Sodium, potassium and chlorine are further subclassified as "electrolytes."

TRACE ELEMENTS include iron, zinc, copper, manganese, iodine, chromium, selenium, molybdenum and fluorine. While these substances are essential for life it is important to remember that the right balance is needed for good health. Both too little and too much is harmful to health. None of these chemicals are taken in their pure form. They are normally found in organic foodstuffs, and certain foods are particularly rich in certain minerals and trace elements. Traditional medical text books state that while certain minerals are necessary in trace amounts, any adequate diet easily supplies the traces. But this is now widely challenged by researchers who maintain that highly processed foods which, in their opinion, are often grown in mineral depleted soils, do not provide these minute chemicals in the proper amounts needed for good health.

Many vitamin supplement preparations are available with minerals, such as *UNICAP-M*, *THERAGRAN-M*, or the store brand multivitamins with minerals. As a matter of fact, if you are going to supplement your diet with a multiple vitamin, why not get one with minerals? That way you are getting everything from A to Z, and they do not cost much more. Some of the most common minerals found in vitamin products are:

Calcium

Calcium is the main component of teeth and bones, and it also plays a major role in clotting the blood. Deficiencies of this mineral can cause brittle bones or soft teeth. Calcium is available without a prescription in the form of **CALCIUM CARBONATE, CALCIUM GLUCONATE**, and **CALCIUM LACTATE**. However, calcium should only be taken by itself under the orders of a physician, because it may be toxic and if high levels build up in the urine, could cause the formation of kidney stones. Calcium is from the Latin word calx, meaning "lime" (lime is the oxide of calcium). It is abundant in the earth's crust occurring as the mineral calcite (calcium carbonate) found in chalk, limestone, marble, eggshells, coral, stalactites and numerous other substances. One of the "macro" (meaning large) minerals in the human body, about 99 percent of all calcium is incorporated into the bones and teeth as **CALCIUM PHOSPHATE**. On a weight basis, the human body is about 2 percent calcium, with only a very small fraction of this in the blood at any one time. At one time it was reported that about 60 percent of calcium in the American diet was supplied by milk, cheese, and other dairy products. However, over the years there has been a steady decline in the amount of dairy products consumed in the United States, which means that other sources of calcium need to be added to the diet. Broccoli, citrus fruits, and legumes are a fair source of calcium.

The growth of the skeleton requires slightly higher amounts of calcium in the blood than is ordinarily needed until peak bone mass is reached. Mineralization of bone continues for some years after lengthwise bone growth has stopped. Most of the accumulation of bone mineral occurs in humans by about 20 years of age, but some bone mineral is added during the third decade of life. Bone mass then begins to decline slowly in the 50s in both sexes, as evidenced by progressive reduction of bone density. The rate of loss increases greatly about the time of menopause in women and remains high for several years. Bone loss increases much later in men. This results in a gradual loss of bone strength and increased risk of fractures. The risk of fracture is less at a given age in people who have developed greater bone mass when they were in their early years. Adequate calcium intake during this stage of bone development is very important.

According to the National Academy of Science's Food and Nutrition Board, the most promising nutritional approach to reduce the risk of **OSTEOPOROSIS** in later life is to ensure a calcium intake that allows the development of each individual's genetically programmed peak bone mass during the formative years. It is important to meet recommended allowances at all ages, but special attention should be given to amounts of calcium intake throughout childhood to age 25 years.

CALCIUM PHOSPHATE or **CALCIUM CARBONATE**, both minerals found in nature, are usually the source when supplied in commercial mineral or vitamin-mineral supplements. CALCIUM LACTATE may also be used and it is prepared commercially from lactic acid (a natural component of milk) and calcium carbonate. Calcium lactate, however, supplies only one-half as much calcium compared to an equal weight of calcium carbonate. So you would have to take more. Look for the amount shown on the label in terms of calcium content. Your pharmacist can help you with these comparisons, which can get confusing.

Chromium

Chromium is an interesting metal and trace element that is required for proper utilization of glucose to produce energy for the body. Elemental chromium is the same shiny metal that is used on automobile bumpers but this form is rarely found in nature. The body cannot use this elemental form of chromium, but rather requires it in combination with vitamins and amino acids, which is how we get it in a balanced diet. It has been identified as the critical component of the "glucose tolerance factor," a combination of chromium, amino acids and the vitamin **NIACIN.** This is the only known function for chromium in our body at the present time, however it might help to metabolize fat. Good sources of chromium are dried brewer's yeast, whole grain cereals and liver. It is usually incorporated into vitamin-mineral tablets as a soluble salt, such as **CHROMIUM CHLORIDE.**

Copper

Copper is a metal that has been of economic importance since the earliest recorded writings of humankind. The reddish metal is found in nature and it occurs combined in many minerals. Copper, considered a trace element in humans, is important for healthy blood in humans because it is involved in the storage and release of the iron needed to form hemoglobin for red blood cells. Copper, in an average healthy adult, is distributed somewhat evenly among the liver and brain, muscles, and other tissues. Its concentration in the human body must remain small in order for good health to prevail. Copper, while being transported in blood from various tissues and organs in the body, combines with proteins to make enzymes required for vital body processes. Copper is found in oysters, nuts, liver, kidney, and peas and beans. Some drinking waters also contain trace amounts of copper.

Chlorine

Chlorine is supplied in the diet as ordinary table salt, which is **SODIUM CHLORIDE**. In vitamin-mineral supplements **POTASSIUM CHLORIDE**, a white crystalline salt is used as a source of both potassium and chlorine. Chlorine is found in abundance in sea water and in minerals combined with sodium, such as rock salt. Chlorine, the word itself meaning "greenish-yellow," is actually a poisonous gas in the molecular form, but in combination with sodium forms one of the essential electrolytes necessary for life. Only infants who have been fed commercially prepared formula lacking in chloride have suffered deficiencies, otherwise deficiency is not known to occur in humans. However, numerous disturbances in the balance of chlorine with other electrolytes, such as potassium can occur in certain disease conditions, although this is different from deficiency in the sense of a dietary shortage. The exact minimum daily requirement of chloride is not known.

Fluoride

The National Research Council lists fluoride as an essential trace element, but there are independent researchers who disagree that fluoride is essential to health. Dentists and parents alike know that in areas where a very small amount of fluoride is added to drinking water it protects against dental caries. In areas where water is not fluoridated you can get the same effect with supplements by taking 1.5 mg per day. Slightly higher intakes may result in mottling of teeth in young children and while this is cosmetically bad and undesirable it is apparently not dangerous to health. Serious poisoning from fluoride can happen at much larger amounts. Controversy continues over the need for and safety of adding fluoride to drinking water and it is safe to say that this will continue for some time.

Iodine

Iodine is an essential micronutrient or trace element because not getting enough leads to enlargement of the thyroid gland (goiter). Iodine is a part of the hormones (thyroxin and triiodothyronine) which have roles in maintaining the metabolic rate of the body. Iodine deficiency and thus goiter was a national problem in the early 1900s. This eventually led to the voluntary iodization of table salt in the United States by 1940. Most Americans now consume at least twice the amount of iodine recommended by the Food and Nutrition Board of the National Academy of Science. So we really do not need to add iodine to our diet in the form of vitamin supplements. Good sources are seafoods. Vegetables are usually low in iodine. Iodine is usually listed in over-the-counter vitamin and mineral supplements as potassium iodide.

Iron

Iron plays a vitally important role in moving and using oxygen in the body. About 75 percent of the body's iron is used in hemoglobin to carry oxygen and make enzymes and other proteins. The remaining 25 percent is stored in the liver, spleen and bone marrow. Iron is absorbed through the gastrointestinal tract. It is carefully recycled by the body, and the only way you lose iron is when you lose blood. Iron deficiency is common and causes iron deficiency anemia.

IRON DEFICIENCY ANEMIA is a widespread problem. Although it has caused few deaths, it causes people to feel run down. Iron deficiency anemia may result from inadequate dietary intake, inability to absorb iron from the intestines, pregnancy and nursing, or blood loss. Early symptoms of iron deficiency are fatigue and weakness. (These symptoms could also be related to other illnesses.) Other symptoms of anemia are, pale color, headache, frequent infection, chest palpitations, sore tongue, mouth inflammation with difficulty in swallowing, difficulty in breathing, coldness, and numbness of the fingers and toes. Usually women need supplemental iron more than men, especially if they have heavy menstrual periods.

If iron products are suggested, there are many to choose from. Which one is best to use? A multivitamin with iron, or an iron supplement by itself. If you decide to use an iron supplement, look at the ingredients. In vitamin supplements iron is usually supplied as **FERROUS SULFATE, FERROUS FUMARATE** or **FERROUS GLUCONATE**. Of these three popular salts, **FERROUS SULFATE** is the only one that occurs naturally. It is the most well absorbed and therefore most often recommended by doctors, even though it sometimes irritates the stomach causing nausea and stomach pain. **FERROUS FUMARATE** and **FERROUS GLUCONATE** are a little less irritating to the stomach, but also less well absorbed. If you take iron and find that it causes nausea or upset stomach, it might help to take it while eating or immediately after finishing a meal. If that does not help the nausea, check with a doctor. It may be necessary to change to a slow-release form or try one of the other salts. You may have a very sensitive stomach.

No matter what iron preparation you choose, one common side effect is constipation. Remedy this by taking a stool softener periodically or making sure you drink plenty of water during the day. Another thing you might notice when taking iron is that the stool becomes black and tarry. This is the result of the unabsorbed iron the body is eliminating. Check with a physician, however, since black, tarry stools could also represent gastro-intestinal bleeding. If after taking it for one month, there is no improvement in the way you feel, check with your doctor. You should notice some relief of anemia symptoms in 30 days. By the same token, if you are just starting to take an iron product, only buy a month's supply, so that if it does not work, you will not be wasting money.

Some iron products are available in combination with **VITAMIN C**, which helps the body use iron more effectively.

Iron may react with certain prescription drugs, such as the antibiotic **TETRACYCLINE**, causing the antibiotic not to be absorbed properly. It is also recommended that you avoid taking iron if you are taking **ALLOPURINOL** *(ZYLOPRIM)* for gout.

Problems with Too Much Iron

It is also possible to get too much iron. When taken in overdose (particulary in children), iron injures the gastrointestinal tract. This allows larger amounts of iron to be absorbed which causes changes in the blood vessels, resulting in lowered blood pressure (shock) and finally damage to the liver, which can cause death. This can happen in children who accidentally get into mom's prenatal vitamins and swallow as few as 10 tablets.

Magnesium

Magnesium is one of the macro-minerals required by the body in both bones and soft tissue. Magnesium plays an important role in all living cells, particularly in maintaining electrical operations of nerves and muscles, but also for the function of enzymes, the making of new protein, and the storage and release of energy. The average adult human body contains about an ounce of magnesium, most of which is in the bones and teeth. Magnesium deficiencies are not well understood. Some researchers claim that there are magnesium deficiencies to a large extent in the population but it is seldom diagnosed because doctors are not looking for it. Magnesium is supplied in vitamin/mineral supplements as **MAGNESIUM SULFATE** (also known as **EPSOM SALTS**), or **MAGNESIUM OXIDE**.

Manganese

Manganese is one of the trace elements and is an essential part of the enzyme systems involved in protein and energy metabolism. It also seems to be important for bone growth and development, and reproduction. Deficiencies have not been reported in humans, but we know it is necessary for life. Manganese is in nuts, seeds, whole grain cereals and legumes. It may be put in vitamin supplements as **MANGANESE SULFATE**.

Molybdenum

Molybdenum is another trace element that is needed in the body by several important enzymes. It plays important roles in fat and protein metabolism. **SODIUM MOLYBDATE** is a salt of **MOLYBDENUM** frequently used in over-the-counter vitamin-mineral supplements.

Phosphorus

Phosphorus, the name which comes from Greek and means "light bearing", is in the elemental form a semitransparent, soft, waxy solid that glows in the dark. Phosphorus is essential to life and is present in the body as **CALCIUM PHOSPHATE** in bones and teeth. Bones consist of about half as much phosphorus as the calcium content. Phosphorus forms phosphate which is important to cell membranes and to the nervous system. Phosphate plays a key role in energy exchange in the human body. Good food sources are fish, meats, nuts, dairy products, legumes and whole grain cereals. In order for good health to prevail phosphorus needs to be taken in a balanced way with calcium. **CALCIUM PHOSPHATE**, a naturally occurring mineral is used as a dietary supplement of both calcium and phosphorus.

Potassium

Potassium is essential for the life of every cell in the human body. In fact, about 98 percent of total body potassium is found inside our cells. Potassium controls electrical activity of the heart, muscles and nervous system. It works with sodium and other electrolytes outside of the cells to regulate blood acidity, water balance, acidity of the urine and may other functions. Good sources of potassium are green, leafy vegetables, wheat germ, beans and nuts, and most fruits. **POTASSIUM CHLORIDE** is the most common form of potassium in both prescription and nonprescription supplements, the only difference being the amount used per dose.

Selenium

Selenium is one of the essential trace elements and some researchers believe Americans are facing a serious nutritional shortage in their diets. The only function of selenium known at present is as part of an enzyme which protects vital parts of cells against damage by oxidation. Selenium deficiency may be associated with skin and hair disorders. It may also be connected with a form of cardiomyopathy (abnormal heart muscle). Good sources are seafood, whole grains and some vegetables. Protection against cancer and heart disease involving selenium have recently been reported and it may somehow strengthen the immune system. However, much more investigation needs to be done with this element. **SODIUM SELENATE** is one type of salt used in vitamin-mineral supplements.

Zinc

Zinc is an essential nutrient in humans. It is necessary for enzymes that are involved in many important functions. Zinc is also found in large amounts in bone. Signs of zinc deficiency are loss of appetite, failure to grow, skin changes, slow healing of wounds, and decreased taste. Meat, liver, eggs, and seafood (especially oysters) are good sources of zinc, whereas whole grain products (whole wheat or rye bread, oatmeal, whole corn) contain less zinc. Zinc is supplemented in the diet in vitamin formulations as **ZINC SULFATE**. Zinc sulfate when taken in doses of 250 mg or greater can cause stomach irritation and vomiting, in fact the drug was once frequently used as a vomiting agent in poisoning. However, zinc has been administered to people in doses ten times the recommended dietary allowances (RDAs) for years without ill effects.

Megavitamins

Although megavitamin therapy has been used with some success for certain illnesses, there is no evidence to indicate that large doses of vitamins ensure good health. Indeed, some serious side effects have been reported. One sees many new products, such as **GINSENG, KELP, LECITHIN**, etc., in the vitamin sections of drugstores. However, the nutrients in these products have not been proven medically, and chances are that you are getting more than enough of the ingredients in these products in your normal diet. Since some of these products cause problems for people suffering from diabetes or high blood pressure, do not be swayed to use them without proper medical advice. Most of the people promoting these products are more interested in your money than your health.

We truly believe that nutrition is important for good health and that more research should be done in this area. But remember that fad diets are no substitute for sound medical care.

Symptom Index

Bibliography

Books and Reference Works

American Hospital Formulary Service (AHFS) Drug Information. Bethesda, MD, 1994. American Society of Hospital Pharmacists.

W.E. Benitz and D.S. Tatro, *The Pediatric Drug Handbook*, Second Edition. Chicago, 1988. Year Book Medical Publishers, Inc.

N.F. Billups and S.M. Billups, *American Drug Index*. St. Louis, MO, 1994. J. B. Lippincott Company, Facts and Comparison Division.

FDA Consumer, Vol. 22, no. 1, 1988–Vol. 28, no. 5, 1994. Rockville, MD. US Food and Drug Administration.

E.G. Feldmann (Ed.), *Handbook of Nonprescription Drugs*, 9th Edition. Washington, DC, 1994. American Pharmaceutical Association.

J.F. Grogan, *The Pharmacists Prescription*. New York, 1987. Avon Books.

Handbook of Pharmaceutical Excipients. Washington, DC, 1986. American Pharmaceutical Association.

A.L. Hunting, *Encyclopedia of Shampoo Ingredients*. Cranford, NJ, 1983. Micelle Press, Inc.

Indications Index. Oradell, NJ, 1994. Medical Economics Company, Inc.

B.R. Olin (Ed.), *Facts and Comparisons*. St. Louis, MO, 1994. J. B. Lippincott Company, Facts and Comparison Division.

Physician's Desk Reference for Nonprescription Drugs. NJ, 1994. Medical Economics Company, Inc.

Quick Reference to Discontinued Drugs. St. Louis, MO, 1988. J.B. Lippincott Company, Facts and Comparison Division.

Recommended Dietary Allowances, Subcommittee on the Tenth Edition of the RDAs, Food and Nutrition Board, Commission on Life Sciences, National Research Council, 10th Edition. Washington, DC, 1989. National Academy Press.

Report of the Committee on Infectious Diseases, 22nd Edition. Elk Grove Village, IL, 1991. American Academy of Pediatrics.

P. Sanberg, *Over-the-Counter Drugs—Harmless or Hazardous?* New York, 1986. Chelsea House Publishers.

The New Medicine Show. Mount Vernon, NY, 1989. Consumers Union.

United States Pharmacopeia Drug Information for the Consumer. Mount Vernon, NY, 1989. Consumers Union.

USP DI Drug Volume I, Information for the Health Care Professional, Rockville, MD, 1994. The United States Pharmacopeial Convention, Inc.

USP DI Volume II, Advice for the Patient, Drug Information in Lay Language. Rockville, MD, 1994. The United States Pharmacopeial Convention, Inc.

A. L. Wan, *Non-Prescription Drugs.* Boston, 1990. Blackwell Scientific Publications.

H. N. Wigner, *Over-the-Counter Drugs.* Los Angeles, 1979. J. P. Tarcher, Inc.

J. B. Wyngaarden and L. H. Smith (Ed.), *Cecil Textbook of Medicine,* 18th Edition. Philadelphia, PA, 1988. W.B. Saunders Company.

J. H. Young, *American Self-Dosage Medicines—An Historical Perspective.* Lawrence, KS, 1974. Coronado Press.

Index

Index

RD5BR